acclaim for james frey's

a million little pieces

"A frenzied, electrifying description of the experience."
— *The New Yorker*

"We finish *A Million Little Pieces* like miners lifted out of a collapsed shaft: exhausted, blackened, oxygen-starved, but alive, thrillingly, amazingly alive." — *Minneapolis Star-Tribune*

"One of the most compelling books of the year. . . . Incredibly bold. . . . Somehow accomplishes what three decades' worth of cheesy public service announcements and after-school specials have failed to do: depict hard-core drug addiction as the self-inflicted apocalypse that it is." — *New York Post*

"Thoroughly engrossing. . . . Hard-bitten existentialism bristles on every page. . . . Frey's prose is muscular and tough, ideal for conveying extreme physical anguish and steely determination."
— *Entertainment Weekly*

"Incredible. . . . Mesmerizing. . . . Heart-rending."
— *Atlanta Journal-Constitution*

"A rising literary star . . . has birthed a poetic account of his recovery. [*A Million Little Pieces* is] stark . . . disturbing . . . rife with raw emotion." — *Chicago Sun-Times*

"Frey will probably be hailed in turn as the voice of a generation."
— *Elle*

"We can admire Frey for his fierceness, his extremity, his solitary virtue, the angry ethics of his barroom tribe, and his victory over his furies. . . . A compelling book." — *New York*

"An intimate, vivid and heartfelt memoir. Can Frey be the greatest writer of his generation? Maybe." — *New York Press*

"Incredible. . . . A ferociously compelling memoir."
—*The Plain Dealer*

"Insistent as it is demanding. . . . A story that cuts to the nerve of addiction by clank-clank-clanking through the skull of the addicted. . . . A critical milestone in modern literature."
—*Orlando Weekly*

"At once devastatingly bleak and heartbreakingly hopeful. . . . Frey somehow manages to make his step-by-step walk through recovery compelling."
—*Charlotte Observer*

"A stark, direct and graphic documentation of the rehabilitation process. . . . The strength of the book comes from the truth of the experience."
—*The Oregonian*

"A virtual addiction itself, viscerally affecting. . . . Compulsively readable."
—*City Paper* (Washington, DC)

"Powerful . . . haunting . . . addictive. . . . A beautiful story of recovery and reconciliation."
—*Iowa City Press-Citizen*

"An exhilarating read. . . . Frey's intense, punchy prose renders his experiences with electrifying immediacy."
—*Time Out New York*

"Describes the hopelessness and the inability to stop with precision. . . . As anyone who has ever spent time in a rehab can testify . . . he gets that down too."
—*St. Louis Post-Dispatch*

"Frey comes on like the world's first recovering-addict hero. . . . [His] criticism of the twelve-step philosophy is provocative and his story undeniably compelling."
—*GQ*

"[A] gruesomely absorbing account, told in stripped-down, staccato prose."
—*Details*

"Frey has devised a rolling, pulsating style that really moves . . . undeniably striking. . . . A fierce and honorable work that refuses to glamorize [the] author's addiction or his thorny personality. . . . A book that makes other recovery memoirs look, well, a little pussy-ass."
—*Salon*

j a m e s   f r e y

a   m i l l i o n   l i t t l e   p i e c e s

James Frey is originally from Cleveland.
He is also the author of *My Friend Leonard*.
He is married and lives in New York.

a

million

little

pieces

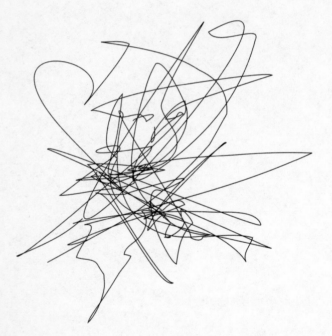

a

million

little

pieces

james frey

ANCHOR BOOKS

A DIVISION OF RANDOM HOUSE, INC.

NEW YORK

FIRST ANCHOR BOOKS EDITION, MAY 2004

Copyright © 2003 by James Frey

All rights reserved under International and Pan-American Copyright Conventions.
Published in the United States by Anchor Books, a division of Random House, Inc., New
York, and simultaneously in Canada by Random House of Canada Limited, Toronto.
Originally published in hardcover in the United States by Nan A. Talese, an imprint of
Doubleday, a division of Random House, Inc., New York, in 2003.

Anchor Books and colophon are registered trademarks of Random House, Inc.

The Library of Congress has cataloged the Nan A. Talese / Doubleday edition as follows:
Frey, James, 1969–
A million little pieces / James Frey.—1st ed.
p. cm.
1. Frey, James, 1969– 2. Narcotic addicts—Rehabilitation—Minnesota.
3. Narcotic addicts—Minnesota—Biography. I. Title.
HV5831.M6F74 2003
362.29′092—dc21
2002044393

Anchor ISBN: 1-4000-3108-7

Interior art by Terry Karydes

www.anchorbooks.com

Printed in the United States of America
10   9   8   7   6   5

a

million

little

pieces

The Young Man came to the Old Man seeking counsel.

I broke something, Old Man.

How badly is it broken?

It's in a million little pieces.

I'm afraid I can't help you.

Why?

There's nothing you can do.

Why?

It can't be fixed.

Why?

It's broken beyond repair. It's in a million little pieces.

I wake to the drone of an airplane engine and the feeling of something warm dripping down my chin. I lift my hand to feel my face. My front four teeth are gone, I have a hole in my cheek, my nose is broken and my eyes are swollen nearly shut. I open them and I look around and I'm in the back of a plane and there's no one near me. I look at my clothes and my clothes are covered with a colorful mixture of spit, snot, urine, vomit and blood. I reach for the call button and I find it and I push it and I wait and thirty seconds later an Attendant arrives.

How can I help you?

Where am I going?

You don't know?

No.

You're going to Chicago, Sir.

How did I get here?

A Doctor and two men brought you on.

They say anything?

They talked to the Captain, Sir. We were told to let you sleep.

How long till we land?

About twenty minutes.

Thank you.

Although I never look up, I know she smiles and feels sorry for me. She shouldn't.

A short while later we touch down. I look around for anything I might have with me, but there's nothing. No ticket, no bags, no clothes, no wallet. I sit and I wait and I try to figure out what happened. Nothing comes.

Once the rest of the Passengers are gone I stand and start to make my way to the door. After about five steps I sit back down. Walking is out of the question. I see my Attendant friend and I raise a hand.

Are you okay?

No.

What's wrong?

I can't really walk.

If you make it to the door I can get you a chair.

How far is the door?
Not far.
I stand. I wobble. I sit back down. I stare at the floor and take a deep breath.
You'll be all right.
I look up and she's smiling.
Here.
She holds out her hand and I take it. I stand and I lean against her and she helps me down the Aisle. We get to the door.
I'll be right back.
I let go of her hand and I sit down on the steel bridge of the Jetway that connects the Plane to the Gate.
I'm not going anywhere.
She laughs and I watch her walk away and I close my eyes. My head hurts, my mouth hurts, my eyes hurt, my hands hurt. Things without names hurt.
I rub my stomach. I can feel it coming. Fast and strong and burning. No way to stop it, just close your eyes and let it ride. It comes and I recoil from the stench and the pain. There's nothing I can do.
Oh my God.
I open my eyes.
I'm all right.
Let me find a Doctor.
I'll be fine. Just get me out of here.
Can you stand?
Yeah, I can stand.
I stand and I brush myself off and I wipe my hands on the floor and I sit down in the wheelchair she has brought me. She goes around to the back of the chair and she starts pushing.
Is someone here for you?
I hope so.
You don't know.
No.
What if no one's there?
It's happened before, I'll find my way.
We come off the Jetway and into the Gate. Before I have a chance to look around, my Mother and Father are standing in front of me.
Oh Jesus.
Please, Mom.

Oh my God, what happened?

I don't want to talk about it, Mom.

Jesus Christ, Jimmy. What in Hell happened?

She leans over and she tries to hug me. I push her away.

Let's just get out of here, Mom.

My Dad goes around to the back of the chair. I look for the Attendant but she has disappeared. Bless her.

You okay, James?

I stare straight ahead.

No, Dad, I'm not okay.

He starts pushing the chair.

Do you have any bags?

My Mother continues crying.

No.

People are staring.

Do you need anything?

I need to get out of here, Dad. Just get me the fuck out of here.

They wheel me to their car. I climb in the backseat and I take off my shirt and I lie down. My Dad starts driving, my Mom keeps crying, I fall asleep.

About four hours later I wake up. My head is clear but everything throbs. I sit forward and I look out the window. We've pulled into a Filling Station somewhere in Wisconsin. There is no snow on the ground, but I can feel the cold. My Dad opens the Driver's door and he sits down and he closes the door. I shiver.

You're awake.

Yeah.

How are you feeling?

Shitty.

Your Mom's inside cleaning up and getting supplies. You need anything?

A bottle of water and a couple bottles of wine and a pack of cigarettes.

Seriously?

Yeah.

This is bad, James.

I need it.

You can't wait.

No.

This will upset your Mother.

I don't care. I need it.

He opens the door and he goes into the Filling Station. I lie back down and I stare at the ceiling. I can feel my heart quickening and I hold out my hand and I try to keep it straight. I hope they hurry.

Twenty minutes later the bottles are gone. I sit up and I light a smoke and I take a slug of water. Mom turns around.

Better?

If you want to put it that way.

We're going up to the Cabin.

I figured.

We're going to decide what to do when we get there.

All right.

What do you think?

I don't want to think right now.

You're gonna have to soon.

Then I'll wait till soon comes.

We head north to the Cabin. Along the way I learn that my Parents, who live in Tokyo, have been in the States for the last two weeks on business. At four A.M. they received a call from a friend of mine who was with me at a Hospital and had tracked them down in a hotel in Michigan. He told them that I had fallen face first down a Fire Escape and that he thought they should find me some help. He didn't know what I was on, but he knew there was a lot of it and he knew it was bad. They had driven to Chicago during the night.

So what was it?

What was what?

What were you taking?

I'm not sure.

How can you not be sure?

I don't remember.

What do you remember?

Bits and pieces.

Like what?

I don't remember.

We drive on and after a few hard silent minutes, we arrive. We get out of the car and we go into the House and I take a shower because I need it. When I get out there are some fresh clothes sitting on my bed. I put them on and I go to my Parents' room. They are up drinking coffee and talking but when I come in they stop.

Hi.

Mom starts crying again and she looks away. Dad looks at me.

Feeling better?
No.
You should get some sleep.
I'm gonna.
Good.
I look at my Mom. She can't look back. I breathe.
I just.
I look away.
I just, you know.
I look away. I can't look at them.
I just wanted to say thanks. For picking me up.
Dad smiles. He takes my Mother by the hand and they stand and they
come over to me and they give me a hug. I don't like it when they touch
me so I pull away.
Good night.
Good night, James. We love you.
I turn and I leave their Room and I close their door and I go to the
Kitchen. I look through the cabinets and I find an unopened half-gallon
bottle of whiskey. The first sip brings my stomach back up, but after that
it's all right. I go to my Room and I drink and I smoke some cigarettes
and I think about her. I drink and I smoke and I think about her and at a
certain point blackness comes and my memory fails me.

Back in the car with a headache and bad breath. We're heading north and west to Minnesota. My Father made some calls and got me into a Clinic and I don't have any other options, so I agree to spend some time there and for now I'm fine with it. It's getting colder.

My face has gotten worse and it is hideously swollen. I have trouble speaking, eating, drinking, smoking. I have yet to look in a mirror.

We stop in Minneapolis to see my older Brother. He moved there after getting divorced and he knows how to get to the Clinic. He sits with me in the backseat and he holds my hand and it helps because I'm scared.

We pull into the Parking Lot and park the car and I finish a bottle and we get out and we start walking toward the Entrance of the Clinic. Me and my Brother and my Mother and my Father. My entire Family. Going to the Clinic. I stop and they stop with me. I stare at the Buildings. Low and long and connected. Functional. Simple. Menacing.

I want to run or die or get fucked up. I want to be blind and dumb and have no heart. I want to crawl in a hole and never come out. I want to wipe my existence straight off the map. Straight off the fucking map. I take a deep breath.

Let's go.

We enter a small Waiting Room. A woman sits behind a desk reading a fashion magazine. She looks up.

May I help you?

My Father steps forward and speaks with her as my Mother and Brother and I find chairs and sit in them.

I'm shaking. My hands and my feet and my lips and my chest. Shaking. For any number of reasons.

My Mother and Brother move next to me and they take my hands and they hold them and they can feel what is happening to me. We look at the floor and we don't speak. We wait and we hold hands and we breathe and we think.

My Father finishes with the woman and he turns around and he stands in front of us. He looks happy and the woman is on the phone. He kneels down.

They're gonna check you in now.

All right.

You're gonna be fine. This is a good place. The best place.

That's what I hear.

You ready?

I guess so.

We stand and we move toward a small Room where a man sits behind a desk with a computer. He meets us at the door.

I'm sorry, but you have to leave him here.

My Father nods.

We'll check him in and you can call later to make sure he's all right.

My Mother breaks down.

He's in the right place. Don't worry.

My Brother looks away.

He's in the right place.

I turn and they hug me. One at a time and hold tight. Squeezing and holding, I show them what I can. I turn and without a word I walk into the Room and the man shuts the door and they're gone.

The man shows me a chair and returns to his desk. He smiles.

Hi.

Hello.

How are you?

How do I look?

Not good.

I feel worse.

Your name is James. You're twenty-three. You live in North Carolina.

Yeah.

You're going to stay with us for a while. You okay with that?

For now.

Do you know anything about this Facility?

No.

Do you want to know anything?

I don't care.

He smiles, stares at me for a moment. He speaks.

We are the oldest Residential Drug and Alcohol Treatment Facility in the World. We were founded in 1949 in an old house that sat on the land where these Buildings, and there are thirty-two interconnected Buildings here, sit now. We have treated over twenty thousand Patients. We have the highest success rate of any Facility in the World. At any given time, there are between two hundred and two hundred and fifty Patients spread through six Units, three of which house men and three of which house women. We believe that Patients should stay here for as long a term as they need, not something as specific as a twenty-eight-day Program. Although it is expensive to come here, many of our Patients are here on scholarships that we fund and through subsidies that we support. We have an endowment of several hundred million dollars. We not only treat Patients, we are also one of the leading Research and Educational Institutions in the field of Addiction Studies. You should consider yourself fortunate to be here and you should be excited to start a new chapter in your life.

I stare at the man. I don't speak. He stares back at me, waiting for me to say something. There is an awkward moment. He smiles.

You ready to get started?

I don't smile.

Sure.

He gets up and I get up and we walk down a hall. He talks and I don't.

The doors are always open here, so if you want to leave, you can. Substance use is not allowed and if you're caught using or possessing, you will be sent Home. You are not allowed to say anything more than hello to any women aside from Doctors, Nurses or Staff Members. If you violate this rule, you will be sent Home. There are other rules, but those are the only ones you need to know right now.

We walk through a door into the Medical Wing. There are small Rooms and Doctors and Nurses and a Pharmacy. The cabinets have large steel locks. He shows me to a Room. It has a bed and a desk and a chair and a closet and a window. Everything is white.

He stands at the door and I sit on the bed.

A Nurse will be here in a few minutes to talk with you.

Fine.

You feel okay?

No, I feel like shit.

It'll get better.

Yeah.

Trust me.

Yeah.

The man leaves and he shuts the door and I'm alone. My feet bounce, I touch my face, I run my tongue along my gums. I'm cold and getting colder. I hear someone scream.

The door opens and a Nurse walks into the Room. She wears white, all white, and she is carrying a clipboard. She sits in the chair by the desk.

Hi, James.
Hi.
I need to ask you some questions.
All right.
I also need to check your blood pressure and your pulse.
All right.
What type of substances do you normally use?
Alcohol.
Every day?
Yes.
What time do you start drinking?
When I wake up.
She marks it down.
How much per day?
As much as I can.
How much is that?
Enough to make myself look like I do.
She looks at me. She marks it down.
Do you use anything else?
Cocaine.
How often?
Every day.
She marks it down.
How much?
As much as I can.
She marks it down.
In what form?
Lately crack, but over the years, in every form that it exists.
She marks it down.
Anything else?
Pills, acid, mushrooms, meth, PCP and glue.
Marks it down.
How often?
When I have it.
How often?
A few times a week.
Marks it down.
She moves forward and draws out a stethoscope.
How are you feeling?
Terrible.

In what way?

In every way.

She reaches for my shirt.

Do you mind?

No.

She lifts my shirt and she puts the stethoscope to my chest. She listens.

Breathe deeply.

She listens.

Good. Do it again.

She lowers my shirt and she pulls away and she marks it down.

Thank you.

I smile.

Are you cold?

Yes.

She has a blood pressure gauge.

Do you feel nauseous?

Yes.

She straps it on my arm and it hurts.

When was the last time you used?

She pumps it up.

A little while ago.

What and how much?

I drank a bottle of vodka.

How does that compare to your normal daily dosage?

It doesn't.

She watches the gauge and the dials move and she marks it down and she removes the gauge.

I'm gonna leave for a little while, but I'll be back.

I stare at the wall.

We need to monitor you carefully and we will probably need to give you some detoxification drugs.

I see a shadow and I think it moves but I'm not sure.

You're fine right now, but I think you'll start to feel some things.

I see another one. I hate it.

If you need me, just call.

I hate it.

She stands up and she smiles and she puts the chair back and she leaves. I take off my shoes and I lie under the blankets and I close my eyes and I fall asleep.

I wake and I start to shiver and I curl up and I clench my fists. Sweat runs down my chest, my arms, the backs of my legs. It stings my face.

I sit up and I hear someone moan. I see a bug in the corner, but I know it's not there. The walls close in and expand they close in and expand and I can hear them. I cover my ears but it's not enough.

I stand. I look around me. I don't know anything. Where I am, why, what happened, how to escape. My name, my life.

I curl up on the floor and I am crushed by images and sounds. Things I have never seen or heard or ever knew existed. They come from the ceiling, the door, the window, the desk, the chair, the bed, the closet. They're coming from the fucking closet. Dark shadows and bright lights and flashes of blue and yellow and red as deep as the red of my blood. They move toward me and they scream at me and I don't know what they are but I know they're helping the bugs. They're screaming at me.

I start shaking. Shaking shaking shaking. My entire body is shaking and my heart is racing and I can see it pounding through my chest and I'm sweating and it stings. The bugs crawl onto my skin and they start biting me and I try to kill them. I claw at my skin, tear at my hair, start biting myself. I don't have any teeth and I'm biting myself and there are shadows and bright lights and flashes and screams and bugs bugs bugs. I am lost. I am completely fucking lost.

I scream.

I piss on myself.

I shit my pants.

The Nurse returns and she calls for help and Men in White come in and they put me on the bed and they hold me there. I try to kill the bugs but I can't move so they live. In me. On me. I feel the stethoscope and the gauge and they stick a needle in my arm and they hold me down.

I am blinded by blackness.

I am gone.

I sit in the chair by the window staring. I don't know what I'm staring at and I don't care. It's dark and it's late and I can't sleep anymore. The drugs are wearing off.

The Nurse comes in.

Can't sleep?

She checks my pressure and pulse.

No.

We have a Lounge.

She hands me some pills.

You can watch TV.

She hands me a robe and slippers.

And you can smoke.

I turn and I stare out the window.

Get changed and let me show you where it is.

All right.

She leaves and I take the pills and I change and when I open the door, she's waiting for me. She smiles and she hands me a pack of smokes.

These all right?

I smile.

Thank you.

We go to the Lounge. A television, two couches, an easy chair, some vending machines. The television is on.

You want a soda?

I sit in the chair.

No.

You're okay?

I nod.

Thank you.

She leaves and I can feel the pills kicking in. I watch television but nothing registers. I smoke a cigarette. It burns.

A man walks in and he walks up to me and he stands in front of me.

Hey, Buddy.

His voice is deep and dark.

Hey, Buddy.

Tracks crisscross his forearms.

I'm talking to you.

Scars run the length of his wrists.

I'm talking to you.

I look in his eyes. They're blank.

What?

He points.

That's my chair.

I turn back to the television.

That's my chair.

The pills are kicking in.

Hey, Buddy, that's my chair.

Nothing registers.

HEY, ASSHOLE. THAT'S MY FUCKING CHAIR.

I watch TV and he's breathing heavy and the Nurse comes in.

Is there a problem here?

This Asshole is in my chair.

Then why don't you sit on the couch?

Because I don't like the couch. I like the chair.

James is in the chair. There's the couch or the floor or you can leave. You decide.

Fuck James. Make him move.

Do you want me to call Security?

No.

Then you decide.

He walks to the couch and he sits down on it. The Nurse watches him.
Thank you.

He laughs and she leaves and we're alone and I'm watching television and smoking a cigarette. He stares at me and he chews his nails and he spits them at me but the pills are in and the bugs are gone and I don't care. Nothing registers.

I watch the television. Everything slows down. Slows down beyond recognition.

The image blurs, the voices fade. There is no action and no noise, just flickering lights and a symphony of withered voices. I stare at the lights, listen to the voices. I want them to go away and they won't.

My eyelids fall. I struggle to bring them up but they won't come. The rest of my body follows my eyes. My muscles go limp and I slide from the chair to the floor. I don't like the floor and I don't want to be on the floor

but I can't stop myself. As I slide, the surface of the chair holds my robe
and scratches the back of my legs and the robe bunches around my waist.
I lift my hand to adjust the robe and my hand falls back. My mind tells
my hand to move and my mind tells my hand to adjust the robe but my
mind isn't working. My mind isn't working and my hand isn't working.
The robe stays.

The man stops spitting his nails at me and he stands and he walks
toward me and I can see him coming through the slitted lids of my
eyes. I know that he can do whatever he wants to do to me and I know
that I am helpless to stop him. I know that he is angry and I know
from his tracks and his scars and his eyes that he will probably express
that anger through some form of violence. If I were able to move I
would stand and meet him with a dose of whatever he cared to bring
but I can't meet him with anything. With each step he takes toward me
the situation becomes more clear in my mind. He can do whatever he
wants to me, I am helpless to stop him. Helpless to stop him. Helpless.
He stands over me and he stares at me. He leans down and he looks at
my face and he laughs.

You are one ugly Motherfucker.

I try to say something back. I can only grunt.

I could kick your ass right now if I felt like it. Beat you to a bloody
fucking pulp.

My body is limp.

But all I want is the fucking chair.

My mind isn't working.

And I'm gonna fucking take it.

He reaches out and he grips my wrists and he drags me along the floor.
He drags me away from the chair and into the corner of the Room and
he leaves me lying facedown on the floor. He leans over and he puts his
mouth next to my ear.

I could have beat your fucking ass. Remember that.

He leaves and I can hear him sit down in the chair and start changing the
channels on the television. There is a daily sports wrap-up, an infomercial
on hair growth, a late-night talk show. He leaves the talk show on and he
laughs when he is supposed to laugh and he mumbles to himself about
how he'd like to fuck one of the guests. I lie facedown on the floor.

I am awake but I'm unable to move.

My heart beats and it's loud and I can see it.

The bristles of the carpet dig into my face and I can hear them.

The laugh track on the show booms and I can feel it.

I am awake but I'm unable to move.

I fade.

I fade.

I fade.

Morning comes and when I wake I am able to move and I stand and I look for the man. He's gone, but my memory isn't and it won't be for a long time. It has always been a fault of mine. I hold my memory.

I go to my Room and when I open the door I see an Orderly setting a tray of food on the desk. He looks at me and he smiles.

Good morning.

Good morning.

I brought you some breakfast. We thought you might be hungry.

Thank you.

If you want anything else, just call.

Thank you.

He leaves and I look at the food. Eggs, bacon, toast, potatoes. A glass of water and a glass of orange juice. I don't want to eat but I know I should so I go to the chair and I sit down and I look at the food and then I feel my face. Everything is still swollen. I touch my lips and they crack. I open my mouth and they bleed. I close my mouth and they drip. I don't want to eat but I know I should.

I reach for the glass of water and I take a sip but it's too cold.

I reach for the orange juice and I take a sip but it burns.

I try to use the fork but it does too much damage.

I break up the toast and push the pieces down my throat with my fingers. I do the same with the potatoes and the eggs and the bacon. I drink the water, but not the juice. I lick my fingers clean.

When I'm done I go to the Bathroom and I vomit. I try to stop it, but I can't. About half of the food comes up, as does some blood and some bile. I am happy that I have kept half of the food. That is more than I normally keep.

As I walk back to my bed, a Doctor comes into the Room. He smiles.

Hi.

He's wearing a name tag but I can't read it.

I'm Doctor Baker.

We shake hands.

I'm going to be working with you today.

I sit on the edge of the bed.

Are you okay with that?

He looks at my face but not my eyes.

Yeah.
I look at his eyes.
How are you feeling?
His eyes are kind.
I'm tired of that question.
He laughs.
I'll bet you are.
I smile.
These.
He hands me more pills.
Are Librium and Diazepam.
I take them.
They're detoxification drugs and important medically because they sta-
bilize your heart, keep your blood pressure down and help ease you
through withdrawal. Without them you could suffer a stroke or a heart
attack or both.
He leans forward and looks at my cheek.
You'll be taking them every four hours, in decreasing doses, for the next
five days.
I look at his eyes.
We're going to take some tests.
He's seen this before.
And start planning a Program for you.
All right.
First though, we need to try and fix you up a bit.
We go to a Room. It has bright fluorescent lights and a large surgical bed
and boxes of supplies. I sit on the bed and he puts on a pair of latex
gloves and he examines my cheek. He picks away the scabs. He opens my
mouth. His finger fits through the hole. He gets a needle and some string
and tells me to clench my fists and close my eyes. I leave them open and I
watch as the needle runs through. Inside and out. My cheek, my lip, my
mouth. Forty-one times.
We're through and he's on the phone with a Surgical Dentist and I'm sitting on the bed and I'm shaking from the pain. I can taste heat and the
string and the blood. He sets a date and he hangs up the phone and he
starts washing his hands.
We're gonna take you into Town in a couple of days and get your teeth
fixed.
I run my tongue along the stitches.
I know the Dentist and he'll take good care of you.

I run my tongue along the remnants of my teeth.
You'll look as good as new.
I let my tongue sit where it belongs.
Don't worry.
He puts on a new pair of gloves and he turns around.
Now I need to check your nose.
I take a deep breath. He steps forward and he starts looking at my nose.
He touches it and I cringe. I can no longer feel my cheek.
This is bad.
I know.
I'm gonna have to break it and reset it.
I know.
The sooner the better, but if you want we can wait.
The sooner the better.
All right.
He spreads his feet and he firms himself and he puts both of his hands on my nose. I grab the sides of the bed and I close my eyes and I wait.
You ready?
Yeah.
He jerks his hands forward and up and there's an audible crack. Cold white light shoots through my eyes and through my spine and into my feet and back again. My eyes are closed but I'm crying. Blood is streaming from my nostrils.
Now I have to set it.
He moves his hands to the side and I can feel the cartilage move with them. He moves them again. I can feel it. He presses up and it seems to fit. I can feel it.
There.
He reaches for some tape and I open my eyes. He puts the tape across the bridge of my nose and it holds the cartilage in place. It feels solid.
He grabs a towel and he wipes the blood from my face and my neck and I stare at the wall. My face is throbbing and I'm squeezing the sides of the bed and it hurts my hands. I want to let go but I can't.
You all right?
No.
I can't give you any painkillers.
I figured.
The Librium and Diazepam will take the edge off, but you're gonna hurt.
I know.

I'll get you a new robe.
Thank you.
He steps back and he throws the towel in the garbage can and he leaves. I
let go of the bed and I hold my hands in front of my face and I stare at
them. They shake, I shake.
The Doctor comes back with a Nurse and they help me change and
they tell me about the tests they're going to give me. Blood, urine, stool.
They need to know how much damage I've done to my insides. The
thought revolts me.
We leave and we go to a different Room that also has a Bathroom. I piss
in a cup, shit in a plastic container, take a needle in my arm. It's simple
and it's easy and it's painless.
We emerge and the Unit is busy. Patients wait in line for drugs, Doctors
go from Room to Room, Nurses carry bottles and tubes. There is noise,
but everything is quiet.
I go to my Room with the Doctor and I sit on the bed. He sits in the chair
and he writes on a chart. He finishes writing and he looks at me.
Except for the Dentist, the worst of it is over.
All right.
I'm going to put you on two hundred and fifty milligrams of Amoxicillin
three times a day and five hundred milligrams of Penicillin VK once a
day. These will prevent any possible infection.
All right.
Go to the Dispensary and they'll give them to you, or if you forget, a
Nurse will come find you.
Okay.
Thank you for dealing this morning.
No problem.
Good luck.
Thanks.
He stands and I stand and we shake hands and he leaves. I go to the
Dispensary and I stand in line. A young woman stands in front of me.
She turns around and she looks at my face. She speaks.
Hi.
She smiles.
Hi.
She holds out her hand.
I'm Lilly.
I take it. It's soft and warm.
I'm James.

I don't want to let go, but I do. We step forward.
What happened?
She glances toward the Dispensary.
I don't remember.
She turns back.
Blacked out?
Yeah.
She grimaces.
Shit.
I laugh.
Yeah.
We step forward.
When'd you get here?
I glance toward the Dispensary.
Yesterday.
The Nurse is glaring.
Me too.
I motion toward the Nurse and Lilly turns around and she stops talking and we step forward and we wait. The Nurse glares at us and she hands Lilly some pills and a cup of water and Lilly takes the pills and she drinks the water. She turns around and as she passes me she smiles and she mouths the word bye. I smile and step forward. The Nurse glares at me and asks me my name.
James Frey.
She looks at a chart and she goes to a cabinet and she gets some pills and she hands them to me with a cup of water.
I take the pills.
I drink the water.
I go to my Room and I fall asleep and I spend the rest of the day sleeping and shoving food down my throat and waiting in line and taking pills.

It's still dark when my body wakes me. My insides burn and feel like fire. They move and the pain comes. They move again and the pain becomes greater. They move again and I am paralyzed.

I know what's coming and I need to get up but I can't walk, so I roll off the bed and I fall to the floor. I lie there and I moan and it's cold and silent and dark.

The pain subsides and I crawl into the Bathroom and I grab the sides of the toilet and I wait. I sweat and my breath is short and my heart palpitates. My body lurches and I close my eyes and I lean forward. Blood and bile and chunks of my stomach come pouring from my mouth and my nose. It gets stuck in my throat, in my nostrils, in what remains of my teeth. Again it comes, again it comes, again it comes, and with each episode a sharp pain shoots through my chest, my left arm and my jaw. I bang my head on the back of the toilet but I feel nothing. I bang it again. Nothing.

The vomiting stops and I sit back and I open my eyes and I stare at the toilet. Thick red streams stick to its sides and brown pieces of my interior float in the water. I try to slow my breathing and my heart but I can't, so I sit and I wait. Every morning it's the same. I vomit and I sit and I wait. After a few minutes I stand and I walk slowly back into the Room.

Night is leaving and I stand at the window and I watch. Orange and pink streaks sail across the blue of the sky, large birds silhouette themselves against the red of the rising sun, clouds inch their way toward me. I can feel blood dripping from the wounds on my face and I can feel my heart beating and I can feel the weight of my life beginning to drop and I realize why dawn is called mourning.

I wipe my face with my sleeve and I take off my robe, which is now covered with blood and whatever I just threw up and I drop it on the floor and I go to the Bathroom. I turn on the shower and I wait for the warm water.

I look at my body. My skin is sallow and white. My torso is covered with cuts and bruises. I'm thin and my muscles sag. I look worn, beaten, old, dead. I didn't always look like this.

I reach in and I feel the water. It's warm, but not hot. I step inside the shower and I turn off the cold water and I wait for the heat.

The water runs down my chest and along the rest of my body. I take a bar of soap and I lather up and as I do, the water becomes hotter. It slams into my skin and burns my skin and turns my skin red. Although it hurts, it feels good. The heat, the water, the soap, the burns. It hurts but I deserve it.

I turn off the water and I step out of the shower and I dry myself off. I climb into bed and I climb under the covers and I close my eyes and I try to remember. Eight days ago I was in North Carolina. I remember picking up a bottle and a pipe and deciding to go for a drive. Two days later I woke up in Washington, D.C. I was on a couch at a House belonging to the Sister of a friend of mine. I was covered in piss and puke and she wanted me to leave so I borrowed a shirt from her and I left. Twenty-four hours later I woke up in Ohio. I remember a House, a Bar, some crack, some glue. I remember screaming. I remember crying.

The door opens and I sit up and the Doctor brings in a pile of clothes and my pills and he sets them on the table.

Hi.

I reach for the pills.

Hi.

I take them.

We got you some fresh clothes.

Thanks.

He sits at the table.

We're going to move you down to a Unit today.

All right.

Usually when a Patient moves down to a Unit his contact with us is limited, but in your case, we need to continue to see you.

Okay.

For the next week, you'll need to come up here twice a day, after breakfast and dinner, to get your antibiotics and your Librium. What I'm giving you is your last dose of Diazepam.

Got it.

He looks at my mouth.

We're taking you to a Dentist tomorrow.

I haven't looked at my mouth yet.

He knows what he's doing and he's a friend of mine. He'll take good care of you.

I'm scared to see myself.

Stay strong and you'll be fine.

Scared of the hate that my own image can conjure.
You should get changed and go wait in the Lounge.
All right.
They'll send someone up from the Unit to get you.
I can't wait.
He laughs and he stands up.
Good luck, James.
I stand.
Thank you.
We shake hands and he leaves and I change into the clothes he brought
me. A pair of khakis, a white T-shirt, some slippers. They're warm and
soft and they feel good. I almost feel human.
I leave my Room and I walk through the Medical Unit, where nothing
has changed. There are bright lights, there is whiteness. There are
Patients and Doctors and lines and pills. There are moans and screams.
There is sadness, insanity and ruin. I know these things and they no
longer affect me. I walk into the Lounge and I sit down on a couch. I'm
alone and I watch television and the latest batch of pills kicks in.
My heartbeat slows.
My hands stop shaking.
My eyelids drop.
My body is limp.
Nothing registers.
I hear my name and I look up and Lilly is standing in front of me. She
smiles and she sits down next to me.
Remember me?
Lilly.
She smiles.
I wasn't sure you would. You look pretty juiced.
Librium and Diazepam.
Yeah, I just got off it. I hate that shit.
It's better than nothing.
She laughs.
Talk to me in a couple days.
I smile.
I doubt I'm gonna last a couple of days.
She nods.
I know the feeling.
I don't respond. She speaks.
Where you from?

I reach for my cigarettes.
North Carolina.
I draw one out.
Got one of those for me?
I hand her a cigarette and I light them and we smoke and Lilly tells me
about herself and I listen to her. She's twenty-two and grew up in Phoenix.
Her Father left when she was four and her Mother was a Heroin Addict
who supported her habit by whoring herself to whoever would pay. She
started giving Lilly drugs at ten and started forcing her to whore herself to
whoever would pay at thirteen. At seventeen, Lilly ran away to her
Grandmother in Chicago, where she's lived since. She's addicted to crack
and quaaludes.
A man walks into the Room and we stop talking and the man stops in front
of me. He is thin, preppy, nearly bald. He has small nervous eyes.
James?
He smiles.
Yeah.
He seems very happy.
Hi, I'm Roy.
He holds out his hand.
Hi.
I stand and I shake his hand.
I'm here to take you down to the Unit.
All right.
Do you have any bags?
No.
Any extra clothes, books?
I have nothing.
A dob kit?
Nothing.
He smiles again. Nervously.
Let's go.
I turn and I look at Lilly, who is pretending to watch television.
Bye, Lilly.
She looks up and she smiles at me.
Bye, James.
Roy and I leave the Lounge and we walk down a short, dark, carpeted
Hallway. As we walk, Roy watches me carefully.
You know that's against the Rules.
I stare straight ahead.

What?

Talking to women.

Sorry.

Don't be sorry, just don't do it again.

All right.

The Rules here are for your own good. I suggest that you follow them.

I'll try.

Do better than try or you'll be in trouble.

I'll try.

We come to a large door and we walk through it and everything changes. The Hallways are long and lined with doors. The carpets are plush and the walls bright. There is color and light and a feeling of comfort. There are people walking everywhere and they are all smiling.

We walk through a series of Corridors. Roy stares at me and I stare straight ahead. He tells me about the Unit and its Rules.

There are between twenty and twenty-five men on the Unit at any given time, three Counselors and a Unit Supervisor. Each man has a Counselor who oversees his Recovery Program and the Unit Supervisor oversees them. Each man is required to attend three Lectures a day, eat three meals a day, and participate in all Unit activities.

Each man has a job that he is required to complete each morning. Mood-altering chemicals are not allowed on the Unit. If you are caught using them or possessing them, you will be asked to leave.

Mail is passed out once a day. Unit Counselors reserve the right to open and search any and all mail.

Visitors are allowed on Sundays between one o'clock and four o'clock. The Staff reserves the right to search and examine any gifts or packages that you are given by Visitors.

The women are housed in separate Units and contact with them is not allowed. If you see them in the Halls, hello is okay, how are you is not. If you violate this Rule, you may be asked to leave.

Roy stares at me.

The Rules are serious business. If you want to recover, I'd recommend following them.

I stare straight ahead.

I'll try.

We walk through a door marked Sawyer and we enter the Unit. We walk down a Hall with doors on both sides. Some of the doors have names on them and some of them are open. I can see men in the Rooms.

We leave the Hall and enter a large open Room with two levels. On the

Upper Level there is a soda machine, a candy machine, a large coffeepot, a Kitchen and a large table surrounded by chairs. On the Lower Level there are couches and chairs, arranged in a circle, a television and a blackboard. Against the far wall there is a Telephone Booth and there are large sliding-glass doors built into two of the other walls. The doors open onto large expanses of grass and trees, in the distance I can see a Lake. Men sit at the tables and on the couches. They're reading, talking, smoking cigarettes and drinking coffee. When I enter the Room, they all turn toward me and they stare at me.

Roy smiles.

Welcome to Sawyer.

Thanks.

It's a good place.

I want to leave.

You'll get better here.

Run away.

Trust me, I know.

Get fucked up.

Yeah.

Die.

Let's go to your Room.

We walk from the Upper Level of the Room to a Hall off its far end. The Hall is lined with Rooms in which I hear People talking, laughing, crying. We stop at a door and Roy opens the door and we enter the Room. The Room is fairly large and contains four beds, one in each of the corners. Next to each bed is a small nightstand and a small dresser. A Bathroom is off to one side. There are two men sitting on one of the beds playing cards and they both look up when we enter.

Larry, Warren, this is James.

The men stand and they walk over to where I am standing and they introduce themselves. Larry is short and powerful looking, built like the butt of a sledgehammer. He has long brown hair and a thick beard and a southern accent. He looks as if he's about thirty-five. Warren is in his fifties and he is tall and thin and tan and well dressed and he has a large smile. We shake hands and they ask where I'm from and I tell them. They ask if I want to play cards and I say no. I tell them I'm tired and I want to rest and I thank Roy and I walk over to the empty bed and I lie down. Roy leaves and Larry and Warren go back to their cards.

I close my eyes and I take a deep breath and I think about my life and how I ended up this way. I think about the ruin, devastation and wreck-

age I have caused to myself and to others. I think about self-hatred and
self-loathing. I think about how and why and what happened and the
thoughts come easily, but the answers don't.
I hear footsteps, feel a presence. I open my eyes and there's a man
standing over me. He's in his thirties. Medium height and thin like a
reed with long bony arms and delicate hands. He's clean-cut, short hair,
clean shave.
You're new.
He's nervous and hyper.
Yeah.
And his eyes are empty.
What's your name?
James.
I sit up.
I'm John.
He sits on the edge of the bed and he hands me a card.
That's my card.
I read it. It says John Everett. Sexual Ninja. San Francisco and the
World.
I laugh.
Wanna see something?
He reaches for his wallet.
Sure.
He opens it and he draws out a faded newspaper article and he hands it
to me. The article is old and from the *San Francisco Chronicle*. It has a
picture of a man standing in the middle of a Street holding a sign. The
headline reads Man Arrested On Market Street With Sign Reading
Cocaine For Sale Three Hours After Being Released From San Quentin.
That's me.
I laugh again.
I went back for three more years.
I hand him the article.
That sucks.
He pockets it.
You ever fuck anybody in the ass?
What?
You ever fuck anybody in the ass?
What are you talking about?
I got into it in Prison and now I'm addicted to it. That and rock cocaine.
I thought you should know right off the bat.

I stare at him.

Honesty and openness are very important here. They're part of
the Program and since I'm working the Program, I wanted to tell you.
Is that okay?

I stare hard.

It's fine.

He gets nervous, stands, looks at his watch.

It's time for lunch. You want me to show you the Dining Hall?

I stand without a word. I just stare.

We leave and we make our way through the Unit and down another series of
Halls. As we walk, John talks about himself. He's thirty-seven and he is from
Seattle. He grew up in a wealthy and powerful Family that has cut him off.
He has a twenty-year-old Daughter whom he hasn't seen in ten years. He
spent eight years in jail. His Father started molesting him when he was five.
We enter a long Hall with glass walls on either side of it. In one of the
sections, women sit eating their lunches, in the other sit the men. At
the end of the Hall is a Common Area with a salad bar and two
cafeteria-style lines where food is served. John grabs two trays, hands
one of them to me and we get in line.

As we move forward, I take in my surroundings. There are men and
women. There is food. There is talking, but there are no smiles. There are
round tables surrounded by eight chairs. There are People sitting in the
chairs, there are plates and glasses and trays on the tables. There are about
a hundred and twenty-five men in the Male Section spread among tables
that probably hold two hundred. There are about a hundred women in
the Female Section spread among tables that hold about one hundred and
fifty. I get a bowl of soup and a glass of water and as I walk through the
Room, I can feel People staring at me. I can only imagine what I must
look like.

I find an empty table and I sit down and I'm alone. I take a sip of the water and I begin spooning the soup into my mouth. It's hot and each
spoonful shoots a wave of pain through my lips, my cheek, my gums and
my teeth. I eat slowly and deliberately and I never look up. I don't want
to see anybody and I don't want anybody seeing me.

I finish the soup and for a moment, at least, I feel good. My stomach is
full and I am warm and content. I stand and I take my tray and I put it
with a pile of other trays and I leave the Dining Hall.

I walk back to the Unit. As I pass an open door, someone calls my name.
I stop and I go back to the door and a man stands and he comes from behind a desk and he walks toward me. He's in his early thirties. He's very

tall and very thin. He has dark hair pulled into a small ponytail and he wears round black glasses. He is dressed in a black T-shirt, black pants and black tennis shoes. He looks like a grown-up version of a kid who spent his childhood sitting behind a computer and hiding from Bullies.

You're James.

He reaches out to shake my hand. We shake.

I'm Ken, your Unit Recovery Counselor.

Nice to meet you.

He turns and he walks toward his desk.

Come in and sit down.

I follow him in and I sit down in a chair across from him and I look around his Office. It's small and cluttered and there are piles of paper everywhere and there are files everywhere. The walls are covered with schedules and small pictures of either people or landscapes and there is a framed copy of the Twelve Steps of Alcoholics Anonymous hanging behind him. He reaches for a file and he sets it on his desk and he opens it and he looks at me.

You settling in okay?

Yeah.

Anything we can do to make you more comfortable?

No.

We need some more information to round out our file. Do you mind answering a few questions?

No.

He picks up a pen.

When did you start using drugs and alcohol?

I started drinking at ten, doing drugs at twelve.

And when did you start using heavily?

At fifteen I was drinking every day, at eighteen I was drinking and doing drugs every day. It has gotten much much heavier since then.

Do you black out?

Yes.

How often?

Every day.

How long has this been happening?

Four years or five years.

Do you get sick?

Every day.

How often?

When I wake up, when I have my first drink, when I have my first meal and a few more times after that.
How many times is a few?
Anywhere from three to seven.
How long has this been happening?
Four or five years.
Do you ever contemplate suicide?
Yes.
Have you ever tried it?
No.
Have you ever been arrested?
Yes.
How many times?
Twelve or thirteen.
For what?
All kinds of shit.
Such as?
Possession, Possession with Intent to Distribute, three DUIs, a bunch of Vandalism and Destruction of Property charges, Assault, Assault with a Deadly Weapon, Assaulting an Officer of the Law, Public Drunkenness, Disturbing the Peace. I'm sure there's some other shit, but I don't remember exactly what.
Are any of the charges still outstanding?
Most of them.
Where?
Michigan, Ohio and North Carolina.
Have you been going to Court?
No.
Are you out on Bail?
I skipped Bail.
Where?
Everywhere.
Why?
I've been to Jail. I don't like it and I don't want to go back.
You're gonna have to deal with the charges at some point.
I know.
We'll encourage you to do it while you're here. Or at least start the process.
I'll think about it.

How have you been making a living?
Selling drugs.
That will have to stop.
I know.
Have you ever been to Treatment before?
No.
Why?
I was never willing to go. I told my Parents if they tried to put me in I'd
leave and they'd never see me again. They believed me.
He pauses and he sets down his pen. He looks me in the eye and I can
feel that he's testing me, waiting for me to look away, so I don't.
Do you want to get sober?
I think so.
You think so?
Yeah.
Does that mean yes?
It means I think so.
Why?
My life is Hell, has been Hell for too long. If I keep going I'm going to
die. I'm not sure I want to be dead yet.
Are you willing to do whatever it takes?
I don't know.
I'll ask again. Are you willing to do whatever it takes?
I don't know.
I'll ask one more time. Are you willing to do whatever it takes?
I don't know.
He stares at me, angry I won't give him the answers he wants to hear. I
stare back.
If you're not willing to do whatever it takes, you might as well leave. I
would rather you not, but we can't help you until you're ready to help
yourself. Think about it and we can talk more. If you need anything
come find me.
I will.
He stands and I stand and he comes around the desk and we leave the
Office and we go back into the Unit. Men are returning from lunch and
are gathering in small groups at the tables, on the couches, in small
clumps of fold-out chairs. Ken asks me if I want to meet anyone and I
tell him no and he leaves and I watch him walk over to another man and
start talking to him. I find a chair and I light a cigarette and I take a long
deep drag and I look at the men sitting around me. They are black and

white and yellow and brown. They have long hair, short hair, beards and mustaches. They are well dressed and they wear rags, they are fat and they are thin. They are hard, weathered, worn-out and desperate. Intimidating and thuggish, addicted and insane. They are all different and they are all the same and as I sit there smoking my cigarette, they scare the living shit out of me.

Ken is finished talking to the man and he announces that it's time for the Lecture so the Men stand and begin filing out. My drugs are wearing off and I need some more so I skip the Lecture and I walk back to the Medical Wing and I get in line. As the line moves forward I start to feel anxious and nervous and angry. With each step closer to the drugs, the feelings become stronger. I can feel my heart beat faster and I look at my hands and they're shaking and when I get to the counter I can hardly speak. I want something, I need something, I have to have something. Anything at all. Just fucking give it to me.

The Nurse recognizes me and she reaches for a chart and she looks at it and she turns around and she gets my pills from a cabinet. She hands them to me with a small plastic glass of water and I take them as quickly as I can and I step away from the counter and I wait. Almost immediately I feel better. My heart slows, my hands stop shaking, the nervousness, anxiety and anger disappear.

I turn and I leave and I walk toward the Unit and I go to the Lecture Hall where I sit and I listen to a man explain the relationship between a healthy diet and a sound mind. None of it makes any sense because of the drugs and at a certain point the Lecture ends and I stand up and I leave and I go back to the Unit with the rest of the men. One of them looks like a Movie Star and I think I talk to him but I'm not sure. The afternoon and the early evening slide by in a lidded daze where the ability to think in any identifiable way disappears and where every moment seems to be an eternity. Shortly after dinner I climb into bed and for the first time in several years I am conscious of the fact that I'm going to sleep.

I open my eyes. My Roommates are sleeping and the Room is silent and calm and dark. I sit up and I run my fingers through my hair and I look down at my pillow and I see that it's covered with blood. I touch my face and I realize that I'm bleeding.

I stand and I slowly walk steps to the Bathroom and I open the door and I go inside and I turn on the light. I recoil from the brightness and I close my eyes and as I wait for them to adjust, I step forward and I grab the edges of the sink. I open my eyes and I look up into the mirror and for the first time in five days I see my own face.

My lips are cut and cracked and they are swollen to three times their normal size. On the left side of my cheek a row of crusted scabbed stitches hold a deep, inch-long gash together. My nose is bent and swollen beneath its bandage and red lines stream from my nostrils. There are black and yellow bruises beneath both of my eyes. There is blood, both wet and dry, everywhere.

I reach for a paper towel and I wet it and I begin softly wiping. Streaks crisscross my cheeks and scabs break and I wince in pain and the towel becomes soaked. I throw it away and I reach for another. I do it again.

I do it again.

I do it again.

I finish and I throw away the last towel and I wash my hands and I watch the red drift from my skin into the sink and down the drain. I turn off the water and I run my hands through my hair and they're warm and they feel good and I try to look at myself again.

I want to see my eyes. I want to look beneath the surface of the pale green and see what's inside of me, what's within me, what I'm hiding. I start to look up but I turn away. I try to force myself but I can't.

I turn and I walk out of the Bathroom and into the main Room. Larry and Warren and John are all awake and in various stages of dressing. They say hello and I say hello and I walk back to my bed and I get inside of it. As I start to get comfortable, John walks over and stands in front of me.

What are you doing?

What's it look like I'm doing?

Going back to sleep.

Exactly.

You can't do that.

Why not?

We gotta go do our jobs.

What jobs?

We each got a job. We get up in the morning and we do our jobs.

Now?

Yeah.

I get out of bed and I follow John into the Upper Level of the Unit. Roy sees me and he walks over to me and he takes me to the Job Board and he shows it to me and he explains how it works.

There's a job, there's your name. The longer you're here, the easier the job. Since you just arrived, you have to clean the Group Toilets.

I ask him where the cleaning supplies are and he shows me. As I collect them and I head toward the Group Toilets, he speaks.

Make sure they're clean.

I will.

Really clean.

I heard you.

I find the Group Toilets, two Bathrooms off the Upper Level that are used by the Counselors, the men who don't feel like going to their Rooms and Visitors. They are small, with one toilet and one urinal each and one sink each. I go inside and I scrub the toilets and the urinals and the sinks. I take out the trash and replace the toilet paper. I mop the floor. It's not fun, but I've cleaned toilets before, so I don't mind.

I finish the job and I return the supplies and I go back to my Room and I go to the Bathroom and I get sick. I haven't had a drink in three days and I haven't done coke in five so the sickness isn't as bad as normal, but I'm starting to feel sick in other ways. I close the lid of the toilet and I flush it and I sit down on the toilet seat and I stare at the wall. I wonder what is happening to me.

I stand and begin pacing back and forth across the length of the Bathroom. I cross my arms and begin rubbing my body. I get cold and a chill shoots up my spine. One second I want to cry, one second I want to kill, one second I want to die. I think about running but there's nowhere to run so I pace and I rub my body and I feel cold.

Larry opens the door and tells me it's time for breakfast so I leave and I follow him and Warren and John to the Dining Hall and I get in line and I get some food. I find an empty table and I sit down and I begin eating a bowl of warm sugary oatmeal and drinking a glass of water. The feelings have subsided, but not entirely. I think that I'm going insane.

I finish my oatmeal and I sit back in my chair and I look around the Dining Hall and I see Ken talking to a man from my Unit. The man points to me and Ken walks over to my table and he sits down across from me.

You feeling all right?

I'm fine.

Have you done any thinking about our conversation?

Yeah.

Any conclusions?

No.

Keep thinking then.

I will.

You have an appointment this morning with the Dentist.

All right.

I'll walk you up to the Medical Unit and after you get your meds, I'll take you to a van. The Driver will take you to your appointment, wait for you and bring you back.

Okay.

Then, after you have lunch, we're going to have you take a test called the MMPI. It's a standard psych test that will give us some insight as to how we can help you.

Okay.

He stands.

You ready?

I grab my tray and I stand.

Yeah.

I put my tray away and we leave and we walk back to the Medical Unit. I get my pills and I take them and we go to the front Entrance of the Hospital where a white Transportation Van sits waiting. Ken gives me a jacket so I won't be cold and we go outside and he slides open the side door of the Van and he talks to the Driver while I climb into the front seat and make myself comfortable. Ken says good-bye and I say good-bye and he shuts the door and the Driver starts to drive and we pull away. The weather has gotten worse. Black clouds fill the Sky and patches of snow gather along the Ground. What once was green is brown. What once had leaves now has none. It's cold and it's winter and the World has gone to sleep.

I stare out the window at the drifting frozen landscape. A mist from my breath collects itself on the glass and I begin to shiver. I huddle up and I look at the Driver who is also huddled up and is driving slowly and watching the Road.

You think we could get some heat in here?

The Driver looks over at me.

You cold?

I return his look.

Goddamn right I'm cold.

He laughs.

It's coming, Kid. Once the engine is warm, we'll be warm.

We stop at a lonely intersection where the light is red and the roads are empty and the wind sends scraps of paper and leaves whipping through the air. The Driver looks ancient. He has messy white hair and a messy white beard and bright blue eyes. His skin looks as if it's made out of leather. He has thin forearms, but they look strong, and despite his age, he looks strong. He reaches out to shake my hand.

I'm Hank.

We shake hands.

I'm James.

What happened?

Don't exactly know.

You fucked up?

What's it look like?

Looks like that might be an understatement.

Looks are not deceiving.

We laugh and the light turns green and Hank continues driving and we continue talking. He's from Massachusetts, where he spent most of his life as the Captain of a Commercial Fishing Boat. He was always a Drinker, but after he retired it got worse. He lost his House, his Wife, his Family, his mind. He came here to get help and after he got well he decided to stay and see if he could help others. He's an easy talker and as the ride drags on, I begin to think of him as a friend.

We drive into a small Town and turn onto what seems to be its Main Street. There's a Grocery Store, a Hardware Store and a Police Station. Halloween decorations hang from the Streetlights, and People, who all seem to know each other, wander in and out of the Shops. Hank pulls into a parking spot in front of a Bait-and-Tackle Store and we get out of the Van and we walk to a small door next to the main Entrance of the Store. Hank opens the door and we walk up a flight of stairs and we go through another door and we enter a small dark Room with two couches, a sliding-glass Reception Area and a small table littered with magazines and Children's books.

Hank heads to the Reception Desk and I walk over to one of the couches and I sit down and I begin looking through the magazines. On the other couch a woman sits with a young Boy looking through a picture book about Babar the Elephant. When I find a magazine and I lean back to start reading it, I can see the woman watching me out of the corner of her eye. She moves closer to the Child and she puts her arm around him and she leans over and kisses his forehead. I know why she does it and I don't blame her and as I open my magazine my heart breaks and I hope that the little Boy doesn't grow up to be anything like me.

Hank comes back from the Reception Desk.

They're gonna take you right now.

I set down the magazine and I stand.

Okay.

I'm scared and Hank can see it.

You all right?

He puts his hand on my shoulder.

Yeah.

He looks me straight in the eye.

I know this is a podunk Town, but these people know what they're doing, Kid. You're gonna be fine.

I look away.

A Nurse calls my name and Hank moves his arm and I walk toward an open door where the Nurse waits for me. Before I go in I turn around and I see the woman and the Child staring at me. I look to Hank and he nods and I nod and for a brief second I feel strong. Not strong enough to face myself, but strong enough to keep going.

I walk through the door and the Nurse shows me to a clean white Room and I sit down in a large dentist's chair in the middle of the Room and the Nurse leaves and I wait. A few seconds later the Dentist walks in. He's in his forties and he is tall and he has dark hair and dark eyes and rough skin. Except for the white coat and the clipboard, he looks like a Lumberjack.

You're James?

He pulls up a chair and sits in front of me.

Yes.

Doctor David Stevens, nice to meet you.

We shake hands.

You too.

He puts on a pair of thin clear latex gloves.

I got some info on you from the Doc at the Treatment Center.

He grabs a small flashlight from his pocket.

But I need to check you out more myself, see what exactly we've got going on here.

He leans forward.

Can you open your mouth?

I open my mouth and he turns on the flashlight and he moves toward my face.

Can I lift your upper lip?

I nod yes and he sets down the flashlight and he lifts my lip and he picks up a long thin metal tool with a sharp end.

This might hurt.

He touches the shards of my outer teeth with the end of the tool and he starts pushing into some of the damaged areas of my gums. The pain is instant, sharp and overwhelming. I want to close my mouth and make him stop, make the pain go away, but I don't do it. I close my eyes and ball my hands into fists and I squeeze. I can feel my lips quivering and I can taste blood and when the Dentist touches my teeth, they move. He finishes the exam and I hear him set the tool in a tray. I lean back and I open my eyes.

We need to do some X-rays, but from what I can see with my eyes, we're going to have to do some surgery.

I squeeze my fists. Squeeze tight.

The outer two teeth are broken, but the roots seem to be intact.

My lips quiver.

We can cap those and you should be fine.

I can taste the blood.

The front two, though, are dying.

I run my tongue along my upper gum.

We're going to need to do root canals and build a bridge.

I feel the remains of my teeth. Short sharp shards of teeth.

It won't be pleasant, but unless you're comfortable without teeth, it's the only option.

I nod.

I'll set up an appointment for you in a few days. The swelling in your lips should be gone by then and we can't do this until it is.

I nod.

Nice to meet you, James.

Nice to meet you too.

He stands and we shake hands and he leaves. Another Nurse comes in and she washes out my mouth and she stuffs it with cotton wads and plates and she takes some X-rays. When she's finished the cotton wads are covered in blood and my mouth feels as if it's been brushed with sandpaper and slammed with a hammer. She tells me I can go and she leaves and I stand and I walk back into the Lobby. Hank is sitting on one of the couches reading a magazine about the personal lives of Movie Stars and I walk over and I sit down next to him and he sets down the magazine and he looks at me.

How'd it go?

It was fine.

They gonna fix you up?

They say they are.

I'm gonna go find out when you gotta come back.

He stands and he walks to the Reception Area and he talks to the Receptionist and he comes back and we leave the Office and we get in the Van and start driving back to the Clinic. Hank tries to be friendly and talk to me but I tell him my mouth hurts so he leaves me alone. I stare out the window.

I think about her. I think about the first time I saw her. I was eighteen and at School and I was sitting by myself under the orange and yellow of a fading October tree. I had a book in my hand and I was reading and for some reason I looked up. She was walking alone across the lawn of the School with an armful of papers. She tripped and the papers fell to the ground and as she bent over to get them she looked around to see if anyone had noticed. She didn't see me, but as she scrambled to pick up her papers, I saw her. She didn't see me, but I saw her.

The Van pulls up to the Entrance to the Clinic and Hank and I get out of the Van and I walk over to Hank and I thank him for driving me and helping me. He tells me I look as if I could use a hug and I laugh at him and he ignores me and steps forward and puts his arm around me and hugs me. I warm at the simple pleasure of human contact and for the first time in a long time I actually feel good. It makes me uncomfortable so I pull away and I say good-bye and I thank him again and I walk back into the Clinic. The Receptionist tells me it's lunchtime so I go to the Dining Hall and I get in line and I get a bowl of soup and a glass of water and I find an empty table and I sit down by myself and I do the best I can to force some food past the bloody wreckage of my mouth.

Hey, Kid.

I look up. A man stands across from me. He's about fifty, medium height, medium build. He has thick brown hair that is thinning on top and a weathered face that looks as if it has taken a few punches. He's wearing a bright blue-and-yellow silk Hawaiian shirt, small round silver glasses and a huge gold Rolex. He stares at me. He sets his tray down. He looks pissed.
Remember me?
No.
You been walking around the last two days calling me Gene Hackman. Now I know they got you doped up on that detox shit, but I'm not Gene Hackman, I've never been Gene Hackman, I'll never be Gene Hackman, and if you call me Gene fucking Hackman again, we're gonna have a big fucking problem.
I laugh.
Something funny?
I laugh again. He looks like Gene Hackman.
You think this is funny, you Little Fuck?
I stare at him and I smile. I have no teeth and the thought makes me smile more.
You think this is fucking funny?
I stare at him. He has hard, angry, violent eyes. I understand his eyes and I know how to deal with them. This is familiar territory.
I stand and my smile disappears. I stare at the man and the Room becomes quiet. I speak.
I don't know you. I don't remember ever seeing you, I don't remember ever speaking to you and I certainly don't remember ever calling you Gene Hackman, but if I did, yeah, I think it's funny.
I can feel that most of the People in the Dining Room are watching us and my heartbeat increases and the man stares at me and his eyes are hard, angry and violent. I know I'm in no shape for this, but I don't care. I feel myself getting ready. I tense up, clench my jaw, stare straight ahead, eyes fixed, focused and unblinking.
If you're gonna force me to beat your ass, Old Man, we might as well get on with it.
He's shocked. Not scared or unwilling, just shocked. I stare straight ahead.
What'd you just say?
Eyes fixed, focused and unblinking.
I said if you're gonna force me to beat your ass, we might as well get on with it.
What's your name, Kid?

James.

James, I'm Leonard.

He smiles.

I don't know if you're the stupidest fuck I ever met or the bravest, but if you answer one question for me, I'll consider letting that last remark slide.

What's the question, Leonard?

Are you fucked up, James?

Yeah, Leonard, I'm fucked up. I'm fucked up real bad.

Good, cause I'm fucked up too. I like fucked-up people and I try to associate with them as much as I can. Why don't we sit and have lunch together, see if we can forget about our differences and become friends. I could use a friend in here.

All right.

We sit and we eat our lunches and Leonard talks and I listen to him talk. Leonard is from Las Vegas and he has been here for a week. He's addicted to cocaine and has been planning his stay here for over a year. For the last twelve months he's done nothing but eat rich food, drink expensive wine, play golf and snort enormous amounts of blow. He has done enough, he says, that if he does it again he will die. I don't know what he does for a living, but I know it's not legal and I know he does it well. I can see it in his eyes, hear it in his words, recognize it in the easy way he speaks of things most people would consider horrific. I am comfortable with Leonard. More comfortable with him than anyone else whom I have met in here. He speaks easily of horror. He is a Criminal of some sort. I am comfortable with him.

We finish eating and we put our trays away and we leave the Dining Room and we go to the Lecture Hall. Female Patients sit on one side of the Hall, males on the other, and the total number of Patients is around two hundred and fifty. Everyone sits with their Unit and as Leonard and I sit down among the twenty men of Sawyer, a Doctor on a Stage starts speaking to us about the concept of Alcoholism and Addiction as a disease.

I start to feel sick. Waves of nausea pulse through me. I get cold. I close my eyes and I open them and I close them again. I do it quickly, I do it slowly. I start to shiver and I stare at the seat in front of me and it's moving. It starts to talk to me so I look away and I see blue and silver lights dancing everywhere. I close my eyes and the lights dance through my brain. I can feel my blood crawling slowly through my heart and I think I'm going to pass out so I grab my face with one of my hands and I squeeze my face. It hurts, but I want the pain because it makes this nightmare a reality and it keeps me from going insane. The pain is immense, but I need it because it keeps me from going insane.

The Doctor finishes speaking and the Patients start clapping and I let go of my face and I take a deep breath and I stare straight ahead. Leonard taps me on the shoulder.

You all right?

No.

You need some help?

No.

You look like you do.

I need something, but it's not help.

As the Doctor onstage answers questions I stand and I walk out of the Lecture Hall. I head back to the Unit hoping to make it to my bed and hoping that my bed will make me feel better. As I walk by Ken's Office he calls for me and I ignore him and I keep walking. He comes into the Hall and he calls for me again.

James.

I stop.

What?

I lean against the wall.

You all right?

He walks toward me.

I feel like shit, I need to lie down.

He stops in front of me.

You can lie down later. It's time for your test.

What test?

The MMPI. I told you about it this morning.

I don't want to take it.

Why?

Because I feel like shit and I need to lie down.

You're gonna feel like shit for a while.

Maybe, but I still don't want to take your test.

It's not optional.

I can't take it later?

No, we need you to take it now. It helps us know how to help you, and we want to start helping you right away.

Fine.

We walk past the Lecture Hall and through a maze of carpeted Corridors and we enter a small bare white Room with two chairs and a table. Ken sits down and I sit down. On the table in front of us is a large stapled booklet and a form answer sheet and a pencil. Ken speaks.

It's a very simple test. All of the questions are true or false, you can take as long as you want to answer them. When you're finished come back to my Office and if I'm not there, leave your responses on my desk. A staff Psychologist will analyze everything and in two days we'll go over the results together.

All right.

Any questions?

No.

Ken leaves and I grab the pencil and the answer sheet and I open the booklet and I start reading it. The pages are filled with questions and I begin answering them.

I am a stable person.

False.

I think the World is aligned against me.

False.

I think my problems are caused by others.

False.

I don't trust anybody.

False.

I hate myself.

True.

I often think of death.

True

Suicide is a reasonable option.

True.

My sins are unpardonable.

I stare at the question.

My sins are unpardonable.

I stare at the question.

My sins are unpardonable.

I leave it blank.

I finish five hundred and sixty-six of the five hundred and sixty-seven true-or-false questions of the test and I close the booklet and I lay down my pencil and I take a deep breath. Hours have passed and I am exhausted and I want a drink. Vodka, gin, rum, tequila, bourbon, scotch. I don't care. Just give me a drink. A nice strong alcoholic drink. I tell myself that I only want one but I know it's not true. I want fucking fifty.

I grab my answer sheet and I stand and I leave the Room and I walk back to Ken's Office and I leave my test and my answer sheet on his desk and I walk into the Unit. The day's activities are done and the men are spread out in small groups across both of the Levels. They are playing cards, talking shit, smoking cigarettes and drinking coffee. The phone is free and I haven't talked to my Parents, my Brother or any of my friends, so I walk down to the Lower Level and I grab a chair and I sit down by the phone and I pick up the receiver and I start making collect calls.

I call my friend Amy. I call my friend Lucinda. I call my friend Courtney. They were all originally her friends but when she left and everybody else left they stood with me. I love all three dearly and the conversations upset me. I call, they answer. I tell them that I got hurt, that I came here, that I'm going to try to get better. I tell them I don't know if I can. They cry and they ask me if I need anything and I tell them no. They ask if they can help in any way. I tell them they've given me enough. We hang up.

I call my Brother. He asks me how I am and I tell him that I'm holding up. He tells me that he's worried about me and that he wants to come and see me. I tell him I don't know what today is but that Visiting Day is on Sunday and I'd like it if he came. He tells me to be brave and I tell him that I'm trying. He tells me that he's proud of me and I say thanks. I tell him I need to go and he says to call if I need anything and I thank him. We hang up.

I call my Parents at a Hotel in Chicago and my Mother answers the phone.

Hello.

Hi, Mom.

Hold on, James.

I hear her call my Father. My Father picks up the phone.

Hi, James.

Hi, Dad.

How are you?

All right.

How is it there?

It's fine.

What's happened so far?

I'm being detoxed and that sucks, and yesterday I moved down to a Unit and that's been fine.

Are you feeling like it's helping?

I don't know.

I hear my Mom take a deep breath.

Anything we can do?
I hear my Mom break down.
No.
I listen to her cry.
I gotta go, Dad.
I listen to her cry.
You're gonna be okay, James. Just keep it up.
I listen to her cry.
I gotta go.
If you need anything, call us.
Good-bye.
We love you.
I hang up the phone and I stare at the floor and I think about my Mother
and my Father in a Hotel Room in Chicago and I wonder why they still love
me and why I can't love them back and how two normal stable people could
have created something like me, lived with something like me and tolerated
something like me. I stare at the floor and I wonder. How did they
tolerate me.
I look up and I see most of the men leaving the Unit to go to dinner so I
stand and I walk through the Halls to the Dining Hall and I get in line
and I get some soup and a glass of water and I sit down at an empty table
and I eat. The food tastes good, and when I finish my bowl I want more.
My body is craving and wanting and requiring and though it can't have
what it normally has, it needs something. I get a second bowl and then a
third and then a fourth. I eat them all and I want more. It's always been
the same, I want more and more and more and more.
I finish eating and I leave the Dining Hall and I go to the Lecture Hall
and I sit with Leonard and I listen to a woman tell her life story. The
woman has been to seventeen Treatment Centers in the last decade. She
lost her Husband, her Kids, all of her money and spent two years in Jail.
She's been clean for eighteen months and says she's happy for the first
time in her entire life. She says she's devoted her life to God and to the
Twelve Steps and that each new day is better than the last. Good luck,
Lady. Good fucking luck.
She finishes her story and People clap and I stand and I go back to the
Unit and I go to my Room. I want to go to bed but I can't so I play cards
with John and Larry and Warren. Larry, who has a Wife and newborn
twin Girls waiting at home for him in Texas, is grief-stricken. He found
out this afternoon that he has the HIV virus, which he probably con-
tracted during ten years of mainlining crystal meth and fucking whores.

He wants to tell his Wife but he's scared to call her so he sits with us and he plays cards and he talks about how much he loves his Children. I want to try to comfort him but I don't know what to say so I say nothing and I laugh when he makes jokes and I tell him his Girls are beautiful when he shows me their picture.

It gets late and we put away the cards and we get into our beds. My body still wants what I cannot give it and I'm unable to sleep so I lie on my back and I stare at the ceiling. I think about where I am and how I got here and what the fuck am I going to do and I listen to Larry cry and pound on his pillow and curse God and beg for forgiveness. At a certain point my eyes close and at a certain point I fall asleep.

I sit alone at a table. It's dark and I don't know where I am or how I got here. There are bottles of liquor and wine everywhere and on the table in front of me is a large pile of white cocaine and a huge bag of yellow crack. There is also a torch, a pipe, a tube of glue and an open can filled with gasoline.

I look around me. There is blackness, there is alcohol, there are drugs. There is an abundance of all of them. I know I'm alone and there is no one to stop me. I know I can do as much as I want of whatever I want. As I reach for one of the bottles, something inside of me tells me to stop, that what I'm doing is wrong, that I can't do it anymore, that I'm killing myself. I reach anyway. I grip the bottle, bring it to my lips and take a long deep draw that burns my mouth, my throat and my stomach.

For the briefest instant I feel complete. The pain I carry with me disappears. I feel comfortable and at rest, confident and secure, calm and composed. I feel good. Goddamn it, I feel fucking good.

The feelings are gone as quickly as they came and I want them back. I don't care what I have to do, what I have to take, what I have to endure. I'll do anything. I just want them to come back.

I take another drink. It doesn't work. I grab a different bottle, take a larger drink. It doesn't work. I seize bottle after bottle, take drink after drink, nothing works. Instead of feeling better, I feel increasingly worse. Everything I felt that was good has become bad and it has been magnified beyond any point of reference or comprehension. My only option is to try and kill. Kill what hurts. Kill it.

I switch to the drugs. I take a deep breath and I bury my face in the pile of coke and I inhale and my nostrils turn to fire and the back of my throat becomes an inferno. I take a breath, inhale, take a breath, inhale, take a breath, inhale. Too much too fast and my nose starts bleeding. I wipe the blood away and I take a breath and I inhale. I do it again. The killing has started, but I'm not close to being done.

I rip open the bag of crack and I pull out a handful of small yellow rocks. I wipe the blood again and I snatch the pipe, which is a long straight piece of glass and a screen filter and I start stuffing rocks into it. I fill it, wipe the blood again, fire up the torch, put the pipe in my mouth, bring the white flame to its tip. I inhale. Hot peppermint honey mixed with napalm followed by a rush a thousandfold stronger than the purest powder, a thousandfold more dangerous. I hold and the rush gains speed and power and it grows, consumes and overwhelms me. I feel good again, perfect, magnificent and invincible, like the power of every orgasm I've ever had, could ever have and will ever have has been concentrated into a single moment. Oh my God, I'm coming. Oh my fucking God, I'm coming. Let it come let it come let it come let it come. Let it fucking come.

It's gone as fast as it came and I know it's gone for good, replaced by fear, dread and a murderous rage. Any pretense of experiencing pleasure disappears. I grab rocks, stuff the pipe, hit. I grab rocks, stuff the pipe, hit. The torch is white and the glass is pink and I feel the skin of my fingers bubbling but it doesn't bother me. I grab rocks, stuff the pipe, hit. I do it until the bag is empty and then I stuff the bag into the pipe and I smoke the plastic. I have a murderous rage and I need to kill. Kill my heart, kill my mind, kill myself.

There is glue and there is gasoline and I want them both. I grab the glue and I put the end of the tube below my nose and I lay a thick line on the skin between my nostrils and my lip. Each breath brings the stench of Hell and death, each breath brings on the desire for more. I am killing quickly and efficiently now, but not quickly or efficiently enough.

I lean over and place my nose just above the shimmering surface of the gasoline and I stare into the face of chemical annihilation. This face is my friend, my enemy and my only option. I take it.

Breathe in, breathe out, go faster and faster and faster and faster. I don't feel anything anymore or what I do feel is so powerful that my mind and my body are incapable of allowing it to register. I am comfortable here. This is what I want, what I need and what I must have, and this is where I have been living the last few years of my life.

I realize that I'm cold and I snap and I open my eyes. The Room is dark and quiet. A clock near John's bed reads six-fifteen. I can hear Warren snoring. I sit up and I rub my body and I shiver. Goose pimples cover my arms and the hair on the back of my neck stands straight and I'm scared. Scared of my dream, scared of the morning, scared of this place and the People in it, scared of a life without drugs and alcohol, scared of myself, scared to deal with myself, scared of the day that lies ahead, scared shitless, scared out of my mind. I'm scared and I'm alone and it's early in the morning and no one is awake yet.

I get out of bed and I walk to the Bathroom and I take a shower and I dry myself off and the pain hits me and I drop to my knees and I crawl to the toilet and I get sick. The sickness is worse than usual. Thicker, bloodier, more chunks of stomach, more painful. Each wrenching ejection burns my throat and sends a sharp pain through my chest and makes me feel as if I'm choking. It makes me feel as if I'm choking and I almost wish I was because then it would stop. I just want it to stop.

The sickness ends and I sit down on the floor and I lean back against the front of the toilet. Waves of emotion begin streaming through me and I can feel the welling of tears. Everything that I know and that I am and everything that I've done begins flashing in front of my eyes. My past, my present, my future. My friends, my enemies, my friends who became enemies. Where I've lived, where I've been, what I've seen, what I've done. What I've ruined and destroyed.

I start to cry. Tears begin running down my face and quiet sobs escape me. I don't know what I'm doing and I don't know why I'm here and I don't know how things ever got this bad. I try to find answers but they aren't there. I'm too fucked up to have answers. I'm too fucked up for anything. The tears come harder and sobs become louder and I curl up on the cold tile floor and I hug myself. I hug myself and I wail and it's morning and I'm somewhere in Minnesota and I haven't had a drink in five days and I don't know what the fuck is happening to me.

The tears stop and the sobs stop and I sit up and I wipe my face. I can hear talking outside and I don't want to be seen this way so I stand up and I take a deep breath and I tell myself I'm all right and I leave.

I walk into the Room. Warren and John are standing by Larry's bed. Warren hears me and he looks over at me.

Have you seen Larry?

No.

His stuff is gone.

I haven't seen him.

We think he left.

I don't know what to tell you.

We're going to find the Counselors to tell them. If you see him, will you send him after us?

Yeah.

They leave and I walk to my bed and as I put on my clothes, I think about Larry. He's gone. Definitely gone and definitely not coming back. He's out, alone in the cold, probably on the side of a Highway, carrying his bags, his thumb out and raised. He's thinking of his Wife and his beautiful little Girls.

He wants to see them and hold them and hug them and kiss them. He wants to tell them he's sorry and that everything is all right, that he's ready to be the Husband and the Father he knows he could've been. He's praying that they don't have what he has because if they do, they're dead. Maybe not tomorrow or next week or next month or next year, but sooner or later they're dead, and they're dead because of him. Bless you, Larry, my thoughts are with you. May you make it home safe, may your Wife and Daughters be HIV-negative, may the rest of your days on this Earth be the happiest you've known. Bless you, Larry. Bless you.

I finish dressing and I leave the Room. I collect the cleaning supplies and I go to the Group Toilets and though they don't seem dirty, I get down on my knees and I start cleaning them.

Hey.

I turn around. Roy is standing at the door.

You did a shitty job yesterday.

I lay down my sponge.

What?

I stand.

You did a shitty job yesterday.

Roy steps forward.

They looked clean to me.

He steps forward again.

They were dirty. Do a better job today or I'm telling on you.

The Bathroom is small.

You hear me. You clean these toilets well or I'm telling on you.

I feel trapped.

I'll clean them well. I promise.

Like a rat in a cage.

YOU'LL CLEAN THEM BETTER THAN WELL. YOU'LL MAKE THEM SPARKLE OR I'M GETTING YOU THROWN OUT.

Like a rat in a cage who wants to get out.

GET THE FUCK OUT OF MY FACE.

He steps forward again. I can smell his breath, feel his spit on my cheeks. The Fury rises.

I'LL GET YOU THROWN OUT OF HERE ON YOUR FUCKING ASS, YOU LITTLE SHIT.

I reach up and I grab Roy by the throat and I squeeze and I throw him against the wall of the Bathroom and he hits with a thud and he starts screaming.

HELP HELP HELP HELP.

I grab him again and I shove him through the door. He hits the wall outside the door and he slumps to the ground and he continues screaming.

HELP HELP HELP HELP.

I step through the door and I stand over him.

How clean are the toilets now, Motherfucker?

I wanna beat him.

HELP HELP HELP HELP.

I wanna kick his fucking face in.

How clean are the toilets now, Motherfucker?

I want to tear his limbs off and stuff them down his fucking throat.

HELP HELP HELP HELP.

I want to kill him. Reduce him to crushed bone, torn flesh and blood.

HOW CLEAN ARE THEY NOW, MOTHERFUCKER?

Fucking kill him.

HOW CLEAN ARE THEY NOW?

HELP HELP HELP HELP.

Two men rush into the Hall and they grab me and they pull me back. I push them away.

DON'T FUCKING TOUCH ME.

More come. They lift Roy to his feet, stand between us, stare at me as if I'm a monster. I stare back. I stare through them and straight at Roy.

He attacked me, he's crazy, get him away from me.

Roy is crying and sobbing. Tears are streaming down his face and he's breathing quickly and heavily. The men try to comfort him.

I came to help him with the toilets, I just wanted to help and he attacked me. I didn't do anything wrong.

They stare at me. Stare at me as if I'm a monster.

I turn and I walk back to my Room and it's empty and I begin pacing and my body shakes and I try to control myself. Half of me wants to go back to the Hall and fight whoever is there and either destroy or be destroyed, half of me wants to hide. All of me wants the liquor and the wine and the coke and the crack and the glue and the gasoline that I had in my dream.

The Fury has risen. I pace and I shake and I try to control myself. I need to calm down, but I don't know how. The outlets I depend on, use for survival and have become addicted to are gone, replaced by Doctors and Nurses and Counselors and Rules and Regulations and Pills and Lectures and Mandatory Meals and Jobs in the morning and none of them do a fucking thing for me. Not one fucking thing.

I stop pacing. I stare at the floor. I ball my fists and I squeeze and every cell in my body tenses and prepares and it's coming the Fury is coming and I don't know what to do or where to go or how to stop it and it's coming and it's coming and it comes. Explosion.

I scream. I see a bed. I grab the end of the bed and I lift it and I flip it and the mattress goes and I grab the simple metal frame and I lift it and I throw it down with everything everything everything and it snaps but it's not enough so I stomp it stomp it stomp it and it snaps again again again and there are only broken bars and bolts and screws and I'm screaming and it feels good and I'm just getting started. I move to a nightstand. I pull out the drawers and throw and they're on the other side of the Room and they're no longer drawers but pieces of drawers and the nightstand is still there so I pick it up and I slam it and it's just pieces of a nightstand. There is someone by the door and that someone is yelling but I don't hear him. I am beyond hearing, beyond sight, beyond feeling, beyond thinking. I am deaf, dumb and blind. Unconscious, unaware and uncontrollable. There is a dresser, there are pieces of a dresser. There is another bed and I flip it and I destroy it. There is more yelling and then there are Men in White and there are arms and they're holding me and I'm screaming. There is a needle.

I am in a new Room. It is simple and white and empty, but for a bed. I don't know how I got here or how long I have been here or what day it is or what time it is. I do know that I'm still at the Clinic. I know this because I can hear the screams. The screams of the Addicted without their addictions. The screams of the dead who are somehow still alive.

I lie on my back and I stare at the ceiling. I have been sick twice today but it wasn't bad. There was no blood and no bile and no chunks, just acid and water. I find this encouraging. It is the only thing about my current situation that I find encouraging.

I am waiting for someone to come and tell me that it is time for me to leave. I am trying to decide what I'm going to do. I have no place to live, nowhere to go. I have no money, no resources, no job. I have no hope for money, no hope for resources, no hope for a job. I have no self-confidence, no self-esteem, no sense of self-worth. My sense of self-preservation was gone a long time ago. I won't bother with my Parents or my Brother or the few friends I have left. They will write me off once I leave here. I will write me off once I leave here.

There is a knock at the door and I ignore it. There is another knock and I ignore it again. I don't want to see anybody or speak to anybody or have anything to do with anybody. I need to decide what I'm going to do.

The door opens and Ken and a man and a woman walk in and I sit up. The man is taller than Ken and his body is thick with muscle and he has short black spiky hair. He wears large black boots, faded black jeans and a black shirt that has a picture of a Harley on the front and reads Ride Hard, Ride Sober. His arms are covered with tattoos and his knuckles are covered with scars. The woman is short and plump and she has long gray hair pulled into a ponytail and she looks like Mona Lisa. She wears thick baggy clothing and wool socks and Birkenstocks and she wears silver rings on her fingers and a turquoise pendant around her neck. I see no tattoos and I see no scars. Ken speaks.

Hi, James.

Hi.

Mind if we sit down?

I don't care.

Ken sits on the end of the bed, the woman sits cross-legged on the floor, the man stands. Ken speaks.

This is Lincoln.

He motions to the man. The man stares at me.

He's the Unit Supervisor on Sawyer.

I stare back.

And this is Joanne.

Lincoln stares at me.

She's a Staff Psychologist.

I stare back.

We'd like to talk about what happened yesterday.

Lincoln stares, I stare back.

Then talk.

Lincoln speaks. His voice is deep and hard, sounds like a rusty metal spike.

We want you to talk. We wanna hear your side of things.

You gonna throw me out of here?

Ken looks at Lincoln, Lincoln looks at Joanne. Joanne speaks.

Right now we just want to talk.

Where should I start?

Lincoln speaks.

Where did the trouble start?

I had a dream, a bad dream, and it completely fucked me up. I guess it started there.

Ken speaks.

What was the dream?

I was in a Room alone and I didn't know where I was or how I got there and I was drinking and doing drugs and I got annihilated. It seemed real and when I woke up I was scared.

Joanne speaks.

You had a User Dream.

What's a User Dream?

When Alcoholics and Addicts stop drinking and using drugs, their sub-conscious minds still crave them. That craving is sometimes manifested in dreams that can seem startlingly real and, in a sense, are real. Although you didn't use, some part of your mind did. You'll probably continue to have them for as long as a year.

That'll be fun.

Lincoln speaks.

Then what?

He's staring at me.

I went to the Bathroom and I got sick and I felt worse. I tried to look at my face and I got sick in a different way and I felt worse again. Then I went to clean the Toilets.

He's still staring.

And then you attacked Roy.

I turn, stare back.

Roy got in my face. I got him out of my face.

Ken speaks.

Why'd he get in your face?

No idea.

He just did it?

He's been giving me shit the whole time I've been here. I have no idea why.

What's he been doing?

Telling me I'm breaking all the Rules, telling me I'm doing everything wrong, telling me he's gonna get me thrown out of here.

Lincoln speaks.

And you don't like that, do you?

I didn't do anything. He had no right to say shit to me.

And did you have any right to attack him?

Once he got in my face I did.

What if I got in your face?

I'd get you out of it.

Lincoln stares.

The Tough Guy act isn't gonna get you very far.

I stare back.

Won't get you very far either.

Ken speaks.

Roy told us he was helping you and you went after him without a reason.

Roy's a fucking liar.

Lincoln speaks.

Watch your mouth.

Fuck you.

What did you say?

I said Fuck You.

WATCH YOUR MOUTH.

FUCK YOU.
Ken speaks.
Calm down, James.
Fuck you too, Ken.
Joanne speaks, looks at Ken and Lincoln.
Would you leave us alone for a while?
Lincoln speaks.
We're not done yet.
Joanne speaks.
I think it would be best if you left us alone for a little while. We'll talk as a group again soon.
Lincoln turns and walks out of the Room without a word. Ken looks at me and he speaks.
If you need to talk, I'll be in my Office.
He follows Lincoln out and he shuts the door and I'm alone with Joanne. She leans against the wall and she closes her eyes and she takes a deep breath and she exhales and I sit on the bed and I watch her and she just sits there and she breathes and I get tired of the silence and the sound of her breathing. I want to be alone and I need to figure out what I'm going to do. I speak.
What do you want?
She opens her eyes.
Just thought I'd sit with you for a few minutes. See if there was anything you wanted to talk about.
There's nothing.
Okay.
She stands.
Is there anything I can help you with before I leave?
Yeah.
What?
I want to stop taking Librium.
Why?
It makes me crazy, makes me feel like everything is a bad fucking dream. I'd rather have nothing than that shit.
I'll tell the Nurses to end your cycle.
Thank you.
Anything else?
What am I supposed to do?
Today is another day. Breakfast starts in about ten minutes, then the Lecture. You have an appointment with the Dentist at ten-thirty and

need to be back here to meet the Driver at ten o'clock. Just go about your day and if you need to talk about anything, I'm in Room three twelve. Thank you.

She moves toward the door.

I'll see you soon?

Maybe.

She leaves and I'm alone and I'm surprised to be here and part of me is relieved and part of me is disappointed and part of me is confused and I don't know what I'm going to do. I can either leave or stay. I can either leave or stay? Leaving means going back to addiction and facing either death or Jail. Staying means leaving addiction and facing something that is unknown to me. I'm not sure which scares me more. I get up and I open the door and I see I'm in the Medical Unit. I get in line and I start to go about my day and I remember Joanne's room number. Three twelve.

I take my antibiotics and they go down easier than they have been going down and I walk through the clean bright empty Halls to the Dining Hall. As I enter the glass Corridor I see that I'm late and I see People look up and stare at me and I ignore them and I get a bowl of gray mushy oatmeal and I dump a large pile of sugar on top of it and I find a place at an empty table and I sit down. I know that People are still staring at me and I ignore them. Leonard motions to me and he walks over with two men. The first man is short and thick and wears a black bandana around his head. Long dark hair hangs out of the back of the bandana. He wears jeans and a black T-shirt and has a scar running the length of one of his cheeks. The other man is tall and thin and wears tight black jeans, a black button-down shirt and black cowboy boots. His face is tight and drawn and blue veins stick out from beneath the skin of his arms. Both of the men look violent and angry. Both of them are far more frightening than the average Patient here. Leonard sets his tray down on my table.

Hey, Kid.

Hey.

This is Ed.

He motions to the short man.

And this is Ted.

He motions to the tall man.

The men nod. I nod back.

Mind if we eat with you?

I don't care.

Leonard sits down.

Thanks.

Ed and Ted follow his lead. Leonard speaks.

Heard you beat Roy's ass yesterday.

I stare at my oatmeal. I don't respond.

I hate that Asshole, so don't worry about me telling anybody anything.

I look up at Leonard. I don't respond.

Ted speaks. He has a deep southern accent.

You shoulda seen him afterward. He was fucked up. All crying and moaning and screaming and shit. He got so scared he pissed his pants.

I look at Ted. I don't respond.

Ed speaks. His voice is low and worn. A blue-collar voice.

What'd you do to him?

I look at Ed.

I ain't gonna say nothing to anybody.

I look at the scar. It's deep and brutal.

I just wanna know what you did to him.

I asked him if the Toilets were clean enough, pushed him around a bit.

Leonard speaks.

That's it?

Yeah, that's it.

I stand and I pick up my tray and I walk to an empty table and I sit down and I start eating. The oatmeal is gray and mushy and disgusting but the sugar tastes good. It soaks into my tongue and its sweetness is the first taste I have recognized aside from whiskey or wine or smoke or vomit since the evening of my accident. I like the sweet and the taste means that some of my senses are coming back. They will all come back if I stay here. I'll be able to taste and smell and experience normal sensations that normal people experience every day. If I stay.

I shovel the last sweet spoonful of oatmeal into my mouth and as I swallow it, I can feel my stomach trying to send it back up. I clench my jaw and I hold my breath and I squeeze my abdominal muscles and I try to stop it. I start gagging, having small violent painful heaves. I feel a mass move up my throat and it no longer tastes so sweet and I take a breath and I swallow again and the mass moves back down. As soon as it is down it tries to come back up. I repeat the process. Clench, squeeze, breathe, swallow. Clench, breathe, squeeze, swallow. My body is fighting what it needs to get better. I am fighting what I need to get better.

The mass finally settles and it's uncomfortable and I take a deep breath and I lean back in my chair. My stomach is full and burning. It's not used to keeping so much food and it's not used to keeping so much food so

regularly. It feels as if it's stretching and it begins draining me of all of my
energy. The simple act of digesting a bowl of oatmeal is draining me of all
my energy. I have been awake less than an hour.

Around me the other Patients are filing out of the Dining Hall and heading to the Lecture. I stand and I put my tray away and I follow them
down the glass Corridor and through the maze of Halls and past the
streaming windows and the open doors and the smiling faces of the Staff.
I look at no one and I acknowledge no one. I'm in my head and in my
head I'm alone. I'm trying to decide what I'm going to do.

I find a seat among the men of my Unit and I sit down. There is nobody
on either side of me and that is the way I want it. It is also the way the
men of the Unit seem to want it. I can feel them looking at me and when
I look back they look away. They look away quickly and I stare at them
until they can feel me staring and they can feel the message behind my
stare and they know not to look at me anymore. They don't look at me
anymore. Roy is sitting two rows in front of me and is whispering to a
man I don't know and he is leering at me out of the corner of his eye. I
stare at him. His whispering becomes more animated and is accompanied
by angry gestures. The man starts leering at me. Roy punctuates a sentence
and they start laughing. I am in no mood.

Hey, Roy.

Roy stops talking, stares at me.

Is there a problem?

The rest of the men of the Unit stare at me.

No, there's no problem.

If you've got something to say, come say it to my face.

I don't have anything to say.

Then why don't you and your little Butt-Buddy shut the fuck up.

Roy gasps, the man is shocked. I hear several People laugh. I stare at Roy
until he and the man turn around. They look straight ahead and there is
no more whispering.

A woman steps onto the Stage and the Lecture starts. The woman talks
about sex and addiction and how Alcoholics and Addicts often have
cross-addictions between their drug of choice and their sexual activity of
choice. She talks about how the connection can drive both activities to
dangerous and deviant places. Physical places and figurative places. Places
without exits and places from which it is impossible to return.

The Lecture ends and I sit and I wait and I watch everyone leave and I
stand and I walk out and the food is still soaking in and the last remnants
of the past days' Librium are seeping out. I feel heavy and slow but be-

neath there are the beginnings of something fast and needy and scared and shaky and fragile and anxious and angry and desperate. For now the heaviness is holding it back, but I know that it's only for now.

I go back to the Medical Unit and I find a Nurse and I tell her I have to go to the Dentist and she checks the outside appointment book and it checks and she sends me to a Waiting Room and I wait. The Waiting Room has windows and I can see outside. Though it is late in the morning, it is still dark. I can hear thunder and see sleet. The wind is whipping whatever lies on the ground into the air. The trees look as if they want to hide. It is ugly and it's going to get uglier.

Hank walks into the Waiting Room. He's bundled in a thick, warm, waterproof jacket. He wears wool-lined rubber boots.

Hey, Kid.

Hey, Hank.

We shake hands.

How ya been?

Been better.

I stand.

Bet ya been worse too.

I smile.

Yeah, I've been worse too.

You ready?

Yeah.

Let's go.

We walk out of the Waiting Room and through a short Hall and outside. The Van is twenty feet from the Exit and I run toward it. The sleet and the wind pound into my skin, the thunder shakes my bones.

I open the front passenger door of the Van and I jump inside and the Van is running and it is warm. There is an old weather-beaten jacket similar to the one Hank is wearing sitting on the seat. I pick it up and put it on and settle in and clutch myself. After a few seconds, Hank, who did not need to run, opens the driver's door and climbs in.

You found the coat.

It was hard to miss.

I used to wear it when I worked on my boat.

It has that look.

It's a good coat.

It's working great right now.

I know you don't have one, or have anything from what I'm told, so I want you to use it while you're here.

Thank you, Hank. I appreciate that.

Don't mention it.

I really appreciate it. Thank you.

Don't mention it.

Hank puts the Van into gear and we pull away from the Clinic and we start making our way toward Town. Hank concentrates on the road and I stare out the window and I think. A few days ago the land was shutting down and preparing for winter and dying. Now it's shut down and prepared and dead. There are no leaves on the trees, no living vegetation on the ground, not an insect or a bird or an animal in sight. The thunder is getting louder and closer and the sleet is getting harder and faster and the wind is trying to push the Van into a ditch. Hank keeps it on the road. I stare out the window and I think.

I knew the facts within a month of first laying eyes on her. She was from Connecticut, her Father was a prominent investment banker in New York, her Mother played tennis and bridge and was the President of the local Junior League. She had gone to a prestigious all-girls prep school in New Hampshire. She had an older Brother and an older Sister. She had never had a boyfriend.

I met her when a friend of mine asked me if I could get him some dope. He wasn't a smoker so I asked him who wanted it and he told me it was for a girl named Lucinda who lived in his dorm and I told him I would have to meet her first so he gave me the Room number and I went to the Room and I knocked on the door and the door opened and she was standing there. Tall and thin, long blond hair like thick ropes of silk, eyes cut from the Arctic. I didn't know Lucinda and I didn't know she lived with Lucinda and I couldn't speak and she was standing there. She was standing there.

Hi.

I just stared.

Can I help you with something?

I started to open my mouth and my mouth didn't work and my heart was pounding and my hands were shaking and I felt dizzy and excited and scared and insignificant. She was standing in front of me. Right in front of me. Tall and thin, long blond hair like thick ropes of silk, eyes cut from the Arctic.

I turned and I walked away without a word. I didn't look back and I went to my Room and I got a strong bottle and I took a strong drink. My heart was still pounding and my hands were still shaking and for the first time in my life it wasn't because of alcohol or drugs and for the first time in my life alcohol and drugs wouldn't make it go away.

We pull into town and it is empty. There are no parked cars, no shop-pers, no young Mothers walking with Children, no old men on benches with coffee and words of wisdom. The Stores are open, but they're not doing business. The only things out are thunder and sleet and wind. They are getting stronger.

We park in the same spot in front of the same Building and Hank turns off the Van and reaches over and opens the glove compartment and re-moves two old, yellow tennis balls. He hands them to me.

I thought you might want these.

Why?

I don't know much about anything except for fishing and driving, but I have a feeling whatever you're getting done this morning is gonna hurt.

Probably.

You're not gonna get painkillers or anesthesia, at least not while you're still a Patient at a Treatment Center. I've found the next best thing is those balls. When it starts hurting, start squeezing.

I hold the balls in my hand, give them a squeeze.

Thanks.

Sure.

He opens his door and he gets out and I do the same and we shut the doors and we walk into the Building and we walk up the stairs to the Dentist's Office. The door is open and we go inside and I sit on one of the couches in the Waiting Room and Hank goes to Reception and he starts talking to the Receptionist. The Babar the Elephant book is sitting in front of me. I pick it up and start reading it. I remember reading it as a small Boy and enjoying it and imagining that I was friends with Babar, his constant Companion during all of his adventures. He went to the Moon, I went with him. He fought Tomb Raiders in Egypt, I fought alongside him. He rescued his elephant girlfriend from Ivory Hunters on the Savanna, I coordinated the getaway. I loved that goddamn Elephant and I loved being his friend. In a childhood full of unhappiness and rage, Babar is one of the few pleasant memories that I have. Me and Babar, kicking some motherfucking ass.

Hank comes back and he sits down next to me.

They're ready for you.

All right.

You ready for them?

I hold up the tennis balls.

Yeah.

It'll be interesting to see what you look like with teeth.

It'll be interesting to have them again.

I stand.

I'll see you in a while, Hank. Thanks for everything.

Don't mention it.

I walk toward a door where a Nurse stands waiting for me. As I walk past her she is careful not to touch me and I am brought back from the happy afterglow of pachyderm memories and I am reminded of what I am. I am an Alcoholic and I am a drug Addict and I am a Criminal. I am missing my front four teeth. I have a hole in my cheek that has been closed with forty-one stitches. I have a broken nose and I have black swollen eyes. I have an Escort because I am a Patient at a Drug and Alcohol Treatment Center. I am wearing a borrowed jacket because I don't have one of my own. I am carrying two old yellow tennis balls because I'm not allowed to have any painkillers or anesthesia. I am an Alcoholic. I am a drug Addict. I am a Criminal. That's what I am and I don't blame the Nurse for not wanting to touch me. If I weren't me, I wouldn't want to touch me.

She leads me into a small Room. The Room is like many other Rooms I have been in lately, except that it seems cleaner and whiter. There are stainless steel cabinets along the walls, trays of sharp sparkling instruments on top of the cabinets, a large halogen lamp hanging from the ceiling. There is a surgical chair sitting in the middle of the floor. It is metal and it has green cushions and long menacing arms and all sorts of straps and buttons and levers and gears. It looks like a medieval torture device. I know it is for me. I walk past the Nurse and I sit down in the chair and I try to make myself comfortable but it's not possible. Torture devices are not made to be comfortable.

Doctor Stevens will be here in a minute.

All right.

Can I get you anything while you wait?

A Babar book.

Excuse me?

I would like a Babar the Elephant book. You have them in the Waiting Room.

I'll be right back.

Thank you.

She leaves and I'm alone and as I settle into the chair and look around the Room, I start to panic. The last of the Librium is nearly gone and the food in my stomach has been broken down to the point that it no longer holds and everything speeds up. My heart, my blood pressure, the thoughts in my head. My hands are shaking, but it is not the heavy shaking of withdrawal. It is a quick and fragile form of shaking, a form of shaking that comes from fear. Fear of this Room, fear of the chair, fear of what the cabinets hold, fear of what the instruments do, fear of what's going to happen to me here, fear of a pain so great that I need to squeeze tennis balls to make it go away.

The Nurse returns with the Babar book and she gives it to me and she leaves. I set the tennis balls in my lap and I open the book and I try to read it. As I turn the pages, I can see the words and I can see the pictures but I can't read the words and I can't understand the pictures. Everything is speeding up. My heart, my blood pressure, the thoughts in my head. I can't concentrate on anything. Not even Babar.

I close the book and I clutch it against my chest and wait. Everything is shaking. My hands, my feet, the muscles in my legs, my chest, my jaw, my remaining teeth. I pick up the balls and I squeeze them and I try to force the strength of the shaking into the balls and the balls start shaking. Everything is shaking.

The door opens and the Lumberjack Dentist Doctor Stevens walks in and he is followed by another Dentist and two female Nurses. Doctor Stevens pulls up a stainless steel stool and he sits down on the stool near the bottom of the chair. The other Dentist and the Nurses begin collecting bins and instruments and opening cabinet doors and closing cabinet doors. The noises they are making are sharp and I don't know what exactly they are doing but I know the sum of it will be going into my mouth.

Hi, James.

Hi.

Sorry for the wait. We were reviewing the procedures we're going to do today.

No problem.

The other Dentist leans down and whispers something in Doctor Stevens's ear. Doctor Stevens nods. The sum of it will be going into my mouth.

The first thing we want to do is cap the outside two teeth. We looked at the X-rays again and the roots seem to be intact, the bases stable. Once they're capped, they should be fine.

Okay.

After we do that, we need to do root-canal surgery on the middle two. The roots are unstable and if we don't do the surgery, your teeth will turn black and die. After they die, they will fall out. I'm assuming you don't want that to happen.

No, I don't.

I'm sorry to be so blunt.

I appreciate your bluntness.

I want you to know exactly what we're doing and why.

I don't want to know any more.

There is one thing.

What?

This is going to be incredibly painful. Because you're currently a Patient
at a Drug Treatment Center, we can't use any anesthesia, local or general,
and when we're done, we can't give you any painkillers.

I hold up the balls, give them a light squeeze.

I know.

And you think you can deal with that?

I've been through worse.

What?

I've been through worse.

Doctor Stevens stares at me as if what I have said is incomprehensible to
him. I know what I'm about to experience is going to be horrible and I
don't know if I've been through anything worse, but in order to do this, I
have to believe that I have. I stare back.

Let's go, Doc. Bring it.

He stands and begins talking in hushed tones to the other Dentist and to
the Nurses and he helps them prepare the bins and instruments for their
use in my mouth. I sit and wait and my body slows down and my mind
slows down and I stop shaking and I stop squeezing the balls and I am
calm. I have accepted that this is going to happen and that I need it to
happen and that it's going to hurt. A calm descends, a calm the
Condemned must experience just before Execution.

Doctor Stevens steps forward and stands over me.

I'm going to lean you back a bit.

Okay.

He reaches down and he pulls a lever and he slowly and gently leans me
back. The halogen light is directly over me and it is blinding in its brightness and I close my eyes. I am holding the balls and the Babar book is
resting on my chest, just above my heart.

Do you mind if I move this book?

I'd rather you didn't.

That's fine. We'll work around it.

I hear the shuffling of feet and the placement of bins and someone lifts my
head and places the strings of a bib around the back of my neck and clips
them and places the bib on top of the book. The chair moves farther down

and farther back and a small firm pillow is placed beneath the base of my skull.

A female voice. A clinical manner.

I need you to open your mouth.

I open my mouth.

If it hurts, say so.

Okay.

Now stay still.

I stay still as someone's hand pulls my bottom lip out and stuffs the space between my lip and gum with cotton. I can feel the stitches stretch and blood start to seep. The same procedure is done with my upper lip and my cheeks and it feels as if my mouth is full of soft fibrous dirt and almost instantly, everything is dry. A spray of water moistens it, but not enough. It is dry and it will stay dry no matter how many sprays I get.

I lean back into the chair and I close my eyes and I open my mouth wide and someone hands me the tennis balls and I take a spray and I hear low quiet words and the sound of a drill being tested. The drill goes on and off, on and off.

Check the sander.

A sander goes on and off, on and off.

Check the secondary drill.

The secondary drill goes on and off, on and off.

I feel the presence of People standing over me. A hand grabs my upper lip and gently pulls it so that my gum is exposed. A spray covers the remains of my teeth.

Here we come, James.

The spray continues and the sander is turned on and as it comes in toward my mouth it gets louder and the noise is high and piercing and it hurts my ears and I start squeezing the balls and I try to prepare for the sander and the sander hits the fragment of my left outside tooth. The sander bounces slightly and white electric pain hits my mouth and the sander comes back and holds and pain spreads through my body from the top down and every muscle in my body flexes and I squeeze the balls and my eyes start to tear and the hair on the back of my neck stands straight and my tooth fucking hurts like the point of a bayonet is being driven through it. The point of a fucking bayonet.

The sander moves its way around the contour of the fragment and I stay tense and in pain and I can taste the grit of the bone on my tongue and the spray is spraying and it collects the grit and sends some of it down my throat and some of it into the space beneath my tongue. It continues, the sanding and the spraying and the grit and the pain, and the constant electricity of it keeps me tense and hard. I sit and I squeeze the tennis balls and my heart beats even and strong as if it needs the test of this ordeal to prove that it works correctly. The sander stops and I relax and I take a deep breath. There are soft voices and there are instruments being picked up.

I think there's a cavity here, James. I need to check.

The cotton in my mouth has shifted enough to allow me to speak comprehensibly.

Then check.

It's gonna hurt.

Get it over with.

I prepare for more but I'm not prepared for what hits me. As a sharp pointed instrument pokes around one of the sanded edges of my tooth it finds a small hole and it penetrates the hole. The electric pain shoots and it shoots at a trillion volts and it is white and burning. The bayonet is twenty feet long and red hot and razor sharp. The pain is greater than anything I've ever felt and it is greater than anything I could have imagined. It overwhelms every muscle and every fiber and every cell in my body and everything goes limp. I moan and the instrument goes away, but the pain stays.

It's definitely a cavity. We need to fill it to cap the tooth correctly.

Every fiber and every cell is limp.

James?

Every fiber and every cell is white hot and burning.

James?

The pain is greater than I could have imagined.

James?

I take a deep breath.

Do what you need to do. Just get it over with.

Low muffled voices, the opening and closing of cabinets, the changing of instruments. The drill is turned on. I sit and I wait.

The drill comes and the drill hits and I squeeze the balls so hard that I think my fingers are fucking breaking and I moan. I moan in a steady tone that fills my ears so that I don't have to hear the drill but I still hear it and I concentrate on the sound of the moan so that it will distract me from the pain but it doesn't. Bayonet bayonet bayonet bayonet bayonet. The drill makes a hole and moves around the circumference of the hole and makes it wider and the grit mixes with the spray and moves down my throat and collects beneath my tongue. Bayonet, bayonet, bayonet. The hole gets larger and larger. Bayonet bayonet bayonet. There's a fucking drill in my mouth. Bayonet.

The drill stops, the pain continues, the squeezing continues, my moan continues. Doctor Stevens tells the Nurses and the other Dentist to move quickly and they do. They stuff the hole with some sort of putty and they wipe it away and they stuff it and they wipe it away. The stuffing buffers the open pain of the hole and the piercing pain fades and a dull throbbing agony remains and my heart beats strong and steady and the agony beats along with it and it doesn't bother me. I have lived with agony for so long that as it beats along with my strong and steady heart, it doesn't bother me.

I stop moaning and I open my eyes and through the deep well of tears resting atop them I can see some sort of blue light being held above me and being focused on the putty. The putty gets hard and closes and melts around the hole and I hear the sander and see it moving in and I close my eyes and the sander hits and the chemical grit of the putty fills my mouth. The process repeats itself. Putty, blue light, sander. Putty, blue light, sander. I become immune to it and immune to its pain and I squeeze the tennis balls and I wait for it to end and it ends. One down, three to go.

Now we want to cap the outside right tooth.

I nod yes.

Do you want a break before we do it?

I shake my head no.

A moment of preparation and then the sander comes back and I endure it easily. There is no cavity and no drill so the putty and the light come back and they're nothing. I'm holding the balls but not squeezing, the steady moan is gone, my heart rests. An easy and seamless rebuilding on the outside right. Two down, two to go.

I hear the shuffling of feet and the shuffling of instruments and the opening and closing of cabinet drawers and I open my eyes. Doctor Stevens is speaking with the other Dentist and the Nurses are putting the used instruments in a small sink for sterilization. Doctor Stevens finishes talking and the other Dentist leaves the room.

Is there a problem?

No, there's no problem.

I sit up.

Where's he going?

Doctor Stevens pulls up the stool.

I didn't want to tell you this until we were ready to start, but I want to strap you down while we're doing the root canals.

Why?

Aside from the factor of pain, one of the reasons we anesthetize Patients during root-canal procedures is so they don't move. We need you to be still to work, and I'm not sure you'll be able to be still if you're not strapped down.

Fine.

You're sure you're okay with it.

Yeah, I'm fine.

The Dentist returns carrying two long thick blue nylon straps with large pressure-secure buckles. They are the kind of straps used to hold large objects onto the roofs of cars, to hook boats up to trailers, to keep the doors of animal cages shut. They have seen some use and they are the only thing in the Room besides me and the tennis balls that is not sparklingly clean.

I lean back in the chair and the Dentist steps forward. The Nurses have stopped cleaning the instruments and they are staring at me.

Could you hold your arms at your sides?

I put my arms along the sides of my body.

The Dentist lays the straps across my body so that the buckles fall beneath the chair. He crouches down and he hooks the loose end and he pulls it and the straps start to tighten around my body.

Let me know when it's secure.

He continues to pull, the straps get tighter and tighter. When I can't lift or move my arms in any way and when the straps start digging into my skin and pressing the Babar book into my chest, I let the Doctor know the straps are secure. He locks the buckles and he stands and he walks to the sink to wash his hands. Doctor Stevens and the Nurses step forward.

We're going to try and do this as fast as we can.

Make sure you do a good enough job so that I don't have to come back here.

I'll definitely do that.

Let's go.

I close my eyes and I try to settle in and make myself comfortable. There are wads of cotton in my mouth and there is a throbbing agony from the earlier drilling and there are thick blue nylon straps digging into my skin and pressing a book into my chest. There are fingers grabbing my upper lip and pulling it back and there is a cold spray dousing the exposed remains of my front two teeth. There is a tennis ball in each of my hands and there is the knowledge that I'm about to undergo a dual root-canal procedure without any anesthesia. There is the sound of my heart beating ever more quickly. There is anticipation. There is fear. There is no comfort.

The drill is back on and it is working through the fragment of my left front tooth. It is moving through a thinner, more fragile section of bone, so it works quickly. It shoots the grit, makes the hole, penetrates. At the point of penetration, a current shoots through my body that is not pain, or even close to pain, but something infinitely greater.

Everything goes white and I cannot breathe. I clench my eyes and I bite down on my existing teeth and I think my jaw might be breaking and I squeeze my hands and I dig my fingers through the hard rubber surface of the tennis balls and my fingernails crack and my fingernails break and my fingernails start to bleed and I curl my toes and they fucking hurt and I flex the muscles in my legs and they fucking hurt and my torso tightens and my stomach muscles feel as if they're going to collapse and my ribs feel as if they're caving in on themselves and it fucking hurts and my balls are shrinking and the shrinking fucking hurts and my dick is hard because my blood hurts and my blood wants to escape and is seeking exit through my dick and my dick fucking hurts and my arms are straining against the thick blue nylon straps and the thick blue nylon straps are cutting my flesh and it fucking hurts and my face is on fire and the veins in my neck want to explode and my brain is white and it is melting and it fucking hurts. There is a drill in my mouth. My brain is white and it feels as if it's fucking melting. I cannot breathe. Agony.

The drill comes out and a vacuum starts sucking the dying flesh surrounding my root from the canal that holds it. The agony does not subside. The vacuum stops and the remaining flesh is scraped from the interior of the canal with some sort of sharp pointed instrument. The agony does not subside. The vacuum goes back and comes out, the scraping continues. The agony does not subside. The root has to be clean to heal correctly. Please clean the Motherfucker fast. Please please please clean the Motherfucker fast. The agony does not subside.

I start to fade into a state of white consciousness where I am no longer directly connected to what is being done to me. My arms are no longer my arms, my legs are not my legs, my chest is not my chest, my face is not my face, my teeth do not belong to me. My body is no longer my body. There is white. Everywhere there is white. There is agony. It is agony that is unfathomable. I try to will myself back to reality and back to the drills

and the vacuums and the instruments and the cotton stuffing and the
spray and the grit and the Doctors and the Nurses and the rebuilding of
my teeth, but I can't come back. My body won't let me come back. It is as
if it is sparing my mind what it can and pushing into a realm that is horrible, but somehow less horrible. I give up and I give in and I am consumed by the whiteness and the agony and I am there for what seems to
be eternity. The whiteness and the agony. The whiteness and the agony.
The whiteness and the agony.

I am brought back by the screaming pitch of the drill. I can feel a tooth
on the left front side of my upper gum and I know the drill is coming in
to fix the right. It hits and penetrates and I am conscious during the penetration and the process of endurance repeats itself. I lose the air and the
ability to breathe it. I clench my eyes and I bite down and I squeeze the
tennis balls and every single cell of my body feels as if it is going to explode from the force of the pain. If there was a God, I would spit in his
face for subjecting me to this. If there was a Devil, I would sell him my
soul to make it end. If there was something Higher that controlled our
individual fates, I would tell it to take my fate and shove it up its fucking
ass. Shove it hard and far, you Motherfucker. Please end. Please end.
Please end.

The vacuum sucks and the instrument scrapes and I endure. The interior of
the canal is cleaned and drained and I endure. The canal is filled with new
flesh and the root is protected and I endure. There is putty and blue light
and a sander, putty and blue light and a sander, putty and blue light and a
sander. I endure. I'm somewhere in Minnesota and I'm a Patient at a Drug
and Alcohol Treatment Center and I'm having my front four teeth rebuilt
and I'm strapped into a chair because I can't have any anesthesia. All I can
do is endure.

I feel water flowing off what must be teeth and the last of the grit washes
down my throat. The cotton is removed from my cheeks and my gums and
I hear muffled voices and the sink is running and cabinet doors are opening
and closing. I open my eyes. I see flashes of white and I have trouble focusing. The halogen is still on. There is movement and the halogen is off and
something moves away from me and other things move toward me. I hear
the buckles on the straps release and the straps are pulled off and the Babar
book is removed and my body is now free to move and function as it
wishes and I am immediately cold and I am immediately shaking. I try to
sit up and I am unable to sit up. I try to lift my head and I am unable to
lift my head. I try to focus my eyes and my eyes won't focus. I'm cold and

getting colder. I'm starting to shake harder. I am still clutching the tennis balls. The agony has yet to subside.

Someone lifts me and wraps a blanket around me. The blanket is warm and the warmth brings on an intense nausea and I can feel it coming and there's nothing I can do to stop it and it comes. It comes easily, and somehow its coming loosens my stomach and my lungs and my torso and although I still can't focus my eyes, I can see that it's red. It comes and comes and comes. Red red red. All over the blanket, all over the chair, all over the floor, all over myself. I let go of the tennis balls and I try to lift my hand to wipe my face but my hand is shaking and my face is shaking and I can't make them meet. My hand falls to my side.

Get some more blankets and get some water. Hurry.

I lie back on the chair.

Are you okay, James?

I moan.

Can you understand me?

I moan again, nod yes.

You need to go to the Hospital. I'm going to call an Ambulance.

I don't want to go to a Hospital, so I gather whatever strength I have and I push myself up and I open my eyes. Doctor Stevens is standing in front of me.

No Hospital.

You need Medical Attention. Attention we can't give you.

The chair.

What?

Lower the chair.

Doctor Stevens lowers the chair. I put my feet on the floor. I am cold and I am shaking and everything hurts. I'm sick of Doctors and Dentists and Nurses and chairs and tests and halogen lights and instruments and clean Rooms and sterile sinks and bloody procedures and I'm sick of the attention the weak and the injured and the needy receive and I don't want to go to a Hospital. I have always dealt with pain alone. I will deal with it alone now.

Get Hank and get me back to the Clinic.

You need Medical Attention.

I'll be fine.

If you leave here, it will be against my direct advice.

I understand.

I push myself from the chair. The muscles in my legs are twitching and my

legs are unsteady. I take a small, slow step and I stop. I take the blanket off
and I drop it on the chair and I take another small, slow step and I stop.
Can you make it?
Yeah.
Do you need help?
No.
My eyes are focusing and my stomach is settled. I'm still shaking and I'm
still cold and I'm still hurting, but being away from the chair makes me
feel better. I look at the door. If I can get to the door, I'm closer to being
out of here. I want to be out of here.
I take another step. My legs are jelly. Another step. They weigh a million
pounds apiece. Another step. They hurt. Another step. They throb.
Another step. Each movement is a titanic effort. Another step. After each
I don't know if I can do it again. Doctor Stevens is watching me and the
Nurses have returned and they are watching me and I know if I falter I go
to the Hospital. Another step. Another step.
I get to the door and I stop. To my right is a mirror. I glance toward it
and catch a glimpse of myself. I am white as chalk. My face is hideously
swollen. The area around my mouth is splattered with flakes of dried
blood. There are stitches protruding from my lower lip and my eyes are
black. There is a bandage across the bridge of my nose. I am too thin for
my frame and what flesh I have is loose and limp. The white T-shirt I'm
wearing is caked with brown and red vomit stains. The tan pants I'm
wearing are caked with brown and red vomit stains. I look like a fucking
monster.
I turn to Doctor Stevens and the Nurses. The Nurses look away, Doctor
Stevens does not. I speak slowly.
Thank you for helping me.
No problem. It's what I do.
I'm not what you do. You went beyond what you do today. Thank you.
Doctor Stevens smiles.
No problem.
I smile back. It is my first smile with my new teeth. I'm amused by this and I
smile wider and I point toward my mouth. Doctor Stevens laughs and he
walks toward me and he puts his arms around me and he hugs me. We are
two men who have just been through a terrible ordeal together. Although it
was worse for me, I know it wasn't easy for him. This hug is our bond, our
bond to learn from what we have just been through and become better and
stronger because of it. I know he will keep the bond, I don't know if I can. I
pull away.

Thanks again.

Take care of yourself, James.

I'll try.

I turn and I slowly walk away and I don't look back. It has always been a fault of mine, but it is the way I am. I never look back. Never.

I move down a Hallway, gripping the side of the wall for support. Each step is more difficult than the last, each step hurts more. My face is throbbing to the rhythm of my heart, the rhythm of my heart is not as strong or as steady as it was. It is speeding up and slowing down, beating with irregular strength, sending sharp messages through my left arm and my jaw. It held when it needed to hold, but it's not going to hold much longer. I'm not going to hold much longer.

I get to a door and I push it and I walk though it and into the Waiting Room. Hank is sitting on a couch chatting with an elderly woman and when they look up the elderly woman gasps. Hank stands and he walks over to me and I put my hand on his shoulder. Without his shoulder, I would fall.

Jesus Christ.

Get me out of here.

You all right?

Not even close.

What can I do?

Get me the fuck out of here.

Hank puts my jacket on and he places my arm around his shoulder and his arm around my shoulder and he holds me up and we leave the Office and we walk down the stairs. When we get to the bottom my legs stop functioning and Hank drags me toward the door. He leans me against it and he pushes it open and he pulls me outside.

The Storm, which was growing when we entered, is now raging. The wind is whipping sheets of frozen rain and sleet through the air. The Sky is black. There is shattering thunder and shocks of lightning. Hank drags me toward the Van and my feet drag along the cold and wet of the ground and the cold and the wet soak into my shoes. When we get to the Van he leans me against the passenger door.

Can you stand?

He reaches into his pocket for the keys.

Yeah, but hurry.

He pulls the keys from his pocket and he unlocks the Van and he opens the sliding side door and he helps me through and he sets me down on the length of the three-man seat and he shuts the door and he runs around to the Driver's door and he opens it and he climbs inside the Van. He sits down and he puts the keys in the ignition and he starts the engine and the Van pulls out.

As we drive through Town, I lie on my back and I shake and I freeze. My heart beats irregularly and it hurts. The bayonet is in my mouth and I'm tired beyond exhaustion. I'm going back to the Clinic and I don't want to go back to the Clinic. If I leave the Clinic, there is either death or Jail. This is not the life I want or who I want to be but I don't know anything else. I have tried to change before and I have failed. I have tried to change again and again and again and I have failed over and over and over. If there was something to make me think this time was different, I would try, but there isn't. If there was a light at the end of the tunnel, I would run to it. I am worse than I have ever been before. If there was a light at the end of the tunnel I would run to it. I am an Alcoholic and I am a Drug Addict and I am a Criminal. There is no light at the end of the tunnel.

After a few moments the Van is flooded with heat and the heat slows the shaking and kills the freezing and I'm tired beyond exhaustion and I close my eyes. It is dark. I close my eyes. There is no light at the end of the tunnel. I close my eyes. It is dark. I close my eyes. There's no light. I close my eyes. Dark.

I close my eyes.

I close my eyes.

I close my eyes.

I'm in another white Room and I hate it. I'm in another white robe and I want to tear it to shreds. There is another bed and another desk and another chair and I want to destroy them. There is a window. I want to throw myself through it.

I follow my usual routine. Crawl to the Bathroom. Vomit. Lie on the floor. Vomit. Lie on the floor. Vomit. Lie on the floor. Some of the vomit gets stuck in my new teeth and it hurts cleaning it out. After the cleaning, I vomit again and I clean again and I crawl back to bed.

It is still black, still storming. The rain and sleet and the wind are pounding the window. An endless series of clicks and clacks, an endless shriek. I hate the noise and I want it to stop. Click, shriek, clack, shriek, click, shriek, clack, shriek. I hate it. I want it to fucking stop.

I get out of bed. My clothes have been washed and they are sitting on the desk. I take off the robe and I put them on. They are looser today than they were yesterday.

I open the door and I walk out and I'm on the Medical Unit. It is the middle of the night and the Unit is almost empty. There is a Nurse on duty. She is reading a fashion magazine and she doesn't notice me.

I walk out of the Medical Unit and I make my way through the Halls. Though the Sky is dark with night and weather, the Halls are still light. The overhead lamps are light, the walls are light, the carpet is light, the hanging pictures are light, the signs on the doors are light. I am uncomfortable in the light. It exposes too much.

I go back to Sawyer. It is quiet and dark. All of the lights are off, all of the doors to the Rooms are closed, all of the men are sleeping. I walk to the Main Room and I sit down on a couch and I turn on the television. There's a show about weight loss, an infomercial for a Motivational Speaker, some woman talking about some psychic bullshit, a professional wrestling extravaganza. There are several channels with static. The static is the most interesting thing I see on the screen. I watch it. For an hour. The static.

I turn off the television and I look for something to do. I'm not tired and I don't want to sleep and I don't want to go back to the Medical Unit and

I don't want to walk the Halls. The Halls are too light and the light makes me uncomfortable.

There is a set of shelves filled with books against one of the walls. I learned to read at a young age and I have always read voraciously. It is one of the few things, aside from getting fucked up and getting in trouble, that I have done consistently throughout my entire life. I am drawn to the books. I stand and I walk over to the shelves and I sit down in front of them.

There are three shelves with about forty books on each shelf. As I look through them, I am hoping for something that will take me away from here. I want and I need to get the fuck out of here for a while. If I can't do it physically, I would like to do it in my head. Just a little while. Get me the fuck out of here.

There are self-help titles such as *Let it Out Now: Curing by Crying, Denial Is Not a River in Egypt, Angels and Addicts: Letting God's Helpers Help You!!!* and *Daddy Didn't Love Me: A Tale of Addiction.* There is a series of books on each of the Twelve Steps. *Step One: No Control, Step Three: Let Go and Let God, Step Six: Get Ready for Action, Step Eleven: Make Contact.* There are several well-thumbed copies of the New Testament. I have read the New Testament. I will not waste my time on it again.

I reach for a thick, worn blue book. It has no cover and no title and there is a symbol on the front that has a triangle on the inside of a circle. I have been given this book before. I have been given this book by friends, by friends of friends, by people who thought they could change me. It is called *The Big Book of Alcoholics Anonymous,* the symbol on the front of it is the symbol of sobriety. I have never read it before, nor even bothered opening it. When it was given to me, I threw it in the gutter or stuffed it in the bottom of the nearest garbage can. I have been to AA Meetings and they have left me cold. I find the philosophy to be one of replacement. Replacement of one addiction with another addiction. Replacement of a chemical for a God and a Meeting. The Meetings themselves made me sick. Too much whining, too much complaining, too much blaming. Too much bullshit about Higher Powers. There is no Higher Power or any God who is responsible for what I do and for what I have done and for who I am. There is no Higher Power or any God who will cure me. There is no Meeting where any amount of whining, complaining and blaming is going to make me feel any better.

I am an Alcoholic and a Drug Addict and a Criminal. I am worse than I have ever been in my life. I am in a Clinic somewhere in Minnesota. If I leave the Clinic my Family and my remaining friends will write me off. If

I leave the Clinic my options are limited to death or Jail. I'm alone and it's the middle of the night and I don't want to go back to the Medical Unit and I can't sleep. I want a drink. I want fifty drinks. I want a pipe and some rock. I want a long fat line of meth, I want ten hits of acid, a tube of industrial-strength glue. Give me a bottle of pills, give me some dope laced with PCP. Give me something. Anything. I need to get out of here. If not in body, at least in mind. I need to get the fuck out of here. I pick up the book. I stare at it. I know it can't hurt me and I know I have nothing to lose. I begin reading.

It starts with a Doctor's note, written by an Expert on addiction. The Doctor says that profound Alcoholism is basically incurable. He says the only thing he knows of that will get someone sober and keep them sober is AA.

It moves on to the story of Bill, who is the founder of AA. Bill is the Jesus Christ of the movement, the Savior and the Messiah, and although Bill did not die on the cross, he certainly lived on it. Bill was a bad drunk with a bad life and bad problems. He searched and searched for a cure for his Alcoholism and he came up empty. At his lowest point, he came across an old drinking Buddy who had found God and gotten sober. His friend's conversion reminded him of an experience he had in a French Cathedral after serving as a Soldier in World War I. As he sat in a pew during sunset, Bill was filled with a peace and serenity unlike any he had ever known and unlike any he had thought possible. He was filled with the Glory of God. The memories of that moment and the sobriety of his converted friend had a profound effect on Bill. He became convinced that trusting in God, or in some form of a Higher Power, could transform his life. He decided at that instant to turn his will over and place himself unreservedly under God's care and direction. He never drank again, he developed the Twelve Steps and the concept of Alcoholics Anonymous, and he devoted his life to spreading the word. It is a touching story, and it is written more to convince than to tell. I am not convinced. No way, not at all. Not at all.

I read the rest of the book, which is mostly about the Twelve Steps. There are chapters with titles like There Is a Solution, How It Works, Into Action, and Vision for You. It is all very simple. If you do what the book says, you will be cured. If you follow their righteous path, that path will lead you straight to redemption. If you join the club, you're the lucky winner of a lifelong supply of bullshit Meetings full of whining, complaining and blaming. Praise Be the Glory. I want to get down on my knees. Praise Be the Glory Hallelujah.

Near the end, there is a section of testimonials. There is one by a Dentist, one by a European Drinker, one by a Salesman, one by an Educated Agnostic. They were all Alcoholic disasters, they all found God, they all started dancing the Twelve Step, they all got better. As with most testimonials like this that I've read or heard or been forced to endure, something about them strikes me as weak, hollow and empty. Though the people in them are no longer drinking and doing drugs, they're still living with the obsession. Though they have achieved sobriety, their lives are based on the avoidance, discussion and vilification of the chemicals they once needed and loved. Though they function as human beings, they function because of their Meetings and their Dogma and their God. Take away their Meetings and their Dogma and they have nothing, Take them away and they are back where they started. They have an addiction.

Addictions need fuel. I am not convinced Meetings and a Dogma and a God can fuel mine. If what the Doctor says at the beginning is true, and joining AA is the only way to cure me, then I'm completely fucked. Fucked fucked fucked.

I put the book back on the shelf. I stand and I go to the Job Board and I see my name is still listed next to the Group Toilets. I get the cleaning supplies and I go to the Group Toilets and they haven't been cleaned in a couple of days and they are disgusting. There is spit in the sink, dried piss on the floor, bloody toilet paper in the garbage cans, shit stains on the porcelain bowls. I am sure Roy had something to do with this, but I am in no mood for game playing and retaliating, so I take the supplies and I start cleaning. It is a foul endeavor. I vomit twice and I have to clean my own vomit as well as the spit and the piss and the bloody tissue and the shit. When I am done, and the walls and the sink and the floor and the garbage can and the porcelain are sparkling, I feel no sense of accomplishment or satisfaction. I will not do this again. No fucking way.

I leave the Group Toilets and I return the cleaning supplies and I walk to my Room. I open the door and I step inside. The furniture I destroyed has been replaced. Larry, whose whereabouts are still unknown, has been replaced. There is a short Bald Man in his bed and the short Bald Man is snoring. Warren and John are sleeping in their beds. John is mumbling and twitching, Warren is still. My bed is untouched, though a Bible and another copy of the *Big Book* have been placed on the nightstand next to it. I walk to the nightstand and pick up the Bible and the Big Book and I go to the window and I open the window and I throw the books into the darkness outside. The Storm is still raging.

I close the window and I go to the Bathroom and I turn on the shower and take off my clothes and drop them in a pile on the tile floor. I walk over to the mirror. I want to see myself. I want to look into the pale green of my eyes and see not my physical self, but the self that lives beneath. I look at my lips. They are slightly swollen, but almost normal. I look at the stitches and the hole. The hole is starting to heal, the stitches are doing their job. I look at my nose. I take the bandage off and I throw the bandage in the garbage can. My nose is straight, though there is a new bump along its ridge. I look at the area beneath my eyes. The black is starting to fade and is turning yellow, the swelling is nearly gone. I start to look up. I want to look into the pale green of my eyes. I want to see not my physical self, but the self that lives beneath. I move closer. Closer. I want to look into the pale green of my eyes. I want to look into the self that lives beneath. Closer, closer. I can't do it. No fucking way.

I turn away and I walk to the shower and I step into the shower and I am pummeled by the heat. It burns me and it turns my skin red and it hurts but I won't step away from it. I deserve this hurt for not being brave enough to look at myself. I deserve this hurt and I will stand and I will take it because I am not brave enough to look into my own eyes.

When I get numb, I add the cold and I sit down on the floor and I let the water run over my body and soothe the burns. The burning is tiring and the cold tires me more. I close my eyes and I let my body shut itself down and I let my mind wander. It wanders to a familiar place. A place I don't talk about or acknowledge exists. A place where there is only me. A place that I hate.

I am alone. Alone here and alone in the world. Alone in my heart and alone in my mind. Alone everywhere, all the time, for as long as I can remember. Alone with my Family, alone with my friends, alone in a Room full of People. Alone when I wake, alone through each awful day, alone when I finally meet the blackness. I am alone in my horror. Alone in my horror.

I don't want to be alone. I have never wanted to be alone. I fucking hate it. I hate that I have no one to talk to, I hate that I have no one to call, I hate that I have no one to hold my hand, hug me, tell me everything is going to be all right. I hate that I have no one to share my hopes and my dreams with, I hate that I no longer have any hopes or dreams, I hate that I have no one to tell me to hold on, that I can find them again. I hate that when I scream, and I scream bloody murder, that I am screaming into emptiness. I hate that there is no one to hear my scream and that there is no one to help me learn how to stop screaming. I hate that what I have turned to in my loneliness lives in a pipe or a bottle. I hate that what I have turned to in my loneliness is killing me, has already killed me, or will kill me soon. I hate that I will die alone. I will die alone in my horror.

More than anything, all I have ever wanted is to be close to someone. More than anything, all I have ever wanted is to feel as if I wasn't alone. I have tried many times, tried to kill my loneliness with a girl or a woman, and it was never right. We would be together and be close to each other, but no matter how close we were, I still felt alone. They felt that loneliness and it made them want to get closer. When they tried, I either ran or did something to destroy what we felt for each other. I can run fast when I want to run fast, and I've always been good at destroying things. Not one of them would be willing to speak to me today.

The last one was the only one who made me feel the way I always wanted to feel. She made me feel better than I have ever felt, better than I imagined I could feel, and it scared me, scared me to the point of paralysis. When she offered herself to me, I failed. That failure drove me to destruction. I destroyed her, destroyed me, destroyed the two of us together. I destroyed the hope of a future. She will not speak my name now, nor will she acknowledge my existence. I don't blame her.

I start talking to an old friend, an old dear friend. I say hello, how are you, how have you been doing, what's new. My voice reverberates in the shower and I feel stupid, but I keep talking. I say I miss you, I wish you were here. My friend's name is Michelle and I haven't seen or spoken to her in over a decade. I say you have been on my mind lately. I say I may see you soon. I say please be there when I arrive, I'm looking forward to spending some time together. It has been too long. Over a decade. It has been far too long.

I met Michelle when I was twelve and my Family had just moved to a small Town. I had spent my entire life in a big City and the adjustment wasn't smooth. I didn't relate to any of the Kids in the Town, they didn't relate to me. I didn't lift weights, I hated heavy metal, I thought working on cars was a waste of fucking time. At first I made an effort to fit in, but I couldn't pretend, and after a few weeks, I stopped trying. I am who I am and they could either like me or hate me. They hated me with a fucking vengeance.

I started getting taunted, pushed around and beat up. I taunted back, matched every push with a push, every punch thrown with one of my own. Within a month or two I had a reputation. Teachers talked about me, Parents talked about me, the local Cops talked about me. They did not say pleasant things. I responded by egging their houses, blowing up their mailboxes and vandalizing their cars. I responded by declaring War

on them and their Town and by fighting that War with everything inside
of me. I didn't care whether I won or lost, I just wanted to fight. Bring it
on, you Motherfuckers, bring everything you've got. I'm ready to fucking
fight.

Six months into my time there I became friends with a Girl named
Michelle. She was popular, beautiful and smart. She played sports and she
was a Cheerleader and she got straight A's. I don't know why she wanted to
be my friend, but she did. It started when she passed me a note in English
class. The note said you don't seem as awful as I hear you are. I passed one
back that read: beware, I am as awful as people say and worse. She laughed
and I had a friend. She didn't become my Ally, and I didn't ask her to or
want her to, but she became my friend, and that was more than anyone else
was willing to do.

We started talking on the phone, passing notes in class, eating lunch together, riding in the same seat on the Bus. People wondered why she
bothered with me and wondered what she saw in me and told her she
shouldn't waste her time with me, but she ignored them. She had too
much going for her for anyone to make her suffer for our friendship, so
they pretended that it didn't exist.

Halfway through the Eighth Grade, Michelle got asked out on a date by a
Guy in High School. She knew her Parents wouldn't let her go, so she
told them she was going to the movies with me. I had never done anything to them and I had always been pleasant and polite in their presence,
so they agreed and they drove us to the Theater. I went inside and I
watched the movie with a pint of whiskey and I walked Home by myself
when it was over. Michelle got picked up and went on her date. She and
the Guy parked and drank beer and as he was driving her back to the
Theater, he tried to beat a Train across a set of tracks. His car got hit and
Michelle was killed. She was popular, beautiful and smart. She played
sports and she was a Cheerleader and she got straight A's. She was my
only friend. She got hit by a Train and killed. She got hit by a fucking
Train and killed.

I found out the next day. I got blamed by her Parents and by their friends
and by everyone else in that fucking hellhole. If she hadn't lied and if I
hadn't helped her, it would not have happened. If we hadn't gone to the
Theater, she would not have gone on the date. The Guy was unhurt and
was a local football Hero and everyone felt sorry for him. I got taken
down to the local Police Station and questioned. That was the way it
worked there. Blame the fuck-up, feel sorry for the football Hero. Vilify
one forever, forget the other had anything to do with it. I took a lot of

punches for that bullshit, and every time I threw a punch back, and I threw one back every single time, I threw it back for her. I threw it back as hard as I fucking could and I threw it back for her.

I still think about Michelle and I still miss her. I wish I could hear her voice or hear her laugh or see her smile. I wish I could sit next to her or call her or pass her a note. I wish I could smell her, touch her hair, look into her eyes. I wish I could hear her say calm down, it's not worth it. I wish I could hear her say walk away, don't give them the pleasure. I wish I could hear her say it's okay, Jimmy, everything is going to be okay. I wish I could tell her I love her because I did and I do and I never did it when she was still alive. She was my only friend. She got hit by a Train and killed.

I don't believe she's in Heaven and I don't believe she's in a better place. She's dead and when we're dead, we're gone. There are no blinding lights, there is no happy music, there are no Angels waiting to greet us. St. Peter is not at the Pearly Gates with a big fat fucking book, our friends and Relatives are not holding a seat for us at some divine dinner table, we do not get a tour of Heaven. We are dead and that is it. No more. That does not, however, prevent me from talking to Michelle. I talk to her and I ask her questions and I tell her about my life. I tell her I miss her and I tell her that I think about her every day and I tell her that I love her. I tell her that I'm still throwing back and that I'm still throwing hard and that I'm still throwing for her. I will always throw for her. Always.

I talk to Michelle and I tell her these things in the worst times of my life. I talk to Michelle and I tell her these things when I no longer have hope. I talk to Michelle and I tell her these things when I feel as if I'm going to die. I know that when I'm dead I'll be dead and I know that I'm close to death now. I know it is simple, and that when I die there will be no more. I know I'll never meet Michelle in Heaven or anywhere else, but I talk to her anyway. I have been talking to her a lot lately.

The shower door opens and someone steps inside and I am brought back from my mind and my loneliness, brought back to this moment this now this goddamn shower. I open my eyes and John is standing in front of me. I stand and I stare at him. We are both naked. I speak.

What the fuck are you doing?

No one else is up yet.

What the fuck are you doing in here?

I heard you and thought you might want some company.

Get the fuck out of here.

I won't tell anyone. I promise.

GET THE FUCK OUT OF HERE.

John steps out of the shower and he shuts the door. I step out of the shower behind him and I reach for a towel and I wrap it around my waist. The Bathroom is filled with steam and the sink and the toilets are dripping with condensation. John is sitting on the radiator with a towel on his lap. He looks nervous and scared, like a little puppy expecting to get smacked.

I'm sorry.

Don't do that again.

A lot of men in here get lonely. You seemed lonely to me.

I'm not.

I'm sorry.

Don't be sorry, just don't do it again.

Do you hate me?

No, I don't hate you, and I don't care what you do with other people. Just don't expect to do it with me.

Are you gonna hit me?

No, I'm not gonna hit you.

Sometimes People hit me.

I'm not gonna hit you.

You can hit me if you want to.

I'm not gonna hit you.

John starts crying.

I'm sorry. I'm so sorry.

Don't be sorry, just don't do it again.

I pick up my clothes and I walk out of the Bathroom and I go to my section of the Room and I dry myself off and I get dressed. I can hear John whimpering in the Bathroom, Warren and the Bald Man are still sleeping, the Storm is still at full strength. When I finish dressing, I lie down on top of my bed and I am surprised by how tired I am and I close my eyes and I am asleep.

The dream comes fast. I am back in the Room and I am back at the table. I have booze, coke, crack, glue and gas. I am using them all. I am using as much as I can as fast as I can. I am screaming and I am laughing and I am cursing. I am shaking my fist at the Sky and calling God a piece of shit Motherfucker, I am calling God a bitch. I am jumping up and down and I am running around the table. There is so much of the booze, coke, crack, glue and gas that I am rubbing it into my skin and I am pouring it all over myself. I am full of it and I am covered with it. I am fucked up beyond comprehension. I am comfortable for the first time in days.

I find a gun beneath a large bag of cocaine. I pick it up and hold it in my hand. It is a thirty-eight-caliber revolver. It is a gun I have held in my hand before, a gun that I know how to use. I sit down in the chair and I open the cylinder. The cylinder is full, there is a bullet in every chamber. I close the cylinder and I spin it and the clicking noise of the spin makes me smile. I have held this type of gun before and I know how to use it. A thirty-eight-caliber revolver.

I put the barrel in my mouth. The barrel is cold and it is dirty and the metal tastes good in my mouth. I spin the cylinder again. The click click click click click makes me smile. Every chamber is full. There is no doubt as to the outcome. The cylinder stops. I hook my thumbs around the trigger. I am full of booze, coke, crack, glue and gas. I am fucked up beyond comprehension. My thumbs are twitching, twitching, twitching. Boom.

I wake, eyes open to the ceiling, shaking and short of breath. I reach for my nose and there is a drop of blood beneath my nostril. My head is spinning and I'm dizzy. My stomach is on fire. I am fucked up beyond comprehension.

I get out of bed and I walk to the Bathroom. I am having trouble walking and I fall through the door. Warren is standing at the sink brushing his teeth and someone is in the shower. I start gagging and as I gag, I crawl to the front of the toilet. When I get to the toilet, I vomit. The vomit is full of bile and brown shit that I have never seen before. It is full of blood. It burns my stomach, my throat and my mouth. It burns my lips and my face. It won't stop. I heave and it comes, the burning vomit comes and comes again and again. It keeps coming. I want it to stop, but it won't.

Warren steps over and kneels down and he puts his arm around me and he tries to hold me steady. The Bald Man has stepped from the shower and he is staring at me and he is stunned by the violence of my sickness. It keeps coming. It keeps coming and coming. It won't stop. It won't fucking stop. My heart is racing and it's racing irregularly and there is pain with every beat and there is pain with every irregular beat and the pain shoots through my left arm and the left side of my jaw. The liquid has stopped flowing through my body and out of my mouth, but the action of vomiting has not stopped. It feels as if my stomach and my throat are coming out or they are trying to come out. It feels as if my body is trying to rid itself of itself. It is trying to rid itself of me.

I can't do this anymore. I cannot continue to live this way. I am an Alcoholic and I am a drug Addict and I am a Criminal. My body is falling apart and my mind fell apart a long time ago. I want to drink and I want to smoke crack even though I know drinking and smoking crack are killing me. I am alone. I have no one to talk to and no one to call. I hate myself. I hate myself so much that I can't look myself in the eye. I hate myself so much that suicide seems like a reasonable option. My Family is ready to write me off, my friends are ready to write me off, I have destroyed every meaningful relationship I've ever had. I am vomiting for the seventh time today. The seventh fucking time. I cannot continue to live this way. I cannot continue to live this way.

The gagging slows down and I start breathing. Warren is holding me steady and the Bald Man is staring at me. I raise my hand and I motion for Warren to step away and he stands and he steps away and I lean my head against the front of the toilet. I breathe. I take in as much air as I can. I know the air will slow my heart and calm me down, so I breathe. I take in as much air as I can. Calm me down. Calm me down.

Warren speaks. The Bald Man stares.

Are you all right?

I nod.

Do you need help?

I shake my head.

I'm going to get someone.

I speak.

No.

You need help.

No.

James, you need help.

I stand. I am unsteady.

I decide what I need. Not you.

I take a deep breath and I stumble to the sink and I turn on the water and I wash my face and I clean the vomit out of my mouth. When I finish, I turn off the water and I turn around. Warren is staring at me and the Bald Man is staring at me. I walk past them and I walk out of the Bathroom. Warren follows me out and he heads to his area of the Room.

Let me at least give you a shirt.

I look at my shirt. It is white and brown and red. Covered with streaks of bile and patches of shit that I have never seen before and streams of blood.

Here.

Warren tosses me a shirt. I catch it. It is a starched white oxford. I look at it and I look at him. He speaks.

It's the only clean shirt I've got left.

I look at the shirt. It is not a shirt I would wear. I laugh and I look back to Warren.

Thank you.

He laughs.

No problem.

I take off my T-shirt and I toss it on the floor next to my bed and I put on the oxford and it is huge. It envelops my withered frame like a tarp and it hangs near my knees. I roll the sleeves to the middle of my forearms and I run my hands down its front. It is stiff from the starch, but soft beneath. The cotton is expensive and finely woven, probably made in some faraway Country. It is the cleanest, nicest thing I have worn in as long as I can remember, and I feel as if I don't deserve to have it on my sick body. Warren is sitting on the edge of his bed clipping his toenails, a pair of black socks sit next to him. I walk over and I stop in front of him and I run my hands down the front of the cotton. I speak.

It's very nice. I'll take good care of it.

Warren smiles.

Don't worry about it.

I will worry about it, and I appreciate you lending it to me. Thank you.

Don't worry about it.

I'll take good care of it. Thank you.

Warren nods and I turn and I leave the Room and I walk through the Unit. Men are doing their morning jobs, getting ready for the day, walking to breakfast. Roy is standing in front of the Job Board with his friend. I walk past him.

James.

I keep walking, don't look back.

You still have to do the Group Toilets.

I keep walking and I don't look back and I raise my middle finger over my shoulder so he can see it.

James.

I keep my finger raised.

JAMES.

I make my way through the Halls toward the Dining Hall. With each step I take, a profound need for a drink or something harder or both or everything grows on me. My feet get heavy and my pace slows. My mind is filled with one thought and it runs through over and over and over. I need to get fucked up. I need to get fucked up. I need to get fucked up. I need to get fucked up.

I walk through the Glass Corridor that separates the men and the women and I get in line. I can smell the food, it is breakfast food. Eggs and bacon and sausage and pancakes and French toast. It smells fucking good. I see the oatmeal in a big crock off to the side. Fuck that oatmeal. Disgusting gray mushy bullshit. I can smell the food, it is breakfast food. Eggs and bacon and sausage and pancakes and French toast.

I move forward. I move closer, closer, closer. My need to get fucked up has grown exponentially. It has grown to the point that it is no longer a thought and it has grown to the point that I don't have any thoughts. There is just a base instinct. Get something. Fill me. Get something. Fill me.

Someone bumps into me and I look at them and the Girl I met a few days ago is standing in front of me and she's dropped something. Get something. Her name is Lilly. Fill me. I pick up whatever she dropped and I see it's a small piece of folded white paper. Get something. I hand it back to her. Fill me. She starts to say something. Get something. I ignore her. Fill me. I step forward. Get something. Fill me.

I grab a tray and I ask the woman working behind the Glass Counter for eggs and bacon and sausage and pancakes and French toast. She doesn't give me enough, so I ask for more. She gives me another helping, but it's still not enough. I ask again. She says no, the plate won't hold anything else.

I grab a stack of napkins and some silverware and I find an empty table and I tuck the napkins into the front of Warren's shirt and I sit down and I get a bottle of syrup and I cover the eggs and bacon and sausage and pancakes and French toast with the syrup and I start devouring the food. I don't look at what it is and I don't taste it and I don't care what it is or what it tastes like. It doesn't matter. What matters is that I have something and I'm going to take as much as I can as fast as I can. Get something. Fill me.

I finish the plate. My face and my fingers and the napkins protecting Warren's shirt are covered with eggs and bacon and sausage and pancakes and French toast and syrup. I lick my fingers and I wipe my face and I pull the napkins out of the shirt and I ball them up and I drop them on my tray and I lick my fingers again. I want more, but for the moment, my needs have been met. I lean back in my chair and I look around me. Men and women are streaming through the Glass Corridor. They bump into one another, exchange glances, share the same space, but they do not speak. There is obvious tension.

The women's area is nearly filled. Some of the women have showered and made themselves up, some of them have not, and they have divided themselves up according to Socioeconomic Class. The rich sit with the rich, the middle with the middle, the poor with the poor. There are more rich than middle, more middle than poor. The rich women talk and laugh and hardly touch their food and they behave as if they are on some sort of vacation. The middle women are less animated, but they also look as if they're enjoying themselves. The poor women are not made up at all and they hardly talk. They concentrate on their food, as if these are the best meals they have seen and the best meals they are going to see.

Although my table is empty, most of the tables in the men's area are filled. The divisions among the men are not made by class, but by drug of choice. Drunks sit together, Cokeheads sit together, Crackheads sit together, Junkies sit together, Pillpoppers sit together. Within each of these groups, there are two other divisions. One group is made up of the Hardcore. They are the heaviest users and the truly fucked up. The other group is made up of the Wussies. They are the functional and the potentially saved. The Hardcore make fun of the Wussies and tell them they don't belong here. The Wussies don't respond with words, but with looks that say thank God I'm not one of you. Ed and Ted and John sit among the Hardcore, Roy and his friend and Warren and the Bald Man sit with the Wussies.

I sit alone watching them all, wondering what the fuck I am doing here, desperately wishing I had something that would fuck me up. The food has killed the instinct for the moment, but I know it will come back and I know it will come back stronger. Get something. Get something hard and get something fast. Fill me. Fill me till I die.

Leonard sits down at my table. He is wearing a different Rolex and a different Hawaiian shirt. His plate is covered with sausage and bacon and nothing else.

Hey, Kid.

He unfolds a napkin, places it on his lap.

Hi.

He takes another napkin and he cleans his knife, his fork and the edge of the glass of orange juice.

When'd you get the teeth?

Yesterday.

What'd they have to do?

Cap the outside two, fill a cavity on this one.

I point to my outside left tooth.

Root canals on these.

I tap the middle two. They are firm.

They give you good drugs?

They didn't give me anything.

No fucking way.

Yeah.

They didn't give you anything?

No.

You got root canals on your two front teeth without any drugs?

Yeah.

Leonard looks at me as if what I have said is incomprehensible to him.

That's the worst fucking thing I've ever heard.

It sucked.

Sucked isn't the word I would use.

It fucking sucked.

He laughs, sets down his fork.

Where the fuck did they make you, Kid?

What's that mean?

Where does someone like you come from?

I've lived a lot of places.

Like where?

Why do you care?

Just wondering.

Stop wondering.

Why?

I don't want to make friends here.

Why?

I don't like good-byes.

You gotta say them though.

No, you don't.

I stand and I take my tray and I get back in line and I get more food and I get more napkins and I make my way toward an empty table in the corner and I sit down and I eat my food. I eat slower this time. With each bite I take I feel my stomach expanding. It is an awful, uncomfortable feeling, but I can't stop. I take bite after bite, I feel worse and worse. I look at the food and I don't want any more, but it doesn't matter. I take bite after bite, I feel worse and worse. Get something. Fill me. That is all that matters. Fill me.

I finish the plate and I stand and I walk slowly, slowly, slowly across the Dining Room and I put my tray on the conveyor belt to the dishwasher. When I turn around, Lilly is standing in front of me. Although I saw her a little while ago, I didn't really see her, and although I have met her twice before, I have never really looked at her. She has long black hair to the middle of her chest and she has blue eyes. Not ice blue, water blue. Deep clean water blue. She is pale white, pale pale pale white, and her lips are thick and blood red, though she is not wearing lipstick. Her jeans are old and worn and her black sweater is old and worn and her combat boots are old and worn and everything is too big for her body, which is small and thin. She is holding a tray and smiling. Her teeth are straight and white, and they are straight in a way that came without braces and white in a way that has nothing to do with toothpaste. I smile back. She speaks.

You have teeth.

Yeah.

They look nice.

Thanks.

You doing all right?

Not even close. You?

Yeah, I'm okay.

Good.

I step around her and I walk away. I know she is watching me, but I don't look back. I make my way through the Halls and I go to the Lecture Hall and I find a seat among the men of my Unit and I sit down. Leonard sits next to me and I get up and I move so that there is a seat between us. He looks at me and he laughs. I ignore him.

The Lecture starts. It is about Letting Go and Letting God. The man giving the Lecture has been sober for a decade. Whenever he is troubled or something is going wrong in his life, he turns it over to God and goes to an AA Meeting. God does with it what he will, resolving it for better or for worse, and the man doesn't worry about it or try to control it. He just waits and trusts, waits and goes to Meetings, waits and assumes whatever happens is what is supposed to happen. When he talks of God and of his trust in his mighty male God, his eyes glaze over. It is a glaze I know and have seen many times before, usually when someone is fucked out of their skull on strong, hard drugs. His God has become his drug and he is high, high as a Motherfucking kite, and he rants and raves, paces back and forth, God this and God that, blah blah blah. If I was closer to him or if I could get at him, I would punch him in the mouth just to make him shut the fuck up.

He finishes and everyone is impressed and everyone claps. I get up and I leave. When I get outside the door, Ken is waiting for me.

Hi, James.

Hi.

Could you come with me for a little while?

Why?

Your test results have come back and Doctor Baker wants to speak with you.

Okay.

We walk back through the light of the Halls and it makes me uncomfortable and Ken tries to make small talk and I ignore him. I ignore him because my need to get fucked up is growing and it is screaming at me and it is all I can think about and all I can concentrate on. I would kill for a drink right now. Kill. Drink. Kill. Drink. Kill.

We walk into the Medical Unit and Ken takes me to the Waiting Room and he tells me to wait. He leaves and I smoke a cigarette and I watch television. The cigarette tastes good and it burns my throat and my lungs and though it is the lowest and weakest drug that I am addicted to, it is still a drug and it feels fucking good. I don't care what it's doing to me, it feels fucking good.

There is a coffee machine in the corner and I get up and I get myself a cup. I pour sugar into it to the point of saturation and I take a sip and it is hot and it hurts to drink it and I like it. My heart speeds up almost immediately, and though it doesn't speed up like it normally does, and though I am not addicted to coffee, it is still a drug and it feels fucking good. It feels so fucking good.

Ken comes back to the Room and he says the Doctor is ready and I stand and he leads me through the Medical Unit to a small, clean, white Examination Room. There are three chairs and a window and a set of shiny steel shelves with instruments on them and an examination table against one of the walls and an X-ray viewing machine hanging near the door. Doctor Baker is sitting in one of the chairs with a file. He stands when we enter.

Hi, James.

He offers his hand. I shake it.

Hello, Doctor Baker.

We sit.

Can I see your teeth?

I smile.

They look good. Doctor Stevens said you were very brave.

Doctor Stevens was good to me. Thank him for me next time you speak to him.

I will.

Now tell me why I'm here.

Dr. Baker opens his file.

I have the results from the tests we took a few days ago.

How bad is it?

He looks at the file, he takes a deep breath. He leans back in his chair and he looks at me. He speaks.

You have done significant damage to your nose, your throat, your lungs, your stomach, your bladder, your kidneys, your liver and your heart. I have never seen so much and such extensive damage in someone so young. We would need to do more tests to know the specific extent of it, and if you want them done we can facilitate that, but from what I have here, I know a few important things. The first is that you are lucky to be alive. The second is that if you ever have another drink or use any type of hard drug again, there is a good chance that you will die. The third is that if you start drinking or using drugs regularly, you will be dead within a few days. Your body has suffered from a pattern of such profound and prolonged abuse that it will not hold up anymore.

Ken is staring at me, Doctor Baker is staring at me. I look past him and out the window where the Storm is still raging. I finally know with absolute certainty what I have suspected for a long time. I am almost dead. It's a happy fucking day.

Doctor Baker speaks.

This is not a joking matter, James.

I look at him.

I know it's not, but what the fuck am I supposed to say? I have received my sentence.

Ken speaks.

What's that mean?

What do you think it means?

We're here to help you, James. We're here to help you get better and to help you learn how to stop killing yourself. If you do what we tell you to do and you follow the Program we prescribe, you will live a long and happy life.

I have received my sentence.

It doesn't have to be carried out. Just trust us.

I look at Doctor Baker.

You got anything else to say to me?

I hope you'll trust us, I hope you'll give us a chance to help you, and I hope to God you're here tomorrow.

I stare at him. His eyes are thick and wet and breaking. He is obviously sad and obviously disappointed. I'm tired of making people sad and I'm tired of disappointing them and I'm tired of seeing them break. I have seen this too many times. He will be the last.

I appreciate your time and your efforts. Both of you. Thank you.

I stand and I open the door and I walk out of the Room and I shut the door behind me and I head back to my Room. Although I have just been told that further use of alcohol and drugs is going to kill me, and kill me soon, what I want right now is a nice strong drink and a blast of rock. I want them badly. Get something. I want them so badly. Fill me. I would kill for them. Get something. Kill for them. Fill me. I am completely fucked.

All around me, People are going about their day. Patients are going to counseling and to therapy, Doctors and Therapists are giving them whatever they need. People are either getting help or giving help and they are all doing it willingly. Their bodies are recovering and their minds are recovering and they are rebuilding their lives and they are following the Program and they are trusting in the Program. They have turned themselves over and they believe and whether it works or not in the long run doesn't matter. For now, they believe. I do not know how they are doing it.

I get to my Room and I see that someone has retrieved the Bible and the *Big Book* that I threw out the window and placed them back on my bed. They are soggy and wet, the pages swollen, the covers warped. The fact that they are back and that someone has brought them back makes me angry. I pick them up and I carry them to the Bathroom and I stuff them in the garbage can beneath the used razors, the brown Q-Tips and the dirty snot rags. If I could, and if my body would cooperate, I would stuff them into the toilet and I would shit on them.

I walk back to my bed and I lie down and I close my eyes and the finality of Doctor Baker's words start to sink in and the words clear my mind and kill my urges and slow my heart. I have received my sentence. A few days of regular drug and alcohol abuse is going to kill me. I will be dead, gone, no more. I will cease to exist in any way, shape or form. I will meet the blackness and the blackness will be eternal. Somehow I always knew I would meet my end this way. Somehow I always knew that I would kill myself with drugs and alcohol. I knew each time I took a drink, I knew each time I snorted a line, I knew each time I hit a pipe or sniffed a tube or took a pill. It is nobody's fault but my own. I knew each and every time. I could never stop.

I can imagine my obituary. The truth of my existence will be removed and replaced with imagined good. The reality of how I lived will be avoided and changed and phrases will be dropped in like Beloved Son, Loving Brother, Reliable Friend, Hardworking Student. People will change their view of me, from reckless Fuck-Up to helpless Martyr, from dangerous Fool to sad Victim, from addicted Asshole to unfortunate Child. They will say things like my God, what a waste. Oh, what he could have been. He had so much going for him, what happened? And it will be fucking false, every single word of it will be false.

I know who I am and I know what I've done and I know why I am about to die. I have faced the reality and the reality is simple. I am an Alcoholic and I am a drug Addict and I am a Criminal. That is what I am and who I am and that is how I should be remembered. No happy lies, no invented memories, no fake sentimentality, no tears. I do not deserve tears. I deserve to be portrayed honestly and I deserve nothing more and I start to write an honest obituary in my own mind. I write the obituary that should appear, but never will. I start at the beginning and I stick to the facts and I move to what I know will be my end.

James Frey. Born in Cleveland, Ohio, September 12, 1969. Started stealing sips from drinks at seven. Got hammered for the first time at ten. Vomited from abuse for the first time at ten. Smoked dope at twelve. By thirteen was smoking and drinking regularly. Blacked out for the first time at fourteen. At fifteen got arrested three times. For Driving Without a License, for Vandalism and Destruction of Property, for Public Intoxication and Possession of Alcohol as a Minor. Went to Jail for a night. At fifteen tried cocaine, acid and crystal meth for the first time. Got arrested three more times at sixteen. Started drinking and doing drugs before School. Started selling liquor and drugs to his fellow Students. Blacked out and vomited regularly. Three more arrests at seventeen. Got first DUI. Blew a .36, and set a County Record. Went to Jail for a week. Drank and did drugs every day. At School, at Home, everywhere. Vomited and blacked out several times a week. Made first attempt to quit. Experienced delirium tremens. Drank to make them go away. Two arrests at eighteen. First drug overdose, first case of alcohol poisoning. Tried to quit again, lasted two days. Vomited blood for the first time, had first cocaine-induced bloody nose. Nineteen. Blacked out five days a week, vomited five days a week. Pissed bed for the first time. Shook visibly when not drinking. Woke up for the first time without knowing where he was or how he got there. Twenty. Blacked out seven days a week. Vomited several times a day, seven days a week. Smoked cocaine for the first time, smoked methamphetamine for the first time, smoked PCP for the first time. Twenty-one. Three arrests. Assault with a Deadly Weapon, Assaulting an Officer of the Law, Felony DUI, Resisting Arrest, Attempted Incitement of a Riot, Possession of a Narcotic with Intent to Distribute, Felony Mayhem. Skipped bail on everything. Smoked crack for the first time, started smoking crack regularly. One overdose, three cases of alcohol poisoning. Twenty-two. Accelerated alcohol abuse, accelerated crack abuse. Took anything and every-thing possible, whenever possible. Was constantly sick. Vomiting and shit-ting blood daily. Tried to quit four times. Never lasted longer than twelve hours. Twenty-three. Continued acceleration of abuse, continued decline in health. Two overdoses, constant alcohol poisoning. Rarely knew where he was or how he got there. Tried to quit twice, lasted a total of six hours. Fell down fire escape and destroyed face. Checked into Treatment Center. Left Treatment Center. Died two days later. Fatal dosage levels of alcohol and co-caine found in system. Death ruled accidental overdose. Should have been ruled suicide. Intentional Suicide. He is survived by no one. His Family had written him off, his friends had written him off.

My mind is clear and my urges are gone and my heart is beating slow and steady. In my mind, my obituary is done. It is done and it is right. It tells the truth, and as awful as it can be, the truth is what matters. It is what I should be remembered by, if I am remembered at all. Remember the truth. It is all that matters.

My mind is clear and my urges are gone and my heart is beating slow and steady. I have made my decision and I am comfortable with my decision. It's what I always knew would happen, though the details are just now coming into focus. I am going to leave here and I am going to kill myself. I am going to leave here and I am going to find something to drink and I am going to find something to smoke and I am going to drink and smoke until I die. I am going to leave here and I'm not going to look back and I'm not going to say good-bye. I have lived alone, I have fought alone, I have dealt with pain alone. I will die alone.

I think about when I'm going to leave. I don't want to be seen and I don't want to be followed, I want to disappear quickly and quietly and without any drama, I want as much time in the darkness as I can possibly have. The darkness provides cover, the darkness provides places to hide and the darkness provides comfort. Darkness usually comes around dinner, but dinner would be too obvious. We are required to show up and we are required to eat and though I don't fraternize during dinner, it would be noticed if I were gone. The Lecture follows and the Lecture would be better. People get up and leave during Lectures all the time. They get up and go to the Bathroom, head outside for a smoke, leave to meet with a Counselor or a Shrink, run to get sick. It would not be noticed if I left, and by the time anyone realized I was gone, which would probably be three or four hours later, I would be far enough away that there would be no bringing me back. I would be in the darkness. I would be alone. I would be comfortable. There would be no bringing me back.

My mind is clear and my urges are gone and my heart is beating slow and steady. I am going to leave here and I am going to kill myself. The thought makes me smile. It makes me smile because it is sad and horrible. It makes me smile because the mystery of my death is gone and without the mystery it isn't scary anymore. It makes me smile because I would rather smile than cry. It makes me smile because it's going to be over. It is finally going to be over. It is finally going to be over. Thank you.

I take a deep breath and I wonder how many breaths I have left. I feel my heart beat and I wonder how many more. I run my hands along my body and my body is warm and soft and I know that soon it will be cold and hard. I feel my hair, my eyes, my nose, my lips. I feel the whiskers growing on my cheeks. I touch the skin on my neck, my chest, my arms. It will all be rotting soon. Decomposing and disintegrating. Disappearing. Every trace will cease to exist. Ashes to ashes, dust to dust. We return from which we came. I will be rotting and decomposing and disintegrating soon.

I hear the door open and I sit up. Roy and Lincoln walk in. Roy is smirking and Lincoln looks pissed. Lincoln speaks.

What are you doing?

Sitting here.

Why aren't you in group?

I needed some time alone.

You should have told somebody.

I didn't feel like telling anybody.

Things here aren't always about what you feel like doing.

If you're here to bitch at me about group, I'll go right now. If you're here to bitch about something else, let's get it over with.

Lincoln turns to Roy.

Roy.

Roy steps forward.

You didn't clean the Group Toilets this morning.

I laugh. Roy looks at Lincoln. Lincoln speaks.

What's so funny?

His dumb-ass attempt to get me in trouble.

Roy speaks.

I'm not attempting anything. You didn't clean the Group Toilets this morning.

I laugh again.

Fuck you, Roy.

Roy looks at Lincoln. Lincoln looks at me.

They're not clean, James. He just showed them to me.

I look at him.

I cleaned them at about four o'clock this morning. Cleaned them till they fucking sparkled. If they're dirty now it's because somebody used them or somebody, most likely him, fucked them up to get me in trouble.

Roy speaks.

Not true.

I laugh.

Fuck you, Roy.

He turns to Lincoln. Whines like a spoiled little boy.

It's not true.

Lincoln speaks.

Whether they were clean earlier is irrelevant. It's your job to keep them clean all the time and right now they're dirty as hell. You need to go clean them again.

No way.

Absolutely yes.

No fucking way.

Right now.

You're fucking crazy if you think I'm gonna touch those toilets. I cleaned them earlier and Roy fucked them up to get me in trouble. Let Roy clean the goddamn things this time.

Lincoln steps forward, I lean against the back of the bed. He looms over me, puts on his fighting face.

You're going to clean them whether you want to or not and you're going to do it right now and you're not going to say another word about it. You understand me?

I push myself off the bed and I stand and I stare him in the eye.

You gonna force me?

I stare him in the eye.

You gonna try to force me?

I stare him in the eye.

Come on, Lincoln. What are you gonna do?

We stare at each other, breathe slow, clench our jaws, wait for a jump. I know nothing is going to happen and that gives me the advantage. I know that if he touches me he'll lose his job. I know the job is too important to him to risk for me. I know he's gotten soft after years of sobriety and I know that at this point, the black clothes and the boots and the haircut are little more than a costume. I know nothing is going to happen and that he has taken this so far is humorous to me. I laugh in his face.

He speaks.

This is not a laughing matter.

I laugh again.

I'm not cleaning your fucking toilets, Tough Guy. No fucking way.

I step around him.

James.

I start to leave.

No fucking way.

I walk past Roy and I walk out of the room and I go to the Upper Level of the Unit and I drink a cup of coffee and I smoke a couple of cigarettes and the nicotine and the caffeine feel good inside of me. They speed up my heart, slow down my brain, settle my hands, jump-start my feet. They are strong enough so that I can feel their effects, but not strong enough to really do anything significant. I like them and I like the combination they form. One speedy and manic, the other slow and depressing. They ebb and flow so that I experience them on both ends of the spectrum. Fast as I can go, low as I can go, everything in between. It's fun playing with the doses and the levels and it's fun manipulating the buzz. It's like firing a gun at a target. I get the feeling and I get the rush and I get the experience, but there's no danger. I am in complete control of what I'm doing and what I'm feeling. As in a gunfight, I know that when I switch to the real thing there will be no controlling anything. No fucking way. As much as I can as fast as I can. Till I die.

Men begin filing in from their groups and heading to the Dining Hall for lunch. I follow them and I eat with Leonard. He asks me a lot of questions and I don't answer any of them. He thinks it's funny and I think it's funny and at a certain point he gives up and he tells me stories about our fellow Patients. They are all the same. Had it all, got fucked up, lost it all. Trying to recover. The Great American Sob Story.

After lunch we go to the Lecture, which is about exercise and sobriety. I don't listen to a single word of it, don't care one fucking bit, and Leonard throws pennies at the Bald Man who is now my Roommate. He aims for his head and he gets excited when he hits the center of the bald spot on the top of the man's skull. For some reason the man tolerates it.

The Lecture ends and we go back to the Unit and I attend my first Group Therapy Session. The topic is amends. The group is led by Ken and they discuss the necessity of making amends. Ken believes they are imperative, as do most of the men in the group. Making them allows one to start with a clean slate, to get rid of the guilt Addicts accrue with their actions, to shed the skin of their previous life. Whether they are accepted or not isn't important. What is important is the act of apologizing, the act of admitting fault, the act of asking for forgiveness.

The men who don't believe in amends are the worst of the group. They know that most of what they have done shouldn't be forgiven and won't be forgiven. They don't want to make the effort of asking because the pain of re-jection and the reminder of their actions will hurt too much. They want to move on and forget, even though forgetting is impossible. I am in their class. I know I won't be forgiven and I'm not going to bother to ask. My amends will be my death. No one I have hurt will ever have to see me, hear from me, or think about me ever again. I won't be able to damage them or fuck up their lives anymore, I won't be able to cause them the pain I have caused pre-viously. Forget me if you can. Forget I ever existed, forget I did whatever it was I did. My suicide will be my apology. Even though it is impossible, please forget me. Please forget.

After the group all of the men of the Unit gather in the Lower Level and there is a Graduation Ceremony. Roy and his friend are both leaving. They have done their time, worked their Programs and they are ready to rejoin the outside World. They both receive a Medal and a Rock. The Medal signifies their current term of sobriety, the Rock their resolve to stay sober. They both give small speeches. About half of the men despise them and think they're full of shit, the other half admire them and wish them the best. I sit in the back of the Room with Leonard, who reads the USA Today sports page and swears under his breath.

The Ceremony ends and everybody claps and Roy walks around giving out hugs and good-byes. He avoids me, as does his friend. They both seem very happy and they both have the glazed eyes of the Converted. They clutch their Medals and their Rocks, have their friends sign the backs of their copies of the Big Book. They both look scared and they both look fragile. They both look as if they're running from something and they both look as if they're hiding from something. They both look as if they know they're going to get caught. I give them a month before they're both so fucked up that they can't see straight. I give them a month at best.

Most of the men head to their Rooms and start getting ready for dinner. I head to mine to get ready to leave. I take off Warren's oxford and put on my T-shirt and I write Warren a note of thanks and I put it in the front pocket of the oxford and I walk over to his area and I fold the oxford and I set it on his bed. I go back to my area and I write another note that has Hank's name and the address of the Clinic and says Please Return This Jacket and thank Hank for his kindness and friendship. I put this note in the front pocket of the jacket he lent me so it will be found when I am found and I put the jacket on and I look around for anything else I might have, but there's nothing. I look in the drawers, on the bed, under the bed, under the sheets, in the medicine cabinet, in the shower. There is nothing. I have nothing.

I walk to the Dining Hall and I get in line and I grab a tray and I take a deep breath and the smell of the food floods my body and I am hungry, hungry, hungry and I want to eat and I want to eat a lot. Tonight's meal is meat loaf and mashed potatoes and gravy and brussels sprouts and apple pie. It is a meal I like and it is suitable for what will probably be the last real meal that I eat. I get as much as the woman behind the counter will give me and I get utensils and napkins and I find an empty table and I sit down and I spread the napkins on my lap and I take a deep breath. This is probably going to be the last real meal I ever eat.

The meat loaf is good and wet and juicy and the potatoes are real potatoes and the gravy is warm and thick and tastes deeply of beef. I eat slowly, savoring each bite, letting each bite sit in my mouth until it dissolves. My Mother made meat loaf for my Brother and me when I was a Child, made this exact meal about once a week. Eating it now and eating it as my last meal brings back the memories of those dinners and of many more. My Father would be working or away somewhere on some trip, my Brother and I would be at School or running around whatever neighborhood we happened to live in at the time. At six-thirty every night, we'd have dinner with my Mother. She made great dinners, and she loved the routine of sitting down and eating with us. After dinner we'd watch television or play games or my Mother would read to us. When my Father made it home we would spend time together as a whole and then it was off to bed for my Brother and me. We were a Family, a happy Family, and we stayed that way until I stopped showing up. It would be nice to have my Family here with me now. It would be nice, despite the disintegration of our relationship over the past years, to have a final dinner with them.

Though I doubt we would talk much, it would be nice to look each of them in the eye and say good-bye to them. Though I doubt we would talk much, it would be nice to hold each of their hands, tell them that I'm sorry, that me being who I am wasn't their fault. Though I doubt we would talk much, I would like to tell them to forget me.

I finish eating and I lean back in my chair and I see Leonard walking toward me with a tray of food. He sets down his tray on the table and he sits across from me and he starts unfolding napkins and cleaning his silverware.

How are ya, Kid?

I'm good.

You're good?

Yeah, I'm good.

That's the first time I ever heard you say that.

I'm coming to terms with some shit.

What?

None of your business.

One of these days you're gonna talk to me.

No, I'm not.

You'll get tired of being an Asshole and you'll get tired of not having any friends and you'll talk to me.

No, I won't.

I'm gonna keep sitting with you until you do.

I laugh.

I'm gonna keep sitting with you. Mark my motherfucking words.

I grab my tray, stand.

Have a nice life, Leonard.

What's that supposed to mean?

Have a nice life.

I turn and I walk my tray to the conveyor and I drop it on the belt and I start to walk out of the Dining Hall. As I head through the Glass Corridor separating the men and women, I see Lilly sitting alone at a table. She looks up at me and she smiles and our eyes meet and I smile back. She looks down and I stop walking and I stare at her. She looks up and she smiles again. She is as beautiful a girl as I have ever seen. Her eyes, her lips, her teeth, her hair, her skin. The black circles beneath her eyes, the scars I can see on her wrists, the ridiculous clothes she wears that are ten sizes too big, the sense of sadness and pain she wears that is even bigger. I stand and I stare at her, just stare stare stare. Men walk past me and other women look at me and Lilly doesn't understand what I'm doing or why I'm doing it and she's blushing and it's beautiful. I stand there and I stare. I stare because I know where I am going I'm not going to see any beauty. They don't sell crack in Mansions or fancy Department Stores and you don't go to luxury Hotels or Country Clubs to smoke it. Strong, cheap liquor isn't served in five-star Restaurants or Champagne Bars and it isn't sold in gourmet Groceries or boutique Liquor Stores. I'm going to go to a horrible place in a horrible neighborhood run by horrible people providing product for the worst Society has to offer. There will be no beauty there, nothing even resembling beauty. There will be Dealers and Addicts and Criminals and Whores and Pimps and Killers and Slaves. There will be drugs and liquor and pipes and bottles and smoke and vomit and blood and human rot and human decay and human disintegration. I have spent much of my life in these places. When I leave here I will find one of them and I will stay there until I die. Before I do, however, I want one last look at something beautiful. I want one last look so that I have something to hold in my mind while I'm dying, so that when I take my last breath I will be able to think of something that will make me smile, so that in the midst of the horror I can hold on to some shred of humanity.

A woman walks over to Lilly and she leans over and she whispers something in her ear and Lilly shakes her head and she shrugs. The woman looks as if she has some sort of Authority and I don't want to get Lilly in trouble because of what I want, so I wait until she looks back at me and I smile and she smiles a beautiful perfect smile back and I have the image I want. Good-bye, Lilly. I will hold your image dear. Good-bye and thank you.

I walk to the Lecture and I find a seat in the back row of the Lecture Hall and I sit down and I stare straight ahead and I ignore everything and everyone around me. In fifteen minutes I'll be out of here, gone for good on a beeline to Hell. In the simplest terms, what I'm doing shouldn't be hard. Stand up, walk out, keep walking. The abstract, however, is starting to sink in. The abstract is starting to sink in and it is starting to make this harder for me.

I am going to die. When I die I will be dead, gone, no more. There will be no more thinking, no more breathing, no more feeling of any kind. There will be blackness and the blackness will be eternal. There will be silence and the silence will last forever. I am going to die.

I take a deep breath. I am doing the right thing. I am doing the right thing. I am doing the right thing. It is time to end this charade, it is time for me to leave. I can't take my life anymore, I can't take myself anymore.

I can't look into my own eyes, I can't bear to face my own image. I have tried to get better and I can't. It is time for me to die.

Leonard sits down next to me and he stares at me. I stare straight ahead.

Why you wearing that big coat?

I ignore him.

You cold?

I ignore him.

Why you wearing that big coat?

He stares.

Talk to me, you Little Fucker.

I stare straight ahead.

Why you wearing that big coat?

I ignore him. He reaches for me and he puts his hand on my shoulder and he shakes me.

Why'd you tell me to have a nice life?

I remove his hand from my shoulder and I forcefully set it in his lap and I turn and I look him in the eye.

Leave me the fuck alone.

He looks back, right in my eye.

Why'd you tell me to have a nice life?

Leave me alone, Old Man. Leave me the fuck alone.

I turn away from him and I stare straight ahead. I can feel him continue to stare at me. I don't know why he's doing this or why he cares or what he thinks it is going to achieve. If he tries to stop me, I will prevent him from doing so and I will leave anyway. It is time for me to die.

The Lecture starts and he turns away from me. On the Stage, a man about my own age starts telling his life story. He drank some beer and smoked some pot as a Kid and got sober when he was fourteen. He joined AA and he found a Higher Power and it changed his life. He got straight A's in High School and he went to Harvard. Now he's an Investment Banker and he's engaged to be married. He still goes to Meetings, places all of his trust in his Higher Power, and he gets down on his knees every night and he prays before he goes to bed. As he speaks of his nefarious past, he refers to pot as grass and beer as brew. He talks about having the spins and taking sips from a flask at a School Dance. He talks about the guilt and shame he felt in committing these acts.

I do not relate to this man in any way whatsoever. I do not relate to drinking brew and smoking grass and the spins and sips from a flask. I do not connect these things to any sort of true and dangerous addiction, I do not connect these things to any sort of need for recovery. I suspect that

this man would have joined a Twelve Step Group had he felt he had been
watching too much television or eating too many hot dogs or playing too
much Space Invaders or picking his goddamn nose too many times a day.
I suspect that had he not found the Twelve Steps, he would have found
the Jehovah's Witnesses or the Pentecostal Christians or the Hassidim or
the UFO Redemption Group. I suspect that his membership in AA
doesn't have anything to do with brew and grass or any sort of addiction
to them, but to a desperate need to belong to something. Belonging is
not something I have ever concerned myself with and is not something I
give two shits about. I have lived alone. I am about to die alone.

I stand and I start to make my way out of the Aisle. As I pass Leonard, he
reaches for my arm. I push his hand away and I keep going, past the rest
of the seated men, toward the door, out and into a Hall, toward another
door that leads outside. I reach the door and I open it and I am hit by the
cold and the rain and the wind and the sleet and I am hit by the darkness
and I am hit by what lives within the darkness.

I button up the jacket and I flip the collar and I take a deep breath and I
stare into the black. They are waiting for me. The drink and the drugs and
the Dealers and the Addicts and the Criminals and the Whores and the
Pimps and the Killers and the Slaves and the pipes and the bottles and the
smoke and the vomit and the blood and the human rot and the human decay and the human disintegration. They are there in the darkness and they
are waiting for me.

I step out from beneath the cover of the door and I start walking. One step
at a time, away away away. The cold is quick and bitter, the rain and sleet are
hard and wet, the ground a mosaic of mud and rock and water, the darkness
the darkest darkness. Away away away, one step at a time, it is waiting for
me, it is waiting for me. About twenty feet from the Entrance, I hear the
door open and I turn around and I see Leonard coming outside. He's not
wearing a jacket and he's immediately drenched and he is heading straight
toward me.

Hey, Kid.

I turn away from him and I keep walking. I hear his footsteps in the wetness and I hear the pace of them increase and I hear them getting closer
to me. I keep walking.

Wait up a second, Kid.

I don't wait, don't stop, don't turn around.

Where you going?

Footsteps closer.

Where you going?

A hand on my shoulder. I push it off.

Stop for a second, Kid.

A hand on my shoulder. I push it off. Hands on both my shoulders.

Stronger than I expected. They stop me and they turn me around.

Leonard is drenched and dripping. He speaks.

Where you going?

I push his arms off of me.

Leave me alone.

I start walking.

Where you going?

He follows me.

Away from here.

What are you gonna do?

Get fucked up.

No way I'm letting that happen.

You think you're gonna stop me?

Yeah.

I stop, turn around, grab him by the throat, squeeze his Adam's apple. I don't want him following me, don't want him trying to stop me. I am in the darkest darkness. I am going Home.

Leave me alone, Old Man.

I let go, push him to the ground. He grabs his throat, gags. I start walking and the lights of the Clinic start to fade and the black begins to envelop me. I hear Leonard stand and start after me again and I clench my fists and prepare to use more persuasive means to stop him.

I can see the fist, Kid, and it's gonna take a whole lot more than that to take me down.

I keep walking.

And even if you can take me down, I'll have you found and brought back here.

He follows.

And I'll keep doing it as many times as you leave and as many times as it takes to get your goddamn head on straight and make you start fixing yourself.

I keep walking.

You don't know me and you don't know who I am, but I have the resources and I'll fucking use them. I'll bring you back again and again and again.

I stop and I turn around. He's a few feet behind me. He stops and he stares at me.

Again and again and again, Kid. I'll keep doing it.
I told you to leave me alone.
Come back inside.
No.
Where you gonna go?
I'm gonna go get fucked up.
And then what?
I'll see what happens.
You'll end up dead.
Maybe.
When you're dead, you're dead.
I know.
There's no coming back.
I know that.
That's not what you want.
It's my only option.
No, it's not.
He steps forward.
One more step and I'll drop you.
I'll get back up.
No you won't.
What are you scared of, Kid?
Fuck you.
He steps forward.
What are you scared of?
Take a step back, Old Man.
He stares at me, I stare at him. He steps back and he speaks.
I'm not scared of anyone and you scare the shit out of me. Ed and Ted
won't eat with me anymore 'cause they're worried that you might snap on
them, and all day all anybody talked about was how you stared Lincoln
down and laughed in his face when he tried to get rough with you. As
much as I admire it in a certain sense, it's no good being the way you are.
It's no good at all.
I am what I am.
That's not what's inside of you.
Fuck you.
You can't fool me.
Fuck you.
You can't fool me.

FUCK YOU.

Fine, fuck me. Go find some booze and whatever else it is you do and get fucked up and go die in the gutter with piss on your pants and shit in your drawers. That's a good way to go, Kid, an honorable way out. Be proud.

It's my choice.

If you think you're making that choice, you're wrong. Your choices are made by the shit that controls you and by the shit you can't quit. You walk out of here and that shit's gonna kill you and that's fucking wrong.

Maybe, maybe not.

Maybe not, my ass. How about walking back in and being a fucking man? How about walking back in and putting up a fucking fight? How about walking back in and doing what's decent and right and honorable and showing a little pride, just a little bit of fucking pride?

Not possible.

Why?

It's just not.

You're strong enough to get your teeth drilled without drugs and you're strong enough to scare the shit out of a bunch of hardened fuck-ups and you're strong enough to do whatever the fuck you've had to do to end up like you are and you can't walk back into that Clinic and try?

No.

Why?

I've tried before. I can't do it.

Why?

It's too hard.

Life is hard, Kid, you gotta be harder. You gotta take it on and fight for it and be a fucking man about how you live it. If you're too much of a pussy to do that, then maybe you should leave, 'cause you're dead already.

I stare at him and he stares back. Unlike most of the eyes that look upon me, there is no pity in his, no sadness, no sense that he's looking at a lost cause. There is an anger and there is a hardness and there is a resolve.

There is truth, and that is all that matters. The truth. I don't know why he's out here or why he's doing this but I know by his eyes that he means what he says, that he will follow through with his words.

Why do you give a shit?

Because I do.

Why?

It doesn't matter why. All that matters is that I'm here and that I'm not gonna accept any of your bullshit or any of your excuses. You can make this easy, and come back right now, or you can make this hard, and make me call out my dogs. Either way, you're here till you get better.

I can't promise that's gonna happen.

Promise that you'll try.

I stare at him.

Trying can't hurt, Kid.

There is truth in his eyes. Truth is all that matters.

And trying's nothing to be scared of.

Truth.

Just try.

I take a deep breath. I stare at him. I am in the darkest darkness and I am comfortable. Except for my time inside, I have been sober for a total of four days in the last six years. My attempts at sobriety were weak at best. There was always liquor around, there were always drugs around, I was always around people who were using them. I am profoundly physically, mentally and emotionally Addicted to two separate substances. I am profoundly physically, mentally and emotionally Addicted to a certain way of life. I don't know anything else anymore, I don't remember anything else anymore, I don't know if I can be anything else at this point. I am scared to try. I am fucking scared to death to try. I have considered my options to be in Jail or death. I have never considered quitting to be an option because I have never believed that I could do it. I am scared to death to try. I stare at Leonard. I don't know him. I don't know who he is or what he does or what he has done to arrive at this moment. I don't know why he is here or why he has followed me or why he gives a shit. What I know is in his eyes. What I know is an anger, a hardness, a resolve and truth. What I know is that I respect his eyes and I believe his eyes. What I know is that what's in his eyes is different from any of the other eyes that have looked at me, judged me, pitied me and written me off over the last years. What I know is that I can trust his eyes because what lives in them, lives in me.

Twenty-four hours.

Twenty-four hours what?

I'll stay here for twenty-four hours. If I feel the same way I feel now, I'm gone.

I'll call out my dogs.

Call them. I'll bite their fucking heads off.

He smiles.

You're a scary Motherfucker, Kid.

Don't forget it, Old Man.

He laughs.

Come here, I'm gonna give you a hug.

I stay where I am.

I agreed to twenty-four hours. That doesn't mean I'm hugging you and that doesn't mean we're friends.

He laughs again, steps forward, puts his arms around me, hugs me.

All you got to do is try.

I pull away, he motions toward the faded lights of the Clinic.

It's fucking cold out here and I'm soaking wet and I don't want to get sick. Let's go inside.

I'm not going back to that Lecture.

I don't care if you do or you don't, as long as you're inside, I'm happy.

We walk back to the door and I open it and we go inside. The lights are bright and I don't like them and I am scared to death.

I am scared to death.

Scared to death.

Scared.

Fucking scared.

I am outside. I am sitting on a wooden bench in back of the Main Building of the Clinic. There are empty benches on either side of me, a small Lake in front. I am cold and I am shaking and there is sweat running down my forehead and my chest and my arms and my legs and my heart is speeding up and slowing down and my teeth are chattering and my mouth is dry and there are bugs in my coat and in my pants and in my shirt and in my shoes and in my socks. Even though I can see them and hear them and feel them, I know they're not really there. I'm cold. I can see the bugs and I hear the bugs and I feel the bugs, but I know they're not really there. I'm cold.

I have not slept, will not be sleeping anytime soon. I tried to sleep and Warren was snoring and the Bald Man was snoring and John was moaning and turning and twitching and crying out in his dreams and I was thinking about my decision to stay here for twenty-four more hours. My mind was fine with my decision and my heart was fine with my decision and my mind and my heart were ready to keep my word, but my body wasn't fine or anywhere near fine and it wasn't ready to keep anything. My body wanted drugs and alcohol, my body wanted large amounts of them. I stood and I paced to the symphony of snores and moans and cries in an attempt to wear my body down and make it fine, but it didn't work. My body wants what it wants and it could give a fuck about twenty-four hours. I have eighteen hours left. I am not wearing a watch and I can't see a clock, but I know. I have eighteen hours left.

I left my Room and I left the Unit and I went outside and I walked around the Buildings and the Units a couple of times. The Buildings and the Units were dark and quiet except for the Medical Unit. It was light and there were screams coming from within it. I stood and listened to the screams and I screamed back at them. I screamed as loud as I could scream. Nobody heard me and nobody responded. I screamed as loud as I could, but nobody heard me.

I found the bench and I sat on it and I have been sitting on it and the wet wood has been soaking into the backs of my legs. I am staring at the Lake. The surface is dark and smooth and there are long, thin, fragile

sheets of ice floating among dead leaves and broken sticks. It is the deepest part of night, just before the dawn, and the Storm has broken and the
wind and the rain and the sleet are gone. I am staring into the Lake and
I'm sweating and my teeth are chattering and my heart is speeding up and
slowing down and it hurts and there are fucking bugs everywhere. There
is nothing I can do that will make them go away.

I am thinking about her. I am thinking about her even though I don't
want to think about her. I am thinking about her because I can't forget
her, because I continue to look back at her. She is the only one. I can't let
go of what once was and what will never be again. I can't face the fact
that she is gone gone gone, I can't face that it was me who drove her
away. I was with her. I loved her. I drove her away. I am thinking about
her even though I don't want to think about her.

Two days after my first trip to her room, I went back. Before I arrived, I drank
a bottle of wine and I smoked a pack of cigarettes and I rehearsed what I
would say when she opened the door. When I got to the door I stood and I
stared at it. My heart was pounding and my hands were shaking and I felt
dizzy.

I knocked and a voice that wasn't her voice said just a minute and I stood
and I waited nervous scared nervous scared and the door opened and a
tall Girl with thick red lips and a big smile and brown hair and brown
eyes stood before me. It was not her.

I was hoping you'd come back.

Who are you?

Lucinda. Ed's friend. You want to come in?

Yeah.

I stepped into a typical Dorm Room with two desks and two windows and
two used couches and stacks of papers and books and a couple of pizza
boxes and some empty beer cans and tapestries on the walls and a stereo in
the corner with a pile of CDs and a loft with two beds looming over everything. As I looked around the Room I saw that she was reading a book in
one of the beds. Light streamed through one of the windows and across
her face and I had never seen anything or anyone so beautiful in my life. If
my heart had stopped at that moment I would have fallen happy and fallen
full and I would have seen in life all that I had wanted to see and all that I
needed to see. Fall. Let me fall.

Lucinda opened a small fridge and she pulled out a couple of beers.

Want one?

No.

Mind if I have one?

I don't care.

Lucinda cracked one of the beers and she of the eyes set her book down and they both watched me as I reached into my pocket and pulled out a quarter bag of dope. It was good dope, the best I could get, and better than anything that was floating around the School. Green, hairy and pungent, the odor was strong enough that it drifted through the clear plastic of the baggie. I tossed it to Lucinda.

Where'd you get this?

She opened the bag.

A friend.

Took a deep breath.

How much?

Closed the bag.

Don't worry about it.

No way.

Yeah.

Why?

I'm in a giving mood.

Thank you.

I'll give you a number. If you want more, call it and tell them you're my friend. They'll hook you up.

Thank you.

Don't give the number out. I normally don't do this and they don't like people they don't know calling them.

Okay.

Lucinda sat down on one of the couches and reached under it and pulled out some rolling papers and set them on her lap and started picking buds out of the bag.

You want to smoke with us?

I could feel her watching me from her loft. I was scared.

I don't smoke dope.

Really?

I stood.

Really.

I opened the door.

Bye.

Thank you.

I nodded and as I closed the door I looked up at her and she was looking

at me and our eyes met and she smiled and I knew I wasn't the only one
who was nervous and scared and whose hands had been shaking. I
wanted to fall. I wanted to fall hard. I knew.

Darkness retreats and the Sun rises. Red, yellow and orange creep into
clear blue, the sweet airborne calls of waking birds echo across the black
mirror of the Lake, a crisp draft carries the bitter of cold into the reserve
of night. I stand and I walk back to the Unit and the dew on the dead
grass soaks through my shoes and I watch my feet break the crystalline
perfection of the morning's drops and the drops are just another thing
I've destroyed, another thing I can't fix or bring back, another beautiful
thing ruined by my carelessness. I don't stop. I don't stop destroying and I
don't change my course and I don't look back. Looking back hurts too
much, so I just keep going.

I open the door and I head inside and it is quiet and no one is awake
yet. I walk to my Room and I go the Bathroom and I take off my clothes
and I step into the shower and I turn on the hot water. Same old bullshit.
The water burns and it turns my skin red and it hurts and it hurts and it
hurts and I stand there and I take it because I deserve it and because I
don't know anything else. It hurts and I deserve it. Same old bullshit.

I step out and I dry off and I walk to the mirror and I wipe the steam
away and I look at myself. The black beneath my eyes is fading. The
swelling around my nose is gone, though the bump is there and will stay
there. The swelling in my lips is down and my lips are starting to look almost normal. The reduced swelling in them makes the stitches around
my gash more prominent. The stitches are old and black and crusty and
they look like barbed wire, the gash has sealed itself and a scar is starting
to form. I pull down my lower lip to look at the rest of the cuts and the
rest of the stitches. The stitches are black and they weave in and out of
one another like a vicious fence. The cuts are closed bright white against
pale red. They're no longer bleeding, no longer oozing, and scars are starting to form.

I start to look up. I want to see my eyes. I want to look beneath the surface of the pale green and see what's inside of me. As I get near I turn
away. I try to force myself back, but I can't do it. I have not consciously
looked into my eyes for years. Although I have wanted to look into them,
I have not had the strength to do so. I try to force myself, but I can't. I do
not have the strength now and I do not know if I will ever have the
strength. I might never look into the pale green of my eyes again. There
are places from which you cannot return. There is damage that can be irreparable.

I wrap a towel around my waist and I walk into the Room to see if anyone is awake. Warren is sitting up and the Bald Man is sitting up and they're talking to each other. John is still sleeping and is curled into the fetal position and he is clutching himself and sucking his thumb. I walk over to Warren.

Good morning.

Hi, James. How are you?

I'm okay.

You look tired.

Didn't sleep much.

He nods.

It happens here.

I was wondering if I could borrow something from you?

What do you need?

A Swiss Army knife or some nail clippers or something sharp.

Why do you need something sharp?

I just do.

Are you going to hurt yourself?

I smile.

If I was gonna hurt myself, I'd use something that does a whole lot more damage than a Swiss Army knife or a pair of nail clippers.

He looks at me, smiles.

Yes, I guess you would.

He leans over and he opens his dresser and he withdraws a pair of small, shiny nail clippers. He hands them to me.

Thanks, Warren.

I walk back to the Bathroom. The steam has dissipated and the mirror is clean. I walk over to it and I look at the stitches around my gash. They are black and crusty and they look like barbed wire. I want them gone. I am tired of looking like Frankenstein. If I pull them out the scar will be worse, but I don't mind scars and another scar isn't going to hurt me.

I set the clippers on the white porcelain of the sink and I turn on the hot water and I grab some toilet paper and I wet it and I start wiping the dried blood off the stitches. They need to be clean to come out, need to be free of the crust so that they will slide through their entry points without tearing new and larger holes. I have made the mistake of not cleaning stitches properly before and the results were less than pleasant, so I take my time with these. I wet the paper, dab, repeat. Wet, dab, repeat. Wet, dab, repeat. When the scabs receive the water they become blood and the blood smears across my chin and my cheek. I leave it on my cheek because there is more work to be done.

After about ten dabs, the stitches are clean. I pick up the clippers and I open them and I start cutting. There are twelve on the outer gash and they come apart easily and without a problem. When they are cut, I pull them out. The entry points are clean and there is little blood. The scar will be visible, but it won't be bad. A small half circle on the side of my face. Another reminder of the life I live. There is more work to be done. I pull down my lower lip. The cuts are worse and they have not healed as well. The constant exposure to spit and food and movement of my mouth and the activity at the Dentist's office has prevented the stitches from doing their job properly. At this point, they are useless.

I look for the stitch that is closest to the flesh. It is in the lower corner of my mouth, near the base of my gum. As I hold my lip with one hand, I use my other hand to bring the clipper down and in and I insert the blade between the flesh and the stitch and I squeeze the clipper and the stitch snaps and I wince and a small trickle of blood starts to flow from the entry points of the thread. I move methodically through the rest of twenty-nine stitches within my mouth. When I am done cutting, I pull the stitches out and the flow of blood from the entry points fills my mouth and I turn on the cold water and I take a sip of it and I flush it through my mouth and I spit it out. The sink is bright pink, there is red smeared across my face, the remnants of the stitches lie on the side of the porcelain and the clippers are in my hand. I am in pain, but not much.

The Bathroom door opens and I turn around and the Bald Man walks in and he sees me and he falls to his knees and starts screaming he's killing himself, he's killing himself and I can hear commotion and the door flies open and Warren rushes into the Bathroom.

What are you doing?

I'm taking out my stitches.

Warren walks toward me. The Bald Man crawls toward the toilet.

You said you weren't going to hurt yourself.

I didn't.

It looks like you did.

I didn't.

You should have let a Doctor do that.

I've done it before, it's not a big deal.

The Bald Man starts vomiting. Warren walks over to him and he kneels next to him. I reach for some paper and I wet it and I wipe my face. I finish and I toss the bloody tissue into the garbage and I walk over to the toilet and I watch the Bald Man vomit. Although part of me wants to laugh, I don't want to make the Bald Man feel any worse than I've already made him feel. When he stops retching, I speak.

I'm sorry.

He looks up at me, wipes his face.

I didn't mean to upset you.

You're sick.

I don't respond.

You're a sick, sick person.

I don't respond because he's right. I'm a sick, sick person.

I want you to get away from me.

I didn't mean to upset you.

Get away.

I turn and I walk out of the Bathroom and I go to my part of the Room. John is awake and staring at me.

What happened?

I start getting dressed.

I was cutting my stitches out and the Bald Man walked in and saw the blood and thought I was trying to commit suicide and panicked.

John smiles.

I tried to commit suicide once.

That's too bad.

It wasn't bad, it was funny.

Suicide isn't funny, John.

I was hanging myself while I masturbated and after I came I decided to just let myself hang. My Mom walked in and screamed.

That's awful.

It wasn't awful, it was funny.

It's not funny, John.

I finish dressing and I leave John with his memories and the Bald Man with the toilet and Warren with the Bald Man and I go to the Supply Closet and I get a mop and a bucket and a bottle of cleaner and some paper towels and I make my way toward the Group Toilets. Although I don't want to clean them, I am still here and while I'm here, I will live up to my responsibilities. I will show up at meals. I will eat. I will go to the Lectures. I will do my Job. I will attend whatever I am supposed to attend. I will not drink and I will not do drugs. I have fifteen hours left.

I open the door to the Group Toilets and I set the supplies down. There are a few stains on the bowls and some tissue on the floor, but beyond that, there is nothing. This will be quick and easy.

I start scrubbing the stains. They come off easily. I flush the dirty paper towels down the bowl. Towel meet pipe, towel meet sewer. They are friends of mine. They will destroy you, towel.

I clean the sinks and the sinks sparkle. I mop the floor and the floor shines with a thin layer of water and soap. I take out the garbage and I dump it into a larger can of garbage. There is a ton of fucking garbage here. There is more every day.

I walk back to the Toilets. I stare at them. They look clean to me, they are done. I am done. I grab the bucket and the towels and I put the supplies back in their places and I walk to the Dining Hall. I get in line and I get breakfast and I find an empty table and I sit down and I start eating. I have now been eating regularly for two weeks. Three meals a day, every day. I can feel my body reacting to the food in a positive way. I feel stronger. I have slightly more energy. I am gaining weight. I get hungry after a few hours. I haven't been hungry for food in a long time. I have been hungry for other things, and I have fed that hunger mightily, but food was always an afterthought. Humans are said to seek only food, shelter and sex. Humans are said to have only these as their primary urges. I have lived in a state where I went without all, sought none. I do not know what that makes me.

I see Leonard walking toward me and I set down my fork and he's smiling and he looks as if he didn't expect to see me here and he waves at me. I give him the finger and as he sits down, he laughs at me.

Good to see you're still here.

Got fourteen more hours.

You're keeping track?

Part of me is.

Which part?

The part that'll kick your ass if you try to stop me again.

It'll take more than an ass-kicking for me not to stop you.

Why is that?

Because I can take an ass-kicking.

I mean why do you give a shit?

I just do.

Why.

That's none of your concern right now.

You try to control me, try to tell me what I can and can't do, I consider that my concern.

You're looking at it the wrong way, Kid. I'm just trying to help you.

Why?

Leonard leans back in his chair.

Are we friends?

No.

He chuckles.

You want to hear a story that I might tell someone who was a friend?

If it'll explain why you won't leave me alone.

He chuckles again, stares at me for a moment, speaks.

I grew up in the Bronx, just off Arthur Avenue, which is a working-class Italian neighborhood. My Pop mowed lawns and polished shoes at a fancy Country Club in Westchester to pay our bills, and my Mom stayed home and took care of me. We didn't have any dough, but we loved each other and we had a good life together. When I was eleven, my Pop got hit by a Cement Truck as he was walking across the street and he died. My Mom was heartbroken, and two months later, she got hit by a Subway Train. The Authorities called it an accident, said she slipped or something, but I knew better. My Mom just couldn't survive without my Dad, and she went to find him.

I had to live in an Orphanage, which was awful. Nobody there gave two shits about me. I started skipping School and following this guy around my neighborhood whose name was Michelangelo, but who was better known as Mikey the Nose. I thought Mikey was a God. He drove a Caddy, always had a blonde riding shotgun, and he carried a huge wad of cash in his pocket. He did good things for people in the neighborhood who needed them done. He paid their rent, gave them coats and hats and gloves in the winter, delivered food to people who were hungry. I knew he did bad shit too, but I was too young to understand what might be involved in that.

One day, at one of his stops, Michelangelo got out of his car and came up to me and asked me why the fuck I followed him around all the time. I was so scared I couldn't talk. He asked again, and this time he added that he wasn't going to hurt me, he just wanted to know. I told him it was because I wanted to figure out what he did and do it myself so I wouldn't have to live in the Orphanage anymore. He laughed and he asked me my name and I told him and he said following me around all the time is stupid, if you want to see what I'm doing, come ride with me tomorrow. So the next day, instead of a blonde riding shotgun, there was me, and that's all I did from that point on, ride around with Michelangelo and learn what he did for a living.

A couple months after that, I left the Orphanage and moved in with him. I don't think anyone noticed that I was gone. A year later, Michelangelo got married to a woman named Geena, who was the greatest woman that

I have ever known. I lived with them just like I was their Son, though I figured once they had Kids I'd be gone. Turned out Geena couldn't have Kids, so they asked me if I might want to stay with them permanently. I said yes, Michelangelo pulled some strings and he and Geena adopted me, and for the rest of my childhood, they treated me like I was their real Son. They gave me a life, they gave me a home, they gave me a future, and they gave me love. They gave me lots and lots of love.

Leonard stops speaking, looks down at the table. I wait for him to start again, but he doesn't. I speak.

That's a very touching story, Leonard, very sweet and tender.

He looks up at me.

But I'm not a Kid and I'm not an orphan and I don't want to be your fucking project. You understand me?

He smiles.

You need help, Kid.

Find someone else, Leonard.

You like football?

Find someone else.

I heard you, I understood you, I'm changing the subject. You like football?

Yeah.

Who's your team?

The Cleveland Browns.

Really?

Yeah.

Why the Browns?

I was born in Cleveland

He nods.

They're playing Pittsburgh today, should be a good game. You wanna watch with me?

Not if it's part of your project.

It's not.

Then maybe.

You got plans?

No.

Then watch with me.

We'll see.

I notice Lincoln walking across the Dining Hall. He's staring at me and he's not carrying a tray. I stare back at him. Leonard sees me staring and he follows my eyes.

Looks like another fight.

There was never a first one.

Lincoln arrives. He looks at Leonard.

You mind giving me and James a minute alone?

Leonard looks at me.

That okay with you, Kid?

Yeah.

He stands, picks up his tray.

I'll be right over there if you need me.

He motions to the next table.

I'm not gonna need you, Leonard.

Leonard laughs and he walks to the next table and he sits and he watches my table. Most of the men in the Dining Hall are watching my table.

Lincoln pulls out a chair and he sits down.

You and Leonard friends?

Sort of.

You know anything about him?

Not really.

It might not be such a good idea for you to be around him.

Is that why you're here? To tell me who I should and shouldn't be around?

No.

Then what do you want?

Eric came and talked to me yesterday.

Who's Eric?

Eric was Roy's friend. He left yesterday right after Roy.

What'd he have to say?

He told me Roy was obsessed with getting you thrown out of here, that he thought Roy started the fight the two of you had, and that he saw Roy trash the Group Toilets after you had cleaned them.

That's interesting.

I thought so too, and I owe you an apology. Roy was a model Patient here and I don't know why he would have done what he did and I was wrong for assuming he was telling the truth and you were lying. I'm sorry for doing that, and I'd like to try and start over with you and see if we can't try to understand each other a bit better.

That's fine with me.

He stands.

Start over?

I stand.

Sure.

We shake and we let go and he walks away and I sit back down with my breakfast and as I take my first bite, Leonard sits back down and he wants to know what happened and I tell him it was nothing and he doesn't believe me and he bugs me about it and I ignore him and I finish eating. When I'm done, I stand and I take my tray and I drop it on the conveyor and I walk back to the Unit. On the Lower Level, men are gathering around the television watching a pre-game football show. Some of them are smoking, some of them are drinking coffee, some of them seem excited, some of them seem bored out of their fucking skulls. No matter what they are doing, no matter what their attitude may be, they are staring at the images on the screen. Addictions need fuel. Sometimes anything, even base images on a dull screen, will do. Fuel. I have thirteen and a half hours left.

I get a cup of coffee and I find a place on a couch and I light a cigarette and I watch the football show. I don't really know what the men on the show are saying and I doubt they do either, but they seem to think it's important, so I try to pay attention. Within a couple of minutes, I am almost catatonic. I stare at the screen. I drink my coffee. I smoke my cigarettes. I don't even try to figure out what the fuck the guys on the screen are talking about.

Leonard walks in with the Bald Man and hollers I am open for business and men start placing bets with him and the Bald Man writes down the bets on a small pad and he takes the money for the bets and he places it in a small bag with a large zipper. At one point, Lincoln walks through the Room and all the activity stops. When he's gone, it starts again. Men without money bet cigarettes or their Job duties, one man bets a pair of slippers, another bets his sunglasses. Addictions need fuel. The television isn't enough.

When the games start the men argue over which game we're going to watch and the argument ends when Leonard says we're watching the Pittsburgh/Cleveland game. Nobody wants to watch the Pittsburgh/Cleveland game and there is a volley of complaints, but Leonard says the decision is final and everyone shuts up and turns their attention to the screen.

When I was a Child, my Father always had season tickets to the Browns. Although he could have used them for business, he never did. Each Sunday in the fall, he and my Brother and I would put on Browns jerseys and Browns hats and take the Train downtown from our House in the Suburbs and walk from the train to the Stadium. My Dad held our hands the whole way, and because he had only two seats, he'd carry

me into the game and I'd watch it from his lap. We'd yell and scream
and cheer and sing songs when the Browns won, we'd cry when they
lost. When I got too old to be carried into the Stadium, my Brother
and I would alternate games. One week him, one week me. If my Dad
was out of Town, my Mom would take us. I loved the motherfucking
Browns as a kid, and although I haven't watched football in a long time,
part of me still does. I loved my Family as a Kid, and although I haven't
in a long time, the same part of me that still loves the Browns and the
same part of me that remains human and the same part of me that remembers what love is, still loves them as well.
I sit and I silently watch the game and I relive the memories of the games
I attended with my Mother and my Father and my Brother. Around me,
men cheer and yell according to their bets. One man complains about
having to watch Cleveland/Pittsburgh and he calls Cleveland the Mistake
on the Lake and he says that it is the shittiest City he's ever seen and that
it's full of the shittiest People he's ever had the displeasure of encountering
and he yaps endlessly about how pissed he is that he has to watch a crap
Team from a crap City and on and on and on. After about half an hour,
the memories and the love disappear and I lean over and I stare at him
until he turns to me and I tell him that if he doesn't pipe down, the only
mistake spoken of today will be the fact that he couldn't shut his fat fucking mouth. Part of me still loves. More of me doesn't.
Lunch rolls around and most of the men go to the Dining Hall and
they get sandwiches and they bring them back and they continue to
watch football on the television. As I get ready to do the same, Ted
walks up to me and tells me that someone from Administration is looking for me and that I'm wanted at the Front Desk. I ask him if he
knows why and he tells me he has no idea why.
I get up and I go to the Front Desk and I tell the Receptionist my name.
She smiles and she tells me that I have Visitors and she leads me through
a short Hall toward a door.
They're in there.
Who are they?
They asked me not to tell you.
Thank you.
She walks away and I stare at the door and I take a deep breath. I do not
look forward to seeing People from my past. They rarely have kind things
to say to me and I have always done something to deserve their disdain. I
take a deep breath and I open the door and I hear laughing and the
laughing stops and I step into the Room and my Brother is sitting at a

table with a couple of formerly close friends of mine who live together in
Minneapolis. My Brother stands.

What's up, Buddy?

I smile.

Nothing.

He hugs me and I hug him back. It feels good.

What are you doing here?

We separate.

It's Visiting Day. I wouldn't miss Visiting Day.

I turn to my friends. Their names are Julie and Kirk.

What are you Guys doing here?

Julie smiles.

We wouldn't miss Visiting Day either.

I smile.

Thanks.

Kirk stands and he hugs me and Julie follows him and we separate.

There are a number of wrapped packages on the table. My Brother motions toward them.

It's time for you to open your presents.

I sit.

You bring me these?

I brought a couple and they brought a couple.

I look to Julie and Kirk.

I didn't think you'd ever speak to me again after last time.

Kirk laughs.

People do stupid things when they're fucked up. We don't ever need to talk about it again.

Thank you.

He pushes forward a box.

Now open.

The box is beautifully wrapped. The paper is bright and colorful and it says Get Well Soon and has a ribbon around it. I open it slowly and carefully and I almost wish I didn't have to open it at all. It would be nice just to carry it around.

Beneath the paper there is a plain cardboard box. I open the box and inside of it there are three small wrapped packages. I pull them out and I look at Kirk and Julie.

You really didn't have to do this.

Julie smiles.

We wanted to.

I smile and I look at the packages and I start to open them and I have
to stop myself from crying. I do not deserve this kindness. I do not deserve it.

Inside the packages there is a pair of wool slippers, two cartons of cigarettes, a box of chocolates. I look at Julie and Kirk and I thank them and
my voice cracks and they smile and my Brother pushes his boxes forward
and they're not as perfectly wrapped, but they're beautiful as well.

I open them and there are two pairs of khakis and two pairs of wool socks
and two white T-shirts and two pairs of boxer shorts and a black wool
sweater and a pair of pajamas and a black ball-cap with the Cleveland
Browns logo on the front. There is a toothbrush and some toothpaste and
some shampoo and some soap and a can of shaving cream and a razor. There
are some books.

I stare at all of my presents and I try to speak, but I can't. I look up at my
Brother. He's smiling.

You like everything?

Yeah.

You need anything else?

No, this is great.

I stand and I walk to my Brother and I lean over and I give him a hug
and I whisper thank you in his ear and I do the same with Julie and Kirk
and I gather up my things and I walk toward the door.

You want me to show you around?

They stand. My Brother speaks.

That'd be great.

They follow me out and we walk through the maze of bright, light, clean,
uncomfortable Halls and Julie tells me that she has been here before because one of her closest friends was here a couple of years ago. It was an
awful time and her friend was in awful shape, but she got better and she
is still better today. The memories are bittersweet.

We find our way to the Unit and I go to my Room to put my stuff away
and my Brother and Julie and Kirk wait for me on the Upper Level.

When I walk in, the Room is empty. I go to my corner and I set down
my new things on my bed and I sit down on the bed and I stare at them.
They are simple things. Necessities to most people. Clothes and toiletries.
Food. Some books to occupy my mind. Simple things. I touch them and
I hold them and I feel them. They are the nicest things I have had in a
long time.

I know my Brother and Julie and Kirk are waiting for me, so I leave the
Room. I walk to the Upper Level of the Unit and when I arrive, my

Brother and Julie and Kirk aren't there. Ed and Ted are sitting at a table playing cards and drinking coffee and smoking and I ask them if they know where they went and I hope hope hope they didn't have second thoughts and leave and Ted tells me that they're watching football and I look over the rail and I see them sitting on the couches with Leonard and with the other men of the Unit and they're all watching the end of the Cleveland/Pittsburgh game. I walk down and I sit on the floor in front of the couches and I watch the game with them and Cleveland wins and the Winners collect their booty and the Losers bitch and moan and increase the size of their bets on the next game. The man who bet his slippers lost his bet. Now he wants to bet his sweater.

Julie doesn't want to watch any more football and suggests we take a walk. Everyone agrees and I go and get Hank's jacket and my new hat and I put them on and we go outside and it's clear and the Sun is out and the air is crisp and the ground is soggy and it's as nice a day as there is at this time of the year in Minnesota.

The Clinic sits on a thousand acres. Aside from the Buildings, which are all interconnected and spread across about five acres, the rest of the Land is for walking and meditating and spending time alone. There are Trails, there are Clearings along the Trails, there are benches in the Clearings. There are patches of dense Forest, two small Lakes, several wide, tall-grass Pastures, there is a Swamp with an Elevated Walk. Julie knows the Trails from her previous visits here so she leads the way. There is little or no talking except for the occasional comment on our surroundings. Leaves and sticks crack beneath our feet. The Sun is warm and bright and shining, the Sky blue blue blue. Animals and birds are calling and screaming and playing, foraging for food. A breeze brings a spell of cold and another breeze carries the cold away. The Earth is still asleep and will be sleeping for the rest of the Winter, but it is stirring and moving. We pass other Patients and we pass other Visitors and there is usually a nod and nothing more. The Land is showing life and everyone wants to soak it in and appreciate it and remember it. Life. Remember showing life.

Our walk takes a still, quiet hour and ends near the back of the Medical Unit. As we emerge from thick wood, we are met by screams, long loud piercing screams. My Brother and Julie and Kirk stare at the dark, barred windows and my Brother asks me what's happening inside and why people are screaming. I tell him that it's the cost of doing business here and I pick up the pace so that we won't have to listen to them, but even after we pass, the screams are still inside all of our heads.

We come around the front of the main set of Buildings and Julie suggests

we sit on the benches, the same benches I was on earlier. As we get close to them, Lilly stands up with a small, frail Elderly Woman. She takes the Elderly Woman's hand and they start walking toward us. Lilly smiles at me.
Hi, James.
Hi, Lilly.
This is my Grandmother.
I smile at her Grandmother, who has long white hair and Lilly's blue eyes.
Hi.
She smiles back. It is a kind smile.
Hello, James.
I motion to my Brother and Julie and Kirk.
This is my Brother Bob, these are my friends Julie and Kirk. This is Lilly and her Grandmother.
Lilly smiles.
Hi.
Bob and Julie and Kirk all smile, say hello. Lilly's Grandmother speaks.
What happened to your face?
I got hurt.
Did you hurt yourself?
Sort of.
Why'd you do that?
I didn't do it on purpose. It's just the cost of doing business.
Her Grandmother smiles and she gently touches my face with her free hand.
I hope that's a business you're leaving, James.
I smile, enjoy the warmth of her hand.
We'll see.
She nods. Her eyes and her hand understand my words, have seen and felt this type of damage before. There is no judgment and no condescension. Just hope.
It was nice meeting you.
You too.
She looks at Lilly and she smiles.
We should go, Sweetheart.
Lilly looks at me and she softly speaks.
Bye.
I return the look, the tone.
Bye.
She looks at Bob and Julie and Kirk.
Nice meeting all of you.

Bob and Julie and Kirk speak together.

Nice meeting you too.

Lilly and her Grandmother leave and I watch them and they hold hands and they walk toward the Buildings. No judgment, no condescension.

Just hope.

When they're out of earshot, Julie playfully pushes me.

Who was that?

That was Lilly.

I know that, but who is she?

A girl who's here and was taking a walk with her Grandma.

Julie pushes me again.

Come on.

I laugh.

I met her when I first got here. I don't really know her.

She likes you.

I walk to the middle bench, sit down.

Whatever.

Bob and Julie and Kirk follow me, sit down.

Kirk speaks.

Have you heard from—

I cut him off.

No, and I won't.

Julie speaks.

It was that bad?

Yeah, it was that bad.

Bob pulls out a cigarette, offers me one.

Smoke?

I take it, light it. The nicotine feels good.

Buddy?

I stare out at the Lake.

I haven't really asked yet, but are you doing okay?

I stare out at the Lake.

I don't know.

There is an uncomfortable silence. I'm not looking at them, but I know that Bob and Julie and Kirk are looking at one another. Julie speaks.

Do you feel okay?

I don't know.

Kirk speaks.

Do you feel better?

I don't know.

My Brother playfully punches my shoulder.
What the fuck, Buddy. You gotta talk to us.
I turn to him.
I don't know what to say.
What are you gonna do?
I don't know.
Julie speaks.
You've got to get better.
I don't know if I can.
Bob speaks.
Why?
Because I'm fucked up and I'm fucked up really bad. I don't know what
happened or how I ever ended up like this, but I did, and I've got some
huge fucking problems and I don't know if they're fixable. I don't know
if I'm fixable.
Julie speaks.
Everything's fixable.
That's easy to say, much harder to do.
My friend did it.
I'm not your friend.
Bob speaks.
You gotta try, Buddy.
We'll see.
No, not we'll see. You gotta fucking try.
I stare out at the Lake, take a deep breath.
I don't want to talk about it anymore.
There is an uncomfortable silence. I'm not looking at them, but I know
that Bob and Julie and Kirk are looking at one another, I know they're
trying to figure out how to proceed. Bob speaks.
Have you talked to Mom and Dad?
I laugh.
I don't want to talk about that either.
Do me a favor and call them.
Where are they?
At the House in Michigan. They go back to Tokyo tomorrow.
All right.
Julie speaks.
Have you talked to anyone else?
Anna, Lucinda and Amy.
How are they?

Fine, I guess. They're all happy I'm here.

A lot of people are happy you're here.

I doubt that.

Kirk speaks.

We've gotten a bunch of calls from People asking about you.

Who?

We kept a list.

Kirk looks at Julie. Julie pulls a list from her handbag and she hands it to me. I put it in my pocket. Julie speaks.

You're not gonna look at it?

I'll look later. I don't want to waste what time we have left looking at a fucking list.

She laughs, looks at her watch.

It's getting late.

What time is it?

Three-fifteen.

When are Visiting Hours over?

Bob speaks.

Four.

I chuckle.

What?

I have five and a half hours left.

Kirk speaks.

Until what?

Nothing.

I stand.

Let's go inside.

They stand and we start walking back to my Unit and my Brother puts his arm around my shoulders and he tells me that he's proud of me and I laugh and he tells me again and I thank him and we go inside and I show them my Room and introduce them to Warren, who is reading a detective novel in bed. Julie needs to use the restroom so I tell her where the Group Toilets are and she goes to use them. Bob and Kirk and I walk down to the television, where we've agreed to meet Julie. We find an empty couch and we sit down and we watch football. I smoke a cigarette. I have five hours and fifteen minutes left.

Julie comes back and she's carrying a card. She sits down and she hands the card to me and she asks me if I know the guy. I look at it. It reads John Everett, Sexual Ninja, San Francisco and the World.

I hand the card back to her and I ask if he made her uncomfortable or did anything offensive and she laughs.

He was really nervous and he stared at my ass the whole time. It was kind of weird and funny.

Kirk takes the card and he reads it and he laughs and he hands it to Bob who reads it and laughs. Kirk asks if I know the Ninja and I tell him he's one of my Roommates and Kirk howls and he takes the card back from Bob and he looks at it again and he howls louder. He asks if he can meet the Ninja and I tell him maybe some other time and Julie looks at her watch and says that it's time to go so we walk through the bright uncomfortable maze of Halls and we find our way to the Front Entrance and I step outside with them to say good-bye.

Thanks for coming. It means a lot to me.

Julie speaks.

We were worried about you.

I don't want you to worry about me.

Kirk speaks.

We will anyway.

You shouldn't.

Bob speaks.

We want you to get better, Buddy.

I know you do.

This place is your only option.

There are others.

What?

I think you know what they are.

Bob puts his hand on my shoulder, stares at me.

Get better. Please get better.

He starts to break and seeing him start to break makes me start to break and I don't want that. He steps forward and he puts his arms around me and he hugs me and I hug him and it feels good and strong and pure and real. This is my Brother, my Blood, the only thing in this World created from that which I was created from, the Person in this World who knows me best, the Person who would miss me most if I was gone. That he cared enough to come here and that he cares enough to nearly break in front of me means something, but in the end, I know that it means only so much.

We separate and he pushes me in the way that Brothers push each other. I don't want you to die, you dumb Little Fucker.

I push him back.

I hear you. Let's leave it at that.

He nods and he knows me well enough to know that's all that he's going to get. I hug Julie and Kirk and I thank them for the gifts and the visit and they tell me they'll be back next week and they tell me that if I need anything I should call them and I thank them again. They walk toward their car. I go back inside. I walk through bright, uncomfortable Halls. I go back to the Unit.

I arrive and all of the men have gathered on the Lower Level. Leonard is standing on the top of a couch and the Bald Man is standing on the floor next to him waving his arms and they're trying to quiet the men down. Leonard sees me and he smiles and he looks at his watch and he points at me.

I thought you were gone. You have four hours left.

I laugh.

Come down here, Kid. Join the party.

I walk down and I find a spot against the wall and away from most of the men and Leonard and the Bald Man quiet them. The Bald Man stops waving his arms and Leonard takes a deep breath and he stares down at the men.

Men, I have had a good day.

There are a couple chuckles.

I watched some great fucking football, won the bulk of my bets and the bulk of your money, and I triumphed personally in a situation where I expected defeat.

A couple more chuckles, a bunch of boos. Leonard laughs.

I understand the boos, but I'm about to turn your anguish and poverty into joy. I like to share my wealth and celebrate my victories, so after clearing it with the proper Authorities, I called Cajun Sam's in Minneapolis and ordered a feast for delivery. Tonight we eat in.

The men cheer.

The food will be here around six. If you don't like turducken, jambalaya and po'boys, then have fun in the goddamn Cafeteria.

The men cheer again.

I'm going to take a nap before the slaughter. See you at six.

Leonard steps down and men start thanking him and asking him questions and he walks toward his room and they follow him. I walk to the Phone Booth and I sit down on a cold steel chair and I close the door and I pull the list Julie and Kirk gave me from my pocket and I look at it. I am surprised that the list exists, that people called them to find out about me. I am surprised by the names on the list.

I pick up the phone and I start making collect calls. Adrienne isn't home, Eben isn't home, Jody isn't home, someone at Matt's House declines my call. I talk to Kevin and I talk to Andy. Both tell me they were with me the night of my accident, both tell me I was a fucking mess. Kevin tells me he doesn't remember much because he was blacked out, but he remembers being with me. He tells me that he wants to come visit me and I tell him it would be nice if he could and I thank him. Andy tells me he found me knocked out and bleeding and he carried me to a car and took me to the Hospital. He begged the Doctor not to call the Police and he begged the Doctor to put me on a plane. He called my Parents and he took me to the Airport and he got me on the Plane. I thank him and I tell him that if I happen to be saved that he will partially be responsible for saving me. He tells me it's no big deal and he tells me that he would do it again if he needed to do it again, but he hopes that he doesn't. I ask him if he knows what I was on or what I was doing in Ohio and he tells me that he found a crack pipe in my pocket and he saw a bloody tube of glue a few feet from where he found me, but beyond that, he doesn't know anything. He had heard I had shown up at ten in the morning and that I was drunk and incoherent and I had disappeared for the day. The first time he saw me was when he found me on the ground. I thank him again. We say good-bye. We hang up.

I call my Parents. My Mother answers the phone and she accepts the call. James.

She sounds frantic.

Hi, Mom.

Let me get your Father.

She holds the phone away, yells for my Father. He picks up.

How are you, James?

I'm fine, Dad.

You're doing okay?

I'm fine.

My Mother speaks.

Are you getting better?

I don't know.

Do you feel any better?

I don't know.

Are you learning anything?

I don't know.

She exhales, exhales frustration. My Father speaks.

James.

Yeah.

Your Mom and I have been talking to some of the Counselors up there and we want to come see you.

No.

Why?

Because I don't want you here.

Why?

Because I don't.

My Mother speaks.

They have something called the Family Program where we would spend three days learning about your sickness and learning about how to help you deal with it. We'd like to come do it.

My sickness?

Alcoholism and Drug Addiction is a disease, James.

Who told you that?

It's in all the books.

Right. The books.

There is an uncomfortable pause. Father speaks.

We'd really like to do the Program, James. We think it could be really good for all of us.

I don't want you here, and if you come, I'll be fucking pissed.

My Mother speaks.

Could you please not swear.

I'll try.

Another uncomfortable pause. I speak.

Go back to Tokyo. I'll call you next week to tell you how I'm doing.

My Father speaks.

We're very worried about you, James.

I hear my Mother start to cry.

I know you are.

We really want to come up there.

Cry.

Do what you want, but don't expect me to participate if you do.

Do you need anything?

Cry.

I need to go.

We love you, James.

I know you do.

My Mother speaks.

I love you, James.

Her voice breaks.

I know you do, Mom.

My Father speaks.

Call us if we can help in any way.

I've got to go, Dad.

Please reconsider the Family Program.

Bye, Dad.

Bye, James.

My Mother sobs.

Bye, James.

Bye, Mom.

My Mother sobs.

We love you.

I've got to go.

I hang up the phone and I take a deep breath and I stare at the floor. My Mother and Father are at a House in Michigan that I've never seen and my Mother is crying and my Father is trying to comfort her and their hearts are broken and they want to come see me and they want to try to help me and I don't want them here and I don't want their help. My Mother is crying because her Son is an Alcoholic and a drug Addict and a Criminal. My Father is trying to comfort her. I have broken their hearts. I stare at the floor.

I walk back to my Room and I sit down on my bed. John is in his area and when he sees me he stands and walks toward my area.

I'm sorry for giving your friend my card.

I'm not mad at you.

It's okay if you are.

We thought it was funny.

I figured out a way to make it better.

I'm not mad.

Let me make it better.

There's nothing to make better.

Please.

He sits down at the edge of my bed, gives me an earnest look.

How old are you?

Twenty-three.

You're so young.

I chuckle.

What's your offer, John?

He takes a deep breath.

This is to make up for all my wrongs.
Okay.
And if it's not sufficient, we can talk about something else.
What's the offer, John?
He reaches into his pocket, pulls out a picture, hands it to me. It is of a beautiful young Girl in a bikini.
What's this?
My Daughter.
She's beautiful, but I don't want a picture of your Daughter.
That's not it.
Then what is it?
I want to give her to you. You can do whatever you want to her.
Goddamn, John.
I hand him the picture.
You don't like her?
You can't give me your fucking Daughter.
My Family supports her and pays all of her and her Mother's bills.
So what.
She'll do what I say.
Go away, John.
She'll do anything I say.
Then tell her to go to School, stay away from drugs and stay the fuck away from you.
That's good advice.
Go away, John.
I'm sorry.
Don't be sorry, John. Just go away.
He stands.
Okay.
He walks to his section of the room and he climbs into bed and he buries himself under the covers and I can hear him cursing himself. He's a poor, sick, sad Motherfucker, but once he was an innocent young Boy. A Boy with a future, a Boy with his whole life in front of him. His Dad was rich and powerful, and one day, one horrible fucked-up day, his Dad decided to molest him. I can imagine young John, alone in his room with a set of army men or stack of Legos or a pile of baseball cards, and I can imagine his Dad coming in and shutting the door and telling John he wanted some private time with him. After it was over, I can imagine John crawling into his bed and burying himself under the covers and cursing himself.

I sit and I listen to John crying and I wish there was something I could do to help him. I sit and I listen to John and I wish there was some way I could make him better. There is no hope for John, no hope at all. He could go to five hundred Clinics and spend ten years working the Twelve Steps and it wouldn't make a bit of fucking difference. He has been broken beyond repair, wounded beyond the point of healing, abused beyond the point of recovery. He will never know happiness or joy, security or normalcy. He will never know pleasure, satisfaction, serenity, clarity, peace of mind or any semblance of sanity. He will never know trust or love. You poor, sick, sad Motherfucker. You will never know. I'm sorry.

I hear voices and activity outside the door to the Room and I know that it is time for dinner. I walk over to John's area and sit down on a chair next to his bed. He is still under the covers, still mumbling and cursing, still thrashing and still punching himself.

John?

He stops, lies still.

John?

Still.

John?

What do you want?

It's time for dinner.

I don't want to eat dinner.

What are you gonna do?

Stay here.

That's stupid.

Go away.

Get out from under there and come have dinner.

Go away.

I'm not leaving until you do.

Go away.

No.

He throws the covers off of himself and he stares at me with his hardest look. I laugh at him.

What's so funny?

Your Tough Guy look isn't very tough.

I'm tougher than you think.

Yeah, you probably are, but you sure don't look it.

He changes his face into a strange grimace and snarls. I laugh at him again.

That's not any better.

It's not?

No.

He relaxes, looks normal.

I wanna be alone.

Being alone won't do any good for you, John.

I wanna be alone.

It's better to be around people. It makes it hurt less.

How do you know?

I know.

No you don't.

Trust me, I do.

John looks at me, looks down at his blanket.

Come on, let's go.

He looks up.

It hurts a lot, James.

I know it does.

I wish it would go away.

I know the feeling.

What do you do?

Deal with it, and hope someday that you don't have to anymore.

He looks down.

Yeah.

He looks up and he swings his legs off the bed and he stands and I stand and we walk out of the Room. We walk into the Unit and we get in the back of a line. The food has been delivered and set up on a table on the Upper Level. The line runs from the table down the stairs that lead to the Lower Level. As the line moves forward, and as I get closer to the food, the smell ignites my hunger. I want to eat and I want to eat immediately and I want to eat until I explode. I want want want want. Fuel. Right fucking now.

As I begin to climb the stairs, my hunger and my need begin to overwhelm me. My hands start shaking, my heart rate increases, I'm nervous, anxious and angry. I stare at the food. I don't see or hear or smell anything else. Each second is an hour long, each step a marathon. I want, want, want, want. Fuel. Right fucking now. I would kill if somebody tried to take the food away, I would kill if somebody tried to stop me from getting to it. Need need need need need.

I reach the end of the table, pick up a plate, stuff a plastic knife and a plastic fork and a paper napkin in my pocket. The food is on trays and in bowls and a man from the Restaurant is serving it and Leonard is stand-ing next to him supervising. He asks me what I want and I say every-thing. He asks me what part of the turducken I like and I tell him I don't know what a turducken is and I don't care what it is, I just want a lot of it. Leonard laughs at me as I ask for more and more and more. I could give a shit about him right now. I want need fuel now.

I sit down on a couch next to John and I pull the fork out of my pocket and I try to use it but my hand is shaking too much to use it so I start shoveling food into my mouth with my fingers. I don't look at it, I don't taste it, I chew it enough so that I can swallow it. It is not impor-tant to experience it or enjoy it. It is important to fill. That is all I want out of this meal. Enough to fill.

I finish my plate and I get another one. I finish that plate and I get an-other one. I finish that plate and I get another one. I finish that plate. I am beyond full, beyond stuffed. I have moved beyond need and into abuse and I am comfortable. My heart and my hands are slowing down, my senses and the ability to think are returning, the nerves, anxiety and anger are fading away. Beyond need and into abuse. It is nice to be comfortable. It is nice to be Home.

I take a deep breath. I can feel my stomach stretching. I know it's not going to stretch enough. It hasn't come yet, but it will. It will come fast and hard.

I stand and John asks me where I'm going and I tell him that I'll be right back and I start walking back to the Room. I walk up the stairs, through the Upper Level, down a short Hall. As I open the door, it starts to come. Hard and fast. I'm twenty feet from the toilet.

It comes and I keep my mouth closed and I breathe through my nose. I didn't taste it on the way down, but I can taste it now. Rice and beans and pieces of fish and meat. Hot spices and hunks of bread.

I breathe through my nose and I rush toward the toilet. I try to swallow what's in my mouth, but more is coming and forcing it forward. I start to choke. I push the Bathroom door open and I lean over and I flip the toi-let seat up and I explode. Hard and fast. A steady stream. Over and over and over. It burns my face and my lips and the inside of my mouth. My heart sends messages through my ribs, left arm and jaw. My throat con-tracts, my stomach contracts. Over and over and over. Over and over and over.

The stream stops and I take a couple of deep breaths and I reach up and I flush the toilet and I stand and I walk over to the sink and I wash my face and I wash the remaining chunks out of my gums and my teeth and my throat and my nose and I take a long sip of cold water and I swallow it and it cools the burning.

My shirt is stained so I take it off and I go to my section of the Room and as I put on one of my nice new shirts, John opens the door and sticks his head inside.

James?

Yeah.

You have a phone call.

Who is it?

I don't know, I didn't answer it.

I'll be right there.

I finish putting on the shirt and I walk back to the Phone Booth. I open the door and I sit down and I pick up the phone.

Hello?

A female voice.

Hi.

I know the voice, but can't place it.

Who is this?

You don't know?

No.

I'm hurt.

You shouldn't be.

Did you have a nice day?

Who is this?

My Grandmother thought you were handsome.

I place the voice. I smile.

That was nice of her.

She said you had pretty eyes.

I wouldn't know.

Why?

Long story.

How long?

Twenty-three years long.

That's long.

Yeah.

A pause. I'm still smiling.

Well, I just called to tell you what my Grandmother said.

I'm glad you did.

I'll see you tomorrow?

Probably.

Why probably?

Long story.

She laughs.

I hope I'll see you tomorrow.

That would be nice.

Bye.

Thanks for calling.

Sure.

I hang up the phone and I stare at it and I'm still smiling. I stand and I open the door and I step out and I'm still smiling and I walk back toward my Room and John asks me if I want to play cards and I tell him I haven't slept since yesterday and I'm tired but I'll play another time and he says okay. I go back to my room and I'm still smiling and I climb into bed and I pick up the books my Brother gave me. *War and Peace, Don Quixote,* a book on Chinese Religion called *Tao Te Ching.* I open *War and Peace.* I'm still smiling. I have read *War and Peace* before, but it is worth a second trip. I'm still smiling. I start reading. I can't get through the first sentence. I'm still smiling. I haven't slept in forty hours. I'm still smiling. I have fifteen minutes left. I'm still smiling.

My hand drops.

Still.

Eyes close.

Smiling.

I wake and I go to the Bathroom and I take a shower and I wash my hair and I brush my teeth and I shave. I keep waiting to get sick, but I don't. As I walk out of the Bathroom, I stop and I stare at the toilet. The toilet has been my friend and my enemy every morning for as long as I can remember. It has been my receptacle, my support, the only thing besides myself that has known the true extent of my sickness. I'm tired of the toilet. I tell the toilet to go fuck itself. I give it the finger and I laugh at it. I leave the Bathroom.

I put on a set of nice, new, clean clothes. I put on my slippers. I go check the Job Board. My new assignment is coffee. I fill an industrial-size steel coffeepot and I turn it on and I make sure it functions properly. When the coffee is ready, I pour myself a cup. I taste it and it tastes good. Coffee is much easier and more pleasant than the Group Toilets.

I walk to the Dining Hall. I get a bowl of cereal and a glass of orange juice and I look for a place to eat. I see Leonard sitting with Ed and Ted. I walk to their table and I sit down. Leonard looks at me and he speaks. I wasn't sure you'd be here this morning.

I was too tired to go anywhere last night.

Ed speaks.

Where were you going?

To get high.

On what?

Crack and liquor.

Ted speaks.

You a Crackhead?

Yeah.

Me too.

Ed speaks.

That shit's fucking gross.

Ted looks at Ed.

You're gross, you big, dumb, steelworking Motherfucker.

I might be big and dumb—

Leonard speaks.

And you're ugly too.

Ed looks at Leonard and he gives him the finger.

I might be big and dumb and I might be a steelworking, ass-kicking Motherfucker.

Ted laughs. Ed continues.

But I ain't dumb enough to have ever smoked that bullshit, Ghetto drug.

Ted speaks.

Yeah, you so smart you sit around a fucking Steel Mill drinking vodka and handling tubs of molten metal.

I ain't never had an accident.

What about your hair?

That wasn't no accident, that was a fight. I got sucker punched.

Ed is, as he always is, wearing a bandana on his head. I speak.

What happened to your hair?

Nothing.

Leonard speaks.

He doesn't wear that silly bandana because he likes it.

What happened?

Nothing.

Ted speaks.

You can tell him or I'm telling him.

You ain't saying nothing.

I will if you don't.

Ed looks at me, speaks.

I was doing this married lady. One night we're in a bar and her husband walks in. We decide to go outside and as I'm walking out, he cracks me over the head with a bottle. I go down and he kicks my nuts. Now I'm really down. He leans over and grabs my hair right here.

He makes a grabbing motion on the top of his forehead.

And he knows when he grabs that shit that I had plugs put in nine months earlier, and he fucking pulls and pulls till he pulls the Motherfuckers right the fuck out. Now my head's all fucked up and scarred and shit.

I wince.

Fuck.

Ted speaks.

Ask him how he got that Bastard back.

Ed speaks.

Shut the fuck up, Ted.

Tell him how you got him back.

I'm gonna kick your ass in a minute.

Ted looks at me.

He didn't do nothing. Let some Motherfucker pull his goddamn hair plugs right the fuck out of his head and he didn't do nothing to him. I'd a shot that Motherfucker's dick off and served it to his Momma on a sandwich.

Breakfast is the blink of an eye. I sit and listen to Ed and Ted fight and tell stories and I laugh as Leonard eggs them on.

Ed is a Drinker and a fighter who's in Rehab for the fourth time. His Union, which has generous medical benefits, has paid for each of his trips. They sent him here because this is the last time they will pay for him to go to Rehab and they want to give him the best opportunity that they can to get better. He is grateful and says if they can't fix me at this place then I guess I'm fucked. Ed is not married, but he has four children, all of which are boys. He says that all of them are ass-kicking Motherfuckers, just like himself. He says that they are the great love of his life.

Ted is a Drug Dealer and a Car Thief who was recently arrested for the Statutory Rape of a Sheriff's Daughter in Louisiana. He already has two Felony convictions and a third means Life-No-Parole under the Three-Strike Law. He skipped Bail and he came here to try to clean up in order to win some points with the Authorities since the Authorities generally look kindly on individuals who have gone through Treatment. He paid for it with money that he made selling crack. He's not married and he doesn't have any Kids, but he does, as he says, have a whole mess of fine-ass Bitches.

Ed and Ted are good men who happen to be bad men and I like them and I can relate to them. Although we come from three parts of the country, are three different ages, and have distinctly different problems, we are, in many ways, the same. Alcoholics. Drug Addicts. Criminals.

I finish breakfast and I walk to the Lecture and I sit and I listen to a Nurse talk about the effects drugs and alcohol have on the health of the liver and it strikes close to home and when I can't listen to any more of it, I watch Leonard as he throws pennies at the Bald Man's bald spot. He hits the spot about every third time.

The Lecture ends and I get up and as I walk out of the Lecture Hall, I see Joanne standing to the side of the door. She motions for me to come to her and I do.

Hi, James. You remember me?

Yeah.

What's my name?

Joanne.

She smiles.

You mind coming to my Office for a while?

All right.

We walk through the maze of Halls and we stop at a door. The door has a sign that reads Joanne P., 312. Joanne opens the door and we walk inside.

The walls are covered with pictures of baseball players, newspaper clippings related to the Chicago Cubs, pictures of Joanne riding horses and standing on mountaintops, a degree from Harvard, a degree from Northwestern, and two large taxidermied fish. There is a desk cluttered with papers, a bookshelf overflowing with books. There are two large comfortable-looking chairs along one wall, there is a worn couch along another wall. A stuffed duck sits in one of the corners.

You can sit on the couch or the chair. Wherever you please.

I sit on the chair. She walks around the desk and she sits down and she pushes an ashtray toward me.

I'm allowed to smoke in here?

I'm going to. You want some coffee?

Sure.

How do you take it?

Black.

She turns around and she reaches for a coffeepot and she pours two cups of coffee. I light a cigarette. She turns back around and she hands me one of the cups.

Thank you.

Be careful, it's strong.

I like strong.

She laughs, lights a smoke.

You know why you're here?

You wanna talk to me about something.

We have the results of the psych test you took last week. I want to go over them with you.

Okay.

Do you have any questions before we start?

No.

She reaches for a file, opens it.

The test you took is called the MMPI-2, which stands for the Second Edition of the Minnesota Multiphasic Personality Inventory. It's an empirically based assessment of Adult Psychopathology used by Clinicians to

assist with the diagnosis of mental disorders and the selection of appropri-
ate treatment. It can also provide Clinicians or appropriate Interpretive
Personnel with a general psychological assessment of any given individual.
She takes a drag of her smoke.
You with me?
Yeah.
She exhales.
It is used in Schools, Offices, Clinics, Hospitals, Courts, Prisons, in the
Military, and by such esteemed organizations as the NSA, the FBI and
the CIA. It is a standardized and widely used test and is generally consid-
ered the best universal diagnostic tool currently available.
She takes another drag.
Any questions?
Why Minnesota?
She exhales.
It was written and developed by a couple of Professors at the University of
Minnesota. It's also published by the University of Minnesota Press.
What'd it tell you?
You're depressed. You have very low self-esteem. You're confrontational
and tend to be aggressive, you sometimes react to confrontation with vio-
lence. You engage in self-defeating behaviors, you have a low tolerance for
frustration, you internalize stress and deal with it through a process of
self-destruction. You're irresponsible, resentful, manipulative, hostile and
have a psychological predisposition to addiction.
I laugh.
It's not funny, James.
Keep going.
This is not a joke.
It's easier to laugh. Now keep going.
She looks down at the file.
You are also very, very angry. Incredibly angry.
She looks at me.
You are also very intelligent.
I take a sip of my coffee.
Sounds about right.
Does it?
Except for the intelligence part.
Why do you say that?
If I was very intelligent, I probably wouldn't be so fucked up.

Addicts, as a group, generally score far above average on intelligence tests.
Why?
You tell me.
I guess maybe we're smart enough to have figured out how shitty things
are and we decide addiction is the only way to deal with it.
You acknowledge that you're an Addict.
I laugh again.
Yeah.
I wasn't sure you would.
I do.
Good, that's the first step toward getting better.
If it's one of the Twelve, then it's the only one I'm taking.
You're getting angry.
Yeah.
Why?
Right now I'm getting angry thinking about the impossibility of ever
getting better.
Is that all you're angry about?
No.
What else?
Pretty much fucking everything.
She laughs.
Everything?
I smile.
Sounds stupid, but it's true. I'm angry about pretty much everything.
How long have you felt that way?
Forever.
As a Child?
My first memories are of anger and pain.
That's too bad.
It's the way things are.
I think if we can work toward finding the source of your anger we'll be a
long ways toward solving a number of your issues. The only way to get to
your anger is to control your addictions, and the only way, I truly believe,
you'll be able to control your addictions, is by working the Twelve Steps.
Not happening.
She takes a deep breath, leans back. I light another cigarette.
Do you know the success rate of this Hospital?
No.

It's about seventeen percent. That's of Patients who are sober for a year after they leave here.

That sucks.

That's the best success rate of any Treatment Center in the World.

That really sucks.

I've worked in six, I'm an Alcoholic and an Addict myself, and the only thing I've ever seen that works is the Twelve Steps.

You don't seem like an Alcoholic or an Addict.

Everyone that works here is, even the Janitors and the Dishwashers. That way if you need help, everywhere you turn there are people who can help you.

That's comforting.

It's supposed to be.

How long have you been sober?

Sixteen years.

Long time.

You can have that too, you just have to do what we tell you and trust us, even if you think it's ridiculous.

If it involves the number Twelve, it's not gonna happen.

It's the only way, James. The only way.

I'm gonna be honest with you about something.

I would appreciate that.

I walked out of here two nights ago.

Where were you going?

I was gonna go find some shit and kill myself.

Why didn't you?

You know Leonard?

I know of him.

Leonard stopped me.

That surprises me.

Why?

That's a separate issue.

What?

We'll talk about it some other time.

There might not be another time.

You're serious?

Yeah.

Do you really want to die?

I know I can't keep living the way I've been living and I know I won't ever believe in the Twelve Steps. People like you keep saying it's the only way, so I'm thinking that I might as well just put myself out of my misery now and save myself and my Family the pain of the future.

Do you really want to die?

I fucking hate myself. I'm sick of it.

Why are you still here?

I promised Leonard I'd stay for twenty-four hours. Then my Brother and a couple of old friends showed up for visiting hours. I ended up having a good day, the best day I can really remember having for a long time, and when the twenty-four hours were up, I was too tired and too happy to think about killing myself.

You can have more days like that.

Not if I can't stay sober.

You can stay sober.

Not if your way is the only way.

It is, and you can do it.

I shake my head.

Nope.

She leans back in her chair and she lights another cigarette and she stares at me. I stare back. She speaks.

You have two decisions to make, James. The first is whether you want to live, and I believe you do. I believe that deep inside of you, you realize what a horrible waste it would be to kill yourself. I believe that what you present to the World and what you are on the inside are two different things, and that you know that what you are on the inside is something that's worth saving. The second decision is whether you're willing to do what it takes, and what we tell you it takes, to get sober. You need to decide whether you're going to stop being stubborn, and whether you're willing to open your mind to something that you really don't know anything about. Take your time and think. As we both know, you are a very intelligent young man. If you have any questions, come see me. If you decide the answer to your decisions is yes, come see me. If your answer is no, I'm sorry, and good luck to you.

She stares at me, I stare back.

I have a question.

What?

Why didn't you guys throw me out of here after I attacked Roy?

She takes a drag.

Lincoln and Ken wanted to throw you out. I hadn't met you, but I'm good friends with Hank. When Hank heard what had happened he came to me and told me that the person who attacked Roy was not the person he knew. He said the person he knew was kind and gentle and quiet and shy and was the strongest and bravest person he'd ever seen. I trust Hank, and I fought to keep you here because he told me I should.

I like Hank.

He likes you.

You're friends?

We hunt and fish together, play cards. He's sort of my Boyfriend.

I laugh.

Tell him I said hi and that I'm taking good care of his coat.

He'll be glad to hear it.

We done?

I hope not.

I stand.

We'll see.

She stands, hands me a card.

That has my Home phone number on it. If I'm not here and you need me, call.

What if you're at Hank's House?

He sleeps at my House.

I laugh.

Thanks.

I walk to the door and I walk out and I close the door behind me. I walk through the bright Halls and back to the Unit. As I enter the Upper Level, I see most of the men have gathered on the Lower Level. They are sitting on the couches and the chairs and the Bald Man is sitting on a chair in front of them. He's speaking, and Lincoln is standing off to the side watching him. I walk down and I sit on the floor. I am near enough to hear, but far enough away so that I'm still alone.

My worst experience, and the one that I want to share with you, was the one that made me finally decide to come here.

He looks down, takes a deep breath.

I'm from Toledo. Two years ago on Halloween, a little girl in our neighborhood was kidnapped and killed by a man in a lion costume. It really shook everyone up, so to try and prevent it, our Neighborhood Council moved Halloween to October first, the thinking being that we could control things more and prevent another tragedy. My two little Girls, Laura, who is six, and Jennifer, who is nine, love Halloween. They're real dramatic Kids and Halloween is their favorite Holiday, and every year they both get dressed up like Princess Leah and I get dressed up like Luke

Skywalker. I put them in the back of a wagon and I pull them from
House to House and we pretend that they're riding in the Millennium
Falcon and that I'm piloting it.
He stops and he looks at Lincoln. Lincoln nods and he holds up a fist as a
sign of strength. The Bald Man returns the nod and he looks back at us.
A couple months ago, I made a deal with my Wife, whose name is
Terry, to stop drinking. Part of the deal was that I could drink nonalcoholic beer when I really felt like I needed something. Being me, I went
out and bought twenty cases of the stuff, hid nineteen of them, and
kept one in the Garage refrigerator. I have trouble sleeping, and I can't
sleep without drinking, but I found if I drank fifteen nonalcoholics a
night, I got enough in me to put me to sleep.
He takes a deep breath.
So every night for six weeks I ran out to the Garage during commercial
breaks on the TV and I slammed nonalcoholic beers so I could sleep. It
sounds dumb, but you do what you do, and you do what you need to do,
and that's what I did.
A couple of men laugh. Lincoln gives them a hard look. They stop.
The problem with my plan was that because I was drinking fake beer
every night, I never stopped wanting to drink real beer, and if anything,
the fake stuff made me want to drink the real stuff even more.
He stops, looks at the floor. As he speaks, his voice cracks.
Now it starts getting tough.
Lincoln speaks.
You're doing great. Just keep going.
The Bald Man looks at him, nods, and looks back at us.
So my Wife had to go to New Jersey for her niece Tina's Bat Mitzvah. We
would normally go to something like that as a Family, but the Bat
Mitzvah was on the morning after our Neighborhood Halloween, so me
and Terry decided that I would stay home and do Halloween with the
girls and Terry would go to Tina's Bat Mitzvah.
A tear starts running down his cheek.
I took Terry to the Airport and I promised her I wouldn't drink. As soon
as she was on the Plane, I went straight to the Airport Lounge and I ordered a vodka and cranberry.
He stops, wipes his face.
From there I went to the Liquor Store and bought a fifth and some more
cranberry and I drank the whole way Home.
He wipes his face.

Then I snuck into my neighbor Ira's Garage and stole two bottles of
chardonnay and another bottle of vodka and I went down to my basement and I drank both bottles of the chardonnay.

The tears are running.

Then I got dressed up as Luke Skywalker and I mixed the vodka and
some more cranberry into a giant Obi Wan Kenobi mug and went out
with the Girls. They knew something was wrong with me, but they
tried to have fun.

He wipes again.

I don't know when, but at some point I passed out in the wagon while
the Girls were up at someone's door.

He sobs.

They came back and tried to pull the wagon back to our House, but
they're little Girls, and I was too heavy.

Sobs.

They went to our neighbor Len's House to get help, and when they came
back with Len and his wife, Ginny, they found that I had peed all over
my Skywalker costume and all over the wagon.

Sobs.

Len tried to wake me, and when he did, I attacked him. You see, Len has
a big, thick, blond beard, and I was so drunk that I thought he was the
man in the Lion costume from two years earlier.

Sobs.

Oh, God.

Sobs.

Oh, God.

He stops, wipes his face, takes a deep breath. The men spread around the
Room are speechless. He looks up.

Len had to tie me up with a dog leash to control me and my Wife had to
come home from New Jersey before Tina's Bat Mitzvah.

He starts bawling.

I disgraced myself, my Daughters, my Wife.

There are several chuckles.

I'm the laughingstock of the whole Neighborhood.

He completely breaks down, wailing, sobbing, holding his face in his
hands. Several men start laughing. Lincoln looks at them, speaks.

Shut up.

The men laugh harder, more join in. The Bald Man looks up. Lincoln
speaks.

This is not funny.

They laugh harder. More join in. The Bald Man is stunned. Lincoln speaks, his voice louder, his voice harder.

This is not funny.

The Room erupts. The Bald Man stands and he runs, wailing, sobbing and crying, from the Room. Lincoln steps in front of the empty chair.

You people think that was funny?

The men laugh.

It wasn't.

They begin to quiet down.

That was a man spilling his heart to you. Spilling his goddamn heart.

There is quiet.

Opening up and telling you about the worst moment of his life, the moment he hit bottom and knew he needed help.

Silence.

That's a hard thing to do, and he's a brave man for doing it, and he deserves to be given respect, not to be fucking laughed at.

Lincoln shakes his head, lowers his voice.

You think you're all hard-asses because maybe you took harder drugs than him or drank more than him or maybe your bottom was lower than his, but when I asked for a Volunteer to talk about bottoming out, I didn't see any of you step up. You just sat there like scared little Boys.

He points in the direction of the Bald Man's departure.

You should learn from that man, and you should learn from what he did up here today. He was brave and he was open and he was honest and he made himself vulnerable to everyone in this Room. That's what being here is all about, and that's the kind of attitude that is gonna keep him sober.

He starts to walk out.

Think about it. Think long and hard.

He stares as he does.

Long and hard.

He leaves. There is complete silence. The men look at one another, ashamed and embarrassed, waiting for someone to speak. Leonard stands.

Lincoln's right, and we should apologize to the little guy, but I still think that story was fucking funny.

Everyone laughs. Leonard stands, looks at his watch.

It's lunchtime. I'm going to eat.

He leaves and the men stand and begin filing out and heading to the Dining Hall. I stand and I follow them and I get in a line and I get a tray of food. I sit down and I listen to Ed and Ted argue and I laugh as Leonard eggs them on and I finish and I get up and I put my tray on the conveyor belt.

I go to the Lecture. A Priest talks about different forms of confession. I don't like Priests, don't trust Priests, and I don't listen to a single word of what he has to say. I sit and I stare at the floor and I think about the Bald Man. I wonder where he is and what he's thinking, and as I replay his story in my mind, it becomes more and more devastating. Although he wasn't on Skid Row or in a Ghetto or in a Crackhouse, and although he still has a job and a Family and a life, he lost the most important thing a human being can lose, which was his dignity.

I know a bit about the loss of dignity. I know that when you take away a man's dignity there is a hole, a deep black hole filled with despair, humiliation and self-hatred, filled with emptiness, shame and disgrace, filled with loss and isolation and Hell. It's a deep, dark, horrible fucking hole, and that hole is where people like me live our sad-ass, fucked-up, dignity-free, inhuman lives, and where we die, alone, miserable, wasted and forgotten.

The Lecture ends and I leave and I go back to the Unit and I sit through an exercise on Rational Reaction Therapy. Ken leads it and explains that Alcoholics and Addicts tend to react irrationally in situations involving stress. Rational Reaction Therapy is a method of decision making to counteract that irrational behavior. When you're in a situation, consider all options. Take your time, stay calm, choose the option that is the most healthy and productive. It is a very rational philosophy.

After the exercise there is another Graduation Ceremony. Three men I don't know are leaving. They have done their time and they have worked their Programs and they are ready to face the outside World. They are happy as they receive their Rocks and their Medals, two of them cry when they give their speeches.

The Ceremony ends and everyone claps and some of the men start playing cards and some of them start watching television and some of them get changed and go to the Gym on the other side of the Clinic. The Graduates leave. I go to my Room and I put on Hank's jacket and I go outside.

There is no Sun. The life that showed itself yesterday has retreated. The ground is cold and hard, the air oppressive, the Sky black, the trees bent beneath the weight of frozen branches. I walk and I smoke and I find a Trail and I let the Trail lead me. It is dark and quiet beneath the canopy of dense, heavy wood, and the only sound is that of my feet forging through piles of crackled yellow leaves.

I listen to the leaves. I stare at the ground. I try to lose myself. I try to forget where I am and why I'm here, I try to forget about what lies in front of me. I try to forget about death, Prison and recovery. I try to forget that there is a World outside of that which is in my head and I try to forget that there is a World within my head. I try to forget everything. The whole fucking mess. I walk, stare, try to lose, try to lose, try to lose. The crack of leaves fades into a sharp tumbling roll of small stones and the stones lead me to a long, narrow Lake covered with delicate sheets of thin, fractured ice. I stare at the sheets. In the shallows beneath, packs of small fish dance, solitary weeds lie still, algae clings to whatever it can find. A shell sits lonely and silent and I stop and I watch it. Somewhere within there is life. At some point life will shed its shell and reemerge. I stare at the shell in the shallows beneath a delicate sheet of fractures. Life reemerging. I want to forget, but I can't.

I walk again, continue to try, continue continue. The shore drifts into a wide stretch of tall, dead, yellow grass and my feet become silent on an artery of hard, black, packed dirt. As they carry me through the grass, I run my hands along the sharp frozen tips of the grass and they tickle me and I laugh and the sound of my laughter calms me. Forget, lose, forget, please lose. It tickles me and I laugh.

The packed dirt graduates to bog and I step onto an Elevated Walk of faded pine, imbedded screws and tall, firm Rails. The deep stench of Swamp seeps up and through, too strong to be killed by the cold. As I walk, I lean over the Rail and I breathe in stench and I stare across a murky, brown desolation dotted with rotting chunks of tree, turf and prickly gray shrub. There is an Island among the rot, a large, round Pile with monstrous protrusions like the arms of a Witch. There is chatter beneath the Pile and a fat brown otter with a flat, armored tail climbs atop and he stares at me.

Hey, Fat Otter.

He stares at me.

You want what I got?

He stares at me.

I'll give you everything.

Stares at me.

Gimme your Pile and gimme your tail.

Stares.

And I'll give you the whole fucking mess.

Stares.

What do you think?

He sits and he stares, seems to consider, and he disappears back under the Pile. I wait for him to come back, but he doesn't.

You're a smart otter. A smart fucking otter.

I laugh and I let go of the Rail and I continue to walk. The Pine crescendos and it takes me down and leads me to a path of stone and the stone rings another small Lake and I try to look through the ice but there are no fractures and the ice is too thick. If there is life it is hidden beneath a cold, frozen shell.

I think and I forget and my feet carry me through heavier Wood. The air is black and the leaves are thicker and the crackle is hypnotic and though my eyes are open, I don't see anything. I just walk.

I come out of the Wood and the darkness, but not out of my head. There is a brown grass Hill ahead of me I climb to the top the view shows me the Buildings and the benches and the Lake. It shows me moving shadows created by the lights of the bright, clean, uncomfortable Halls. I sit down and the brown grass is wet and I'm not bothered by it and my eyes drift to the screams coming from behind the dark, barred windows of the Medical Unit. The screams soak in and they echo, echo, echo and I lie back and the jacket gets wet and the back of my head gets wet and I close my eyes and I listen and I think. I allow myself to feel to feel completely and the feeling brings lucid, linear streams of thought and image and they run through and out and back and through and out and back. They run through and out and back they run.

Can't stop.

Have to stop.

Can't stop.

Pain.

Gutter.

Priest.

Fuck God.

Her.

Fuck her.

Pipe.

Torch.

Bottle.

Can't stop.

Pain.

Take it.

Rage.

Murderous rage.
Uncontrollable.
Rage.
Sins unpardonable.
Places from which there is no return.
Damage irreparable.
Cry.
Fight.
Mom.
Dad.
Brother.
Cry.
Fight.
Live.
Torch.
Pipe.
Bottle.
Sick.
Sick.
Sick.
Get better.
Impossible.
Stay.
Impossible.
Fuck God.
Fuck her.
Fuck you.
Stay.
Live.
Fight.
Cry.
Decision.
Decision.
Decision.
Bring it.
Take it.
Take it.
Decision.
The streams are lucid and clear and they run back and through and back

and through and they meet and they lose empty forget and there is is is
something something something I hardly know perfect calm. Clarity.
Serenity. Peace.

My urges are gone. My heart is beating slow and steady. Everything I
know and I am and I have seen felt done past present past now then before now seen felt done hurt felt focus into a something beyond words
beyond beyond beyond and it speaks now and it says.

Stay.

Fight.

Live.

Take it.

Cry.

Cry.

Cry.

Sickness drags me from sleep, pushes me out of bed, throws me before my friend and my enemy it throws me before the porcelain. It empties, wracks, hurts, it won't let go of me.

There are chunks of stomach, bile and remnants of last night's dinner. There is acid, snot and spit. There is blood. Streams of blood.

I get in the shower and I turn up the heat and I wash the sickness from my face and my body. It gathers around the drain and I crush it with my feet and I make it disappear. I'm sick of being sick. I want it to disappear. I crush it with my feet.

I brush my teeth. The new ones are just like the old ones. I like them and I'm happy to have them.

A white scar is forming in place of the hole in my cheek. Another reminder of the life I live.

I don't even bother with my eyes.

I get dressed and I make the coffee and I pour myself a cup and I drink it. It's strong and I get sick again, so I take another shower and I brush my teeth a second time. I don't even bother with my eyes.

I change and I get another cup of coffee and I walk to breakfast and I get some oatmeal and I cover it with sugar. I sit down at a table with Leonard and Ed and Ted and a short thin black man. I have seen the black man before, though I can't place him. Leonard speaks.

How ya doing, Kid?

I'm all right.

He motions to the black man.

You meet Matty, yet?

No.

Matty, James. James, Matty.

We reach across the table, shake hands. I say nice to meet you. He says nice to meet you, Motherfucker. I look at him more closely. I speak.

I know you from somewhere.

He speaks. He has a high voice, talks very quickly.

Where the fuck you know me from?

I'm not sure. Where do you live?

Minneapolis.

That's not it. What's your last name?

You ain't supposed to fucking ask me my last fucking name in this fucking place.

It registers. I know where I know him.

Your last name is Jackson.

How the fuck you know that?

I used to watch you on TV. You were the Featherweight Champion of the World.

He smiles.

I sure as fuck was.

I smile.

And they wouldn't ever interview you because you swear so much.

They sure as fuck wouldn't. Cocksucking, motherfucking TV Motherfuckers.

Everyone laughs and breakfast gets pushed aside and we sit and we drink coffee and we talk shit and we laugh. Matty is a wreck, a shell of the man he was two years ago, when he was one of the best boxers in the World. At the time, he held two championships, was rich and famous, married and had two young Boys. At a party celebrating one of his victories, he took a hit from a pipe he was told was full of pot, but was actually loaded with crack. He got hooked immediately, fought one more time and got destroyed, and he disappeared.

It is strange to be sitting across from him. It is strange to imagine that the man I used to watch on TV is the man in front of me. At the height of his career, he was a fighting machine. He was fast, smart, strong and unbeatable at his weight, one hundred and twenty-six pounds. He was handsome, had a big smile, there wasn't an ounce of fat on his body, and he had dark, smooth flawless skin. His confidence was supreme, and he entered and commanded the Ring as if he owned it.

There is nothing left. He is very small, one hundred and ten pounds at the most, his hair is tangled and nappy, his skin is covered with open sores and his teeth are yellow, brown and black. Though his confidence seems to be intact, I doubt he could find a Boxing Ring, much less command it or render someone unconscious within it. I don't ask him about his Wife or his Kids because I don't want to know and he probably doesn't want to tell me.

The Dining Hall empties. We don't notice because of Matty and Leonard and our laughter. When one of the Janitors walks over and he tells us to leave, we walk to the Lecture together and Matty talks and he swears and he makes us laugh. When we get to the Lecture, we sit together, away from the rest of the men of our Unit, and before the Speaker begins, Leonard pulls out a deck of cards and we start playing poker. We don't bet, and except for Matty swearing under his breath, we play silently, signaling each other with hands and our heads.

The Lecture ends and I say good-bye to my friends and I walk through the Halls until I find the door that has Joanne's name on it. I knock, I hear her say come in, and I open the door and step inside.

She and Hank are sitting on the couch drinking coffee and smoking cigarettes. Hank rises when he sees me and he gives me a hug.

How ya doing, Kid?

We separate.

I'm good.

Let me see those teeth.

I smile.

They look nice.

I guess so.

Was it worth it?

I survived.

I don't know how, but I guess you did.

It was worth it.

He laughs, moves toward the door.

Come visit me in the Livery some time.

Where's the Livery?

It's the Van sitting in front of the Entrance.

I laugh. He reaches for the door.

You don't have to leave.

You two probably need to be alone.

I'd like you to stay.

He stops, looks at me, sits next to Joanne. I sit in a chair across from them. Joanne speaks.

What can I help you with?

I've been thinking about our conversation yesterday.

What have you been thinking?

I'm gonna stay here for a while. See what happens.

A while?

I'm not making any promises.

She smiles.

I think that's a good start.

We'll see.

They both smile. Joanne speaks.
What sparked this?
I don't know.
Must have been something?
I don't want to talk about it.
Why?
Because I don't.
Because it makes you feel vulnerable.
Probably.
And you don't like that, do you?
I shake my head.
No.
If you're going to get better, you should get used to it.
You're probably right.
Hank and I aren't going to hurt you.
I know.
Try it. Be vulnerable.
I look at them, take a deep breath. I speak.
I saw a man cry yesterday. I've seen men cry before, but I usually think
it's because they're weak or pathetic. The man who cried yesterday cried
because he was strong and I admired his strength. I know people might
think I'm strong or tough, but I'm really not. I'm a sheep in wolf's cloth-
ing.
I take another breath.
So I was thinking about that and I was out walking around and I was try-
ing to forget this place and I was trying to forget all the shit I've gotten
myself into and I laid down in the grass and I felt calm, very calm, and I
decided to stay for a while.
How'd it feel?
Just like I said. Calm.
You had what is called a Moment of Clarity.
That one of your AA terms?
Yes.
Then no, I didn't have a Moment of Clarity. I just felt calm.
They both laugh. Joanne speaks.
That wasn't so hard, was it?
Guess not.
That's all you have to do and you'll get better. Be honest, be vulnerable,
talk about it.
I think it's gonna be a bit more complicated than that.

A bit, but not really.

We'll see.

There is a moment of silence. I stand.

I gotta go. I just thought I'd come by and tell you what I decided.

Joanne speaks.

We're glad you did.

I move to the door.

I'll see you soon.

They say good-bye and I walk out and back through the Halls to the Unit. I sit down on the floor with the rest of the men and I watch the end of a video. The video is about a famous Football Player who had a drinking problem and quit drinking using the Twelve Steps and is now a State Supreme Court Justice and is very happy. As he speaks, he is sitting in his very official Office and he's wearing his very impressive robe. There are pictures of him in his football uniform hanging behind him and everything is perfect and everything is inspirational. It's a lot like an After-School Special and even though I'm going to try to keep an open mind while I'm here I think the thing is fucking stupid and I wonder if keeping an open mind at this place is the same thing as having an empty mind. Open mind, empty mind. This Football Player turned Judge isn't going to convince me to do anything. No fucking way.

The video ends and everyone claps except for me. I boo and I get a bunch of dirty looks. The looks make me laugh and I get more dirty looks for laughing, which makes me laugh more. Someone I don't know asks me what's so funny and I tell him the video and he tells me to grow up and I tell him that I'm not gonna pretend that stupid shit is anything more than stupid shit and he walks away shaking his head. Open mind, empty mind. I wonder if they're the same thing.

I go to lunch and I get a tray and some food and I eat with Ed and Ted and Matty and Leonard. Matty and Leonard do all the talking and the rest of us do the laughing. By the time we're finished, our table is filled with men who have come over to hear Matty and Leonard.

After lunch there is a Lecture, but I don't pay any attention to it.

After the Lecture Ken asks if he can see me in his Office. I follow him through the Halls and when we get to his Office, I sit down in a chair across from him.

It's been awhile.

Yeah.

Have you thought about what we talked about last time you were here?

I don't remember what that was.

Are you ready to do anything and everything it takes to get sober and stay sober?

Yeah, I thought about it.

Do you have an answer?

No.

Do you have an answer?

No.

Do you have an answer?

Staring at me and asking the same goddamn question over and over isn't going to get us anywhere.

He stares.

Do you have an answer?

I laugh.

No.

Hopefully at some point you will.

We'll see.

He sighs and shakes his head, looks at the papers on his desk.

I want to start getting into the meat of your Program.

All right.

He pulls out what looks like a children's coloring book and he hands it to me.

We'll start with this.

I look at the book

What's this?

It's a First Step workbook.

I laugh.

It's a fucking coloring book.

It's simple, yes, but we think the simplest approach is the best.

You want me to do a coloring book?

Yes.

I laugh.

You got a box of Crayolas I can borrow?

There's some on the Unit.

I hope nobody took the Razzle Dazzle Rose.

What's that?

My favorite crayon color. They have it in the sixty-four box.

You through?

You tired of me?

I'm tired of your jokes.

You don't think they're funny?

No.

I'll stop for a while.

Good.

When's my deadline?

Two days.

Got it.

There's also a Goal Board hanging on the Upper Level. I want you to put your name on it and put down a life goal that you have and hope to achieve through sobriety.

Okay.

You have any ideas?

New set of teeth every year.

Not funny.

Become President of the United Sates.

You'll be lucky to vote with your record.

Make mine the prettiest First Step coloring book ever?

You through?

You tired of me?

Put down a goal. Don't make a joke out of it.

I'll do my best.

I also think a change of scenery might be good for you, so this afternoon, I'm going to switch your Room assignment.

To where?

To a two-man Room. Warren and John are leaving later today, and I think it would be better to fill that Room with newer Arrivals.

I'd like that.

I'll make the switch and tell you the Room number later.

Cool.

You seem better, and you seem to be making headway, but you need to take what we're doing in here a bit more seriously. We ask for progress, not perfection. Just do your best.

I'll try.

Come find me when you finish the book. I'd like to go over it with you.

Okay.

I stand and I leave and I walk back to the Unit. I look for John and Warren and I don't see them so I go to my Room and I walk in. John is standing by his window and Warren is packing. I sit down on my bed.

Hi.

Warren speaks.

Hi.

John stares out the window.

I hear you're leaving today.

Warren speaks.

Yes I am.

You excited?

Yes, but I'm also nervous. I've been a Drinker all my life, and it's gonna be tough not having a nice, strong scotch at the end of each day. Or maybe six nice scotches.

You're better without it.

You're certainly right about that.

I stand, walk over to him. He stops packing.

Good luck, Warren.

I offer my hand. He takes it.

Thanks, James.

We shake. Strong and firm. I speak.

I've really appreciated how cool you've been to me.

It's been a pleasure, James, and I'd do it again.

We let go and I walk over to John's area. John's bags are packed and they're sitting on his bed. He's still standing by the window, staring out at gray nothing.

John.

He turns around. There are tears on his face.

Hi, James.

What's wrong?

I'm scared.

Come here.

He steps over. I point to the bed.

Sit.

He sits down on his bed, looks like a fragile little Boy. I sit next to him.

Why are you scared, John?

Because I know I'm not better.

Why do you think that?

Because I know it in my heart.

Then why don't you stay until you feel like you're better?

Because I know it won't do any good.

Why do you think that?

Because I'll never be any better. I'll never be any more normal and I'll never make the pain go away. Never ever ever.

You can't think like that, John.

You do.

I'm trying not to anymore.

How?

I don't know how. I'm just trying.

He looks at me, looks down at the bed, and he bursts out crying.

I feel safe here. Nobody can do anything to me and I can't do anything to myself.

He looks up at me. A fragile little Boy.

Once I leave here, I know I'm going to do something stupid and I know I'm going to end up back in Jail and I know what's going to happen to me there and I don't want that to happen anymore.

I take one of his hands, hold it, don't know what to say. He cries cries cries, sobbing, tears running down his face, his chest up and down, heavily up and down. I let go of his hand and I put my arms around him and I hug him and he cries and there is nothing I can say.

He stops crying and he settles and I let go of him and he wipes his face.

I'm sorry.

Don't be sorry, John. There's nothing wrong with crying.

I cry a lot.

I know. I admire that about you.

You do?

Yeah, I do. I think men who can cry are strong men.

You think I'm strong?

I think you're stronger than you know.

Thanks, James.

He wipes his face again.

I'm gonna miss it here.

We'll miss you.

Really?

Yeah.

You're not lying?

No, I'm not lying.

He looks at me, reaches into one of his bags, and he pulls out a pen and a card.

Will you do something for me, James?

Of course.

He starts writing on the card.

When you get out of here, will you call my Daughter?

Not this again, John.

No, not that.

He holds out the card.

Will you call her and tell her that I tried real hard this time, as hard as I could, and that I wish I was more to her, and that I'm not as bad a man as everyone tells her I am.

I take the card, look at John.

I'd be honored, John.

And if you're ever in the same place as her, maybe you could take her out to dinner or something, and—

He pauses, starts to cry, holds it back.

And just be nice to her, and—

He can't hold it. He starts to cry. Like a fragile little Boy.

And tell her I'm sorry. I'm so sorry.

I reach out and I hug him and I hold him and I let him cry cry cry and he pushes me away, and he asks me to leave him alone and as I walk out of the Room I look toward him and his head is buried in his pillow and I can hear him sobbing and wailing and saying the word.

No.

No.

No.

I leave him to himself and to his future and as I walk into the Unit I make sure the card is deep and safe in my pocket. I will make that call when I leave here. I will make that call and I will tell that Girl that her Father was a good man. She may not believe me, and there may not be anything to say that would change her mind, but I will tell her.

The Unit is crowded and the men are waiting for John and Warren and for their Graduation Ceremony. I don't want to see it or participate in it and I have said my good-byes to them, so I start walking. Same as yesterday, I just want to forget.

There is no forgetting today. I know that as soon as I enter the Wood. The Fury takes over. It envelops every emotion every feeling every thought that I have. I can't deal with emotions feelings thoughts so I let the Fury deal with them. It consumes them. The sadness I feel turns to rage, the calm to a desperate need. I want to destroy everything I see. That which I can't destroy, I want to ingest. With each step that I take, it grows. Rage and need. Rage and need. Rage. Need.

I want a drink. I want fifty drinks. I want a bottle of the purest, strongest, most destructive, most poisonous alcohol on Earth. I want fifty bottles of it. I want crack, dirty and yellow and filled with formaldehyde. I want a pile of powder meth, five hundred hits of acid, a garbage bag filled with mushrooms, a tube of glue bigger than a truck, a pool of gas large enough to drown in. I want something anything whatever however as much as I can. Want need want need I want need enough to kill annihilate make me lose make me forget dull the motherfucking pain give me the darkest darkness the blackest blackness the deepest deepest deepest most horrible fucking hole. Goddamn it to fucking Hell, give it to me. Put me in the fucking hole.

I leave the Trail, force my way through heavy, frozen wood. I am shaking and my heart is racing and I am clenching my fists and I am clenching my jaw. My feet are snapping twigs and crushing infant sapling trees, my arms are removing whatever stands in front of me. The sharp sounds of destruction, a snap crack snap crack, incense me, enrage me, make me want to break more, destroy more, ruin everything. I want to ruin everything everywhere. I want to fucking ruin.

I break through a stand of thick Evergreen and into a small, tight, circular Clearing. I stop walking forging pushing fighting and I close my eyes and I take a deep breath and I hope that the breath will calm me but it doesn't so I take another and it doesn't another doesn't another doesn't another doesn't. I want to be calm but there is no calm for me.

How I am here. How I have arrived in this place at this moment on this day with this feeling history future problems life this horrible fucked-up good-for-nothing waste of a life how. Fifteen minutes ago I was holding a lifelong Criminal and cocaine Addict who spent his childhood with his Father's dick in his mouth as he cried because he was scared to go back into the World. I ate my lunch with some kind of menacing middle-aged movie-star Look-alike and a three-strike Fugitive and a Steel Worker with torn-out hair plugs and a one-hundred-ten-pound Ghost who used to be the Champion of the World. I was given a coloring book and told it would help make me better. I watched some Judge's stupid fucking video and I was told it would help make me better. I got sick, just like I do every other fucking day, and I am not getting better. I am twenty-three years old and I've been an Alcoholic for a decade and a drug Addict and Criminal for almost as long and I'm wanted in three states and I'm in a Hospital in the middle of Minnesota and I want to drink and I want to do some drugs and I can't control myself. I'm twenty-three.

I breathe and I shake and I can feel it coming and rage and need and confusion regret horror shame and hatred fuse into a perfect Fury a great and beautiful and terrible and perfect Fury the Fury and I can't stop the Fury or control the Fury I can only let the Fury come come come come come. Let it motherfucking come. The Fury has come.

I see a tree and I go after it. Screaming punching kicking clawing tearing ripping dragging pulling wrecking punching screaming punching scream-

ing punching screaming. It is a small tree, a small Pine Tree, small enough that I can destroy it, and I rip the branches from its trunk and I tear them to pieces one by one I rip them and I tear them and I throw them to the ground and I stomp them stomp them stomp them and when there are no more branches I hear a voice and I attack the trunk and it's thin and I break it in half and I hear a voice and I ignore it and I throw the broken trunk on top of the branches and one half of it is still in the ground I hear a voice and I want it out of the fucking ground and I grab it and pull pull pull and it doesn't budge not an inch I hear a voice and I ignore and I pull scream pull and it doesn't budge this fucking tree I want to destroy it and I let go of it and there is a voice I ignore I start kicking kicking kicking and the voice says stop stop stop stop. Stop.
I turn around.
Long black hair and deep clean blue eyes and skin pale white and lips blood red she's small and thin and worn and damaged. She is standing there.
What are you doing here?
I was taking a walk and I saw you and I followed you.
What do you want.
I want you to stop.
I breathe hard, stare hard, tense and coiled. There is still more tree for me to destroy I want that fucking tree. She smiles and she steps toward me, toward toward toward me, and she opens her arms and I'm breathing hard staring hard tense and coiled she puts her arms around me with one hand on the back of my head and she pulls me into her arms and she holds me and she speaks.
It's okay.
I breathe hard, close my eyes, let myself be held.
It's okay.
Her voice calms me and her arms warm me and her smell lightens me and I can feel her heart beat and my heart slows and I stop shaking and the Fury melts into her safety and she holds me and she says.
Okay.
Okay.
Okay.
Something else comes and it makes me feel weak and scared and fragile and I don't want to be hurt and this feeling is the feeling I have when I know I can be hurt and hurt deeper and more terribly than anything physical and I always fight it and control it and stop it but her voice calms me and her arms warm me and her smell lightens me and I can feel her heart beat and if she let me go right now I would fall and the need and confusion and fear and re-

gret and horror and shame and weakness and fragility are exposed to the soft strength of her open arms and her simple word okay and I start to cry. I start to cry. I start to cry.

It comes in waves. The waves roll deep and from deep the deep within me and I hold her and she holds me tighter and I let her and I let it and I let this and I have not felt this way this vulnerability or allowed myself to feel this way this vulnerability since I was ten years old and I don't know why I haven't and I don't know why I am now and I only know that I am and that it is scary terrifying frightening worse and better than anything I've ever felt crying in her arms just crying in her arms just crying.

She guides me to the ground, but she doesn't let me go. The Gates are open and thirteen years of addiction, violence, Hell and their accompaniments are manifesting themselves in dense tears and heavy sobs and a shortness of breath and a profound sense of loss. The loss inhabits, fills and overwhelms me. It is the loss of a childhood of being a Teenager of normalcy of happiness of love of trust of reason of God of Family of friends of future of potential of dignity of humanity of sanity of myself of everything everything everything. I lost everything and I am lost reduced to a mass of mourning, sadness, grief, anguish and heartache. I am lost. I have lost. Everything. Everything.

It's wet and Lilly cradles me like a broken Child. My face and her shoulder and her shirt and her hair are wet with my tears. I slow down and I start to breathe slowly and deeply and her hair smells clean and I open my eyes because I want to see it and it is all that I can see. It is jet black almost blue and radiant with moisture. I want to touch it and I reach with one of my hands and I run my hand from the crown along her neck and her back to the base of her rib and it is a thin perfect sheer and I let it slowly drop from the tips of my fingers and when it is gone I miss it. I do it again and again and she lets me do it and she doesn't speak she just cradles me because I am broken. I am broken. Broken.

There is noise and voices and Lilly pulls me in tighter and tighter and I pull her in tighter and tighter and I can feel her heart beating and I know she can feel my heart beating and they are speaking our hearts are speaking a language wordless old unknowable and true and we're pulling and holding and the noise is closer and the voices louder and Lilly whispers.

You're okay.

You're okay.

You're okay.

And she lets me go and I let her go and she stands and I stay and she stares down at me.

I have to go.

I stare at her.

I'll call you later.

I stare at her.

Bye.

I stare at her and she backs away toward the far edge of our Clearing. When she reaches the edge she turns around and she disappears through Evergreen thick and I hear her step settling and her step is gentle and I hear her voice intermingle and her voice is gentle and I sit and I breathe and I sit and I stare. I am alone, lost and broken. I stare at the Evergreen thick. Alone lost broken.

The Sun is falling and the cold is running and the night is descending and I'm tired, spent and completely empty. I force myself to stand and I make my way through the trees until I pick up a Trail and then I let the Trail lead me. My feet are heavy, my body is tired and my heart is beating slow slow slow. The walk is only a couple hundred yards, but it seems across the Earth.

It takes all my strength to open the door. I step inside and I walk through the Unit and I go to my Room. As I enter, I see that all of my things my new beautiful things have been stacked on a chair near my bed. I flare momentarily until I notice a letter sitting on top of my clothes. I reach for it and I open it and I read it and it is from Ken and it says per our earlier conversation you are being moved to a new Room and it has the Room number.

I pick up my clothes and my books they are my only belongings in the World and I leave. I walk through the Halls surrounding the Unit looking for my new Room. I find the Room and the door is closed and my arms are full so I kick the door open with one of my feet. I walk inside. The Room is smaller than the other Room, but otherwise identical. There are two beds and a Bathroom off to the side. There is a middle-aged black man lying on one of the beds. I have never seen him before. He looks at me and he speaks.

Most people knock before entering a Room.

He has a deep, slow southern accent.

I didn't know anyone was here.

I walk to the empty bed.

You could have knocked anyway.

I sit down.

Sorry.

I start putting my stuff away.

Are you living here?
Yeah.
What's your name?
James.
Hello James, my name's Miles.
Like Miles Davis?
Exactly like Miles Davis.
Exactly?
Yes.
Your name is Miles Davis?
Yes, it is.
I laugh.
You play the trumpet?
No, I play the clarinet.
He motions toward a black case sitting at the foot of his bed.
I played the trumpet when I was younger, but when the other Miles got
famous, I quit. It was a bit too much.
Where you from?
New Orleans. Where are you from?
I live in North Carolina.
Which part?
Wilmington.
Do you like Wilmington?
It's nice, but I don't really give a shit.
He laughs.
What do you do down in New Orleans?
I'm a Judge.
What do you Judge?
I'm a Judge in the Federal Circuit Court of Appeals.
That's heavy.
He shrugs.
It is what it is.
You put people away?
I did when I worked in the Criminal Court, but I don't anymore.
What was that like?
It's hard putting away a man. There's nothing good waiting for him in
Jail, even if he does deserve it.
I nod.
What do you do?
I get in trouble.

He laughs.
What kind of trouble?
All kinds.
You in trouble now?
Wouldn't be here if I wasn't.
He laughs again.
Are you in any other trouble?
Can I plead the Fifth?
If you would like.
I would.
He looks at his watch.
Have you eaten supper yet?
No.
Would you like to eat with me?
I stand.
Let's go.
He stands and we leave the Room. We walk through the Halls to the
Cafeteria and we get in line and we get some food. When we sit down at a
table, I find out that Miles is an Alcoholic and that he's married and he has
two Children and he arrived here this afternoon. He speaks quietly and me-
thodically and he chooses his words carefully and he says as much with his
hands and his eyes and the motions of his head as he does with words themselves. When I speak, he listens carefully, softly interjecting with a nod or a
chuckle or quiet word of validation. He is immediately a friend, which is
strange to me. I have always hated Cops and Judges, or Authority Figures of
any kind, and the last place I would have ever thought I would befriend one
would be in a Treatment Center.
After a few minutes, we are joined by Leonard and Matty and Ed and
Ted. It is a typical meal with them. They laugh, make fun of one another,
tell stories about their pasts, talk shit about the Clinic's other Patients.
Aside from Miles, there are four new men on our Unit, and Leonard and
Matty and Ed and Ted size them up, talk about which ones they like and
which ones they don't like, and make plans to fuck with them. There is
one, a short fat man named Bobby, whom they seem to harbor a particular dislike for, though I don't know why. I do know that I'm glad I'm not
him.
We finish eating and we walk as a group to the Lecture. We sit as a group
in the seats. I sit on the aisle and I watch for Lilly. When she walks in my
heart jumps and my hands shake and me myself inside settles it settles
and those things for which there are no words ignite and they start firing

firing firing. I knew I would be affected when I saw her, but I didn't
know this and I don't know this and I'm surprised and the surprise makes
me nervous and I'm usually not nervous. Usually I'm just pissed. I'm not
pissed right now. They have ignited and they are firing.
A man walks out onstage and everyone starts clapping. I recognize the
man as a famous Rock Star who was once a Patient here. He holds his
arms up in triumph and he smiles and he bows and his black leather is
shining and his long, greasy black hair is hanging and his patterned silk
shirt is flowing and his large, round silver earrings are dangling and everyone is dazzled. He motions for quiet and the clapping stops and he starts
theatrically pacing back and forth across the Stage back and forth.
He stops and he stares at the ceiling for a moment as if there's something
up there besides the ceiling panels and he looks back and he starts speaking in a deep, serious voice. His first words are when I had my first hit
single and I got famous I started to party really fucking hard.
From there he launches into a detailed accounting of his career. He talks
about the number of records sold and the number of women slept with and
the number of awards won. He talks about living on the road and he says it
ain't easy, man, even if you are staying at the Four Seasons. He talks about
the rigors of recording an album and he talks about the pressures of being a
Star. He talks about what he calls the national obsession with his lips and
his hair and he talks about melodic qualities of his voice. After a while, after
far too long a while, he talks about drinking and drugs. When he talks of
heroin, he taps the bend of his elbow with two fingers, when he talks of
coke he sniffs, booze he makes a motion like he has a bottle, pills as if he's
tossing them in. He claims that at the height of his use he would do five
thousand dollars of cocaine and heroin a day mixed with four to five fifths
of booze a night and up to forty pills of Valium to sleep. He says this with
complete sincerity and with the utmost seriousness.
I am tired and I am spent. I am nervous and I am happy. I am calm. Were I
in my normal frame of mind, I would stand up, point my finger, scream
Fraud, and chase this Chump Motherfucker down and give him a beating.
Were I in my normal frame of mind, after I gave him his beating, I would
make him come back here and apologize to everyone for wasting their precious time. After the apology, I would tell him that if I ever heard of him
spewing his bullshit fantasies in Public again, I would cut off his precious
hair, scar his precious lips, and take all of his goddamn gold records and
shove them straight up his ass.
I don't like this man. I don't like what he has to say or how he's saying it.
I don't believe him and his Rock Star status isn't enough to make me buy

the shit he's trying to sell. Four to five thousand dollars a day of anything is enough to kill a Person several times over. Five bottles of strong liquor over the course of a night would render the strongest human on Earth comatose. Forty Valiums to sleep and he'd take a fucking nap from which he'd never return. He'd never return and maybe that would be best.

An Addict is an Addict. It doesn't matter whether the Addict is white, black, yellow or green, rich or poor or somewhere in the middle, the most famous Person on the Planet or the most unknown. It doesn't matter whether the addiction is drugs, alcohol, crime, sex, shopping, food, gambling, television, or the fucking Flintstones. The life of the Addict is always the same. There is no excitement, no glamour, no fun. There are no good times, there is no joy, there is no happiness. There is no future and no escape. There is only an obsession. An all-encompassing, fully enveloping, completely overwhelming obsession. To make light of it, brag about it, or revel in the mock glory of it is not in any way, shape or form related to its truth, and that is all that matters, the truth. That this man is standing in front of me and everyone else in this room lying to us is heresy. The truth is all that matters. This is fucking heresy.

The Lecture ends and there is wild applause and enthusiastic cheers and the Lips, Hair, Leather and Silk on the Stage is smiling and waving and glowing and blowing kisses to his adoring Fans. I am tired. I am spent. I am nervous and I am happy and I am calm. Were I in my normal frame of mind, I'd be sick to my stomach. I hear Leonard mumbling and I ask him what he just said and he laughs and tells me that he's thinking of sending a few of his Associates to have a talk with the Lips about an attitude adjustment. I laugh and I tell him it would be a beautiful thing. Bless you, Leonard. It would be a beautiful fucking thing.

We stand and we start to file out and before I leave I turn to get a glimpse of Lilly but I can't see her and I don't want to make my intentions obvious so I turn back and I keep walking. I wish I could see her. I want to see her. I don't see her. I walk back to the Unit and I go to my Room and I lie down on my bed.

Miles walks in and he sits down on his bed and he reaches for his clarinet case and he starts unpacking it and he asks if I mind if he plays and I say no play whatever you want for as long as you want and I reach for a book one of the books my Brother gave me and I don't bother looking to see what I'm reaching for because I don't care I just want to read and I want to occupy my mind with something. The rage and need are back they have returned are alive as they almost always are living and lingering and eating me away. I need something to occupy my mind. I don't care what it is. Occupy.

I pull the Chinese book, the *Tao Te Ching*, by far the smallest of the three that I have, and the only one that I haven't read before. It is a small, thin paperback. The title is written across the front in simple white type against a black background. I flip the book over and I look at the back and there are quotes on the back from three sources that I have never heard of before but that look like bullshit new-age Hippie Periodicals. There is a publication classification in an upper corner. It reads Religion. I am immediately skeptical. Not only because of the source quotes and the Religion classification, but because I've always grouped books such as this in a category with crap like Astrology, Aromatherapy, Crystalology, Pyramid Power, Psychic Healing and Feng Shui, which at various times in my life have all been suggested as cures for my problems. That anyone would actually believe that these things could solve their problems, really solve them, instead of just making them forget about them for a while, is asinine to me. My Brother gave me this book though, so I'll read it. Had anyone aside from my Brother given it to me, it would be sitting in the bottom of a garbage can.

As I open it, Miles starts playing his clarinet. He plays softly and slowly. The notes are on the low side and he draws them out to the point that I wonder how he's breathing. The notes are on the long side and he makes them sound like they are easy to make, though I know they are not. Low and slow and soft and long and easy. I don't know what it is, but I like it.

I skip the Introduction. If the book goes in the trash, I want it to go because of my thoughts on it, not because of some Asshole's thoughts who wrote the Introduction.

The text begins. It consists of a series of short poems numbered one through eighty-one. The first one says that the Tao is that which has no name and is beyond any sort of name. It says that names are not necessary for that which is real and for that which is eternal. It says that if we are free from desire, we can realize mystery, that if we are caught in desire, we only realize manifestations. It says mystery and manifestations arise from the same source, which is darkness. It says darkness within darkness is the key to all understanding. It is not enough to make me throw it away, but I am also not convinced.

I keep going. I keep going as I listen to low and slow and soft and long and easy. I keep going as I settle in beneath the warmth of my bed and I keep going as I wait for the phone to ring. When the phone rings, I know I will get to hear the sound of Lilly's voice. I want to hear the sound of Lilly's voice.

Number two. If there is beauty, there is ugliness. If there is good, there is bad. Being and nonbeing and difficult and easy and high and low and long and short and before and after need, depend, create and define each other. Those who live with the Tao act without doing and teach without saying. They let things come and they let things go and they live without possession and they live without expectation. They do not need, depend, create or define. They do not see beauty or ugliness or good or bad. There just is. Just be.

Number three. Overesteem men and people become powerless. Overvalue possessions and people begin to steal. Empty your mind and fill your core. Weaken your ambition and toughen your resolve. Lose everything you know and everything you desire and ignore those who say they know. Practice not wanting, desiring, judging, doing, fighting, knowing. Practice just being. Everything will fall into place.

Four. The Tao is used, but never used up. An eternal void, it is filled with infinite possibilities. It is not there, but always there. It is older and more powerful than any God. It is not there, but always there. It is older and more powerful than any God.

I stop reading and I read them again. One through four, again and again. The words and the words together and the meaning and the context are simple so simple and basic so basic and true and that is all that matters true. They speak to me, make sense to me, reverberate within me, calm ease sedate relax still pacify me. They ring true and that is all that matters the truth. Although I am no expert on this or anything related to this or anything at all except being a fuck-up, I seem to understand what this book this weird beautiful enlightened little book is saying to me. Live and let live, do not judge, take life as it comes and deal with it, everything will be okay.

I close the book and I let the sounds of the clarinet carry me carry me carry me. They are low and slow and soft and long and easy, as are the thoughts in my head. They carry me carry me carry me.

Live and let live.

Do not judge.

Take it as it comes.

Deal with it.

Everything will be okay.

Screaming, long and loud and hideous, like a Child being burned alive.

I sit up in my bed. It is silent and dark. I don't know if it's real or a dream. Then it comes again. Like a Child being burned alive.

I get out of my bed and I walk out of my room and I head toward the scream. It's coming from the Main Rooms of the Unit and with each step that I take it becomes louder and more intense. It's like a fucking Child being burned alive.

I'm scared. The hair on the back of my neck is standing and the hair on my arms is standing and my heart is thudding and my ears are ringing and it's louder and more intense with each step. I want it to stop. I'm scared. Poor Child. I'm scared. Poor Child.

I walk into the Upper Level. There are a couple of other men there and they are staring down at the Lower Level with stunned faces. I follow their eyes and the sounds of the screams, which are echoing through the room, and I see Roy standing on top of a couch holding a thick, brutal wooden stick, short like a battering ram, with a bloody, fragmented tip. He is waving the stick around, swinging at invisible enemies, and screaming at the top of his lungs. His clothes, which are old and torn, are covered in dirt and blood, as are his arms and his face and his hair, and his eyes are wide and empty, the whites a deep furnace red, the pupils an endless black.

More men arrive, drawn in by the horrible shrieking screams, and they stand around the Upper Level watching Roy, unsure of what to do or how to react, unsure if there's a way to stop him. He has increased the pace of his madness and he is jumping up and down on the couch, banging the stick against its back with one hand and clawing at his face with the other. Spit is flying from his mouth and particles of blood are staining the carpet and the walls and it appears as if he's pissed his pants or is in the process of pissing his pants. He does not appear to notice that there is anybody else in the Room.

Lincoln arrives with a large man wearing a gray outfit and carrying a handheld radio who I assume is some sort of Security. They stand at the

top of the stairs for a moment, watching Roy and talking quietly. When
they stop talking, they begin descending the stairs and Roy stops scream-
ing and he glares at them and he raises his stick and he waves it at them.
Why are you trying to kill me?
Lincoln speaks. Quietly and calmly.
Roy?
Why are you trying to kill me?
We're not trying to kill you, Roy.
They reach the bottom of the stairs and they stop.
Who is Roy?
Lincoln steps forward, the man stays.
Are you on something, Roy?
Roy jumps up and down on the couch. He shakes his stick.
I AM NOT ROY.
Lincoln steps forward.
Who are you?
**My name is Jack and I'll kill you. I'LL KILL YOU, YOU MOTHER-
FUCKER.**
Lincoln turns and nods to the man and the man starts talking into his
radio. Lincoln turns back to Roy.
Hi, Jack.
I'll bash your head in, you two-faced Bastard.
Why would you do that, Jack?
'Cause I'm a Killer. A cold-blooded mercenary Killer.
Two more men in gray arrive. The original man clears his throat. Lincoln
turns around, motions them forward with his head, and steps toward
Roy. The men reach into their pockets and they draw out latex gloves and
they put them on.
Why don't you give me the stick, Jack?
Roy shakes the stick.
This ain't no stick, it's a cudgel. A man-hammer.
The men move forward.
Why don't you put down the cudgel, Jack.
Pry it from my cold dead fingers, Fuckface.
The men surround the couch, Lincoln stands in front of Roy. He is
scowling and growling and moving in a circle to defend himself.
I'll bash your heads in, you Cocksuckers.
Roy.
I'll kill you to death till you're dead and die, you Sons of Whores.

Roy.

The men are looking at Lincoln, Lincoln at Roy. Roy spins, waving his stick and yelling.

I'm Jack the man-hammer. I'll smash all of you to fucking bits.

Lincoln nods at the original man, who nods to the other two men. When Roy turns his back, one of them tackles him from behind, sending his stick into the air and his body to the ground. The other two immediately jump on top of him and they grab his arms and as they try to subdue him he claws at them and he tries to bite them. When he knows he's done and beaten he starts screaming screaming screaming. Screaming. Like a Child being burned alive.

Most of the Unit's men have gathered on the Upper Level and they are watching as the men pick Roy up. One of them has his legs, one has his lower arms and lower torso, the third has his upper arms and upper torso. They carry him up the stairs and out of the Unit and his screams continue as they move through the Halls. Though they are certainly taking him to an unpleasant place, I doubt it will be any worse than the place he was just in. It couldn't be. His screaming. No fucking way.

Lincoln, who has been silently watching, turns to us.

Show's over, Boys. Go back to bed.

No one moves.

Go back to bed.

No one moves. Ted speaks.

You ain't got nothing else for us?

A couple of laughs. Lincoln stares at Ted.

It's not funny, Ted.

Ted speaks.

I thought it was.

Lincoln ignores him.

Go back to bed, everybody. We'll talk about this tomorrow.

He stands and he stares until some of the men start trickling out. When they do, he walks up the stairs and he leaves. I am wide awake and I am not going back to bed. Even if I went back to bed, there is no way I could sleep. The screams are echoing in my mind. The image of the blood and spit will not leave me. The words I am not Roy are alive inside. The emptiness and insanity in his eyes haunt me. I am not going back to bed. The screams were like a Child being burned alive.

I walk over to the coffee machine and I start making the day's first supply. I fill the filter with cheap, industrial grounds, I fill the tank with tap wa-

ter, I push the on button. I stand and I wait as the water trickles through
translucent brown and gurgles gurgles gurgles. When the water stops, I
pour a cup of the coffee and I take a sip and it's hot and it's bitter and it's
good. No sugar and no cream it's hot and bitter and good. I am not going back to bed. I am going to need the coffee. I am going to need it.
I walk over to a table a few feet away. Some men have gathered at the
table and they are talking about what we just witnessed. I tell them the
coffee is ready and a couple of them stand to get a cup and I sit down
and I listen to them. The focus of the conversation is on what known
drugs could do to a Person what was done to Roy, or more likely, what he
did to himself. Crack could have done it, meth could have done it, PCP
or a large dose of acid could have done it, but nothing else readily available has the necessary power. Ted thinks that it was crack. He has experienced crack-induced psychosis several times, the last when he marched
down the Main Street of a small Town in Mississippi wearing a Santa suit
and throwing bags filled with shit at passing cars and Pedestrians. A man
I don't know thinks it was meth and he believes that Roy probably hadn't
slept in several days and was suffering from a severe case of sleep depriva-
tion. Everyone else thinks it was PCP or acid. Either or both have the
strength to take your mind, make you see and hear things that aren't there
and drive you insane. Either or both can do this to a Person in the short
term or the long term. Either or both can do this to a first-time user. The
Bald Man says that Roy was a Drinker and that he hated drugs and he
hated everyone who used them and that he would never have done them.
He thinks he just went insane. No rhyme, no reason, just a malfunctioning mind that finally lost all. I don't have a theory. I sit and listen and I
drink my coffee and I wait for the screaming to go away.
The men drift back to bed, one by one, tired and tired of talking. They
drift until I'm the last and only one awake, me and the industrial coffee and
the pale, quiet walls and the slow, lonely moments and the living, shifting
dark of the deepest night. I sit at the table and I smoke cigarettes and I sip
my coffee. I listen to the ticking of an unseen clock and I think about how
a malfunctioning mind might finally lose all and I remember. Sit stare
smoke sip listen tick remember. A malfunctioning mind can lose all. It has
lost all. Remember.
I remember her. I remember her tall and thin and long and blonde like
the thickest silk her eyes blue eyes Arctic eyes I remember her. I remember leaving her on the afternoon I dropped off the bag of dope for
Lucinda. I remember seeing her the next day. I remember not speaking to
her, but wanting to speak to her and not being able to speak to her. I re-

member staring at her, recklessly and obviously, eyes locked and loaded and unmoving, my eyes straight into her. I remember not knowing if she noticed. I had fallen deep and hard I had fallen. I didn't know if she noticed.

I kept staring at her for the next year. In the Street, through Hallways, on sidewalks, at a table, outside a Coffee Shop, inside a Bar, morning afternoon night. If I was where she was I stared at her. I wanted to talk to her, but I didn't. Never hello, never how are you, never what's up, never what's new, I never said a word, I just stared at her. After a while I knew that she knew I was doing it, but she never told me to stop. I just stared.

She disappeared at the beginning of our third year. I didn't know where she went and I didn't ask anyone. It wasn't uncommon for Students to spend time away either abroad or working, so I assumed she would be back. If she hadn't come back, I would have left to find her. She was away away and if she hadn't come back, I would have searched to the end of the Earth. I would have searched until I found her.

I saw her again in a Class. It was the first Class of a new Fall, fifteen months from the time of her disappearance. I walked in drunk from the night before and dizzy with dehydration and exhaustion and I took a seat in the back of the Room, away from the rest of the Students, as far away as I could get. I put my arms down on my desk and I put my head down in my arms and I closed my eyes and my head spun my stomach spun my body spun and I tried to keep myself awake and I tried to keep myself from getting sick I didn't want to get sick on the first day of Class. I raised my head when I heard the Professor say hello, and welcome to a new year and she was there, in the front row, with Lucinda and another girl whom I had seen before, but whom I didn't know. She was there. I hadn't seen her in over a year. I would have searched to the end of the Earth. She was there.

I sat and stared at her. I forgot that I was drunk, forgot that I was sick, forgot that I was in Class, forgot that I was in School, forgot that I had friends, Family, a life, a name, a face, a mind. I forgot everything, forgot forgot forgot everything, and I stared at her. Though I was behind her, I could see that she had changed since I last saw her. She had gained weight, grown her hair longer, gotten a tan, and she radiated a quiet, calm confidence that hadn't been there before. She was wearing black and the black made her hair more blonde, and though I couldn't see, I knew it made her eyes more blue. I would have gone to the ends of the Earth. When Class ended I didn't want it to end I just wanted to stare she stood up and she turned around as if she knew I was there two eyes locked and loaded behind her and she stared back at me and I held her stare Arctic blue against pale green. She stared and I held it until the Class was empty and she turned around and she walked out. I took a deep breath and I followed her.

She walked through the Halls of the Building. It was the Humanities Building and it was crowded with the excitement and the noise of a new year. She walked quickly, but held at corners and in stairways long enough to let me see her way and long enough to let me know she wanted me to see her way. Arctic blue against pale green. We had held.

I lost her somewhere near the Main Entrance to the Building and I panicked. I didn't want to lose her and I hurried outside immediately scanning looking where did she go I want to see her stare at her where did she go Arctic blue where where where and I heard a voice say my name say it clear, pure, in a strong simple way like sunlight on a rock in shallow water. Clear pure simple and strong a voice said my name James.

I stopped and I turned around and she was standing on a large, wide, stone stair, the first in a set of ten. She was standing there waiting for me.

James.

What?

Why do you stare at me?

What?

You stare at me. I want to know why.

You already know why.

I don't.

Yes, you do.

No, I don't.

You do, you just want to hear me say it.

Tell me why you stare.

I took a deep breath.

The first time I saw you, my heart fell. The second time I saw you, my heart fell. The third time fourth time fifth time and every time since, my heart has fallen.

I stared at her.

You are the most beautiful woman I have ever seen. Your hair, your eyes, your lips, your body that you haven't grown into, the way you walk, smile, laugh, the way your cheeks drop when you're mad or upset, the way you drag your feet when you're tired. Every single thing about you is beautiful.

I stared at her.

When I see you the World stops. It stops and all that exists for me is you and my eyes staring at you. There's nothing else. No noise, no other people, no thoughts or worries, no yesterday, no tomorrow. The World just stops, and it is a beautiful place, and there is only you. Just you, and my eyes staring at you.

I stared.

When you're gone, the World starts again, and I don't like it as much. I can live in it, but I don't like it. I just walk around in it and wait to see you again and wait for it to stop again. I love it when it stops. It's the best fucking thing I've ever known or ever felt, the best thing, and that, beautiful Girl, is why I stare at you.

We were standing a foot apart, staring at each other, Arctic and pale, locked and loaded. The World had stopped and there was nothing else. Just me and her, Arctic and pale, locked and loaded.

She smiled.

That was beautiful.

It was true.

Thank you.

No problem.

What are you doing now?

I've got another Class. Then I'm gonna go get drunk.

Seriously?

Yeah.

The stories are true?

I don't know what you've heard, but probably.

I was hoping they weren't.

Don't know what to tell you.

I took a step backward, down another stair.

I'll see you around?

She smiled and she nodded.

Yes.

I turned and I walked away and my legs were shaking like jelly with each step down the stairs. I knew she was watching me walk away and waiting for me to turn back for another smile and I would've liked another smile I would have liked the World to stop and she was waiting for it, but I didn't turn around. I kept going, an image in my mind, Arctic and pale, locked and loaded, beautiful magnificent mysterious and wonderful. It was in my mind. I knew it wasn't going anywhere.

I listen to the tick of an unseen clock marking moments of time long passed. It takes me the tick and it holds me and it carries and keeps me like the slow swing of a pendulum before the eyes of an idiot. The World has stopped not like before and not in a good way. It has stopped and is not going forward the same way my life has stopped and is not going forward. It is not going forward or backward or anywhere at all it has just stopped. It has just stopped.

The clock holds me nowhere. Nowhere. Nowhere. There is nothing else but now and the shifting depth of night. I sit at a table alone smoking cigarettes and drinking coffee and listening and surviving. I should not be here or anywhere. I should not be breathing or taking space. I should not have been given this moment or anything else. I should not have this opportunity again to live. I do not deserve it or deserve anything yet it is here and I am here and I have it all of it still. I won't have it again. This moment or this chance they are the same thing. This moment and this chance they are the same and they are mine if I choose them and I do. I want them. Now and as long as I can have them they are both precious and fleeting and gone in the blink of an eye don't waste them. A moment and an opportunity and a life, all in the unseen tick of a clock holding me nowhere. My heart is beating. The walls are pale and quiet. I am surviving.

The dark shifts away from itself and light invades it and conquers. The Unit is empty still but for me. I stand and I want to breathe deeply and breathe without boundary and I walk to the door and I open it and I go outside. I walk toward the Lake which is covered with a frigid mist born from the difference between inside and out. The mist hovers above the clear calm black of the water, moving up but not moving at all, changing shape but staying the same. I like the mist and I want to take it in and let it become me. I want to drink it and be full. I want to swallow it and let it make me. Make me how I should be made mist. Make me what I should be made.

I sit on the middle bench. It is cold on my legs and back, but the cold is a counterpoint to the coffee and the cigarettes and the night. I look out unmoving and strong until a bird sweeps down and sweeps through carving its way like Northern Ice drifting south. It moves up and out and above the mist and it finds a tree and it sits on the tree and it rests looking back not at me but at that which it sought. It is not there now or again so it stays the bird stays on the branch of the tree stiff and true. Looking, seeking, searching, waiting. It stays stiff and true.

There is a noise behind me and I turn to the noise. There is a Figure emerging from the reflection of the glass door. The Figure is bundled beneath layers of cotton and bright blue nylon it wears glasses and a hat. It shuts the door and it sees me and it comes toward me one step at a time purposefully through the thick shimmering dew. I do not want it, the

Figure and whatever it may bring, so I turn away from it and I look out across the water, unmoving and strong. The bird is still there. Looking, seeking, searching, waiting. Sitting stiff and true.

The steps are closer and I can see the cotton and the nylon out of the corner of my eye. I try to ignore it, but there's a voice.

Hey, Kid.

I know the voice.

Hey, Leonard.

He stands in front of me.

Mind if I sit?

I stare at the mist.

They're not my benches.

He laughs and he sits.

Why you up so early?

I stare at the mist.

Couldn't sleep.

Roy?

Among other things.

What are the other things?

Nothing I'm gonna talk about.

You sure?

Yeah, I'm sure.

Leonard stands.

Let's go for a walk.

I stay on the bench.

No thanks.

Come on.

No.

Why.

I look up.

I don't know if I can be seen with you in that sweat suit.

He looks at himself and back at me.

What's wrong with the sweat suit?

What's it made of?

He rubs it, smiles.

It's a rayon/nylon/satin blend.

I laugh.

That's the first thing that's wrong with it.

What's the second?

You got your gold watch on.

I love this watch.

And your silly glasses.

They're Gucci.

I don't care what they are, they're silly.

He takes them off, looks at them, puts them in his pocket.

How's that?

It's better.

He smiles, motions toward the Wood.

Let's go for a walk, Kid.

I stand and we start walking and we find a Trail through the Wood. Leonard asks how I'm doing and I tell him I'm fine. He asks me again and I tell him I'm fine again. He asks me again and I tell him I'm fucking fine and he tells me that fine isn't a good enough answer he wants to know how I'm really doing. I tell him I don't know. He asks me what that means and I tell him I don't know how I'm doing that sometimes I feel good and sometimes I feel something far less far far less than good. He says that if that's what I'm feeling then I'm doing well and I should just keep doing and I'll get better and my life will get better everything will get better and I laugh at him. He asks me why I'm laughing and I tell him I'm laughing because I don't think that he as a coke Addict and a fellow Patient and a Fuck-Up of the First Order is in any position to give me advice. He laughs and he says let's find a place to sit down, Kid. I got a story to tell you.

We walk until we find a bench along one of the smaller Lakes. It is a plain wooden bench that looks as if it has been carved from a single chunk of wood. Its edges are rough, its surface is uneven and like all of the benches at this time of day, it is cold. The Sun has started rising and shafts of yellow and white are burning away a mist. Floating sheets of gray ice are shifting and cracking, the crack like a gunshot, and icicles hanging from extended branches of Oak and Pine are dripping, the drip melting the cover of frost beneath. Though I am lightly dressed, I am warm. My heart is beating and I am surviving and I am warm.

Leonard looks out across the Lake. He is calmer than I have ever seen him, the edge of violence, control and power that he carries is gone. His hands are still on his lap, his breathing is deep and slow and his eyes are focused on something in the distance, though they aren't really looking at it. His eyes are looking inside, reviewing, remembering, figuring out how to tell. Without moving, he starts to speak.

I told you how my Father died. How he got hit by a truck and killed. Before he died, as he lay in a Hospital bed, he took my hand and he told me that the only thing he ever wanted for me was that one day I be successful enough to play the Golf Course he mowed for fifteen years just like I was one of the Members. I promised him that someday I'd do it. Leonard takes a deep breath.

I told you how my Mother died and how Michelangelo and Geena adopted me and raised me like I was their own. On top of raising me, Michelangelo guided me into his business. What that is isn't important for you to know. What's important is that he taught me to do it and he set me up in it. I took care of details for him and he watched over and protected me. An opportunity came up for Michelangelo and Geena to move to Las Vegas. They took it and I went with them. We did very well, very quickly. As Vegas was growing and booming, so were we. We had money, Houses, cars, whatever we wanted. It was all there, everything we ever wanted.

Leonard stops talking, stares at the ground. He takes a deep breath, looks up.

Then Geena got cancer. It was a bad cancer, cancer of the bones, and it took her quickly and brutally. In three fucking months and she went from being the most beautiful woman in the World to a fucking skeleton, and when it killed her, in a certain way, it killed both me and Michelangelo too.

He shakes his head, stares across the Lake.

Nothing was ever the same. Michelangelo lost interest in our business and turned it over to me. I didn't see him much after that. I think we just reminded each other of what we had lost. Those were shitty depressing years. We both started drinking more and doing too much cocaine, but Michelangelo completely lost it.

A day came when I needed to see him, talk to him about something, so I went over to his house. I hadn't been there in months, and when I walked in, I was sick to my stomach. There were mirrors full of coke on tables, bottles and cans everywhere, garbage piles in every room, and blonde Girls with big fake tits sleeping on the couches and lounging by the Pool. I went up to his Room and he was sitting there with a couple of young Girls and a bunch of drugs. I told the Girls to get out and I walked him out to the Pool. I sat him down and looked him in the eye and I said Mikey, you should be fucking ashamed of yourself. You should be ashamed of how you're living and ashamed that you're desecrating the memory of your Wife. Geena would have wanted better for you, and if she's up in Heaven watching you, she's probably crying her eyes out.

He didn't say a word to me. He just turned around and walked out of the

House. I didn't know where he went, didn't hear from him at all, so I started mourning him. My mourning was just like his. I drank too much, did too much coke and did a lot of stupid bullshit.

About a year later, I'm asleep in my bed and I hear someone in my house. I always keep a gun under my pillow, so I reached for it and started walking around. I heard someone in my kitchen and I walked in and there was Michelangelo, fifty pounds lighter, looking better and healthier than I'd ever seen him. He looked at me and he asked why the fridge was so god-damn empty.

I gave him a hug and I asked him where he'd been and he told me he was here, at this Clinic, where you and I are right now. He told me that when he had left his House the day I sat him down, he had planned on driving into the Desert and blowing his brains out, but once he got there, he couldn't do it. He decided that if he was going to die, he wanted to die how he'd lived most of his life, which was with dignity and honor. He had heard about this place and decided he was going to come here. He bought a map and drove up here from Vegas and stayed until he felt he was better. Then he got in his car and he drove around for a few months, saw the White House and Key West and Bourbon Street and Alaska. He saw everything he had always wanted to see but never had.

He had come Home to tell me that he was going to retire and that he wanted me to come here. He said this place changed his life. He said getting sober had been the hardest thing he'd ever done, but next to getting married and spending his life with Geena, it was the best thing he'd ever done. He wanted me to do it, he said he wouldn't ever leave or die until I did.

We spent the rest of the day playing golf and talking about this place. He said when he first got here, he thought he had made a big mistake. He thought about leaving, but didn't. A few days later he felt better and he knew something was working. A month after that he knew he was going to be okay. There were still bad times and rough times and times when he didn't think he was gonna make it, but when they came, he just held on. He held on tight and with everything he had until the good started coming back. When he was finally ready to go, he said he knew he wasn't ever going to drink or use again, he said he walked out of here happy and proud.

For the next few days we talked more about the effect that this place had on him, and we talked more about me coming here. About a week after that, he came by my house and picked me up and told me he was taking

me out to eat at my favorite Restaurant. I don't know how he did it without me knowing, but he had set up a big dinner with all of our friends,
even some of our old ones from New York. When we walked in, they were
all waiting for us. We ate, drank, snorted coke. Michelangelo told me that
he was putting me on a plane the next day, so I really went at it. After a
couple hours, he told me he was going Home. He said he didn't feel entirely right spending an entire evening with so much liquor and so many
drugs. He gave me a hug and said he'd pick me up at noon to take me to
the Airport. I hugged him back and told him I'd be ready and I was
gonna make him proud. He said he already knew.
Leonard takes a deep breath.
He turned and he walked away, headed toward the valet. I watched him
from the door as he waited for his car, hoping that he'd turn around so
that I could wave to him. As he was standing there, a black Lincoln
pulled up and the windows went down. I knew what was happening, and
I tried to yell, but before I could say anything, the barrels came out. They
started blazing away. Just blazing the fuck away.
Michelangelo went down straightaway, and even as he was down, the
guns kept fucking blazing. By the time I got there, he was done, hit sixteen times, twice in the chest, four in the stomach, the rest in his arms
and legs. People were running all over the place, there was blood every-
where, and he was done, shot sixteen times by a carload of cowardly
Fucks.
Leonard's voice cracks and tears start running down his cheeks.
I held him as he bled. Just held him and told him how much I loved him.
He was still conscious and he could still talk, but he knew he was done.
Right before he went, he lifted a bloody hand and he put it on my cheek.
He looked me in the eye and he said, live honorably and with dignity, re-
spect the memories of all your Parents. I want you to play the course of
your first Father and play it like one of the Members, and I want you to
live sober and live free. Do that for me, Leonard. Live sober and live free.
It's gonna be hard and scary and brutal, but if you just hold on, you'll be
okay. Just hold on. And then he died, right in my arms, shot down like a
fucking dog. He died in my arms.
Leonard breaks down and starts weeping. It is a strong shaking sobbing
wracking weeping, the weeping that comes from a wound that will never
heal. I let him weep, leave him be with his memories and his loss and his
pain. I would offer him comfort, but it wouldn't matter. The wounds that
never heal can only be mourned alone.

He regains his composure and with it his edge of violence, control and power. He stares out across the Lake at the burning mist and the floating cracking ice, but with an image of the dead held firm in his mind.

I didn't get on my Plane the next day or any day for a long time. I buried Michelangelo next to Geena and I wept at their graves just like I wept a moment ago and just like I weep whenever I think of them. Then I spent a week locked in my house getting blitzed beyond comprehension. When I emerged after that week, the only thing on my mind was vengeance.

I spent the next year tracking down the Motherfuckers responsible for Michelangelo's murder. Then I found the Motherfuckers they worked for, and then I found the Motherfuckers those Motherfuckers worked for. What I did to them does not deserve to be spoken of, but I will tell you that I did not give them the luxury of being held by someone who loved them when I turned their fucking lights out. I spent the year after that drinking and doing blow and trying to get my ass on that goddamn Golf Course in Westchester. I wasn't able to, so I decided to take a break and come here, the thought being that if I wasn't able to make my first Father proud, I would damn well do it for the second.

It has been incredibly hard being here and doing this, much harder than I imagined it would be. When I got here I was a fucking wreck. Not a wreck like you were, but bad enough. Every second that passed was a miserable Hell. Now it's getting easier, but it's still fucking awful, and there are still a lot more bad times than good times and a lot more bad feelings than good feelings. I don't know what I think about Higher Powers and Twelve Steps and all the rest of what they talk about in here, but I do know that when things are tough, and when I don't think I can last another minute, if I just hold on, hold on tight and with everything I got, the shit gets better. The Old Man was right, just like he was always right, and he spoke the truth with his final words. Just hold on. Just hold on.

Leonard turns and he stares at me. I stare back.

I told you this story for a number of reasons. The most important is that when you get down, or you don't think you can fucking do this anymore, just hold on, and sooner or later, the shit is gonna get better.

We stare at each other.

As I said before, Kid, you walk out of here, and I'm having you brought back. As many times as it takes, I will have you brought the fuck back. You can go ahead and test me on that if you want, but I would suggest you not. The smart thing would be to take my advice. I may be a coke Addict and a fellow Patient and a Fuck-Up of the First Order, but I am giving you good advice. Be smart, be strong, be proud, live honorably and with dignity, and just hold on.

We stare at each other. I am listening to him and respecting him and respecting the words that he is speaking. They are true. They come from a place of experience and feeling. I can believe in those things. Truth, experience and feeling. I can believe in them. Just hold on.

You think you can do that?

I nod.

Yeah, I can do that.

He smiles.

You're not gonna fight me on this.

I shake my head.

No, I'm not going to fight you.

You're getting better, Kid.

I chuckle. I turn and I look back across the Lake. The mist is gone and the ice diminished, the drip of the icicles quick and heavy. The Sun is up and the Sky is blue empty blue light blue clear blue. I would drink the Sky if I could drink it, drink it and celebrate it and let it fill me and become me. I am getting better. Empty and clear and light and blue. I am getting better.

Leonard speaks.

It's about time for breakfast.

Yeah.

Leonard stands. I look up at him.

Thank you, Leonard.

He smiles.

Sure, Kid.

I stand. I think about saying something else, but I don't know any words to express the strong, simple and deep appreciation I feel. I reach up and out and I put my arms around Leonard and I hug him. I don't know any words, so I let my actions speak. Strong, simple and deep appreciation. The actions speak true.

We separate and we start walking back to the Clinic. As we move along the Trail, we pass other Patients and we say hello to them or nod to them or exchange brief pleasantries with them. Most of them seem to be walking for exercise and most of them seem to know where they're going. A few are just walking to walk. A few look lost.

We get to the Dining Hall and we get trays and we get food and we sit down at a table with Matty and Ed and Ted and Miles and a man named

Bobby. Bobby, who is short and fat and has the pink skin and red hair of an Irishman, has a huge plate of food in front of him. In between giant mouthfuls of runny eggs, he is telling stories. Matty and Ed and Ted are egging him on, Miles is sitting and quietly listening.

He doesn't acknowledge us as we join them. He doesn't stop eating or talking, the fat jowl beneath his chin doesn't stop jiggling. He is telling a story about some Mobsters he knows in Brooklyn, claiming that he manages their money through investments in the Stock Market and they get him drugs and women and whatever else he wants. When he talks of amounts of drugs, Matty laughs and says he should have asked for more. Bobby then corrects himself and says that he actually did get more. When he talks of women, Ed tells him that four at a time isn't that big a deal and Bobby says the next time he had eight. He mentions crack and the amounts of it he claims to smoke and Ted asks him what it feels like, that he has always wanted to try it. Bobby says that it feels like really strong weed. In reality, it does not at all. Ted laughs at him, feigning awe and amazement.

Leonard sits carefully and quietly watching and listening. Occasionally Leonard asks Bobby questions about who he claims to know and how he claims to know them. I can't tell if Leonard knows all the people he and Bobby are talking about, but I can tell that Leonard is sizing him up. I don't think he's all that impressed.

Eventually I get tired of Bobby and his bullshit and I snicker at a comment he makes about the amount of money he earns, which he claims to be in the millions each year. He stops talking and he stares at me and he asks me what the fuck I think is so funny. I stare back and I tell him that I find his lies amusing and Miles speaks for the first time since the breakfast began and he says they certainly are. Bobby, like all Liars confronted, is instantly defensive and instantly mad. He asks who the fuck I am and where the fuck do I get off accusing him. I tell him I'm no one and I get off because I have decided that I do. He tells me that he's not the kind of man to let his honor be disrespected in that way and that I best retract my statement or face the consequences of it and the image of him trying to do something to me, all three hundred fat-ass pounds of him jiggling toward me in a fit of primal rage, is humorous. I laugh at him and he stands and he asks me if I want to go come on you little Punk let's go right now and I stand and I say sure, let's go right now. He looks toward Lincoln and Keith, who are eating a few tables away, and he says you're lucky they're here or I'd kick your ass. I laugh at him and I pick up my tray and I walk away.

I put my tray on the conveyor. As I turn around, I bump into Lilly. She drops her tray and it hits the floor and there's a mess and she bends over to clean it up and I bend over to help her. As I reach for an empty coffee cup, she slides her hand across my hand and I can feel a piece of folded paper within her hand. As she slides it away the piece of paper stays. Just like a drug deal on a Street Corner. Two hands exchanging a small folded piece of paper in what looks like a harmless gesture. Her hand hitting my hand. The piece of paper stays.

We pick up a plate and an empty cereal bowl and a fork and a knife and a spoon. We put them on her tray and she puts her tray on the conveyor and I walk away. Just like on the Street Corner, I want whatever is in or on the piece of paper and I want it immediately. Just like on the Street Corner, I know I have to wait till I'm alone. Just like on the Street Corner, I know I shouldn't have it.

I put the piece of paper in the front pocket of my pants and I go to the Lecture Hall and I find a seat in the back row. I am early and the Hall is nearly empty. I reach into my pocket and I pull out the piece of paper. Just like on the Street Corner, my hands are shaking and my heart is pounding, my eyes won't focus I have to concentrate to make them focus, if I don't get whatever is in there and get it fast I'm going to go fucking crazy. My hands are shaking. I unfold it. There is nothing inside, though I'm not sure if I was expecting something inside. If there had been drugs, I don't know what I would have done with them. Part of me would have taken them immediately and with great need, part of me would have run to the nearest toilet to get rid of them. I don't know what I would have done.

I turn the paper over and there are words. I can see words I need to concentrate focus be calm enough to read the words I can read them. They say meet me in our Clearing at four. I read them again. Meet me in our Clearing at four. I read them over and over and they say the same thing over and over. Meet me in our Clearing at four. My hands are shaking shaking and my heart is beating beating and my eyes won't focus I have to concentrate to make them focus. Meet me in our Clearing at four. Again and again. Again and again.

Patients start trickling into the Lecture Hall. I carefully fold the piece of paper and return it to its place in my pocket. I sit staring straight ahead thinking about four o'clock until I am joined by Leonard and Ed and Ted and Matty and Miles. They are laughing and in jovial moods, talking about Bobby and reliving the games they played with him. They tell me that after I left, Ted told him that I was a Yoga Instructor from San

Francisco with an addiction to a rare Indian drug called shampoo, pronounced just like the hair product, but spelled champuu. Bobby's reaction was to say that he's beaten down a Yoga Instructor before, and that he wouldn't hesitate to do it again.

The Lecture starts and it is about the Fifth Step of the almighty Twelve. It is being given by a Catholic Priest. I don't listen to a word of it. I sit and I stare across the Lecture Hall. I sit and I stare at Lilly.

The Lecture ends. I stand and I follow the rest of the Patients out, enveloped in the flood toward the doors, enveloped in the flood of my memories. As I step out and into the Hall, Ken is standing waiting for me, waiting as he always waits, it seems as if he's always standing there waiting for me.

James?

What's up, Ken?

Checking to see if you've completed the First Step workbook.

I have not.

Have you looked at it?

Not since you gave it to me.

I'd like you to spend the morning working on it.

Okay.

Take your time, but if you finish, bring it by my Office. If I'm not there, just leave it on my desk.

Will do.

Any progress on the Goal Board?

No.

Put a little thought into that as well.

Okay.

I'll see you later?

Looking forward to it.

Ken chuckles and he walks away. I turn in the opposite direction and I walk to the Unit. I go to the Lower Level and I get a box of Crayolas and I check for Razzle Dazzle Rose. It's there as are sixty-three other beautiful crayons. As I start back up the stairs, I see the Goal Board hanging on a wall in the Upper Level. I walk over to it and I stand in front of it and I stare at it. It is a large piece of laminated posterboard divided into boxes using vertical and horizontal lines. In each of the boxes is a name, written in erasable marker, and next to the name is a goal. Some of the goals are simple, things such as Find a Job and Keep It, Stay Sober for Sixty Days, Be a Functioning Part of Society. Some of the goals are sad, things like Get My Wife to Talk to Me, Regain the Respect of My Children, Stay

Out of Jail for Six Months. Most of the goals are things like Improve My Relationship with My Friend and Savior the Lord Jesus Christ, Work the Program Right and Live the Steps in Every Moment, Get Myself in Shape: Be Buff in Mind, Be Buff in Spirit, Be Buff in Body. The goal next to Matty's name reads Stop Fucking Swearing, which makes me laugh. The goal next to Leonard's name reads Hold On, which makes me smile. The goal next to Miles's name reads Live, which makes the most sense. The space next to my name remains empty.

In the face of surviving long enough to survive in the long term, there is no goal that comes to mind that means anything to me. I could write Survive, but I would rather hold that word in my heart than write it on some fucking board. When I was laughing earlier, laughing about being a Yoga Instructor and being addicted to champuu, the laughing felt good. When I have laughed at all here, which has been too infrequent an occasion, it has always felt good. I could write Laugh on the board, but I would rather write something that makes me laugh every time I see it, so I pick up a marker and next to my name I write I'm Going to LA to Make All of My Dreams Come True. I'm Going to Be a Laker Girl. When I am finished I laugh. When I step back and I read my words again, I laugh. As I walk from the Upper Level and I enter the Hall which leads to my Room, I laugh. Laughing feels good. I haven't laughed enough and I want to laugh more. I'm Going to LA to Become a Motherfucking Laker Girl.

I walk into my Room and I sit down on my bed and I open the box of Crayolas and I open the workbook and I pull the Razzle Dazzle Rose from the box and I start reading. The first part of the book tells the story of Joe. Joe is a drunk who loses his Wife, his Job, all of his money, and ends up in the Street drinking cheap wine straight from the bottle. All the while, Joe refuses to admit that he has a problem or that he has lost control. The story is told in simple words and in simple pictures consisting of empty outlines of figures and places, the inside of the outlines being the part that needs coloring. The idea, I am guessing, is that while spending time filling in the pictures, I am supposed to grasp the horror of Joe's story and then relate that horror to situations in my own life. If Joe is out of control, I must be out of control as well. If Joe ended up on the Street, I better be careful, or I will end up in the Street with him. In the back of the book, after the conclusion of Joe's story, which has a happy ending when he admits that he has lost all control and he joins AA, is a twenty-seven-question survey about the pattern of an individual's drinking. The questions are simple and all of them require yes or no answers. Did you ever wake up on the morning after drinking and discover that you could not remember part of the evening before? Yes. Are there certain situations when you feel uncomfortable if alcohol is unavailable? Yes. When you are sober, do you regret things you have done while you were drinking? Yes. Do you have the shakes in the morning after drinking? Yes. Do you sometimes stay drunk for several days at a time? Yes, yes, yes, yes, yes. I answer yes to every question, all twenty-seven of them, which, according to the key at the end of the survey, means that I'm in the late stages of chronic and dangerous Alcoholism. Tell me something I don't fucking know.

I put the Razzle Dazzle Rose crayon back in the box and I pull out the Black crayon. Unlike most of the other crayons, Black has hardly been used. People probably avoid Black because it isn't considered a happy color, and in here any form of happiness, even something as base as the color of a crayon, is coveted. I, however, like Black. It is a color that makes me comfortable and the color with which I have the most experience. In the darkest darkness, all is Black. In the deepest hole, all is Black. In the terror of my Addicted mind, all is Black. In the empty periods of my lost memory, all is Black. I like Black goddamnit, and I am going to give it its due.

I flip back the pages of the book until I reach the first page. I pick up the beautiful Black crayon and I write **I** in a large, simple, block style, starting at the top of the page and finishing at the bottom, crossing over and ignoring any and all of the outlined figures. On the next page I write **Don't.** On each of the following pages I write **Need This Bullshit To Know I'm Out Of Control.** When I am finished I review my work. Each page looks perfect and I like it. I close the book. Job well done, James. I don't need this bullshit to know I'm out of control. Job well done.

I have an hour before lunch, so I toss the coloring book on the floor where it belongs and I pick up the *Tao Te Ching*. I look at it, front and back, at the stupid quotes and the silly lettering and the funny name. I wonder if I was suffering from an episode of insanity when I last read it. I wonder if I was just tired or vulnerable from my encounter in the Clearing with Lilly. I wonder if the sound of Miles's clarinet had somehow hypnotized me. I look at the book and I wonder how it affected me the way it did. I read only four pages.

I open it at number five on page five. I let my eyes run across the words. I let my brain process them. I let my heart feel them. Number five is like the rest. There is no good or evil, no Sinner or Saint. There simply is what is and that is it. You can use that to be and that is enough. Don't talk about it or question it. Just let it be. Just be.

It still affects me and it still makes sense. It still moves me and it still rings true. That is all that matters. The truth. Does it ring true it does. I can feel it.

Number six. The Tao is the Great Mother the Great Father the Great Nothing. It is empty and inexhaustible. It is always present you can use it or not. Does it ring true it does.

Seven. Infinite and eternal. It was never born and will never die. It is just there. It wants nothing and it needs nothing, it is just there. Stay behind and get ahead. Detach and become. Let go of all and you will be full. Let go of all and you will be full.

Eight and nine say the good is like water that nourishes without trying. They say in thinking keep to simple, in conflict be fair. They say don't compare or compete simply be yourself. They say fill your bowl to the brim and it will spill, keep sharpening your knife and it will dull. They say chase after money and your heart will never unclench. Care about what other people think and you will always be their prisoner.

These things, these poems, these words, these meanings, they make sense to me. They do not tell me to do anything or be anything or believe in anything or become anything. They don't judge me or try to convince me. There is no righteousness or pretension. They don't fight me or insult me or tell me I'm wrong. There is no Authority and there are no Rules. They are just words strung together on a page sitting and waiting patiently for me to accept or reject them. They don't care if I do either or both or nothing at all. They will never tell me I'm wrong. They will never tell me I'm right either. They just sit there.

I don't read them again. I close the book and I let them sit. I am on my bed and I like my bed. It is soft and warm and I am not soft or warm but I imagine that it would be nice to be that way. I have never known it. I know a cold, hard, raging Fury deep inside of me and I am tired of it. I am tired of the feeling, I want to die so that I don't have to feel it anymore. I would like to be soft and warm. I would be terrified to be that way. I could be hurt if I were soft and warm. I could be hurt by something other than myself. It is harder to be soft than it is to be hard. I could be hurt by something other than myself.

It is nearing noon. I can hear men talking outside my Room. They are walking to the Dining Hall they are laughing about something I wonder what they'll feel when the laughing stops. In here laughing is the only drug. Laughing or love. They are both drugs.

I get out of bed and I take my coloring book to Ken's Office. It's empty, so I leave the book on his desk. I go to the Dining Hall and I get a plate of macaroni and beef and I sit down with the same men I eat with at every meal. Matty, Ed, Ted, Leonard, Miles. It's a typical meal. Stories and swearing and a few laughs. As we're finishing, Lincoln walks over and tells us we don't have to go to the Lecture, that we're having a Unit Meeting instead. Ed asks him why and he says don't worry about it, just show up.

I finish eating and I put my tray on the conveyor. I walk back to the Unit and I join the rest of the men on the Lower Level. They are sitting on the couches smoking cigarettes and drinking coffee. The topic of conversation is Roy. The latest theory making rounds is that he was drunk. Alcohol can do powerful things to a person, but as the various drug theorists point out, Roy did not have the slurred speech and dulled reactions that are indicative of a serious drinking binge. They say it had to be drugs, though they argue among themselves as to what type. Bobby, who wasn't here when the incident took place, tries to end the argument with a proclamation that Roy must have been using a powerful type of diet pills, that he's seen it happen a dozen times before on Wall Street. Matty tells him he's fucking crazy goddamn diet pills can't fucking do that to a motherfucking Person. Bobby asks Matty if he knows what Wall Street is and where it's located. Matty tells Bobby it ain't gonna fucking matter where the fuck Wall Street is when I drop your fat fucking ass with a nice right hand. Bobby laughs and says go ahead, Little Man, it will be the last mistake you ever make. Matty stands up and takes a step forward, but Leonard tells him to sit down, that Bobby isn't worth the trouble. Matty sits down.

Lincoln walks in and he pulls up a chair and he sits at the head of the group. Everyone quiets down and waits for him to start talking. He sits down and he stares at the floor for a moment and he looks up. He speaks. Most of you know Roy and witnessed his behavior last night. For those of you who don't know him or didn't witness it, here's the deal. Roy was a Patient here. For the most part, he was an exemplary Patient. He worked hard on himself, he worked hard on his Program, he listened and he followed all of our Rules. When he left a week or so ago, I, along with most of the rest of the Staff, was confident in his prospects for a long-term recovery.

Last night, at about three-thirty, he snuck past Security, entered this Facility and came down to the Unit. He was carrying a large stick and he climbed on top of that couch.

He points to one of the couches.

He started screaming. Security was called, and I was on the Nightshift, and when we came down here and confronted him, he claimed to be someone named Jack and he threatened to beat us with his stick. He was subdued and removed from the Unit and taken to the Medical Unit and examined. From there he was taken to a Mental Institution.

At this point, we believe with fair certainty that Roy suffers from MPD, which stands for Multiple Personality Disorder. For those of you who don't know what MPD is, it is a psychological condition in which two or more distinct Identities, each with its own pattern of perceiving, relating to and thinking about the environment and self, exist within a single Person. Although some of the personalities know of each other, often they do not, and they can exist entirely independent of one another for great lengths of time. Last night, we observed at least four, and possibly five, separate personalities existing within Roy. One of them was the guy we came to know while he was here.

It was a very sad and upsetting night last night. I was Roy's Counselor, and I was very proud of him and the work we did together while he was here. I hope all of you will say a prayer for him, in whatever way it is that you pray. Any questions?

The Bald Man speaks.

How'd you not know about this with all the tests and everything?

Except for a couple of incidents, which I am viewing differently in retrospect, his primary and dominant personality was the Person who was here. If that Person was taking all the tests and doing all the work, we would have no way of knowing anything else was going on.

One of the new men speaks. He is tall and skinny and wears black designer glasses.

Is this common?

No. I've never seen it before, and as far I know, nobody else here has either.

Miles speaks.

Is there treatment for it?

Long-term psychiatric care, support groups, intensive therapy. Most of the treatment methods are similar to what are used for other profound and incurable mental illnesses.

Ted speaks.

I got a question.

What?

Ted speaks.

I never liked Roy, so I'm wondering if you could bring him back here with his Bitch personality so that I could slap his ass around a bit.

Everybody laughs. Lincoln stares, speaks.

Not funny, Ted.

I ain't trying to be funny. I wanna bitch-slap that Motherfucker.

More laughs. Lincoln shakes his head, tries to ignore Ted.

Any other questions?

Nobody speaks. Lincoln stands.

Let's get our afternoon started. Fourth Step Group stay here, Third Step Group up top, the rest of you do your individual assignments. James, come with me to Joanne's office.

The men go to their areas of group assignment or off on their own. I get up and I walk with Lincoln to Joanne's office. He does not speak to me and I do not speak to him. Neither of us looks at the other. When we get there, he knocks on the door. We hear Joanne's voice from behind.

Come in.

He opens the door, we step inside. Joanne is sitting behind her desk, she motions for us to sit. Lincoln sits on the couch. I take a chair between the couch and the desk. Joanne speaks.

Hi, James. How are you?

Fine. You?

I'm fine.

She holds up my First Step workbook.

Care to explain this?

I laugh.

I think it's pretty self-explanatory.

Lincoln speaks, an edge of anger in his voice.

It's completely unacceptable. That and your goal are an insult to what we're trying to do with you.

I thought that fucking book was an insult to my intelligence, and my goal is a joke. I put it up there because it makes me laugh, and laughing makes me feel good, and that's my only goal, to feel good. When I feel good, I feel like I'm getting better.

Joanne speaks.

I understand your intentions, James, though I'm not sure they're appropriate.

Lincoln speaks.

They aren't.

Joanne speaks.

We try to plan a Patient's Recovery Program and their future after they leave here as they are working through what we do and what we teach. At this point, you're not as far along as we would like. You seem to have some grasp of the First Step.

I laugh.

Why are you laughing?

I speak.

The First Step, if I remember correctly, says we admitted we were power-less over alcohol and drugs, that our lives had become unmanageable. I have a fairly sound grasp of that concept.

Lincoln speaks.

You're sure of that?

I'm wanted in three states. I'm addicted to alcohol and crack. I'm unem-ployed, unemployable and completely broke. I've blacked out every night for as long as I can remember and my time in here is the longest stretch of sobriety I've known since I was ten years old. I am out of control. If you want to hear me say it, I'll say it. I am out of fucking control. My life is un-manageable.

Joanne speaks.

We're not the enemy, James.

I know you're not.

Lincoln speaks.

Don't treat us like we are.

Don't treat me like an idiot, talk to me like I'm a fucking Baby and waste my time with coloring books, and I won't treat you like the enemy.

Lincoln shakes his head. Joanne speaks.

Getting back to the subject, you are not as far along as we would like. You are resistant to everything we tell you. We don't think that you'll be ready to move into a normalized existence once this Program is over. If you're not facing Jail time, and that is something we would like to start working on by contacting the Authorities in the states in which you have issues, we want to put you on a waiting list for a Halfway House.

What would I do there?

It would be a lot like this, except you'd be expected to hold a job during the day.

No way.

Lincoln speaks.

Why?

Because that's not gonna work for me.

Why?

I'm starting to figure out how I think I can do this. I won't know until I'm in the real World and until I can test myself. That test will not be real to me if I know that I can go running back to the safety of some Halfway House.

Joanne speaks.

There is no such thing as safety when you're dealing with a profound and incurable addiction. Halfway Houses offer support and you're going to need all the support you can get. You're going to need it when you leave here, a month later, a year after that, and most likely, for the rest of your life.

I don't want safety or support. I want there to be me and whatever I have to face, be it alcohol or drugs or something else. I want there to be a fight because I know how to fight. There will be a Winner of that fight. If it's me, I walk away and I have beat the shit that I didn't think I could ever beat and I move on with my life. If it's not me, at least I get it over with.

Lincoln speaks.

If you don't survive your little test, you're gonna die. Is that what you want to do, die?

If I can't stay sober it is.

You won't stay sober if you keep doing what you're doing.

Why do you think that?

It's not what I think, it's what I know. I know it because every time someone comes in here thinking they have a better way, they walk out of here and they fall and they don't get back up.

You may be right, but at least I'll fall knowing I did the best I could with what I believed in.

Joanne speaks.

I don't like this idea of a test. I think it's dangerous, foolish and stubborn. I think the stakes are too high for you if it doesn't work out. I want you to think about that. To really think about the idea that your resistance to what we're trying to do with you may cause your death. Meet me here tomorrow after morning Lecture and you and I will talk about things and hopefully move forward.

I stand.

Do I need to do anything else this afternoon?

Just think.

I'll see you tomorrow.

I walk to the door and I walk out and I shut the door behind me and I walk back to the Unit. I go to my Room and I look at the clock next to Miles's bed it reads three forty-two. I am meeting Lilly in eighteen minutes.

I get Hank's jacket. I put it on and I walk through the Unit. I open one of the glass doors and I step outside. I walk through the grass there is no dew and I find the Trail and I enter the Wood there is Sun streaming through gaps in the trees like girders of light. I walk along the Trail. I see broken branches and I see torn leaves spread like crumbs and the torn leaves lead me. The signs of my destruction lead me.

I push my way through the thick and I step into the Clearing. It is empty. I sit down on the dirt and I lie back and I close my eyes. I have not slept enough and I am tired. I need more sleep I am tired. Tired. I am tired.

I feel a hand on my face. It's soft and warm, resting on my cheek, caressing it without moving. Lips follow it on the other cheek, full and wet and soft and gentle. There is sweet breath behind and sweet breath after. They both leave my cheek I wish they would stay. I open my eyes and I slowly sit up. Lilly is next to me, bundled in a large green Army jacket, black hair in braided pigtails, her pale skin reflecting a girder of Sun. She smiles and she speaks.

Hi.

What time is it?

She looks at a cheap plastic Superwoman watch on her wrist. Beneath it I see scars.

Four-ten.

I rub my face.

I fell asleep.

She smiles again.

I woke you up.

I smile.

I'm glad.

She leans forward and she kisses me on the cheek. She holds her lips soft wet warm and gentle. My instinct is to pull away, but I don't. When she pulls away, she leaves sweet breath behind her.

Answer a question for me.

Okay.

Do you have a Girlfriend?

I hesitate, a flash of her, Arctic and blonde.

No.

Why'd you hesitate?

I did, but I don't anymore. I thought of her for a second.

Where is she?

I have no idea.

When was the last time you spoke to her?

About a year ago.

You over her?

No.

Lilly smiles, leans forward and she kisses my lips.

That's too bad.

I smile. I have no words. If I did have words, they would mean nothing.

You want a smoke?

She reaches into one of the pockets of her jacket and she pulls out a pack of cigarettes.

Yeah.

I take one.

You got a lighter?

I reach into my pocket, pull out a lighter.

Yeah.

I flip it, light her smoke, light mine.

You having a good day?

I inhale. I feel the nicotine immediately. It doesn't feel as good as Lilly's kiss.

It's been long.

She inhales, stares at me.

They're all long in here.

My instinct is to look away, but I don't.

Yeah.

Tell me something.

All right.

Why are you here?

Here at this place or here with you?

Either one.

I don't know.

She smiles.

That's a good answer.

My instinct is to look away, but I don't. I speak.

Why are you here?

She smiles.

Here at this place or here with you?

I smile.

Either.

I came to this place because of my Grandma.

She brought you in?

She convinced me to bring myself in.

How'd she do that?

She loved me and she took care of me even though I was a total disaster, and whenever I did something stupid, which was pretty much every day, she told me that when I was ready to learn about freedom, I should come talk to her. A while back something really, really awful happened. It fucked me up bad and I went and found her and I asked her what she meant. She told me that I was a Prisoner of my Mom and all of her problems and a Prisoner of my Dad who I don't remember and she told me that I was a Prisoner of drugs and sex and of myself. She told me that living life as a Prisoner was a waste of life and that freedom, even a second of freedom, was worth more than a lifetime of bondage. She told me if I wanted to learn more, to come talk to her again the next day. I did, and she told me the same thing. A second of freedom is worth more than a lifetime of bondage. Then she said come back again the next day. I did and she handed me a map and she said let's get in the car, you're driving. Eight hours later that map led me here. She said she had been saving money for three years and if I wanted freedom I should walk in the front doors and she'd pay for it. She said if I didn't, we should drive Home. I hate my life. I have never wanted it to be the way it has been, and this was a chance to escape it. I had heard of this place and knew it was the best place like it and really expensive and I knew if Grandma had saved for me to be here that she wanted it for me and I knew I wanted it as well. To be free, even if it's just for a second. So I walked through the doors and here I am.

You free yet?

No, but I'm getting there.

She smiles.

You tell me a story now.

About what?

Tell me about your Girlfriend.

I don't like talking about her.

Why?

Because it hurts too much.

Fair enough. Tell me something else.

Pick something.

How'd you lose your virginity?

Why do you want to know that?

It says a lot about a Person.

It won't say good things about me.

I'm not here to judge you.

Why are you here?

To know you. Or to try.

I stare at her. I stare at her eyes clean water blue and her hair braided jet

black. I stare at her skin pale white and her lips blood red, I stare at her
body beneath the jacket she is so small. I stare at her wrists and the
Superwoman watch and the scars running vertically. I stare at me but not
me. I see the damage and pain of hard years. I see the emptiness and des-
peration of existence without hope. I see a young life that has been too
long. I see me but not me. I trust myself. I can trust her.
I've never told anyone this.
You don't have to tell me if you don't want to.
No, I will.
Stop whenever you want.
I stare at her. I see me but not me. I can trust her. I speak.
I was sixteen, a Sophomore in High School. It was Homecoming and
there was a Football Game and a Dance. I hated the Town we lived in
and my Parents knew I hated it and they felt bad about it. My Mom
would always ask me about friends and Girls because she hoped I would
meet some People and then I'd be happier. I always lied to her and told
her that I had lots of friends and that lots of Girls liked me so that she
wouldn't feel so bad. The reality of the situation was that nobody liked
me. As this Dance was coming up my Mom kept asking if I was going. I
told her I hadn't decided yet, that there were a couple of Girls who
wanted to go with me and I wasn't sure which one I liked most and I
really just hoped she'd stop asking. She didn't. Every day it was the same.
Who are you going to ask, you should decide soon, you need to give the
Girl enough time to get ready, it's a special night you shouldn't miss it.
Finally I just lied to her and told her I was taking someone. She was really
excited and she went out and she got me a suit and she bought me a rose
to pin on my lapel and she washed her car and told me I could borrow it
and she gave me some money to go out to Dinner before the Game. It
fucking sucked because I knew it was all bullshit and I was lying to her.
When the day of the Game came around, I put on the suit and she and my
Dad took a bunch of pictures of me and I waved out the car window as I
drove away. I parked the car near the School Stadium and I sat and
watched all the other Kids, the ones who had dates, as they drove in and
hung around in the Stands or on the Sidelines in their suits and dresses
and I watched the Halftime Ceremony and I watched the King and Queen
get crowned and I watched everyone clap and cheer for them and I
watched everyone be happy. When the Game was over, I didn't have anything to do, and I sure wasn't going to go to the Dance alone, so I drove to
this Ghetto nearby to try and score some drugs because I felt like shit for
lying to my Mom and because I didn't have any friends and I wanted to

make the pain go away. As I was driving around, I saw a whore walking on the Street near a House where I used to buy. She would stare at me and wave at me as I passed and I couldn't find any drugs so I finally just pulled over. She walked up to the car and asked if I wanted a Date and I said how much and she told me and it was just a little bit less than the money my Mom had given me so I said yes. I don't know why I did it. I guess I was just lonely and sad and hoping to find some sort of love that would make me feel better. What happened was awkward and stupid and disgusting. The woman smelled and talked to me in this fake dirty voice and it was over in about two seconds. I took her back to the Street and I drove around for the next couple hours trying to talk myself out of driving full speed into a tree. When I went home I told my Mom and Dad I had a great time and I thanked them for everything they gave me and I went to my Room. When I knew they were asleep, I stole a bottle from their liquor cabinet and drank it and cried myself to sleep.

I take a deep breath, stare at the ground.

It fucking sucked, and to be honest, I want to kill myself right now even thinking about it. I hate that it happened, and like most everything in my life, it was not what I had hoped for.

I stare at the ground. If there was a hole deep enough, I would climb in. If there were drugs that could obliterate all, I would take them until all was obliterated. I want to kill myself right now even thinking about it.

I look up. There are tears running down Lilly's cheek and she is smiling at me. It is a deep smile, not the type of momentary happiness, but the rare kind that comes when something inside without words is woken from slumber and brought forth to live. Though I know it will disappear from her face, it will stay in her and with her long after it does. It has woken and it will live. I reach up and I gently wipe her tears away. Her skin is soft and the wetness is warm on my hand. As my fingers slide from her chin she takes them into her own hand and she holds them. She stares at me with eyes clean water blue thicker now with lament. Her smile not gone she speaks.

That was beautiful.

She is holding my hand.

No, it wasn't.

If she let go, I would fall apart.

It was. It was beautiful because it was honest and it was beautiful because it hurt and it was beautiful because you didn't have to tell it to me.

Fall apart.

It makes me feel like shit.

What if I told you I lost my virginity as a whore, instead of with one.

I would say I'm sorry.

I did.

I'm sorry.

She smiles.

Thank you.

She looks at her watch with her free hand, looks at me.

We should go.

She stands and she pulls me up with her. We stare at each other for a moment and she puts her free hand on my cheek. She does not let go of my hand with her other hand and I am glad she doesn't.

I'll call you tonight.

Good.

You don't have to, but I'd like it if you took the call this time.

I smile.

I fell asleep last night.

You can fall asleep tonight if you want as well, but I hope you don't.

I won't.

She leans forward and she kisses me. Though it is the same as before, it isn't the same at all. It is more, stronger, weaker, deeper, quieter, louder. It is more, vulnerable, impenetrable, fragile, secure, unprotected, completely protected. It is more, open, deeper, full, simpler, true. It is more. True.

She pulls away her lips pull away. Without words we walk hand in hand through the thick Wood. At the dense edge near the Trail she stops and she guides me forward and our hands slide slowly apart until there are two fingers one each of our fingers touching not wanting to let go or be away. I stop. I let my finger the tip of my finger touch hers the tip of her finger. We stare at each other. Her smile has not gone away and mine will not either. It will be there when I'm not smiling it will still be there. A smile and a kiss and the tips of two fingers. Touching.

She nods and I know the nod means it is time to let go and I do. I turn and I walk away. I know she's watching me walk away, smiling, and I know she wants me to turn around. I do. I turn around and she is there and she is smiling. I smile back and it is more than just a smile. It is more.

I make my way back to the Unit. I walk in and I walk through the Halls to dinner. Every meal is now the same.

After dinner there is a Lecture. A man telling his life story. He was bad and he joined AA and now he's good. I have heard it too many times.

I go back to the Unit and I sit and I watch TV. There is a sitcom about some witty New Yorkers who spend all of their time in one Apartment. One of the men praises the show and he talks about how real it is. The only people I know who spend so much time in one Apartment usually have black plastic taped over the windows and guns in the closet and burn marks on their lips and fingers and huge locks on the doors. They are not witty people, though their paranoia can be amusing. I don't see anything like that on this show, but it is supposedly very real. Maybe I don't know what real is anymore.

The phone rings, the phone has been ringing all night. This ring, however, draws my attention. Somehow I know it is Lilly even though I shouldn't and even though I have no reason to know that it is Lilly. I stand and I am walking before the man calls out my name. As he does, I take the receiver and I thank him and I put the receiver to my ear and I speak.

Hi.

Hi.

How are you?

Good. You?

I'm good.

I miss you.

I laugh.

You miss me?

Yeah, I miss you. Why's that funny?

No one has ever missed me before. People tend to be happy when I'm gone.

She laughs.

Not me.

Good. I like that you miss me.

I like it too.

I smile.

What'd you do tonight?

Sat here and watched the clock until I thought I could call you without seeming desperate.

I laugh.

What'd you do?

Sat here and waited for you to call and thought about what I was gonna say to you so that I didn't sound desperate.

She laughs, speaks.

I guess we're desperate.

Probably a bit.

For what?
Freedom. However we can find it.
And you think one of those forms could be each other?
Maybe.
It wasn't what I expected when I came here.
You shouldn't expect anything now. You should just wait and see what happens.
Well said.
Thank you.
You want to meet me again tomorrow.
Sure.
You can tell me another story.
I think it's your turn.
I think you're right.
You got anything in mind?
Ask me a question, same as I did to you, and I'll give you an answer.
And whatever that answer is, I won't judge you.
Thank you.
I'll see you tomorrow.
I miss you.
I like that you miss me.
I like that you like it.
Bye.
Bye.
I put the receiver in the cradle and I stare at the phone and I smile. It's not just a smile of momentary happiness. When it disappears from my face, it will stay with me.
I turn and I walk through the Unit and into the Hall and toward my Room. As I approach it, I can hear the soft sounds of Miles's clarinet drifting through the door. I stop outside and I listen to it. He is playing low like he always plays low. He is holding the notes for longer than I would think he'd be able to hold them. He is repeating a melody over and over each time with variations. It is simple music, made by one man and his lungs and a piece of metal with holes and his fingers moving along the holes. It is just sound low then higher slow then faster slow again and low, repeated with variations. There are no words and there is no singing, but the music has a voice. It is an old voice and a deep voice, like the stump of a sweet cigar or a shoe with a hole. It is a voice that has lived and lives, with sorrow and shame, ecstasy and bliss, joy and pain, redemption and damnation. It is a voice with love and without love. I like the

voice, and though I can't talk to it, I like the way it talks to me. It says it is all the same, Young Man. Take it and let it be.

The song the melody the old, low and slow voice ends. It ends and it trails off into the quiet of a sleeping Hall. I open the door and I step into my Room. Miles sitting on his bed his lips are still holding the reed. He nods to me and I nod back to him. I walk over to my bed. I take off my clothes and I climb beneath the covers of my bed and they are warm and I like them and I close my eyes and I curl into myself my head against the pillow I curl into myself and the voice begins again. Sorrow and shame and ecstasy and bliss and joy and pain and redemption and damnation and love and without.

It is all the same, Young Man.

Take it and let it be.

I have an empty bottle in one hand. I have an empty pipe in the other. I am standing on a Street Corner littered with trash. There are shoes hanging from the telephone wires. The ghosts of the rock are screaming. Dealers are hawking their wares. I have an empty bottle in one hand, I have an empty pipe in the other. I'm looking for more.

I wake shaking and shaken. I know I was dreaming, but it doesn't matter. The liquor was real. The crack was real. The ghosts were real and the dealers were real. It was all real. I am shaking and shaken.

I put my arms around myself. I curl into a ball. I think about what is good in my life. I try to occupy my mind. I have been sober for a few weeks. I have friends. Matty and Ed and Ted. Miles and Leonard and Lilly. I have a Brother Bob. I have some clothes and I have some books. It is more than enough.

Roaring pit bulls straining chains. A dead grass yard. Rats scurry across the floor they bite sleeping faces. An empty House no furniture nothing. It is empty but for empty People. The ghosts of the rock. There is smoke in the air mixed with gas and formaldehyde. I am screaming. Screaming pleading begging for more. Give me more please give me more I want need have to have more. I'll give my life heart soul money future everything please give me more. I want need have to have more. Give me more and I'll give you everything. Give me more and I'll do whatever you want. Give me more. Give me more. Give me more.

I wake shaking and shaken. I know I was dreaming, but it doesn't matter. It was real. The dogs the rats the House the People the rock. The great and terrible rock. It was real and I smoked it. I am shaking and shaken.

I curl tighter try to think of the good. I have more than I need, more than enough. Curl tighter. Think of the good. Think of the good.

Another dream.

Another dream.

Each time I sleep.

Another dream.

They are real.

Real.

Another dream.

I am shaking and shaken. I can see light through the window. I stand. I am unsteady as I walk to the Bathroom. I open the door and I fall to my knees and I crawl to the toilet and I am sick. Over and over again. I am violently sick. It is another reminder of the life I have lived. The sickness and the blood and the bile and the chunks of my stomach. Sitting in the water beneath my nose. Another reminder.

I stand up and I step into the shower and I turn on the heat. I step under the stream and I let the water run down and across and over and off of me. I fight the urge to vomit again I am fucking tired of being sick. They were only dreams. This can't keep happening. They were only dreams.

I step out and I grab a towel and I wrap it around my waist and I walk to the sink and I brush my teeth. The taste of my sickness mixes with the taste of my toothpaste. I wash my mouth, but the taste doesn't go away. I wash it again and it doesn't go away. I wash it again. It is not going away. I stop washing my mouth and I shave. As I stand in front of the mirror with the razor, I look at my body. I am getting bigger. I am acquiring flesh. The veins on my arms are still blue, but they are a lighter blue. The bones of my cheek and the line of my jaw are less defined, the bruises that covered me are gone. There is a thin layer of fat over all of me and I am starting to get a belly. I look less like what I am and more like a human being. I am becoming more like a human being.

I finish shaving and I rinse the residue from my face. I take a deep breath and I look at the base of the mirror and I start to move slowly up. I see my chest, my collarbone, the base of my neck. I want to see my eyes. I see my throat, my Adam's apple, the curve of my neck into my chin I want to see my eyes. I see my lips they are healed. I see my cheek it is scarred. I see my nose no longer swollen. I see the area beneath my eyes. It has bags, but they are gray bags of wear not the black and yellow bags of violence. There is green above them. Pale green. As I move toward it, I stop and I breathe. I hold beneath pale green. I can see the lash below. I can see the white beneath. I breathe. It's there. I hold and it's there. Pale green.

I turn around. I walk out of the Bathroom. Miles is still sleeping I try to be quiet. I get dressed and I walk out of my Room the Hall is still asleep. I walk into the Upper Level of the Unit and I make the coffee. I wait for it to brew. When it is ready, I pour myself a tall cup steaming hot and black. I sit at a table and I light a cigarette. I am alone. I sit and I drink and I smoke. I don't think about what I'm doing or why I'm doing it. I just sit there alone. I drink and I smoke.

One of the sliding glass doors opens. I look down and I see Leonard walking into the Lower Level of the Unit. He is wearing a jogging outfit and his face is red it is dripping with sweat. He looks as if he is in better shape than when I met him. He's thin, his jawline is visible, his cheeks are flush. He looks like a healthy suburban Father coming home from a jog. He sees me, walks toward me.

What's up, Leonard?

Out for a run.

How was it?

It sucked.

He gets a cup of coffee, sits down at the table.

You got one of those for me?

I didn't think you smoked.

I just did something good to my body. Now I want to do something bad to it.

I laugh, hand him a smoke, light it. He takes a deep drag, looks at me.

I hear you're seeing that Girl with the black hair.

What Girl?

The Crackhead.

Where'd you hear that?

I never betray a Source.

We're friends, but that's not going to stop me from beating your ass if you don't tell me who told you that.

He laughs.

Ted told me.

How would he know?

He sneaks out every night and meets some Girl in the Woods. I guess that Girl is on the same Unit as your Girl, and if you didn't know by now, Girls talk about that shit.

There's not much to talk about.

Not much means there's something.

I've met her out there a couple times. We talk. It's no big deal.

You like her?

Yeah.

She good to you?

There's no good or bad, we just talk.

You look different right now. That's a good sign.

I smile.

You're making a big deal out of nothing, Leonard.

I'm only interested in your happiness, Kid. If you're happy, I'm happy.

I'm not happy, but I'm not unhappy.

You'll be happy soon. Just hold on.

We'll see.

He holds up the cigarette, looks at it.

These things are fucking disgusting.

I laugh.

They're all I got left.

He stubs it out, stands.

I'm gonna take a shower. Wait for me and we'll go to breakfast.

He leaves. I sit and I wait and I smoke cigarettes and I drink coffee. I watch men begin to filter in and out of the Unit. Some are doing their morning Jobs, some are getting coffee, some are buying candy or cans of soda from the machines. I don't talk to any of them. I just sit and I stare out a window. I don't know what's outside the window and I don't particularly care, it is but a point on which to focus my eyes while I drink and I smoke. I drink and I smoke.

Leonard comes back into the Upper Level. He is clean and his hair is wet. He says I'm hungry let's eat and I stand and we walk to the Dining Hall. I get in line and I get a plate of eggs and bacon and he gets a plate of pancakes and we find a table. We are joined by our friends. As we eat, we talk about the upcoming Heavyweight Championship. Matty knows the fighters and he speaks of the fight with great enthusiasm, stopping and swearing at himself for swearing, jabbing and moving as if he is in the Ring. We sit and laugh and after a few moments, everyone except Matty stops talking. He talks enough for all of us.

After breakfast another Lecture. We play cards in the back row.

After Lecture, Joanne is waiting for me outside the Hall. She says I am with her this morning and we walk through the Halls toward her Office. The Halls are bright and I do not mind. When we walk inside, she sits down in one of the comfortable chairs and I sit on the couch. She lights a cigarette and I light a cigarette. She leans back, settles in, speaks.

You think about our conversation yesterday?

No.

Why?

Because I'm not going to change my mind and I'm not going to bother thinking about changing my mind.

James, you are an incredibly Addicted Person. You have been told by qualified Doctors that any drug or alcohol use is going to kill you. In all of my experience, I have never seen anyone stay sober and survive in the long term using anything but AA and the Twelve Steps. They may last a week or a month or in the best cases a year, but without the necessary support, all of them start using again and most of them die. Is that really what you want?

I'd rather have that than spend my life sitting in Church basements listening to People whine and bitch and complain. That's not productivity to me, nor is it progress. It is the replacement of one addiction with another, and if I'm gonna be Addicted to something, it's gonna be something I like.

AA is not a replacement addiction. It is a support group based around the Twelve Steps.

You can look at it however you want, but when someone stops doing one thing every day and starts doing another thing every day, that seems like a replacement addiction to me.

She takes a deep frustrated breath.

Would you rather be Addicted to something that makes you a better person and makes you healthier every day, or something that's going to kill you?

You can try whatever tricks you want, taking my position or reverse psychology or whatever else you got in your bag, but I'm not gonna believe in AA or the Twelve Steps. The whole thing is based on belief in God. I don't have that, and I never will.

It is based on a belief in a Higher Power, not God.

Same thing.

God, in our Society, is a man with a long flowing beard who sits on a chair in Heaven. You don't have to believe in that. A Higher Power can be anything you would like it to be or anything that gets you through the day. It could be the Sky, it could be Buddha. It could be the Force from *Star Wars*. AA does not try to push any one Higher Power or Religion or particular belief on you.

Let's get something straight before we talk about this anymore.

What?

Whether you're saying Higher Power or you're saying God, you're saying the same thing.

I think that's too general a statement. It discounts the diversity of the World's Spiritual Thought.

From where I sit, all Religion and Spiritual Thought are the same thing. They exist to make People feel better about living, to give them some kind of moral code, and to help them feel better about dying by promising something better when their life ends, provided they follow all of God's Rules.

Is something wrong with that purpose?

I think it's bullshit. I don't need something that doesn't exist to tell me how to live.

How can you be so sure that something Greater than ourselves doesn't exist?

How can you be so sure it does?

Because I have faith in it.

I don't.

She pauses, takes a deep breath, speaks.

What do you think faith is?

I think for a moment. I speak.

Faith is the belief in something that can't be proven to exist.

Have you ever considered it?

Yes.

And why don't you have it?

I think God is something that People use to avoid reality. I think faith allows People to reject what is right in front of our eyes, which is that this thing, this life, this existence, this consciousness, or whatever word you want to use for it, is all we have, and all we'll ever have. I think People have faith because they want and need to believe in something, whatever that something is, because life can be hard and depressing and brutal if you don't.

You may be right, but what about accepting the idea that faith can make your life better. I know my faith makes my life better, and whether what I believe in exists or not, because I have faith in it, I get the benefits of that faith.

I'm not going to ever have faith in God or anything like God.

Do you have faith in love?

Meaning what?

Do you believe in love?

Yeah.

Do you believe it can make your life better?

Yeah.

Do you have faith in anything else?

Friendship.

You believe in friendship?

Very much so.

Anything else?

What's your point?

You can't prove love or friendship exist, but you still have faith in them.

I'm asking you to try and apply the same principle to something Greater than yourself.

I can feel love and friendship. I can see and touch and talk to the People I love and the People I choose to make my friends. The idea of God doesn't make me feel anything and I can't see God or touch God or talk to God.

Have you ever tried to open yourself up to the idea of faith?

I've read the Bible. It didn't ring true to me. I know People who consider themselves close to God, but I've never understood their feelings. I've spent time in Churches, and I can appreciate their beauty and majesty, but nothing good has ever happened to me in a Church.

What does that mean?

Exactly what I said.

Is there something you aren't telling me?

Nothing that has anything to do with what we're talking about.

She stares at me, I stare at her. She speaks.

I want you to think more about this and try to come to terms with it. I want you to stop intellectualizing it and try to open yourself to it.

I've never believed in God, not even as a little Kid. I'm not going to start now.

Think about it.

Fine.

She stands and I stand and we walk to the door and she opens it.

There are going to be some alterations to your Program, which Ken will talk to you about this afternoon. Come back and talk to me when you're ready.

I walk out and I walk through the Halls. As I head to the Unit, I see Leonard walking toward me. He tells me it's time for lunch so we walk to the Dining Hall and we find a table. We are joined by Ed and Ted and Matty and Miles and Bobby.

Bobby tells stories and talks mountains of shit. I have this, I know this Person, they owe me this much money, on and on and on. At one point he starts talking about Las Vegas and a trip he took there for a meeting with Mikey the Nose. Leonard, who has been ignoring Bobby for most of lunch, starts listening to him. He does not speak, and it is not obvious that he's interested, but I can see him start to pay closer attention. Bobby says that Mikey was a fat, drunk pig, foolish with his money and foolish with his mouth, and that when he was finally taken out, there were parties all over New York. Bobby says that he owed Mikey a fairly large sum of money, and that with Mikey's death, the debt disappeared. Bobby says that the last time he went to Las Vegas, he went and found Mikey's grave and took a piss on it.

I watch Leonard as Bobby says these things. I watch his face remain a mask of calm, I watch his hands stay still upon the table. I know that if Bobby were saying these things about someone whom I loved, I'd be across the table and on his neck. Leonard just sits and listens. Leonard just sits and stares. We finish lunch and we stand and walk as a group to the Lecture. We sit in the back and we play cards. For the first time since I have known him, Leonard loses every hand we play. Ted wins three, Ed and Matty win two, Miles and I don't win any. When the Lecture is over, everyone gives Leonard his money back. We leave.

As we walk through the Halls and toward the Unit, Ken steps out of his Office and he asks to speak with me. I step into his Office and sit down and he does the same.

There are a few things we need to talk about today.

He picks up a piece of paper and he passes it to me.

This is a release so that we can have a Lawyer who works here contact the states in which you have issues and try to begin sorting them out. You need to read it, write down the states and Cities and what you think the problems are, and sign it. You don't have to do it, but we highly recommend that you do.

You got a pen?

Sure.

He picks up a pen and he hands it to me. I take it, start reading the document.

In a related, or somewhat related issue, we've noticed that you've become close to Leonard. We're a bit concerned about that.

I look up.

Why?

You're a young man with a tenuous relationship with the law. We don't think that he's going to be a good influence on you.

Why's that?

Do you have any idea what Leonard does for a living?

He's a Businessman of some sort.

Ken laughs.

What kind of business?

I haven't asked.

Have you ever noticed that people are scared of Leonard?

Yeah.

Why do you think that is?

Because he lives without fear. That tends to scare people.

That's not the reason, James.

What is the reason, Ken?

I'm assuming you know more than you're telling me, but I'll say it anyway. Leonard is involved in Organized Crime. He's a fairly major figure in that world. He has been asked not to discuss or flaunt what he does, and because he has real and serious Chemical Dependency issues, we did not turn him away, but we do keep a fairly close eye on him.

I shrug.

Everybody's gotta make a living.

That's your reaction?

That's my reaction.

We don't think you should spend so much time with him. We believe it's going to negatively impact your recovery.

Leonard and I are friends. I like him and I trust him and I respect him. I can't see how having a friend like that is going to hurt me.

Has he ever asked you to do anything illegal?

I laugh.

No.

Has he ever told you what he does for a living?

He says he's a Businessman, he doesn't say much else.

I would like a definition of much else.

I'm not talking about this anymore, Ken.

It's for your own good, James.

Next issue, Ken.

He takes a deep breath and he looks down at a stack of papers on his desk. He looks up.

Your Parents are coming here. They've enrolled in the Family Program.

What?

We've been talking to them fairly regularly since you got here and they've decided that they want to come to the Family Program. Everyone involved thinks it's a good idea.

You think about checking with me?

We had an idea about what your reaction would be.

When do they get here?

Tomorrow.

They're coming from Japan?

Yes.

I shake my head and I stare at the floor. I let it come and it comes fast. Anger, rage, hatred, shame and horror fusing into the Fury the perfect beautiful and terrible Fury. I can't do anything with it and I can't do anything to stop it unless I drink and kill it or do drugs and kill it or do both and kill it. I clench my jaw and I ball my fists and I fight myself. I want to get fucked up.

You okay?

I look at Ken.

No.

What are you feeling?

I'm angry.

Anything else?

I want to drink.

Anything else?

Get fucked up.

Anything else?

I want to jump over your goddamn desk and knock your fucking teeth down your throat.

Do I need to call Security?

I take a deep breath.

What's going to happen when they get here?

I clench my jaw.

You'll stay on the Unit at night and eat your meals as you usually do, but your day will be spent in the Family Center.

I squeeze my fists.

And what happens there?

You'll engage in Group Therapy with the other Patients and Family Members and you'll spend some one-on-one time with your Parents.

I hold on.

Sounds fucking great.

Why don't you want them here?

Because I don't.

Why?

I'm not talking to you about it anymore.

I look down at the release he has given me, write down the names of the Cities and the states, and I hand it back to him.

Anything else?

I think we need to start working on getting at the source of your anger.

I look at him and I laugh and I stand up and I walk out of his Office.

The Halls are bright and the Fury inside of me wants them down full of holes reduced to rubble. I hate these fucking Halls I want to destroy them destroy myself destroy everything. I breathe deeply and I hold on and I walk toward the Unit. I want to go outside and I want to breathe free air.

I want air that is not of this place and I want space that is not of this place. I want no walls, no Halls, no Units, no Counselors, no Rules, no God, no Higher Powers, no Steps, no Groups, no Lectures, no Dining Hall, nobody to see talk to deal with. I want to breathe. Free empty air.

I walk through the Upper Level and I walk down to the Lower Level and through a Group Session Lincoln is leading and he asks me what I'm doing and I ignore him and I open the glass doors and I step outside and I breathe breathe breathe and the air is free.

I start walking. I have no idea where I'm going, I'm just walking. I take a Trail and I follow it and it leads me into the cover of Evergreen. It's darker in here and I feel less vulnerable and more comfortable. I am breathing deeply, as deeply as I can breathe, and the air is calming me down. The Fury has dissipated and is a walking rage, an anger like fire, entirely controllable, and easy to stop it from burning or hurting anything.

The Sun is high, its light shattered by tree branches, their streams illuminate dirt, dead leaves and rotting plants killed by the Winter's cold. Frost sparkles in the shade waiting to melt. In an hour it will be gone. In ten hours it will return. Another day another cycle here gone back tomorrow gone again. I am cold. Warmth is in the light but I avoid it. As I walk, I'll get warmer. I'm in no hurry.

I follow the Trail and the Trail leads me along the Lake. The Lake is the same as it is each day the same. Sheets of ice, life below, birds above. Noise destroying silence, silence overwhelming noise. Reflections slowly move along the water distorting what is real the object or the image. They are both real and it is all real. It all is in front of me life is in front of me and behind me above me below me surrounding me. I can see it and feel it and hear it and touch it. Inside and outside. Right now.

A bench is empty. I sit down close my eyes open myself. I don't know to what I am opening myself. Is it God or something Higher. Is it me or what is around me. Does it matter do I need to know. It matters because it is what is keeping me together. This opening is allowing me to pick up the pieces of a shattered life. I need to believe in it to continue to believe in me. I need to know what it is. What is it that opens me.

I stand and I walk along the edge of the water until it ends in a Sea of yellow grass. The grass is dead now but will return in the Spring that is the way of the World. Things die and they return. Is that biology or God or something Higher. Are we biology or God or something Higher. I know my heart beats and I listen to it. The beat is biology, but what is the song. Will this song ex-

ist when the beating stops. Will one stay when one is gone, can one live
without the other. Does it matter. It does. I have to believe in something. It
is holding me together.

Up the Pine walk and across the murky desolation of swamp and rot and
life existing because of death. Back down into dense Oak and Evergreen.
The Sun is still hot and high its rays still scattered still dancing across the
floor of earth and my feet are moving easily. The Fury is gone, replaced
with free air and the quiet emptiness of a solitary calm. I am quiet and
empty. I am calm.

If there is anything I seek it is this. The calm. If there is God or something Higher for me it is this. The calm. If there is something that will
hold me when I need to hold it is this the calm. There is no anger, no
rage, no Fury. There is no want no need no desire. There is no hatred no
shame no regret. There is no grief, no sadness, no depression. There is
no fear. Absolutely no fear. When one lives without fear, one cannot be
broken. When one lives with fear one is broken before one begins to live.
The calm I feel right now. What is it?

I am lost in the Woods but still on a Trail. I am seeking that which I have
but will lose again. I have sought it before as a cure for the disease of myself. In a Church as a Child it did not come. I held my Parents' hands
and I felt nothing. Love only brought me loneliness and horror. In bottles
and pipes I found emptiness and pain. At twenty-two after Jail and bond
and flight I went back to a Cathedral where what I sought was calm. The
calm did not come. I have it now. Without God. I have it now.

The Wood fades into brittle brown grass and a slope carries me to a point
where I can see all that surrounds me. I can see trees and Woods and
Swamps and Lakes and birds and animals and men and women and the
Buildings of the Clinic and the Sky and whatever is beyond the Sky. I can
hear the wind and water and the cries of flying birds and the screams of the
Patients locked down and detoxifying. I can feel them and I can feel myself.
I can feel the life in them and the life around me. I can feel it in the beating
calm of my heart. It is not God and it is not something Higher. This feel-
ing of calm is of me, within me, from me and created by me. It is not God.
It is not something Higher.

I sit and I stare at the World. I see it and I hear it and I touch it and I
feel it. It is what it is, dirt and rock and water and Sun and air and waves
of light and waves of sound made up of definable elements. It can be created or reproduced by man at will. Science has given us that power. There
is no mystery to it. We can create it all in a laboratory. There is no mystery anymore as there was at the dawn of history when no one knew what

or how or why. We have answers now. Answers that reveal truth. Truth is
not God and it is not a Higher Power. There is no God. There is no
Higher Power.
I let it in through the open of my calm. There is no God. There is no
Higher Power. I let it in to the deep simple center of what I am which is
biology and energy and a beating heart that sings in a language only I can
speak. I let it in and it mixes and settles with the calm there is nothing else. I
will not fight God anymore. I will not fight anything Higher. Fighting is an
acknowledgment of existence. I no longer need to fight or acknowledge
what I know is not there. There are still fights to be fought, and I will fight
them, but not with the blind faith of a false conversion to a belief in that
which does not, has not, will not ever exist, God or something Higher. I will
fight with me, my heart, my will, myself, my song, I will fight with me. I
may win, I may lose. It doesn't matter either way. What matters is how I do
it. There is no God and there is no such thing as a Higher Power. I will do it
with me. Alone. I will do it with me.
I know it is almost time to meet Lilly. I stand and I walk down the hill past
the screams along the Buildings by the Unit. I walk back to the Trail and the
Trail leads me to the point where I leave it and I push it aside until I am in
the Clearing. She is there waiting for me. She is waiting for me walking
toward me she kisses me kisses me kisses me. She pulls away and she smiles.
Hi.
I smile.
Hi.
Let's sit.
Okay.
We sit.
I missed you.
I smile.
Good.
She smiles. It's a sweet, subtle smile. The type of smile that would break
your heart if you stared at it too long. She is still holding my hand and I
am still calm and now I'm high. High on me and high on her. She speaks.
Can I kiss you again?
Yeah.
She leans. Kisses me kisses me I am high. She kisses me. She pulls away,
speaks.
Tell me a story.
It's your turn.
I want you to start.

Why?

Because you're braver than me.

Why do you think that?

Just tell me a story.

What do you want to hear?

Tell me a story about love.

I'm no expert on love, but I'll try.

Thanks.

I stare into her eyes. They are clear blue like water. They comfort me as if I'm thirsty. I speak.

I went to school with this Girl. I spent three years staring at her and thinking about her and waiting for her to talk to me. I knew she knew I stared at her, but if I was the first to talk, I knew she'd think I was crazy, so I let her be the first. My last year there we had some Classes together, and after the first day of the first Class, she waited for me and we had a short conversation. She asked why I stared at her and I told her what I had been waiting to tell her since the first time I saw her, which was that she was the most beautiful Girl I had ever seen. She asked me if the stories she had heard about me were true and I told her that they probably were. We didn't talk for a while after that, and I stopped staring at her, but I knew she'd miss my stares, and that sooner or later she'd come around to me. I was right. Two months into the semester she asked if I wanted to study for midterms with her. After we studied we went out for drinks with her friends. I didn't bring any drugs with me and drank only enough to control my shakes and tremors and it went well.

We started hanging around together all the time, studying, walking to Class, eating lunch, drinking coffee and smoking cigarettes, drinking beers, doing whatever, and we became really close. My drinking slowed down to night hours only and I also stopped selling drugs.

I take a breath, look at the ground, remember. The memories are good ones, some of the few that I have. I look back at Lilly.

Christmas came around and she went home to Connecticut and I went to Brazil, where my Parents were living at the time. She gave me the number at her Parents' place and told me to call her, and though I wanted to call, I never did. I figured it was better to let her miss me, the idea being that her missing me would somehow work to change things between us. I wanted more, much much more. I thought I would be happy if she loved me, I thought her love would help solve my problems, and mostly I loved her and I wanted her to feel the same thing I did.

Lilly smiles, shakes her head, speaks.

Bad move.

What?

Thinking love could solve your problems.

I nod.

Yeah.

You mad that I said that?

I shake my head.

Hard to be mad when something's true.

She smiles.

I wanna hear the rest.

I chuckle.

When we got back to School, she asked why I didn't call her. I told her I figured she was busy with her family and that I didn't want to intrude. She
smiled and told me that from now on I should intrude whenever I felt like it.
I smiled and tried to be calm, but I wasn't calm. My heart started thumping
and my hands started shaking. She didn't say it, but I knew. She had
missed me.

A couple days later we went to a Bar to meet some of her friends. She sat
closer to me than she normally did, laughed a little louder at my stupid jokes,
touched me more affectionately on my leg, my shoulder, the back of my
neck, my hand. She touched and treated me like I was her boyfriend, and I
loved it.

About an hour after we got there, some Cops walk in with a Guy I'd
never seen before. These were Small-Town Cops, fat stupid Assholes with
mustaches and beer guts and guns and badges. I knew them and they
knew me. In the years I had spent in that Town, I had openly taunted
them and had dared them to try and catch me on something, which they
never had. Now they had this new Guy, and they marched up to me, full
of bullshit Cop bravado, and they pulled out a warrant, and they said I
had to come down to the Station with them to answer some questions.
They said there was another team of People searching my House with
dogs. I laughed and told them to get the fuck out of my face, and the
new Guy pulled out his badge and said Son, I am with the FBI and your
number is up, and he grabbed me and hauled my ass out of there. He did
it right in front of her, and did it right in front of her friends. I was fucking humiliated. After years of being in love with this Girl, I was sure she
would never speak to me again.

The car ride down to the Station was bullshit. I sang the National Anthem at
the top of my lungs, and in between renditions, asked the Cops when we
were stopping for pie. The questioning session was even more ridiculous.

The FBI Agent kept asking me about my trips to Brazil, which had nothing to do with drugs, and about who I knew in South America, and I just alternated answers. I won't speak until I have a Lawyer. Your mustache makes you look like a fucking idiot. Eventually the Search Team came back and they hadn't found anything at my House because there was nothing left to find, and they had to let me go. I walked out, and on my way, I told every Cop I saw to go fuck himself.

Lilly laughs.

What'd they say?

A couple ignored me, a couple said it back, one threw a cup of coffee at me.

Did it hit you?

No.

Did you go see the Girl?

When I came out the front door, she was sitting on the bumper of her car waiting for me.

She upset?

I nod.

Yeah. She had been crying.

What'd you do?

She was smoking a cigarette and staring at the ground and she didn't see me, so I walked up to her and I asked her if she was waiting for someone. She looked up and smiled and threw her arms around me and cried on my shoulder. When she was done crying, she asked if I was in trouble and I said no and she asked if I was all right and I said yes. Then she looked me in the eye and she took my hand and she said if we're going to be together, I have to be with the Person I know, not the Person I have heard stories about. I can't deal with Police and the drugs and the drinking and whatever else you've got going on, so make up your mind right now about who you're going to be. I smiled and I said I want to be the kind of Person that you would be proud to be with. I'm going to do everything I can to be that Person. If you can deal with that, just nod. If you can't, just walk away. If you nod, though, I'm going to kiss you, right here and right now and right on the lips, and that kiss will be my pledge to you that I'll make myself better.

She stared at me and she smiled and she nodded and I took my hands from her hands and I put them on her cheeks and I kissed her and for a while, at least, that kiss changed me, and for a while, at least, she and I were in love.

And then you fucked it up?

Yeah.

What did you do?

I don't want to talk about that right now.

Why?

Just don't.

What do you want to do?

I want to kiss you again.

Because you're thinking of her?

No, because I'm thinking of you.

Lilly smiles and she lets go of my hands and she puts her arms around me and she holds me and she softly kisses the skin of my neck. I feel safe in her arms, safe like I have never felt, and the calm and the power of the calm is still with me. She raises her head slightly she raises it and she softly kisses my lips and pulls me tighter I have never felt so safe and so calm. In her arms. Kissing her.

She lets go and she pulls away. She smiles at me and she runs one of her hands down one of my cheeks.

I wish I was her.

Why?

Because it would be nice to have someone feel that way about me.

You've never been in love?

Not even close.

And no one's ever been in love with you?

Men always want to fuck me, but no one has ever loved me.

I don't believe that.

It's true.

I don't believe it.

She stares at me.

It's true.

I stare back.

If it makes any difference, I don't want to fuck you.

She laughs.

Thanks.

I think you're beautiful, but I wouldn't fuck you because when we were done, I wouldn't want you to feel fucked. I would try to make love to you, and I would probably be clumsy and awkward, but when it was over, I would want you to feel loved.

She smiles.

Thank you, James.

I smile.

Thank you, Lilly.

We smile at each other and we look into each other's eyes and we speak to each other with the silence that lies between us. It is strong, safe and calm. The silence between us.

Lilly looks down at her watch.

It's getting late.

Yeah.

Meet me tomorrow?

I don't know.

Why?

I don't know if I can.

You getting scared?

A little, but that's not why I can't meet you.

What's the reason?

My Parents are coming here tomorrow. I have to do the Family Program with them and I don't know how much free time I have.

You excited?

No.

Why?

I don't get along with my Parents, and I don't want them here.

Adjust your attitude, Boy.

I laugh.

What?

I said adjust your attitude, Boy.

What are you talking about?

You're fucking lucky to have Parents. You're even luckier if they actually love you. If they're willing to take time out of their lives to come here to try and understand why you are the way you are and to try to learn to help you, then you hit the fucking jackpot. Be cool to them and try to understand how they must feel having to come here to see you and how upset they must be about it.

They've always been upset with me. That's part of the problem.

From what I know about you, they probably had every right to be.

Maybe.

Maybe nothing. Adjust your fucking attitude and try to be cool with them and remember how lucky you are to even have them.

I look down, stare at the ground, nod. She grabs my chin and she lifts my face back to hers.

I want you to say okay dearest Lilly, I'll try to be cool to my Parents.

I smile.

You getting tough with me?

She nods.

I'm a Badass, Boy. Don't fucking forget it.

I laugh.

Okay dearest Lilly. I'll try to be cool to my Parents.

She laughs.

Thank you.

I stare at her, let my smile fade it won't fade inside. I have never felt so safe or calm. This hard, damaged, drug-Addicted Badass Girl sitting in front of me with her black hair and her braided pigtails and her clear water blue eyes and her scars her scars the scars on her wrist naked beneath a plastic watch makes me feel safe and calm.

I want to see you tomorrow, but I don't know what this thing with my Parents is going to be like. When you go to lunch, sit so you can see into the Men's Section. If my back is turned, I can't meet you. If I'm facing you, I can meet you, and the number of plates on my tray is the time I'll be here.

What if you can't come till midnight?

Then I'm going to look like a fucking idiot.

She laughs.

Kiss me before you go.

I lean in and I kiss her, kiss her lips soft and wet and warm. I put my arms around her and I hold her tight this little Badass friend of mine.

She pulls away and we stand. She speaks.

Have a good night.

I will.

She turns and she starts to walk away. I speak.

Lilly.

She stops and she looks back.

What?

I'll miss you.

She smiles.

Good.

She turns back and she disappears into the green. I turn the opposite way and I push through and I come out on a Trail and I walk slowly back slowly back. I feel safe and calm and I want this feeling for as long as I can have it. I stop outside the glass door to the Unit. I stare through the glass at the men they are not safe or calm. They are watching television, playing cards, smoking cigarettes and drinking coffee. They are talking shit and telling stories. They are neither safe nor calm. Addictions need fuel. They're filling up.

I know I can't keep feeling this way, it will disappear sooner or later. I choose sooner and I open the door and I step inside the Unit. I walk to my Room. The door is closed so I knock softly there is no reply. I open the door and I step inside. Miles is sitting on his bed. His face is in his hands and he is weeping. I am sure that he heard me come in, but he doesn't acknowledge me. His face is in his hands and he is weeping.

I step back the way I came and I shut the door. I am in the Hall and the lights are on and the walls are white and I wish they were blue clear water blue.

I walk to the Dining Hall. I am early and it is empty. I get a tray and a plate of fish sticks and tartar sauce and I choose a table and I sit down. I start eating. I eat slowly. The fish sticks are warm and soggy, the breaded crust around them tastes like wet sand. With each bite a part of me flares and wants more wants the whole stick at once it screams and begs for five hundred sticks at once sandy crust and all. It doesn't matter how disgusting they are I just fucking want them. I sit and I breathe and I clench my jaw. I stare straight ahead. One bite at a time. Hold on. One bite at a time. It's not that hard. One bite at a time. They're fucking fish sticks. Just hold on.

I finish eating. Men start trickling in, they do not sit with me. I want more food, a lot more food, but I don't get up from the table. I just sit and I hold, sit and hold, sit and hold. I am aware that the battle I am fighting is a petty one, but I am also aware that in order to win that which is great, you must first win that which is small. An addiction is an addiction and a fight is a fight. The same principles apply. Just hold on.

I see Leonard coming off the line. He has beef and noodles instead of fish sticks. He smiles and he nods at me and he comes to my table and sits down. He is freshly showered and his hair is wet and his face is flushed.

How ya doing, Kid?

I'm good. You?

I've had a very good day.

Why?

None of your business.

Why?

Stop asking why.

Can I ask what?

Maybe.

What do you do for a living, Leonard?

He laughs.

You know what I do, Kid.

I want to hear you say it.

Somebody been talking to you?

Yeah.

They talked to me too.

What'd they say?

They said they didn't want me being a bad influence on you.

I told them you weren't.

Thank you.

What do you do for a living, Leonard?

You already know, Kid.

I want to hear you say it.

Leonard takes a bite of his beef and noodles. He smiles while he chews.

I'm the West Coast Director of a large Italian Finance Firm.

I laugh.

Need to know anything else?

No.

That's probably best.

Yeah.

You see your Girlfriend today?

Yeah.

You admit she's your Girlfriend now?

Sort of.

She good?

Yeah, she is.

You like her?

I do.

You love her?

In a way.

Watch your step, Kid. They asked me about her too.

How would they know about her?

They know everything.

How?

It's not hard to know things if you want to know them.

I guess.

You know what I think?

What?

I think love is a rare thing in the World. If you think you can have it with this Girl, then fuck whoever tries to stop you and fuck their Rules. Take the risk and do whatever you can do and try not to get caught. If you do get caught, do it again.

I laugh.

You're being a bad influence, Leonard.

He smiles.

No, I'm not, Kid.

I smile. Leonard smiles. We eat silently nobody sits with us. We finish dinner and we walk to the Lecture and we sit with Ed and Ted and Matty in the same seats we always sit in with them. We play cards and the results are back to normal. Leonard wins, everyone else loses. The stakes are small enough so that no one cares time is slow in here the game just helps the time go by faster. We know Leonard will split the winnings when we're done. Win a couple bucks, lose a couple bucks. Ignore whoever is on the Stage. I don't even bother looking anymore.

The Lecture ends and we walk back to the Unit. I get a cup of coffee and I find a place on one of the couches among several other men and I watch TV. There is a show on about a group of Doctors working in an inner-city Emergency Room. One of the stories on the show is about a female Heroin Addict who has come to the Hospital after an overdose.

She is a beautiful young woman whose body is absent of any bruises, scars or track marks. She wears dirty clothes that are ragged in a glamorous way. She cries whenever anyone talks to her and there are large, black bags under her eyes, though her crying is obviously fake and the bags under her eyes are a different size each time we see her. She started smoking pot on a lark, met a man and fell in love, and the man happened to be a heroin Dealer who got her hooked on his product. Now she can't quit, and after loading up a particularly large dose, she has woken up and found herself in the ER, which is the only part of the story which is even reasonably authentic. She refuses to accept any blame for the situation. She yells it wasn't my fault over and over and over.

As we watch the show, some of the men boo when the Girl makes her appearances, a couple of them clap and laugh, one of them grunts and throws his shoe at the TV, which he then retrieves and holds cocked in his hand until she shows up again. If he had a gun, he would probably blow the television to pieces.

As the episode drags on, the Girl confronts her problems with the help of a handsome young Doctor in the ER. He eases her off the junk, he gets her in AA. He lets her stay in his apartment, comforts her when she cries, brings home special nutritional juices for her each night after work. They fall in love and after an emotional candlelit dinner, they have glorious, romantic and multi-orgasmic sex. By the time the show is finished, she is all better. She has kicked her habit completely and she has a new life. It closes with a shot of her and the Doctor walking down the Street with a young Golden Retriever frolicking at their side.

If I could, I would hunt down the Creators of this utter bullshit fantasy fairy-tale piece of crap and I would lock them in a room and feed them drugs until they were profoundly and chronically Addicted to them. Then I would overdose them, drive them to the nearest inner-city ER, and I would drop them off at the door, right next to the homeless Guys with knives, the Addicts with AIDS and the Cops and the Ambulance Drivers smoking cigarettes. I'd leave them there for a couple of days, and then I'd come back and check on them. If they were still alive or still around, which would be highly unlikely, I'd ask them if their experience has in any way whatsoever resembled the experience they presented to the Public. I'd ask them if they were through detoxification and if they were feeling good. I'd ask them if they had been to their first AA Meeting and if they had found new Jobs and if they had found new Apartments. I'd ask them if they had fallen in love over a candlelit dinner and if they had the best sex of their lives. I'd ask them if they had purchased their new Golden Retrievers. After I received their answers, no no no please what do I do now no fuck me I'm fucked no please help me no no no no, I'd ask them how they were going to present addiction to the Public in the future. I'd ask them if they were going to romanticize it, glorify it, make light of it or portray it in a way that is wholly inaccurate. No no no please what do I do now no fuck me I'm fucked no please help me no no no no. That's what I thought, you Motherfuckers. No. After the show I stand and I walk to my Room. I have not seen Miles since I saw him earlier and I stop and I put my ear to the door before I reach to open it. I hear weeping, soft quiet sobs, mumbled words spoken to the air, a fist pounding a pillow. I would like to be in my bed, under the covers and warm, but I do not want to disturb him, so I let go of the door and I walk back to the Unit.

I get another cup of coffee and I go back to the couch. The Lower Level is empty but for me and two men. I don't know them and I don't speak to them. There is a talk show on the TV and a Movie Star is talking about his love for automobile racing and the Host of the show pretends to be interested in what he's saying. He smiles, nods when he needs to nod, accentuates the Movie Star's remarks with witty responses. The audience of the show is enraptured, and though I know the show is idiotic, I am enraptured as well. I am an Alcoholic and a drug Addict. I need fuel. I'll take what I can get.

I drink another cup of coffee, watch another talk show, fade in and out of sleep. Coffee doesn't affect me anymore and the TV is a narcotic. Its dull flicker feeding me filling me killing me keeping me holding me here and giving me something on which to focus. The two men on the couches next to me are both sound asleep. One of them is twitching and moaning, softly crying a word all too common he cries stop stop stop. The other is snoring and still. I'd think he was dead but for the noise. I fade in and out.

The TV is a narcotic.

In and out.

In.

Out.

In.

Out.

A man selling hair-growth products screams buy buy buy it'll grow grow grow. The head of hair that you've always dreamed of. I can give it to you if you buy buy buy it'll grow grow grow. He is standing on a beach. There are beautiful blondes on each of his arms. He is wearing a cheap suit.

I turn him off. I walk to my Room and I open the door. I step inside. Miles is awake, sitting on his bed. He is reading the Bible. He nods to me and I nod to him. I climb into my bed and I settle beneath the blankets and I curl into myself.

I wake up. There is gray light through the window I squint to avoid it. The first thought I have is of my Parents. I'm fucking pissed.

I get out of bed, shower, shave, brush my teeth. The mirror, myself, my eyes, they are not a consideration today. Not even close.

As I get dressed, Miles walks in carrying two cups of coffee. He hands one of them to me.

I brought you a cup of coffee.

Thanks.

You like it black, right?

Yeah.

I take a sip, set the mug on the nightstand next to my bed, continue dressing. Miles walks to his bed and he sits down and he speaks.

I appreciate you allowing me to have the Room yesterday.

Don't mention it.

I was grappling with some things.

You all right now?

I'm better.

There is dense silence. A moment. Miles looks down at the floor, back at me.

It was shame, James.

What?

I am dealing with feelings of great shame, James. That's why I was in here all day yesterday. It was shame.

You ever need someone to talk about it, I'll do my best.

Thank you, James. I know you will.

I finish dressing, sit down on my bed. Miles is staring at the floor.

You okay?

He nods. He does not look okay.

I stand, walk over to him, sit down on his bed, put my arms around him, hug him. He hugs me back strong and I can feel the shame coming through his arms. I am a Criminal and he is a Judge and I am white and he is black, but at this moment none of that matters. He is a man who needs a friend and I can be his friend. I wait for him to release me, wait for him to get rid of whatever it is, and after a couple of long minutes he does. I stand and I speak.

You need anything, come find me. I'm not good for much, but I'll do my best.

He nods.

Thank you, James.

I walk out of the Room and into the Hall and the Hall brings back my anger. Anger because my Parents are here. Anger because I don't want to see them. I walk into the Unit and I go to do the coffee, but the coffee has been done. I look at the Job Board. The space next to my name reads Family.

I leave the Unit and I walk to the Dining Hall. I get a tray, a plate, a breakfast burrito. I sit down at an empty table. I'm angry and I want to be alone.

I eat quickly. The burrito is stuffed with eggs, bacon, cheese and small clumps of unidentifiable vegetables. It is disgusting, but I eat it anyway. I'd like to eat a hundred of them. The anger is becoming Fury. The Fury is rising.

I finish eating and I leave and I head toward the Lecture Hall. There are men ahead of me and men behind me. I pay them no mind. I just walk. Joanne is waiting for me at the door to the Lecture Hall. She asks me to come to her Office. We walk through the Halls side by side.

How are you today, James?

Fine.

You seem angry.

I am.

Why?

Because I am.

We arrive at her Office. We step inside. She sits in the chair, I sit on the couch.

Your Parents arrived here early this morning. They've been settling in at the Family Center. We have a meeting with them in a few minutes.

Great.

You're not happy about this, are you?

No.

Why?

Because I don't want to deal with them.

Why?

They make me angry.

Why?

I don't know why.

There must be specific reasons.

Whatever reasons there are, they're bullshit. Things like them hassling me
or being worried about me, stupid shit that I've always deserved.

Do you think your feelings have any real validity?

I don't know.

How long have you had them?

I've been pissed at my Parents for as long as I can remember.

Maybe we can figure out why that is while they're here.

I doubt it.

Keep in mind that they're here because they love you and want to help
you. This is not an easy thing for them.

I'll try.

We usually start by sitting everyone down in a Room. If your Parents are
going to understand where you are and what they can do to help you,
they need to know what you've been doing and to what extent you've
been doing it. We would like you to tell them.

That's gonna be a fucking nightmare.

Why do you think that?

My Parents know I drink too much, and they know I do drugs, but
they have no idea how much, and they don't know anything about my
legal problems.

How do they not know?

I never told them.

Do you think they're going to react poorly?

I laugh.

Poorly doesn't describe how I think they're going to react.

Whatever their reaction is, we'll deal with it. That's why they're here,
that's why we're here.

I guess.

I think you're going to be surprised.

I highly fucking doubt it.

She looks at her watch.

We should go.

She stands. I stand.

Okay.

She opens the door and we leave her Office and we start walking through the Halls. They are bright and they make me angry, with each step I get more and more angry. I don't want to see my Parents. I don't want to be in the same Room with them. I don't want to speak to them, I don't want them to speak to me. This is how I've always felt. They're my Parents. I don't want them anywhere near me.

My hands start shaking and my heart starts beating like a Cannon on a Field of War. Joanne senses this and she takes my hand the hand closest to her and she holds it and she smiles. I try to smile back, but I can't smile. The Fury is rising. I don't want to see my Parents.

We arrive at a door. Joanne knocks and a voice says come in. She looks at me and she squeezes my hand tight. I stare at the ground. I'm shaking and my heart my heart my heart. I look up and I take a deep breath and I nod. Joanne opens the door.

We step inside. My Mother and my Father are sitting at a conference table on the opposite side of the Room. I'm shaking. They are with a completely bald man in his thirties who is wearing a black sweater and black jeans. My heart my heart my heart. As he turns to look at me, my Mother stands. She is wearing khakis and a white shirt and a blue blazer and a silk paisley scarf and her hair is perfect and her makeup is perfect and there are diamonds on her fingers and there are diamonds in her ears. She rushes toward me. The Fury is rising. I want to get the fuck out of here. I want out out out.

James.

She hugs me. I don't like it when she touches me and I don't hug her back. She lets me go, but she keeps her hands on my shoulders.

You look great.

I want her hands gone.

You're gaining weight.

Her eyes away.

And your face and teeth are better. You look so much better.

She hugs me again. I want her away. Get the fuck away.

Oh, James.

She lets go of me, stares. My Father steps forward. Khakis, blue oxford, blue blazer. A large, expensive watch. He hugs me. I want him away.

How are you, James?

He lets me go.
I'm fine.
You look much better.
I guess so.
Joanne steps forward.
Mr. Frey?
She reaches to shake his hand. He takes it.
Call me Bob.
Joanne nods.
Bob, I'm Joanne. I'm a Psychologist who has been working with your
Son.
Dad smiles.
He looks better.
Joanne smiles.
He is better, and he's on the road toward getting much better.
Dad smiles.
We're very proud of him for coming here.
Joanne smiles.
You should be.
He nods, looks at me. I look away. Joanne speaks.
Why don't we sit, get started.
My Mother smiles and she nods. My Father says okay. They take their
seats the same seats. I sit on the far side of the table as far away as possi-
ble. I hold my hands in my lap they are shaking. I stare straight ahead
stare at the surface of a bright white wall. Joanne sits between us, looks at
the man in black and nods. The man speaks.
Hi, James. My name is Daniel, and I'm a Counselor at the Family Center.
I stare at the wall.
I'm going to be working with you and your Parents while they're here.
My hands are shaking.
As I believe you know, we like to start our work in the Family Program
by having the individual with Chemical Dependency issues talk to the
Family Members about their habits and their use.
My heart my heart my heart. Like a Cannon on a Field of War.
We'd like you to be as honest as possible and you should take as much
time as you need.
I nod.
Start whenever you'd like.
I look straight across the table. My Mother and Father are waiting for me.
Before I start, I just want to say that I don't want to do this, and I wish

you hadn't come here, and I'm sorry you have to hear what I'm about to tell you.

My Father nods and he squeezes my Mother's hand.

I've been drinking for as long as I can remember. As a young kid, I used to steal sips from beers at football games we went to together and drink leftover glasses of wine at your dinner parties. I don't know why I did it, I just did. It made me feel better about myself for some reason, and I liked it, liked it more than anything I had ever experienced. I did it as much and as often as I could, which was fairly often. We went to a lot of football games and you guys had a lot of parties. I got drunk for the first time when I was ten. You were out at the symphony or at some charity function and I snuck out of the House without the babysitter knowing and I went down the street to a party some High School Kids were having. They thought it was cool that I was there and they fed me drinks till I threw up. I stumbled Home and the babysitter was asleep and I went to bed.

My Mother wipes her eyes, my Father squeezes her hand.

I smoked pot for the first time at twelve. Same thing. I snuck out to a party and the older Kids gave it to me. I didn't like it much, but I liked that they thought I was cool. I did it as much as I could, and because you guys were out or away a lot, it was easy to do. The babysitters never gave two shits and sometimes they did it with me.

My Mother holds a hand to her face, my Father looks down at the table.

I blacked out for the first time at fourteen. I was drinking and smoking in the basement of someone's House and the next thing I knew it was morning and I was Home. By then I was getting fucked up three or four times a week. At fifteen I started using harder stuff, coke and acid and crystal meth. I liked all of them more than pot, so I stopped smoking it, and it's the only drug I've ever quit using. I was also selling drugs and liquor at fifteen. I'd go into the Ghetto over in the Harbor and meet up with this guy named Freddy. He was a low-level dealer and if I gave him a couple bucks, he'd get me whatever I wanted. People knew I could get shit, so they gave me rides. The deal was they had to buy me something too. When I couldn't get rides, I took your car. When I didn't have money, Freddy gave me credit. He liked me and called me White Boy James, and I became known over there as that. It was fucking stupid and dangerous, but I liked it, thought it was cool, and it allowed me to get anything I wanted whenever I wanted it. I wanted it all the time.

My Mother starts crying, my Father stares at me.

Sixteen and seventeen were more of the same. I bought and sold liquor and drugs, did as much as I could of whatever I could get. I got fucked up before school, during school, after school. I got fucked up every single day. I drank and mostly used meth, and when I had that overdose, that's what it was, meth and alcohol. I don't know how much I did because I was blacked out. You never knew what went wrong because I refused to talk to the Doctors. I know you're sitting there thinking you should have known more and you should have stopped me, but I hid things well and you tried, you tried hard. If you remember, you threatened me with Rehab a bunch of times and I told you if you sent me, I'd walk out and you'd never see or hear from me again. At the time, I would have done it. There was nothing you could have done to change me. I wouldn't have stopped.

I take a deep breath. My Mother has moved closer to my Father and is sobbing into her own hands. I can see her makeup streaking through her fingers. My Father is staring at me and his eyes are wet. I have never seen him cry before, never seen him even close.

Eighteen. Same thing, but more. Went away to school in the Fall. No Rules, you weren't around, I got a monthly allowance. I was in Heaven. I blacked out every night, always had a bloody nose from snorting coke all the time, pissed in my bed three or four times a week because I was too drunk to get out of bed. Nineteen, same thing, but probably worse. At twenty I started smoking coke. I used all the money you gave me to buy it and sell it. The FBI started investigating me for dealing and I got questioned by them at the local Police Station five or six times. They never got me on anything. Twenty-one. Bad year. I started smoking crack, which I loved. I smoked it as much as I could, which was basically every day. Crack is a bad drug, and it fucked me up. I was throwing up blood, pissing blood, shitting blood. I was sick all the time. I don't really know how I managed it, but I finished school and you guys got me that job and sent me to Europe. I know you did it because you thought it would be good for me to have a job and good for me to be away, but it wasn't. I didn't really have to work and I spent all of my time getting hammered and getting in trouble. There was no crack over there, but there was freebase, and there was powder, and I did a lot of both of them.

Mother sobs in her hands, tears run down Father's cheeks. He does not wipe them, just stares at me.

While I was there I came back to see my Girlfriend from college. I know you remember her, because you liked her so much, and you had hoped things would work out between us. We had broken up at the end of school and had then reconciled through letters and the phone, and she was planning on coming over and living with me. I was excited about it, and I sort of thought of it as a last chance at redeeming myself. I knew if she came over I would have to straighten up because she was sick of dealing with my shit. I was hopeful and it was good and I was so excited that I broke one of my Rules, which was never call her when I was drunk. Three nights in a row I called and I don't know what I said because I was blacked out. When I called again on the fourth day, her Mom answered and told me never to call again, that she didn't ever want to have anything to do with me. I freaked out and went on a nasty bender and then decided I would come back to the States because I knew she was planning to visit School to see some friends.

I can't look at my Parents anymore, so I look at the table.

I flew from Paris to Chicago, drove from Chicago to Ohio. When I got there I stayed sober until I found her and when I found her, she wouldn't talk to me. She told me to go away, that she never wanted to see me, speak to me or have anything to do with me ever again. I was crushed. I went out and I drank as much as I could and smoked as much crack as I could and when I was good and loaded, I decided to go find her and try to talk to her again. I went to a Bar where we used to hang out and where I knew she'd be. As I was driving up, I saw her standing out front with a few of her friends. I was staring at her and not paying attention to the road and I drove up onto a sidewalk and hit a Cop who was standing there. I didn't hit him hard because I was only going about five miles an hour, but I hit him. She saw me do it, and a whole bunch of other people saw me do it. The Cop called for backup and I sat in the car and stared at her and waited. The backup came and they approached the car and asked me to get out and I said you want me out, then get me out, you fucking Pigs. They opened the door, I started swinging, and they beat my ass with billy clubs and arrested me. As they hauled me away kicking and screaming, I tried to get the crowd to attack them and free me, which didn't happen. When I was sitting in the back of the cruiser, she walked up and looked at me and she was crying and I asked if she'd come Bail me out and she nodded and said yes, I'll come. I stayed in Jail that night and I was arraigned the next morning on charges of Assault with a Deadly Weapon, Assaulting an Officer of the Law, Felony DUI, Disturbing the Peace, Resisting Arrest, Driving Without a License, Driving Without Insurance, Attempted Incitement of a Riot, Possession of a Narcotic with Intent to Distribute and Felony Mayhem. The only thing that was bullshit was the narc charge, and that was bullshit because I intended to use it, not distribute it. She didn't show up, so a Buddy of mine paid my Bail on a credit card and I flew back to Paris. As far as I know, I am still wanted on all of the charges.

I look up. My Parents are both silent and they are both crying. Tears are running down their faces and my Mother's breathing is labored. She breaks down and she starts sobbing. I wait for her to stop, but she doesn't. She just sobs sobs sobs. My Father puts his arms around her and he whispers in her ear, quietly whispers, but it doesn't do any good. My Mother sobs. I watch her and I wait for her to stop. It takes a lifetime. A fucking lifetime. When she is quiet, I speak again.

I stayed in Paris, got fucked up, knew I was killing myself and I didn't care. From there I went to London and did the same thing. When I came back to the States and I went down to North Carolina, I started smoking crack again. Crack is an evil and dangerous drug and I smoked as much of it as I could get. I also drank as much as I could drink, which at that point was quite a bit. I don't remember much of what I did down there because I was so fucked up all the time, but I know I got arrested again. I also know I got arrested in Michigan, though I have no idea what I was doing in Michigan. I skipped Bail in both places, so I guess I'm wanted there as well. For the last six months I've just been drinking and smoking and waiting to die.

My Mother is sobbing and my Father is holding her. I don't wait for her this time, I just want this to end.

I don't blame you for this, and I don't think there's anything you could have done to stop it. I am what I am, which is an Alcoholic and a drug Addict and a Criminal, and I am what I am because I made myself so. You did the best you could with me, and you loved me the best you could, and that's all I could have ever asked for from you. I have no excuses for what I've done or for who I am or for what I've put you through all these years.

My Mother starts sobbing. Louder than before and more wrenching. Her makeup is smeared all over her hands and her face and her clothes, and she is having trouble breathing. She clings to my Father, who holds her and stares at the floor. Tears are running from his cheeks and dripping onto his pants, I can see that his lips are quivering. He shakes his head and he starts to look up at me, but he can't do it.

I sit and watch them. The Fury is in me and has risen it is peaking. I don't understand why this happens, but every time I'm near them, it does happen. They try to love me, I hurt them. They try to be decent and reasonable, I won't be decent or reasonable. They try to help me, I resent them for it. I don't understand why. They are my Parents. They are doing the best they can do.

This is how it has always been with me. Give me something good, I'll destroy it. Love me, I'll destroy you. I have never felt deserving of anything in my life. I have never felt as if I were worth the diseased space I occupy. This feeling has inhabited everything I've ever done, seen or had anything to do with, and it has infected every relationship I have ever had with everyone I've ever known. I don't understand it. I don't understand why it's here. I hate it as I hate myself, and for whatever the reason, my Parents' presence has always made it worse. They are only trying to love me, but they have always made it fucking worse.

Joanne stands and she walks over to me and she leans to my ear.

I think we should go.

I look at my Parents. They are still crying. There are tears dripping from my Father's face and my Mother is having trouble breathing. I would like to do something to make them feel better, but I'm incapable of it. I hate myself too much to do anything.

I stand and I walk out of the room. Joanne is holding the door open and she closes it behind me. As soon as it is shut and as soon as I can no longer see hear feel touch or hurt my Parents, I start to feel better.

We start walking. Joanne doesn't speak and neither do I. We just walk through the Halls. I think about my Parents sitting in that Room crying because of me and we head toward Joanne's Office. When we arrive, she opens the door. We walk inside and I sit down on the couch and she sits across from me.

How do you feel?

Suicide.

What?

It's the only word that fits.

You feel like killing yourself?

I won't, but at this moment, it seems like a reasonable option.

Why?

They're my Parents. When I'm near them I get so angry that I can't control myself. That anger makes me hate myself more than I already do, and that makes suicide seem like a reasonable option.

Do you need supervision?

No, I'm too much of a pansy to actually do it.

You think suicide is an act of bravery?

No, I think it's cowardly, just like I think addiction is cowardly. But I do think that they both require a certain kind of pathetic strength.
Strength?
You have to be fairly strong to feel anything as powerful as hatred or self-hatred. Addiction and suicide are not for the weak.
I think that's ridiculous.
Ridiculous things can be true.
Why do your Parents make you so angry?
I don't know.
Did you experience abuse as a Child?
Not that I remember.
Do you think it's possible?
No.
Why?
I grew up in a safe, sheltered environment. My Parents have always loved me and they've always tried to protect me and they've always tried to do their best by me. They fucking piss me off, but there is no way they ever abused me.
What about someone else?
No.
Are you sure?
Yes.
I pull a cigarette from my pocket, light it, take a drag. The nicotine slows my heart and calms me.
What next?
Lunch, and after that you go down to the Family Center. You'll spend the afternoon in Group Sessions with the Members of other People's Families until dinner. After dinner, we'll sit down with your Parents again.
Why?
To discuss this morning.
That'll be fun.
You were brave this morning. You were very honest and very straightforward and you said a lot of things that probably weren't easy to say. Your Parents reacted in a very normal, natural way, and if they hadn't reacted that way, I would be worried about our ability to make progress with them. Now that they know what they need to know, we can work on healing your wounds and figuring out how you can get along better.
When will we be done tonight?
Depends on what we get into with your Parents.

Give me an estimate.

You trying to meet up with Lilly?

What?

You heard me.

Yeah, I'm trying to meet up with Lilly.

Don't.

Why?

If you get caught, you'll be in serious trouble.

Sounds like I got caught already.

There is an idea that there is something going on. We have not caught
you.

Where'd you get the idea?

I can't discuss that with you.

You want me to discuss things with you, but you won't discuss things
with me. That's fucking bullshit, Joanne.

You think so?

Yeah, I do. You be straight with me, I'll be straight with you. That's the
fucking deal. If it's not, you can go fuck yourself.

I'm not your enemy.

You are if you're not straight with me.

Lilly is very smitten with you. One of the Counselors on her Unit over-
heard her talking to one of her Girlfriends about you. She has since heard
Lilly talking about you a number of other times. It seems that you're all
that Lilly wants to talk about.

I smile.

Why are you smiling?

I like that she's smitten with me.

It's a bad idea, James.

Why?

You should be concentrating on what you're here for, which is getting
sober and rebuilding your life. Lilly is a distraction that takes you away
from that. Both of you are very fragile and vulnerable right now, and if
something went wrong between the two of you, it would jeopardize your
sobriety.

I can handle it.

Overconfidence kills a lot of People.

She makes me feel good, better than I feel with anyone else.

I'm sure she does, but that doesn't change our Policy.

I don't want to let her go.

It's in the best of interests of both of you.

I'll take your advice under consideration.

Take it further than that.

I stand.

I'm going to eat.

She nods.

I'll see you tonight.

I turn and I open her door and I walk out of Joanne's Office. I go to the Dining Hall. As I walk down the Glass Corridor separating the men from the women, I see Lilly sitting at a table. She is staring at me and I stare back, though I make no other sort of acknowledgment. It is hard to stare at her, hard because she's not the distant Girl who smiles at me anymore. She has become more than that, more than I expected her to become and more than I was looking for her to become. She is becoming what I wanted she the last with the Arctic eyes to become, which is someone who loves me. Simply and truly and as I am. It is hard to stare at her because as I know she is starting to love me, I am starting to love her. I don't care what she's done or who she's done it with, I don't care about whatever demons may be in her closet. I care about how she makes me feel and she makes me feel strong and safe and calm and warm and true. It is hard to stare because I am forced to contemplate giving it up. It is hard to stare, but I do it anyway.

I get a tray and I get in line and I get a plate of tuna noodle casserole. I ask for ten, but the Lady in the hairnet says no. I go to the Salad Bar and I get five plates. I put lettuce on one, cottage cheese on another, beets on the third, niblets of corn on the fourth, croutons on the fifth. My tray is full so I get another tray. I put four plates on it, each piled high with portions of pudding, peaches, slices of apple pie and carrot cake. I walk slowly through the Dining Area carrying both trays. They're heavy and I hear a couple of snickers and I hear a couple of laughs. A voice I don't know says that's a sad addiction. I chuckle. I find my friends Ed and Ted and Leonard and Matty and Miles and I sit down with them. Leonard speaks.

Where you been all day?

My Parents are here.

Miles speaks.

Are they here for the Family Program?

Yeah.

How has it been?

Shitty.

Why?

I had to do this confession thing this morning where I told them about all the bad shit I've done.
Ed speaks.
What didn't they know about?
They didn't know much.
What was the worst?
The crack, and the fact that I'm wanted in three states.
Leonard speaks.
What are you wanted for?
A bunch of shit.
Miles speaks.
Do you have warrants out against you, James?
Yes.
Where?
Michigan, Ohio and North Carolina.
Are you doing anything to take care of them?
Somebody here is trying to do something.
Ted speaks.
When I told my Mamma I smoked the rock she asked if I could get her some.
Everyone laughs.
She did. She said I been hearing all about this crack stuff and I wanna try me some. I got a fifty bag and I smoked with her till her eyes were in the back of her head. She didn't want no more after that.
Everyone laughs again, though the image of Ted's Mamma with her eyes in the back of her head is not a funny one. We spend the rest of lunch laughing more, mostly at Matty, who is still struggling to stop swearing. Every third or fourth word he speaks is either goddamn or fuck and is immediately followed by a string of other curses which are directed at himself. Eventually he just stops speaking entirely. By the time lunch is over, the men have devoured the food on all of my plates everything is gone. As we stand to leave, I look across the Dining Hall and through the glass at Lilly. She is smiling at me and the smile hurts. I will not could not don't want to give that smile up. I won't give it up. No fucking way. We walk out of the Dining Hall. My friends head toward the Lecture, I walk through Halls into areas I don't know, following signs that lead me to the Family Center. I arrive at a door. A sign on the door says Welcome Home. I open it and I go inside.
The white walls are whiter the lightbulbs brighter the paintings hanging happier. They are filled with scenes of Families on picnics in wide open

fields of green and wildflowers. The members of the Families in the paintings are smiling, eating French bread, cutting fruit and playing backgam-
mon. Variations of them are along all of the walls. I follow them and they
take me to a large open Room. On one side of the Room, the entire wall
is glass and it looks out upon the Lake. There are chairs in the Room
chairs everywhere. Large plush chairs that look comfortable in their
happy patterned upholstery. There are People sitting in the chairs they are
talking, smoking, drinking coffee and waiting. Waiting for their Family
Members and waiting to get better.

It is easy to tell who is here as part of the Family Program and who is
here as part of their own Program. The Family Program People wear
cleaner clothes have better haircuts nicer watches sparkling jewelry. Their
skin is more flush, their bodies glow, they have flesh on their bones. They
have life in their eyes. The rest of us smoke cigarettes and drink cups of
coffee, our hands shake and we have bags under our eyes. We move
slowly and the only thing alive in our eyes is dread.

I look around the Room. My Parents are huddled in a corner softly
speaking to each other. They see me. I hold up one finger and my Father
nods at me and I go to the coffee machine. I get a cup, black and steaming, and I walk toward them.

They stand as I approach. They are smiling and they have changed their
clothes, though the clothes are more or less the same. My Mother has re-
done her hair and her makeup and it is perfect again and my Father's
blazer is crisply pressed. I can see the effort behind their smiles and with
each step closer, I want to turn and run. My Father speaks.

How are you, James?

Been better. You?

I think we've been better too.

There is silence, smiling. I wish the smiling would stop. My Mother
speaks.

Do you want to sit with us?

I nod, we sit. They are side by side, I am across from them. There is a
table between us, it has an ashtray. I reach into my pocket for my cigarettes and I take them out. My Mother frowns.

Could you not smoke, please?

Why?

Because I just changed my clothes and I don't want them to smell.

Fine.

I put the cigarettes back into my pocket. My Mother watches me.

Are you going to quit those things while you're here?

No.

Why?

Because I don't want to quit these things.

Why not?

I'll give you a choice, Mom. I can either smoke cigarettes or smoke crack. You make the call.

She recoils, obviously hurt. I knew it would happen, but I did it anyway. My Father speaks.

I don't think you need to speak to your Mother that way, James.

Obviously we'd rather have you smoke cigarettes than smoke crack.

Then don't give me shit about it.

Don't speak to us that way.

I reach for my cup of coffee and I drink it in one gulp. It's hot and steaming and it burns my mouth, but I don't care. I pull the cup away and I speak.

I'm gonna get some more coffee. You want some?

My Father looks at my Mother. My Mother shakes her head no and her expression tells me she's still hurt. My Father looks back at me.

I think we're fine.

I stand and I walk back to the coffee machine. As I fill my cup, a tall and thin man dressed like my Father rings a bell hanging near the door. Everyone turns toward him. He tells us that we're going to split into groups and that the groups will meet in separate Rooms. He points to a pair of doors against the wall opposite the glass wall and he starts reading names. When People hear their names called, they stand and they go through the doors. As I walk back to the corner where my Parents are sitting, the man says my name. I continue toward my Parents and when I reach them, I speak.

Looks like I've got to go.

My Father nods, my Mother looks like she's going to cry. I turn and I start to walk away. My Father speaks.

James?

I turn around.

We're sorry about the smoking remarks.

My Mother nods. Tears start running down her cheeks.

We know you've got a lot that you're trying to deal with right now and we know you're doing the best you can, so if you need to, it's okay if you smoke around us.

I smile. This simple gesture breaks my heart.

Thank you.

My Father smiles, and beneath her tears, my Mother smiles. Her smile makes me feel a little better.

I'll see you tonight.

I turn and I walk to my door. I walk through it and I enter another large Room. It is white, bright and cheery. There are inspirational pictures on the walls with phrases like Take It Day by Day, Let Go and Let God, Easy Does It. There is thick carpet on the floor and there are folding chairs spread in a wide circle around the Room. There are People sitting in the chairs. I find an empty chair without anybody on either side of it and I sit down. I am alone for a moment, but then a pregnant woman sits on one side of me and a gray-haired man sits on the other. The Room fills up, and for every Patient here there are about three Family Members. Everyone looks nervous.

A woman walks in she's in her thirties wearing khakis and Birkenstocks and wool socks and a chorded sweater. She has brown hair, green eyes and looks as if she could be a model. She sits in the only empty chair in the circle and she smiles.

Welcome to your first Group Session at the Family Program.

There are nods, a couple People say thank you.

What we're going to do in this session is introduce ourselves and ask each other questions. Family Members often ask those of us in recovery about what we do or why we do what we do or what it feels like to do it, those of us in recovery often ask Family Members how our actions affect them or how they feel when they're dealing with us or why they deal with us in the ways they do or why they deal with us at all. You should feel free to ask whatever you want, as long as it's not intended to hurt someone's feelings. I'll start with the introductions.

She smiles.

My name is Sophie, and I'm an Addict and an Alcoholic.

Everyone says Hello, Sophie. The man sitting next to her smiles, speaks.

I'm Tony, and I'm the Husband of an Alcoholic.

Everyone says Hello, Tony, and the introductions move around the Room. Mother of a Heroin Addict, Meth Addict, Wife of a Crack Addict, Alcoholic, Son and Daughter of an Alcoholic, Vicodin Addict, Pregnant Wife of a Crack Addict. There are all types of relations, all types of Addicts and Alcoholics. After the introductions, the questions are supposed to start. At first, no one speaks. People stare at the floor, stare at their hands, stare at each other. There are awkward smiles and frustrated sighs. After a few moments, a man who identified himself as a Meth Addict asks how long this session is going to last. Everyone laughs. A woman who identified herself as the Wife of an Alcoholic asks the same thing. How long does this last? Sophie smiles and asks her if she's referring to addiction. The woman nods and says yes. Sophie says addiction lasts a lifetime. It lasts a lifetime.

From there the questions start to flow. How does it feel to be Addicted to something. Horrible. Why does it feel that way. Because we know what we're doing to ourselves and what we're doing to you and we can't stop doing it. What does it feel like when you want it. Need, overwhelming need, uncontrollable need, unimaginable need. What does it feel like when you get it. Relief, followed by horror, followed by more need. Why can't you stop. I don't know. Why can't you stop. I don't know. Why can't you stop. I don't know.

There are other simpler, more technical questions. What is crack and how do you use it. Crack is cocaine cooked with ethyl alcohol, gas and baking powder. We smoke it with a pipe. Where do you buy heroin and how much does it cost. You buy heroin from a dealer and it is very expensive. What is meth and how is it made. Meth is speed and it is made by cooking asthma medicine called ephedrine, formaldehyde, sometimes gas or fertilizer, and baking powder. What does it do to you. Robs you of your heart, robs you of your soul, takes away the ability and the desire to eat and to sleep, robs you of your sanity.

The Addicts and Alcoholics give straight, simple answers. We ask no questions. Unlike the Family Members, we already know the answers. We fuck up your lives. We ruin every single one of your days. We are your worst nightmare. You don't know what to do with us. You're at the end of your rope. You don't know what to do. You're at the end of your fucking rope. You don't know what to do.

At the end of the Session, Sophie asks everyone to join hands. An intimacy has developed and we do so eagerly. She has us recite a poem that she calls the Serenity Prayer. She says a line and we follow. God grant me the serenity to accept the things I cannot change, the courage to change the things I can, and the wisdom to know the difference. She smiles we smile everyone smiles. When we finish saying the prayer, she has us do it again. God grant me the serenity to accept the things I cannot change, the courage to change the things I can, and the wisdom to know the difference. She has us do it again and again.

When she stands, everyone else stands. She tells us we're finished and everyone starts hugging each other. There are hugs sealing the bonds hugs healing the wounds hugs in appreciation of knowledge and insight shared hugs of understanding and hugs of compassion extended. After the hugs,

Sophie opens the door and we file out smiling and laughing and in better shape than when we entered. Everyone says good-bye thank you good-bye thank you.

The Primary Patients walk through the Halls to the Dining Hall. We do so as a group. The men talk to the men, the women talk to the women. It is all small talk, meaningless bullshit like where you from, how long you been here, what's your drug of choice. The talk continues as we walk through the Glass Corridor and we form a line. It continues as we get trays and food.

The talk stops when it's time to decide where to sit. Nearly everyone seeks out an empty table. The rest of the Patients have yet to arrive, so there are plenty from which to choose. I find a table where no one is anywhere near me and I sit down. I eat slowly. I stare at my plate, move my fork toward it, scoop, move the fork toward my mouth. I chew. I don't pay attention to what I'm chewing, and after a few bites, it doesn't matter. Everything tastes the same. Fork to plate, fork to mouth. Chew. Everything tastes the same. My plate is empty. The rest of the Patients are arriving and the Dining Hall is starting to fill up. I stand with my tray and I put it on the conveyor and I walk out. I go back to the Unit and I go to my Room. I have some time to burn before I am meeting my Parents. I should be prepared. As calm as I can be in order to control the Fury, which I know will come. Lilly makes me calm, but Lilly is not here. Free air makes me calm. The little book the *Tao* makes me calm and it is sitting near my bed. I sit down on my bed and I open the book at random and I start to read.

Fifteen. Be as careful as crossing frozen water, alert as a Warrior on enemy ground. Be as courteous as a Guest, as fluid as a Stream. Be as shapeable as a block of wood, as receptive as a glass. Don't seek and don't expect. Be patient and wait until your mud settles and your water is clear. Be patient and wait. Your mud will settle. Your water will be clear.

Sixty-three. Act without doing, work without effort, think of the large as small and the many as few. Confront the difficult while it is easy, accomplish the great one step at a time. Don't reach and you will find, if you run into trouble throw yourself toward it. Don't cling to comfort and everything will be comfortable.

Seventy-nine. Failure is an opportunity. If you blame others, there is no end to blame. Fulfill your obligations, correct your mistakes. Do what you need to do and step away. Demand nothing and give all. Demand nothing and give all.

Twenty-four. Stand on your toes and you won't stand firm. Rush ahead and you won't go far. Try to shine and you'll extinguish your light. Try to define yourself, you won't know who you are. Don't try to control others. Let go and let them be.

As I read this book it calms me without effort, fills in the blanks of my strategy for survival. Control by letting go of control, fix your problems by forgetting they're problems. Deal with them and the World and yourself with patience and simplicity and compassion. Let things be, let yourself be, let everything be and accept it as it is. Nothing more. Nothing less. Nothing more.

I am prepared. I am calm. I will accept what comes. I walk out of the Room. My Parents are waiting for me on the other side of the Clinic. I walk through the Halls. My eyes are forward but focused on nothing. Each step is a step and nothing more than a step, a method for taking me from this place to that place. As I turn corners I hear sounds. They sound as they are, they just sound as they sound. The Tao told me what I needed to hear and I listened. The Tao taught me what I needed to be taught and I learned. The sounds just sound.

I stop in front of the door to Joanne's Office. I knock on it. Her voice says come in so I open the door and I go inside. My Mother and my Father are sitting on the couch. They have changed clothes again and they are holding hands. Their eyes are dry and their lips steady. They stand to greet me, but they don't try to hug me. I say hello to them and I don't try to hug them either. I sit down in the chair across from them and they sit back down. Joanne is behind her desk. She's smoking a cigarette.

Your Parents told me about their new smoking policy and they extended it to me. I hope you don't mind.

I pull out a cigarette.

Not at all.

I reach for an ashtray.

We were talking about our Session this morning. Your Parents have some thoughts and feelings on it, but we thought we'd start with yours.

I light my cigarette, take a drag. I exhale.

I hated this morning.

Joanne looks at me.

I think you need to be more specific and I think you need to tell your Parents, not me.

I look at my Parents. They are holding hands and they are looking at me. I'm sorry about what I told you this morning. It must have been terrible for you to have to sit through it. As I was doing it, I felt a number of things. The first was anger. Intense anger. I don't know why, but whenever I'm near you, I feel incredibly and uncontrollably angry. The second feeling I had was horror. Horror because as I get some distance from my-self, I'm realizing what a truly horrible Person I am. I've hidden a lot from you, as much as I could, and I can't imagine what it must have been like for you to have to sit through the details of my monstrous existence.

I take another drag of my smoke. My Mother moves closer to my Father, my Father holds her a little tighter.

I felt shame, enormous amounts of shame. I felt shame because of who I am, what I've done, the way I've lived my life, the crimes I've committed. I felt shame because you're good People and you deserve better than me. I felt shame because I hurt you, have hurt you over and over, and every time I did it, including this morning, I knew I was doing it.

I take another drag.

I felt regret for a lot of the same reasons I felt shame. But also because I have wasted so much of my life and so much of your life, and because on some level, it didn't have to be this way. I don't know what way it should have been or how I could have changed myself, but I know that my life should not have been the way that it has been. I know that it is entirely my fault.

Another drag.

I felt like I wanted to drink. I felt like I wanted to do drugs. I felt like I wanted large amounts of both of them. I feel that way most of the time though, so I don't know if it was specific to our conversation. I felt hu-miliation, disgrace, embarrassment, remorse and sadness.

I finish and I take a final drag of my cigarette and I put it out in the ash-tray. My Father is holding my Mother and my Mother is crying. Tears are running down her cheeks, but her breathing is fine and there is no sob-bing. Joanne looks at my Parents.

Are you ready?

My Father speaks.

Yes.

Why don't you tell James how you felt.

My Father takes a deep breath and he looks at me and he speaks. I wish he would look away.

We were upset. Obviously very upset. The first thing I really felt was sur-prise, and after surprise, I felt shock. I know I work a lot, and I always have, and I'm not around as much as I would like to be, but I had no idea you have been doing some of the things you have been doing and I had no idea as to the extent to which you have been doing them. I think of crack as some horrible Ghetto drug that homeless People and schizophrenics and gang members smoke. I had no idea you did it, and it scares me and it upsets me to think about it. The alcohol. I knew you had a drinking problem, that has been obvious for a very long time, but if you have been getting sick and blacking out for as long as you say you have, and I believe you, you are a very, very serious Alcoholic. I was shocked by the drug dealing. Shocked, horrified and disappointed. If you had been caught you would have gone to Prison for a long time, and you're lucky you weren't caught. You also could have been killed, and I sort of think it's a miracle that you haven't been. As far as whatever your situations with the Law are now, I don't really know what to say. Obviously your Mother and I don't want you to go to Prison, and we'll do whatever we can to help you stay out of it. Aside from shock and surprise, I was disappointed and hurt and very sad. I was disappointed in you and in me and in your Mother. There is something very wrong between us if things have gotten to this point. I was hurt because it hurts to learn things like the things we learned. It hurt because I feel as if I have been lied to and duped for many years, and it hurt to know you thought you had to lie to us and hide things from us. I was mainly sad for you. Sad because you've been through some awful things, and no Parent, especially your Mother and me, would ever want that for their Child.

He looks down, takes a breath, looks back at me.

Part of me wanted to wring your neck this morning and part of me still does. Another part of me, the part I'm trying to let stay in control, wants to give you a hug and tell you everything's going to be all right. Another part of me says I should just give up and let you do whatever it is you're gonna do.

My Father stares at me, I look away. He turns to my Mother, who is staring at the floor. He pulls her in tight, reassuring her through his arms. I speak.

Dad.

He looks back at me.

I'm sorry.

I am too, James. I am too.

He looks back at my Mother. Her tears have stopped, though they have streaked her face.

Lynne.

My Mother nods.

Are you ready?

Mother nods again and she looks as if she's going to break down.

Take your time.

She pulls away from him slightly and she straightens herself out. She wipes her face with a tissue and she takes a deep breath.

Aside from the days when my Parents and my Brother and my Sister died, this morning was the worst morning of my life. I hated it. I hated hearing about all that stuff. I hated thinking about you having done it. I hated thinking about all the lies and the deception. I hated thinking about the drugs. I hated the stuff with the Police. I hated the drinking. I hated thinking it had been going on for so long. I hated everything about this morning.

She is crying. She wipes her face with her tissue again and she takes a deep breath.

I don't know why you do these things. I don't know what drives you to do such terrible things. It makes me think that I'm a terrible Mother and a terrible Person and that I haven't done anything right ever. It makes me hate myself.

Her breathing is becoming more labored. She wipes her face again.

I was shocked and hurt and scared. I feel like I don't know who you are. I don't know who you are and that's awful. You're my Son. You're my Son.

She breathes, cries, wipes.

I'm angry at you for all of this. It's such a mess. Crack and blacking out and selling drugs and fighting with the Police and Jail. It's just such a mess. It's my worst nightmare.

Cries become sobs. Tears a flood.

It makes me feel like a jerk for letting it happen and for defending you for all these years. Whenever anyone said anything bad about you, I defended you and told them they were wrong. I guess I was wrong.

She doesn't bother wiping the tears anymore.

I had so many dreams for you.

She sobs.

You could have been anything you wanted. Anything.

Sobs.

And you're this.

Sobs.

This.

My Father puts his arms around her. She buries her face in his chest. She wails and she heaves, she clutches the sleeves of his shirt. I sit and I watch and I wait. I don't know what to do. I want to give my Parents a hug and tell them I'm sorry, but I can't. I want to beg for their forgiveness, but it's not going to happen. I want to take their hands and tell them everything is going to be okay, but that's not a promise I know I can make. I sit and I watch and I wait. I don't know what to do. I want to touch them, but I can't.

My Mother continues to cry. She cannot will not is unable to stop. My Father holds her and he stares at the floor over her shoulder. Joanne stands and she walks to me and she leans to my ear.

I think you should go.

I stand.

You have a meeting with Daniel and your Parents tomorrow morning. It's in the same Room we were in earlier.

I walk to the door. Before I leave, I turn and I look at my Mother and my Father. My Mother is crying, my Father staring at the floor. Joanne is down on one knee and she is whispering kind words to them, words that I do not deserve to hear.

I open the door and I walk out. I make my way back to the Unit. Night has fallen and the Halls are dark. Overhead lights illuminate them. I hate the lights I want them gone. I wish the Halls were darker. I am craving the dark the darkest darkness the deep and horrible hole. I wish the Halls were fucking black. My mind is black my heart is black I wish the Halls were black. If I could, I would destroy the lights above me with a fucking bat. I would smash them to fucking pieces. I wish the Halls were black.

I open the door to my Room. I walk in and I sit down on my bed. Miles is not here and I am alone. My mind is black and my heart is black and I am alone.

I take off my shoes and I take off my socks. I pull my foot my right foot onto the thigh of my left leg. I look down at my toes. They are dirty and gnarled and foul with sweat. I am alone and the Fury is within me. It is not raging, nor near its height, but it is there. It flows through my veins like a slow, lazy virus, urging me to do damage, but not enough damage to constitute destruction. I want it to go away. I want it to leave me. When it is at its full, I am often at its mercy, but not now. I know what to do to make it go away, I know how to make it disappear. Feed it pain and it will leave me. Feed it pain and it will go away.

With the thumb and forefinger of my right hand, I start pulling at the nail of the second toe of my left foot. I know it's sick, a sick fucking symptom of an infected mind, but I do it anyway. I pull. I pull at the nail.

It is always this toe, always this nail. As it has grown back from my last bout with it, it has grown in a way that makes it easy to do it again. It sticks up a little higher than the rest of my nails, its shape is more ragged. It has edges that I can get beneath, edges that provide leverage. I pull. I pull at the nail. It starts to break away at its tip. It starts to hurt. The Fury inside of me howls with delight. Give me more. Give me more.

I pull and the nail breaks further. It tears the skin that holds it in place, severs the veins that feed it. Blood starts to flow. The pain starts moving. Like the blood, the pain is red. It moves down my toe and into my foot, it dances around my ankle. I can feel the Fury feeding on it. Give me more. Give me more.

I look down. My fingers and my foot are covered in blood. I can see the nail through the red, see it hanging by its base. I know the Fury sees it because I can feel it. It feels like a starving demon. Feed me. Feed me. Feed me that goddamn nail. Feed me, you Motherfucker, or I will ruin you. Feed me that goddamn nail.

I put my finger above the nail and my thumb between it and the exposed pink flesh of my toe. My thumb brushes the flesh and the pain turns from red to white and it shoots up my leg and into my stomach. It is instantly devoured and there is an instant call for more. Feed me, you Motherfucker, or I will ruin you. Feed me that goddamn nail.

I pull. I pull at the nail. One half of it rips from its base. I close my eyes my hand is covered in blood I clench my jaw and I cry out softly I cry. The pain is overwhelming and I am full of it. From the tips of my hair all the way down and through everything everywhere the pain is everywhere. The Fury is gobbling it up. The Demon is drinking. One more tear and it will be full.

I pull. I pull at the nail. It tears free and I cry out my cry is not so soft this time. Pain is everywhere, white and flaming and cold as Hell. Every cell in my body is twitching and electric, full of hate and thankful with relief. The Fury rises briefly rises with a smile and screams bloody murder thank you. It eats the pain. It drinks it. It takes it every way it can. It makes it go away go away now. I have given you what you wanted, go away now.

I let out a deep breath. A deep, deep breath like that after ecstasy, like that after your life has flashed before your eyes. I look at my foot. It is covered in blood, as is my hand. I stand and I walk to the Bathroom. As I step with my damaged foot, I place only the heel on the floor. Every time it hits, there is a throbbing bolt of electric red and white lightning. Every time it hits, the bolt is eaten.

I open the door. I step toward the sink, carefully avoiding the mirror. When I reach the sink, I turn on the cold water. I wait until it gets as cold as it can get. When it arrives, the coldest the sink can provide, I lift my foot into the air and place it beneath the faucet. Drops of blood hit the floor as I lift and I lean over to wipe them with my clean hand.

The water meets the flesh and everything is pink. The pink runs down the drain and more pink follows it. The cold cauterizes the pain, and the

Fury cleans it licks its lips of the last of it and fades away. I stand and I wait. I clean my hand. Everything is pink. Blood is flowing.

After a moment or two a few brief moments, the pressure from the water seals the wounds on my toe and closes the torn ends of the broken vessels. The toe throbs. It's not so bad. I would rather have the throb than the alternative. I would rather feed it than let it run wild.

I turn off the water and I remove my foot from the sink and I walk back to my bed. I put on my sock and I put on my shoe. I leave the Room.

It is almost time for me to leave, almost ten o'clock. I walk into the Unit. Men are scattered about the Room. They are watching TV, playing cards, smoking cigarettes and telling stories, waiting for the phone. Leonard is in the Phone Booth and I can hear complaints about the time he is spending there. Complaints, but no action. Against most men there would be action. I get a cup of coffee. A man dressed in black sweatpants and a black T-shirt is standing against a wall on the Lower Level of the Unit. He is in his mid-twenties and though he is thin, he looks strong. He is smoking a cigarette and he is staring at me. Something in him strikes me as familiar, though I don't know from where, and something in him strikes me as menacing, though I do not know why. He is just standing there staring at me. I stand my ground and I stare back. There is no effort behind his stare, he believes whatever it is that is going through his mind. He's familiar and menacing. I don't know why.

He chuckles and he moves off the wall and he pulls his eyes away from me and he walks toward one of the couches in front of the TV and he sits down. I watch him the entire way. I stood my ground, I have a feeling I will need to stand again.

I walk back to my Room with my coffee. Miles is sitting on his bed polishing his clarinet. He looks up at me when I enter.

What's up, Miles?

Not a thing, James. How are you?

I'm okay.

I sit on my bed, start putting on warmer clothes.

How did it go with your Parents this evening?

Fine, I guess.

How did they react?

Not as badly as I thought they would, but bad enough.

How did you feel about it?

About the same.

But more ashamed than anything else?

Probably.

Shame is a terrible thing. Necessary, but terrible.

You're still fighting with it?

I suspect I am going to be for a long time.

Why?

I am not a good man, James.

You're a Judge. You can't be that bad.

I am a Judge, but in my heart, I know I don't deserve to sit in judgment over anyone.

You're just being hard on yourself.

He shakes his head.

I haven't told anyone this, though the Staff knows, but I have been here before. This is my second term at this Clinic.

When was your first?

The first time was years ago. I came because, like now, I had a very bad drinking problem, a problem that nearly destroyed me. It almost destroyed my career, and in many ways, it destroyed my first marriage, which was to a wonderful woman with whom I had a Son.

How old is he?

He's twelve now. He's a fine young man. I wish I got to see him more.

So you're here again, that is nothing to be ashamed of.

He sets down his clarinet.

It is, James, for me it is.

Why?

It took me years to get over what happened last time. Years of long nights alone looking at myself in the mirror, years of hard work staying sober, and years trying to make up for my indiscretions. Now, after all that, I have done it again.

Why do you think that?

I have mentioned my Wife to you before. She is a great woman. She is smart, beautiful, challenging, independent, successful in her field. She is everything I have always sought in a partner. When I first met her, I knew right away I wanted to marry her. On our first date, I told her of my history. I wanted to be honest with her, and in being honest with her, I hoped to not repeat that history. After I told her, she smiled and said, Miles, you are a beautiful man, and I knew from the first second I saw you that we were going to be together, but if you pull that type of shit on me, I will kick your ass and leave you like yesterday's garbage.

I chuckle, he smiles.

I liked that she said that too, and I liked it even more because I knew she meant it. I thought it would be good for me to know that if I went astray again, I would be punished for my sins. We were married, we lived as Husband and Wife for several years, we decided to have Children, and she got pregnant. I was feeling very confident, perhaps too confident, about who I was and how I could live my life.

He stops, looks at the floor, takes a deep breath.

Around this same time, I went to a conference for Federal Judges. It was in Florida, on the beach, at a very nice hotel. There was a golf course there, and on the first day of the conference, I played golf with some other Judges that I was friendly with, but did not know well. After we finished playing, we went to an outdoor Restaurant for dinner. It was a gorgeous night, and I had played well, and I had just spoken with my Wife, and I was at the pinnacle of my career, and I felt good, very good about who I was and what I had done with my life. When it came time to order, all of the other Judges ordered cocktails. I decided I would as well. I ordered a whiskey and coke. I thought that I could handle it. As soon as I took my first sip, and I felt the alcohol hit me, I knew I was in trouble.

He shakes his head.

I left the table a few minutes later and went to my room and drank most of what was in the minibar. I slept in the next day and skipped the conference and when the minibar was refilled, I did it again. When I went home, I started hiding liquor in my house, in my office and in my car, and I drank as much as I could. Soon enough, I was drinking all day and drinking all night. I started keeping a bottle of bourbon under my Bench. I would put it in a glass and drink it during Court proceedings. I pretended it was water, and I consumed it like it was water. I tried to stop, and I couldn't. I passed out one afternoon during a recess in proceedings, and when I came to, an Officer of the Court was waiting for me. He told me that my Wife had been trying to call me and had left several urgent messages. I immediately went to see her, and when she asked if I was all right, I told her that I was sick with the flu. She knew I was lying and she confronted me. She told me that she had warned me about falling off the wagon and that she had known that I had been drinking very heavily. She had hoped I would stop, but now realized that I wouldn't. I tried to deny there was a problem, but she pulled out several bottles that she had found in various places where I had hidden them and told me it was time to stop lying. Then she told me to leave. I immediately came here.

He takes a deep breath.

My Wife arrives here next week for the Family Program. I am expecting the worst, and I feel like I deserve it. I have now done this more than

once, and I feel it is deplorable, and I feel it is the worst type of crime a
man can commit against his Family. I hate myself for it and I am
ashamed of it, deeply, deeply ashamed. At certain points in my career I
have sentenced men to death by execution. I feel in many ways that
would be a reasonable sentence for me. I know that sounds melodra-
matic, but to me it sounds right.

He shakes his head.

I am ashamed to the point where I don't know if I want to go on living. I
don't know you well, but I sense that you are struggling with some of
these same issues. I can also see you changing, that you seem to be finding ways to handle them. When I ask you questions about what you're
doing, it is because I am seeking a way to give myself hope for some form
of redemption. I am a believer in God, but God no longer seems to believe in me. If you know anything or have anything that you think might
help me, I would be very thankful if you would be kind enough to share
it with me.

I smile.

Why are you smiling?

Because I think it's funny that a Federal Judge is asking me for advice.
We are all the same in here. Judge or Criminal, Bourbon Drinker or
Crackhead.

I guess so.

Do you have anything you might be able to share with me, James?

I got two things.

What are they?

The first thing is Leonard.

West Coast Finance Director Leonard?

I laugh.

Yeah, West Coast Finance Director Leonard. You should go talk to him.
Tell him I sent you and tell him you want to hear about holding on.

Holding on to what?

Just ask him.

I will do that. What is the second thing?

You ever see me reading that little book?

I point to the *Tao*. It is sitting on my nightstand.

Yes.

In about thirty seconds, I'm gonna climb out that window above your
bed.

Miles laughs.

After I'm gone, pick up the book and give it a read. You might think it's nonsense, and it very well may be nonsense, but it seems to do me good whenever I read it.

Why do you think it does that?

It just makes sense to me.

I'll give it a try.

I stand, walk toward his bed.

You mind letting me through?

He moves out of the way.

I'm not going to ask you where you're going or what you're doing.

That's probably best.

Be careful not to get caught.

I open the window and I step through it and I close it behind me. I feel the cold immediately. It is strong, bitter, tense and angry. It bites at my face and the exposed skin of my hands like a termite bites at wood.

I start walking. I walk quickly, avoiding all light and avoiding all windows. In the shadows I am safe and I am strong and I am comfortable. I know I won't get caught in the shadows.

I find the Trail and I let it take me toward the Clearing. I step off where I always step off and I push my way through thick tangles of branches and through a tapestry of Evergreens.

As I approach the Clearing I start to rush. My eyes see but my mind registers moments of the future soon to be in Lilly's arms. A branch strikes me. Across my cheek it tears the skin, not deep but deep enough.

I step into the Clearing and she is there. She is sitting on frozen ground wrapped in a blanket her pale skin shining. She smiles and she stands and without words, she steps forward, opens the blanket, envelops me within it and within her and within myself. She kisses my cheek, the one not torn, she wraps me and she holds me. Her arms are thin but strong. She whispers in my ear.

I'm glad you're here.

So am I.

I missed you.

I missed you too.

She releases me a little, enough to gain space. She steps to my side.

Let's sit.

She stays at my side and she guides me down. We sit on frozen dirt and sharp leaves and brittle sticks. She reaches up and she delicately touches my cut cheek.

What happened?

I ran into a branch.

You couldn't see?
I wasn't paying attention.
You want me to make it better?
How you gonna do that?
I've got special powers.
Really?
You want to see?
Yeah.
She leans forward and she starts to kiss my cheek. I pull away.
What are you doing?
Healing you.
That's a fresh wound.
I know.
That's running blood.
I know.
You're willing to take that risk?
She leans forward.
I am.
I don't stop her. Her lips hit my cheek slightly open. Her tongue dances across the flesh of my face. I close my eyes. She pulls herself toward me her arms holding thin and strong. I move myself toward her my arms open and free. She kisses down my cheek to the edge of my mouth it responds. It says come and we meet. Our open mouths meet. Fast and slow alternating hard and soft pressing and receiving seeking and being sought. Loving and being loved.
We are beneath the blanket. We slide to the ground it is no longer cold. She is on me and I am on her side by side our hands wandering along the length of the other. Our hands meet. Embrace. Hold. Our hands. A current connected physically and otherwise.
She slips her hand away out of mine and it moves down my chest, my stomach, beneath my stomach, down. I like it there feel it there want it there but fear interlopes great fear I am scared. I push her hand away gently push it away. We are still together our lips meeting she moves her hand back I push it away. I am scared. Great overwhelming fear. Fear near panic fear. She pulls our lips apart she speaks.
What's wrong?
I can't go any further.
You're shaking.
I know.
Why?

I'm scared.
Of what?
Everything.
What's that mean?
I'm just scared.
Of me?
No.
She pulls me closer.
I'm not gonna hurt you.
I know.
I'm not gonna leave you.
I know.
Tell me why you're scared.
I look at her face close to me. At her eyes clear blue. Even in the dark
they are clear water blue.
I've never done this before.
What?
What I think we're going to do.
What do you mean?
I've never done it before.
You've never had sex?
I have, but not like this.
What do you mean?
Never sober.
What about that Girlfriend?
Never.
Why?
I don't know.
I'm not gonna hurt you.
I know.
Why?
I take a deep breath. I'm scared. I speak.
She was a virgin when I met her. She had been saving herself until she fell
in love. After a couple of months she decided that she was ready. We
talked about it and we set a date and we went out for a fancy Dinner. I
was really nervous, so I drank through the whole date before to try and
calm myself down. When we got back to her Room she had candles
burning and flowers on her bed and classical music playing on her stereo
and it was like something out of a silly movie. We started fooling around,

and when it came time, I couldn't get it up. I wanted to more than anything in my whole life, but I couldn't do it because I was scared and I was drunk.

I take another breath, start to shake more, feel more scared. I hate the memories and I hate myself for creating them.

We tried again and again and again. We tried every night for a couple of weeks and I could never do it. Each time I failed I felt worse and worse and more and more humiliated and embarrassed. She was offering herself to me, and I couldn't take her because I was impotent. Every time we tried I was fucking impotent.

We stayed together for a while, but we weren't really together, we were just sort of each other's habit. In her case it was a bad habit, in my case it was a good one. The last time we tried to have sex I decided to tell her that I loved her. I thought that if I did that it would make my fear go away and everything would work. We were naked and in bed and I was okay and I looked into her eyes. She had these eyes, very blue, not like yours, but lighter and more like ice, and I looked into them and I said I love you. She didn't say anything back. She just stared at me with those eyes, and they were cold and empty and far away, and they looked as if what I had said had made them sick. I said it again and she pushed me off of her and she got out of bed and she went to the Bathroom. When she came back she smiled and she said I think you're a very special person and she kissed me on the cheek and she turned over and went to sleep.

I take a deep breath.

I had thought for a long time that if I could be with her that she would be enough to make me straighten myself out. I had thought for a long time that somehow she could save me. When I was impotent with her, and I knew I had failed and it was over, I knew that I would never be anything but a drunk impotent embarrassing Asshole and that I might as well start seriously trying to kill myself with alcohol and drugs. So I did, and everywhere I went I saw her eyes, and when I think of her I still see them, her eyes at that moment when I told her I loved her, and I could see that I made her sick.

I stare into the blackness. It offers nothing. I am flooded with the feelings I felt with her they come back just as strong. Humiliation, embarrassment, shame, helplessness, impotence.

Lilly holds me, but leaves me to me. I stare into the blackness and I breathe. There is nothing that will change the past and nothing that will help me forget it. It was what it was and it was what it was because of me.

I wish it were different, but there's nothing I can do. It's in the past. It is time to accept it and let it go.

Lilly pulls back. She looks at me and she speaks.

You stopped shaking.

For now.

When it happens, we'll go slow.

That would be nice.

As slow as you want or you need.

Thank you.

And it'll be nice for me too.

Why?

We sort of talked about this before.

A little.

Do you need more than a little?

I need what you want to give me.

I want to give you everything.

Then tell me what you need to tell me.

She pauses, smiles.

This is scary.

I know.

Really scary.

I'm not gonna hurt you.

She smiles again.

I know.

And I'm not gonna leave you.

I know.

And I'm not gonna judge you.

Thank you.

She smiles, looks away for a moment, looks back. Her smile disappears and the brightness of her eyes fades and she starts speaking. She tells me about her Mother. About her Mother's addictions and her Mother's pain. She tells me about her Mother's work as a prostitute and how her Mother sold her. She was thirteen. A man who paid for her Mother saw her and he wanted her. Her Mother needed drugs. Her Mother sold her to the man for two hundred dollars. Sold her for an hour and sold her for a lifetime. Sold her virginity for a syringe full of dope. Two hundred dollars for a syringe full of dope.

She tells me about the men after that man. How her Mother sold her regularly and stopped working herself. She tells me about the pain and the misery and the horror. Man after man. Day after day. Violation after violation. There were always syringes full of dope. Paid for with her body. She tells me how she started using them. How she hated them and how they helped her. Man after man. Day after day. Violation after violation. The syringes helped.

She tells how she left. After four years of terror. A man beat her and used a loaded gun on her and in her and after he was done, she walked out. She didn't have any money or any belongings, she didn't have a car. She just walked out and kept walking, hitchhiking her way to Chicago, paying for it on her back with a few minutes satisfying Truckers. When she got to Chicago, she called information and she found her Grandmother. She had never met her when she went to her house. She knocked on the door and her Grandmother opened it and they both started crying. There were no words, just tears. She and her Grandmother crying.

She tells me how she went back to School. How the Boys loved her and the Girls hated her. How she felt as if she was so far behind. How hard it was to stay away and stay clean and be decent. How hard it was to forget. How it was impossible to forget. How she met a Boy and she liked him and she started going out with him. How she had hopes and dreams, how she played out fantasies in her mind. The Boy started smoking crack and using pills and she wanted to be with him and she went along with him. She started smoking crack and using pills. He started using her. His friends started using her. Her heart was broken it had never healed it just broke again. She was smoking crack and using pills. He and his friends used her.

Something happened. She starts to speak of it and she starts to cry. It was shortly before she came here. Shortly before her Grandmother made her drive herself toward freedom. She stops speaking and she starts to cry. Heavy violent tears. Heaving sobs. She shakes and I can feel her heart through layers and layers of clothing. Through layers and layers of pain. I hold her and she cries and there are no words anymore not from her or from me. There are no words that mean anything in the face of how she has lived her life. In what she has endured. I hold her and she cries. I am not going anywhere. I'm not going to hurt her. I'm not going to leave her. I'm not going to judge her. I hold her and she cries.

hear my name. I feel someone kicking me. I'm not sure if it is real, I am not sure what to do. My name. A foot. Someone is calling me. Someone is kicking me.

I open my eyes. It is still dark, but getting lighter. Somewhere in the hour before dawn. I see outlines of trees and Lilly in my arms. Someone is calling me. Someone is kicking me.

I look up. Ted is standing above me with a blonde Girl in her late twenties. Both look tired, both have messy hair. Ted speaks.

I thought you were dead, you Little Fucker.

What are you doing here?

Saving your ass.

What time is it?

Time to fucking go.

I gently shake Lilly. She opens her eyes.

What?

We gotta go.

Who are you talking to?

A friend. His name's Ted.

What time is it?

I don't know.

We stand. I'm awake, but not completely. Lilly isn't even close. She knows the Girl with Ted and they say hello. I kiss her good-bye and I tell her I'll miss her. She asks me when we'll see each other again and I tell her tonight.

Ted and I walk through the Woods toward the Trail. I ask him what he was doing and he says getting laid. He asks me what I was doing and I say talking. He laughs. I ask him if he's been out here before and he says every goddamn night. He asks me and I tell him no, it was my first time. We hit the Trail. He says be careful and get ready to run, if we get caught out here, we'll be in deep shit. I haven't run anywhere in a long time. I don't have the lungs for it.

The Trail fades into the grass surrounding the Buildings of the Clinic. We make it inside safely and I go to my Room and I climb into bed. I wish I was still with Lilly. I fall asleep. I wish she was here.

When I wake up, Miles is gone, but there is a note on my nightstand. It is sitting on top of the *Tao*. It reads thank you, James, it made sense. The note makes me smile.

The alarm inside tells me I'm late, so I take a quick shower, brush my teeth, dry off and get dressed. Leave.

I hurry through the Halls to the Dining Hall. When I arrive, it is nearly empty. I get a donut and a cup of coffee and I leave.

More Halls. I hurry. I'm late to meet my Parents. The Fury is with me, but barely. It is still full from its feeding. I find the Room, open the door.

My Parents are sitting at the conference table with Daniel on one side of them, and a man I don't know, dressed like my Father, but slightly younger, on the other side. My Mother is crying.

What's wrong?

She shakes her head. I look to my Father.

What's wrong?

He stands, speaks.

James, this is Randall.

He motions to the man, who also stands.

He's an Attorney who works for the Clinic.

I look at the man.

Hello, Randall.

He reaches over the table.

Hello, James.

We shake hands. My Father speaks.

He's been talking to the Authorities in Michigan, North Carolina and Ohio.

What'd they say?

Why don't you sit down.

I sit down. I'm nervous and scared. They sit down.

What'd they say?

My Father looks at Randall, Randall looks at a file. My Mother cries and she stares at the floor. Daniel stares at me. I'm nervous and scared, starting to shake. The Day of Judgment has arrived. The Day of Judgment. Randall looks up.

I've good news and bad news. Which would you like first?

The good.

Michigan and North Carolina want Misdemeanor Possession. Your time in here will be time served. You'll have some fines, a couple thousand dollars in each place, and your Record will be cleared in three years. The Courts in both places are overloaded and want this to go away. I'd recommend going along with what they've offered.

My Father speaks.

So would I, James.

I nod.

Okay. What's the bad news?

Randall speaks.

You're in a lot of trouble in Ohio. It's a Small Town and they don't see much like what they saw with you. They say that you caused quite a few problems there and made a number of enemies within the Police Department. They are incredibly angry, as angry as any Prosecutors that I have ever had to deal with on a case, and they want to make an example out of you. They don't particularly care that you are here and that you're trying to get your life in order. They say they have an open-and-shut case and they'll be happy to go to Trial. I believe them.

He takes a deep breath.

I'm nervous and scared. Scared to fucking death. The Day of my Judgment has arrived.

If you agree to plead guilty to all of the charges, they'll agree to three years in State Prison, followed by five years of Probation. If you violate your Probation, you will be required to serve the full term of the Sentence, which is an additional five years. You will be required to pay fifteen thousand dollars in fines and to fulfill one thousand hours of Community Service upon release. Your driving privileges in the state will be permanently revoked. Your Record will be permanently marked.

If you force them to go to Trial, they're saying that if you're convicted, they will press for the maximum Sentence, which is eight and a half years. As far as the Trial prospects go, they are claiming to have thirty witnesses, a blood test registering your blood alcohol level at point two nine, and a bag of crack cocaine. If that's true, as they say, it's an open-and-shut case.

The fear is gone, replaced by horror. My Father stares at me, my Mother cries. Daniel looks at the wall, Randall waits for a response.

Fuck.

My Mother looks up.

Could you not say that word, James?

I look at her.

I was basically just sentenced to three years in Prison, Mom. What the
fuck am I supposed to say?
Her lips quiver.
Please.
I clench my jaw.
Fine.
My Father speaks.
Any ideas?
No.
Do you think they have all of that evidence?
Yes.
What do you want to do?
I look at Randall.
What can I do?
He shrugs.
I can go back to them with something, but I'm not optimistic about it.
What's that mean?
It means they probably won't budge.
I shake my head, think about three years in a State Prison. A moment ago
fear became horror. At this moment, the fear has come back and the hor-
ror is still here. Three years in a State Prison. Three years of savagery,
three years of fighting and three years protecting myself every second of
every day. Three fucking years.
What if I run?
My Father speaks.
No more running.
I look at him.
This is my decision, Dad.
No, it's not.
Yes, it is.
You're not paying for whatever it costs.
You gonna be in the cell with me?
No, I'm not.
Then I am paying for whatever it costs.
I look at Randall.
What if I run?
My Father speaks.
I won't allow that to happen.
I ignore him.

What if I run, Randall?

There is a seven-year Statute of Limitations. If you stay out of trouble, at the end of that term, you're a free man. If you get caught for anything at any point during that time, even a traffic ticket, you'll likely be jailed, extradited, tried and forced to serve the full term. I would highly, highly, highly recommend against that course of action.

I put my face in my hands, speak to myself.

Fuck.

My Mother speaks.

James.

I look up at my Mother.

Sorry.

She's crying and her lips are quivering.

My Father speaks.

What would you like to do?

I don't know.

Would you like to mount a defense?

It'd be a waste of time and money.

Why?

Because I'm guilty of all the charges.

Your Mother and I will pay for it.

You've paid enough. I don't want you to pay any more.

What do you want to do?

I need to think.

I stare at the floor. I'm guilty of all the charges. Three years in a State Prison is an eternity, a fucking eternity, and it's likely I'll be put in Maximum Security. I have never been there, but I know people who have been there. They did not come out rehabilitated and they did not come out resembling who they were when they went in. Addicts became Thieves. Thieves became Dealers. Dealers became Killers. Killers killed again. I look up at Randall.

Tell them I'll plead guilty to everything.

My Mother interrupts.

You'll be a convicted Felon.

Doesn't look like I have a choice about that, Mom.

I look at Randall.

I'll plead guilty, but for now, tell them I'll keep running unless I get some placement other than placement on a Maximum Security Block. Try and get the time down, if you can. If there's any sort of choice, which sounds like an incredible longshot, I would rather do more time than go into Max.

Randall nods, speaks.
You said for now, what's later?
I don't know.
He looks to my Father.
Does this sound okay to you?
My Father speaks.
Let's see what happens.
Randall looks at his watch, closes his file, stands.
I need to go. I'll call North Carolina and Michigan and tell them we've
got deals. I'll call Ohio and see what I can do. I can't promise anything.
I stand, reach for his hand.
Thank you.
He takes it.
You're welcome.
My Father does the same and Randall walks out. My Mother is staring at
the floor. She looks as if she wants to cry, but there are no more tears.
Daniel speaks.
Would you like to be alone?
My Father nods.
Yes, please.
Daniel stands.
I'll be at the Family Center if you need anything.
Thank you.
Daniel leaves. My Father stares at the table, my Mother at the floor. I
stare at the wall. There is an awful, uncomfortable silence. The type of si-
lence just after a bomb explodes and just before the screaming starts. We
sit in our chairs. We breathe, we think, we stare. It is awful and uncom-
fortable. The bomb has exploded. We all just sit and stare.
The wall isn't giving me any answers. It just sits there bright and white. I
look up and see my Father take a deep breath and look up at me.
It has been an interesting and enlightening day and a half.
I'm sorry.
He shakes his head.
It's much worse than I thought, James.
I know. I'm sorry.
I don't know if we can help you this time.
I don't think you should.
We're your Parents. It's our instinct to try and help you.
I don't think you can this time, Dad.
He shakes his head. My Mother speaks.

I'm sorry, James.

I look at her.

You've got nothing to be sorry for, Mom.

I am though. I just keep wondering what we did wrong.

You didn't do anything wrong, Mom.

We must have done something.

She starts to break down. My Father stands and he goes to her. He pulls out a chair next to her and he puts his arms around her. She buries her face in his shoulder.

She cries. I watch her cry. I can't take this anymore. I can't take her crying, I can't take the guilt I feel because of it. I can't let her take responsibility for what I am and for what I have done, I can't let her try to accept any of the blame. I created this situation and I made the decisions that led me to where I am today. I made every goddamn one of them. It's not her fault, nor anyone else's fault. I can't take this anymore. I can't take it.

I push my chair back. I stand. My Father is holding my Mother as my Mother cries. She is crying because of me. I step toward them. I step again. I am two steps away I step again. I am one step away. They are not paying attention to me. They are lost in their own sorrow. Sorrow they do not deserve. Sorrow I have dumped down upon them. I step again. I am there. I am next to them. I am there.

The Fury speaks it says no. The Fury speaks it says turn and run. The Fury speaks it says fuck them let them deal with it. The Fury speaks it says I will make you pay. I say fuck the Fury. My Mother is crying. Fuck the goddamn Fury.

I get down on one knee. I am close enough to smell her tears. I reach forward and I touch my Mother's shoulder. It is the first time in all of my memory that I have initiated contact with either my Mother or my Father. I firm my grip so she knows it is there. It is the first time in all of my memory that I have initiated contact with either my Mother or my Father. The first time in my life. She lifts her head and she turns toward me. I speak.

Mom.

She stares at me.

I'm sorry.

She has been broken.

Truly, truly sorry.

Broken by me.

I fucked up your life, all of our lives, and I'm truly truly sorry.

She smiles a smile of happiness and a smile of sorrow, happiness for my gesture and sorrow for my life, and she takes one of her arms from around the width of my Father and she puts it around me. She pulls me in. She hugs me with one arm and I let her and I hug her back. I have never done this before. Hug my Mother. Never in my life.

My Father takes one of his arms and he puts it around me and I do the same. Take my arm and put it around him. My Mother is still crying she can't stop crying her youngest Son has just been sentenced to three years in Prison my Father and I hold her. We hold each other. We are a Family. Though I have been their child for twenty-three years, we have never been a Family. We are now. As we hold each other. As my Mother cries for my wasted life. As my Father tries to figure a way to save it. As I try to accept three years locked in a cell.

My Mother stops crying. Everything is streaked and stained, but she doesn't seem to care. She pulls her arm from my Father and leaves her arm on me and she wipes her face with her free hand. She sniffles. She takes deep breaths. She tries to compose herself. She speaks.

What are we going to do?

Wait and see, Mom.

I don't want you to go to Prison.

I don't either.

What are we going to do?

Let's just wait and see.

She nods and her nod is some form of cue that we my Family all under-stand. We pull away from each other and we sit, though not in our original chairs. We sit close. In a small half circle. We all know some-thing has changed, we are all exhausted. The change has drained us. We sit close. We are a Family.

My Father looks at his watch.

I think it's about time for lunch.

My Mother and I stand. We walk toward the door, open it, step outside the room. My Father speaks.

We'll see you this afternoon.

Yeah.

My Mother speaks.

Can I have another hug?

I smile.

Sure.

She steps forward. I put my arms around her. I am immediately uncom-fortable and I immediately feel as if I'm somewhere I don't belong. I gen-tly squeeze. I am more uncomfortable, feel more foreign and out of place.

She squeezes me, which makes me want to run. This is my Mother. I am hugging her. I don't want to hug her, but I want to try. I hold her tight and I hug her. It is but a small price to pay for all that I have done. She releases me and I step back. I feel better.

I'll see you later.

I turn and I walk away, through the Halls and toward food. I am hungry. Hungry from the cold of last night, hungry from the tension of the morning, hungry to feed just for the sake of feeding. Hungry.

I enter the Corridor. I glance through the glass to the women's side. I see Lilly sitting at a table. She is pretending not to notice me, but I know that she does. I am pretending not to notice her, but she knows that I do. In her arms last night after she cried she clung to me like a lost child. She held me strong and thin and she told me she never wanted to let go of me. She told me that she had never been so open or honest with anyone before and that the feeling scared her to death. She told me that she never wanted to let go. She asked me about my plans for the future and I told her I didn't have any and I didn't know what I was going to do. She told me that she is going to a Halfway House in Chicago, that she doesn't feel strong enough or free enough to live without some form of supervised support. She will be near her Grandmother and being near her Grandmother will make her feel better. She will be able to get a job and she will be able to start building a life in a City where she feels a sense of safety. After she finished speaking, she asked me again if I knew what I was going to do. I told her again I didn't know. She asked me if I had been to Chicago before and I told her yes, that's where both my Parents grew up. She asked if I still had Family there and I said yes. She asked if I would consider moving there and I said yes. She asked if I was considering it because that is where she is going to be living. I smiled and I thought for a moment and I said yes.

I get a tray and I get in line. I get a plate of chipped beef, a plate of chicken strips and rice, a plate of turkey taquitos. I carry the tray to the Dining Room. My friends are at a table in one of the far corners. I walk toward them.

I sit down so I can see Lilly and Lilly can see me. Leonard and Miles and Ed and Ted and Matty are talking about the imminent Heavyweight Boxing Match. They ask me what's new, I tell them about my Sentence. They are all surprised. They figured whatever time I was looking at was likely to be short and easy. Leonard asks what I did and I tell him. Ed and Ted both say nice work, three years for popping a Cop is probably worth it. Matty says he knows some good fighting tricks that will help me once I go inside and he'd be glad to teach them to me. Miles asks in what Jurisdiction the case is located.

We eat. I glance at Lilly. We talk. Prison is the main topic of conversation. Everyone at the table has been to Prison except for Miles and me. Leonard did what he calls an easy four at Leavenworth Federal Penitentiary in Kansas. Matty spent six years in a Juvenile Correctional Facility, where he learned to box. Ed did two years at Jackson in Michigan for Assault with Intent to Inflict Great Bodily Harm, Ted has twice been to Angola State Farm in the swamps of Louisiana. Miles says he has sentenced men to Angola, but he has never been there. He says from what he hears, it is Hell on Earth. It is located in the deep bog, hot, humid and miserable, fifty miles from the nearest town. Cells are often open, the Yard is basically unsupervised, and there are scores of Gangs, usually organized according to race, that are in a constant state of War. The busiest part of the entire Facility is the Morgue. When men aren't fighting or hiding or trying to survive, they work fourteen-hour days in the state-owned fields digging irrigation ditches and growing vegetables. Ted laughs and says it ain't that bad. Miles says if that's what you think, you are either the sickest man alive or you're just fooling yourself. Ted stops laughing and says he's facing Life-No-Parole there under the Third-Strike Law, and that if anything, he's just trying to get prepared for it. Miles asks what the strikes are and Ted says Armed Robbery at nineteen, for which he did four years, Possession of a Controlled Substance with Intent to Distribute and Possession of an Automatic Weapon when he was twenty-five, for which he did three years, and most recently, at thirty, Statutory Rape, after he was caught in the backseat of a Trans Am with the fifteen-year-old Daughter of a Small-Town Sheriff. Miles asks why the District Attorney would push on the Statutory charge if he knew Ted was facing Life-No-Parole. Ted laughs and he says he did the same thing with the DA's two Daughters, but that they were both in love with him and were unwilling to press charges. Miles shakes his head in disbelief and asks if Ted would like him to try and help him. Ted says fuck yes, my life is at stake here. Miles says he'll see what he can do.

We finish eating and we stand. As we walk out, I see Bobby sitting at a table with the familiar man the menacing man the man I know but do not know from where. Bobby is staring at me. The man is staring at me. I stare back. I hold my ground.

We leave the Dining Room. My friends go to the Lecture, I go to the

Family Center. When I enter the Main Room, I see my Parents in the same chairs they were in yesterday. As I walk toward them, they stand and they greet me. Dad speaks.
How was your lunch?
Okay.
Mom speaks.
Who did you eat with?
I have some friends in here.
What are they like?
Do you really want to know that?
Dad speaks.
Of course we do.
My closest friend is some kind of Mobster. My Roommate is a Federal Judge. My other friends are Crackheads and Drunks. I sort of have a Girlfriend, and she's a Crackhead and a Pillpopper and she used to be a prostitute.
My Mother cringes, though she tries to hide it. She speaks.
Are they nice People?
I nod, smile.
They are, and in weird ways, they're the best friends I've ever had.
That's all that really matters, if they're nice People and you like them.
I do. Very much.
Dad speaks.
Aren't male/female relationships against the Rules here?
They are.
Do you think you should be doing it?
There are a lot of Rules here. I try to follow most of them, but this Girl, her name is Lilly, has been good for me. She's cool, she's smart, she listens to me, I listen to her, we understand each other. We're different and we come from different places, but in a lot of ways we're the same. We're both wrecked, we're both trying to get better. We both need help and we're trying to help each other.
My Mom speaks.
Would I like her?
If you could get past what she's done and what she's been through.
I think I could.
Then yeah, you would. You'd like her a lot.
Do you love her?
You know I don't like talking about that stuff with you, Mom.
Maybe you can try, though?

I smile, look down at the floor. I have hidden as much as I could from
my Mother and my Father for my entire life. I don't want to do that any-
more, so I look up and I look at my Mother and I speak.
I haven't told her, but yes, I love her.
My Mother and my Father smile. They are bright, genuine smiles, the best
smiles I have seen since I have been here. My Mother speaks.
I wish we could meet her.
You will someday.
My Father speaks.
Next time you see her will you tell her we said hello.
I smile.
I will.
The bell rings. The man standing next to the bell tells us to go to the same
Rooms we were in yesterday. I stand and I say good-bye to my Parents and
I hug them. I am not comfortable doing it, but I do it anyway.
I walk to the Room. The chairs are arranged in a circle again. I sit down,
a young woman is on one side of me, a middle-aged man on the other.
We nod to each other and we say hello. Sophie walks in and she takes a
seat an empty seat at the head of the circle and she introduces herself.
Around the room we follow. Introducing ourselves.
The introductions end. Sophie stands and she takes two steps backward.
There is a large, white, laminated board on the wall behind her, a tray at its
base is lined with colored erasable markers. Sophie grabs one of the markers
a blue marker and she starts writing on the board. When she's finished, she
steps away. The words read Addiction = Disease, Alcoholism = Disease.
She starts speaking. She tells us that now that we have a general idea about
addictive behaviors and the impact that they have on both the Addicts and
the Family Members of the Addicts, we need to start understanding the
cause of those behaviors. She says that addiction is a disease. Whether it is
to alcohol or drugs or food or gambling or sex or anything else, it is a disease. It is a chronic and progressive disease. It is classified as such by most
Doctors and by organizations such as the American Medical Association
and the World Health Organization. It is a disease that can be arrested, or
placed into a state of remission, but that is incurable. No matter how hard
we try, no matter what action we take, addiction, she says, is incurable.
Absolutely incurable.
She starts talking about the causes of the disease. As with most diseases,
the belief is that the cause is genetic. She says that Alcoholics and Addicts
are born with a gene or a gene structure, precisely which is not yet
known, that, when activated, causes the disease to present itself in an in-

dividual. Once this has happened, and at this point there is no way to know if or when it will, the Addict is at the mercy of the disease. It cannot be controlled, it cannot be held in check by force of will, the decision to use or not use, to indulge or not indulge, to take or do or not take or not do, is not a decision that can be made because the disease makes the decision for you. The Addict always uses, always indulges, always takes, always does. The Addict always wants and always needs and that want and that need is always satisfied. The inability to control and the lack of choice is but a symptom of the disease. A dangerous and horrible symptom, but a symptom nonetheless. It is incurable. If active, there is no way to stop it.

She talks about the environmental aspects of the disease. The Family setting, the prevalence of drinking within the Family, the influence of friends, the availability of drugs and alcohol, factors of stress, the Social reliance and acceptance of chemicals and their use in everyday behaviors and functions. She talks about the control of the environment and its effect on someone who has an active form of the Disease. She says that removing as many triggers, which are environmental factors that may cause relapse, such as bottles of wine in a home or friends who abuse substances, is an important part of maintaining a healthy Recovery Program. When she finishes speaking, Sophie opens the floor to questions. Nearly everyone has one. A young Mother asks about the likelihood of addictive genes being passed from her Husband to their Children. The likelihood is very high. She asks how to deal with it. When they are old enough, talk to the Children and make them aware of it, and try to eliminate as many triggers as possible. The man next to me asks about medication. Are there any that can control the disease the way traditional medications control other diseases. There was one, Antabuse, which made Alcoholics vomit when they drank. It proved ineffective because it could be circumvented by not taking it. A middle-aged woman asks if there are specific groups that are more likely than others to be genetically predisposed to the disease. No, it is an equal-opportunity disease. It affects black, white, yellow, everyone in every culture around the World. A man whose Wife is in her fourth Treatment Center asks why the disease seems to return with greater strength each time she relapses. Sophie says that because of the progressive and chronic nature of the illness, when a state of remission is breached, the illness returns at the same level of strength it had when it remissed. He asks if there is any way to reduce the level of its strength. The answer is no. If active, the disease always becomes stronger.

There are a number of questions about Treatment options. A young man asks if there are any beyond what is traditionally taught in Treatment Centers, which are AA and the Twelve Steps. Yes, of course there are other ways. Do they work? No, they do not. Why? We don't know why, they just don't. AA and the Twelve Steps are the only real options. How successful are they? Fifteen percent of those who try them are sober for more than a year. Fifteen percent seems low. It is. Why? It is an incurable illness. Is there anything else we can do? Beyond loving your Family Member and trying to support them, there's nothing else you can do. Is there any way to increase our chances? Fifteen percent is the best we can give you.

I sit and I listen. I sit and I think. I don't ask any questions and I don't say a word. I would like to stand up and scream bullshit this is all fucking bullshit, but I don't do it. I don't believe that addiction is a disease. Cancer is a disease. It takes over the body and destroys it. Alzheimer's is a disease. It takes over the body and the mind and it ruins them. Parkinson's is a disease. It takes over the body and the mind and makes them shake and it wrecks them. Addiction is not a disease. Not even close. Diseases are destructive Medical conditions that human beings do not control. They do not choose when to have them, they do not choose when to get rid of them. They do not choose the type of the disease they would like or in what form it is delivered, they do not choose how much of it they would like or at what time they would like it. A disease is a Medical condition that must be dealt with using Medical technology. It cannot be dealt with using a Group or a set of Steps. It cannot be dealt with by talking about it. It cannot be dealt with by having Family Members attend three-day seminars about it or by reading books with blue covers or saying prayers about serenity.

Although genetics and a genetic link may be undeniable, everything about us is genetic, and everything about our physical selves is predetermined by a genetic link. If an individual is fat but wants to be thin, it is not a genetic disease. If someone is stupid, but wants to be smart, it is not a genetic disease. If a drunk is a drunk, but doesn't want to be a drunk anymore, it is not a genetic disease. Addiction is a decision. An individual wants something, whatever that something is, and makes a decision to get it. Once they have it, they make a decision to take it. If they take it too often, that process of decision making gets out of control, and if it gets too far out of control, it becomes an addiction. At that point the decision is a difficult one to make, but it is still a decision. Do I or don't I. Am I going to take or am I not going to take. Am I going to be a pathetic dumbshit Addict and continue to waste my life or am I go-

ing to say no and try to stay sober and be a decent Person. It is a decision. Each and every time. A decision. String enough of those decisions
together and you set a course and you set a standard of living. Addict or
human. Genetics do not make that call. They are just an excuse. They allow People to say it wasn't my fault I am genetically predisposed. It
wasn't my fault I was preprogrammed from day one. It wasn't my fault I
didn't have any say in the matter. Bullshit. Fuck that bullshit. There is always a decision. Take responsibility for it. Addict or human. It's a fucking decision. Each and every time.

Sophie finishes answering questions. The mood in the Room is somber.
The words genetic and disease and incurable and fifteen percent success
rate hang in the air like radioactive poison. Everyone looks around.
Everyone looks at each other. We all know that when we leave here,
eighty-five percent of us are going to return to the same problems we had
before we came. We have now been told that the root of them is something that is incurable.

We take each other's hands. We hold tighter than yesterday. We try to
squeeze hope from each other, try to bond in the hope that bonding will
change reality. It won't. Eighty-five percent of us are fucked.

We say the Serenity Prayer. God grant us the serenity to accept the things
we cannot change, the courage to change the things we can, and the wisdom to know the difference. We say it again, we say it again. Sophie has
us say it again and again until the poison lifts, until smiles start appearing
on faces. God, grant us the serenity, God, grant us the serenity. The
People are smiling, but smiles and prayers aren't going to change reality.
Eighty-five percent of us are fucked.

We finish, we stand, we file out of the Room. Primary Patients walk one
way, Family Members another. I walk back to the Unit and I get a cup of
coffee. I sit down at a table. The afternoon Session is just ending, a
Graduation is taking place. The Bald Man is standing before the men giving a speech. He says what he learned here has saved his life. He says that
if he hadn't come, he would have never stopped drinking, no matter what
the consequences, because, although he had tried, he did not know how
to stop. He says he knows how to stop now. He says that AA and the
Twelve Steps and his Higher Power have shown him the way. He says that
after his Wife and his Children, this way, this knowing how to stop, is the
greatest gift he has ever been given. The greatest gift by far. He starts to
cry. The men let him cry. Through his tears he says thank you. Thank
you for letting me come here and thank you for being here for me. He
starts to cry harder. He says thank you over and over. Thank you for my

life. Thank you for my Family. They mean everything to me. Thank you for everything. Thank you.

As he cries, the men sitting in front of him look at each other, unsure of what to do or how to react. I hear a clap. A single sharp sting of hand on hand, flesh on flesh. It is loud, and it pierces the uncertain looks of the men the way words of a Preacher pierce the hearts of Believers. I hear another clap. Another. Another. From around the room, isolated clapping becomes part of a unified expression of admiration and respect. The Bald Man cries. The men salute him.

He stands and he smiles. He wipes his face. The clapping continues. Leonard stands and he cheers and the men follow him. They stand and cheer, salute and respect. The Bald Man smiles wider, cries harder, the joy of the now this moment and of the bright, shining future with his Family lights his face, his skin, the round dome of his skull. It lights him lights through him dimming whatever he has done before the darkness of his past has been overwhelmed. I stand and I clap and I cheer. The hair on the back of my neck is alert and alive, there are chills running down the length of my spine. Good luck, Bald Man. I never knew you well but you showed me how to cry like a man. You were braver than me and the rest of the men here you were braver than all of us good luck. May you go home, be happy, live sober and free, live the life you imagine yourself living. May you love your Wife and Children and let them love you. Good luck, Bald Man.

He runs from the Room. Just like before, but not at all the same. As he runs he smiles and as he runs the men laugh, but it's not like before, not like it at all. He runs sober and free. The bright, shining future lies stretched out before him.

The men stop cheering they are happy and laughing and they start to go their separate ways. I see Miles approach Leonard, tap him on the shoulder, and they walk toward the door. I pick up my coffee and I walk to the phone and I get into the Booth and I sit down and I shut the door. I pick up the phone and I start making calls. I call my Brother. He asks how it's going with Mom and Dad. I say better than I thought it would. He says good, try to be cool, they are only there because they love you. I say I'm trying and he says keep trying, I say I will. I ask him to say hello to Kirk and Julie and he says he will. We hang up.

I call Kevin. Kevin lives in Chicago. He yells into the phone I can tell he's been drinking. It makes me sick and it makes me jealous. He's free. He's drinking. I can imagine the glass in his hand the liquid on his lips the feeling the feeling the feeling. I ask him about Chicago. He tells me it's cold. I ask him if I would like it he tells me I would. There are lots of dark alleys and places to hide. I tell him I'm not hiding I'm going to Jail before I move. He says fuck, man, fuck Jail. I say I have to go to Jail and when I'm out I'm moving to Chicago. He says that's great if you need anything I'll help you out you can stay with me when you get here. I say thank you and we hang up. He was drunk. It makes me sick and it makes me jealous.

I call her friends. The ones who became my friends. Amy, Lucinda, Anna. The conversations are all the same. How are you I'm good. I've been thinking of you thank you. Do you need anything I'm fine. The conversations are tense. As if they know something that they are not telling me. I can feel it, they can feel it. It is best left alone I leave it alone and so do they. It is none of my business anymore. They each say they love me. Not romantically but in the way people love when they have seen too much hard life and they have seen it together. They saw it with me. I say I love them back and I do. When we hang up when I hang up with each of them I feel better. Not because of their relationship with her, but because of their relationship with me.

I am finished with the calls. I have made enough of them and I know that my calls will spread among those who know me. I walk out of the Unit and through the Halls and the Glass Corridor that separates men and women in the Dining Hall. I glance through to find Lilly, she is sitting at a table. She is there with her friends and she is staring at me. Her eyes are red and swollen. There are stains of tears that have been washed away. I can see her hands shaking. She is staring at me as if she wishes I were dead.

I don't want to acknowledge her and risk more than we have risked or give away more than is already known, but she is staring at me. Staring at me as if she wishes I were dead. I stare back, lift my hands and lower my head and say what's wrong without words with my face and with my body. She stares at me. I do it again. I know I can be seen, but I don't care. She just stares at me.

I get a tray and I get in line and I get a plate of chicken casserole. It is covered in crispy Chinese noodles and unidentifiable greens. I walk toward a table I look through the glass. She is still staring at me. Her friends are staring at me. The entire table is staring at me.

I sit down with Ed and Ted and Matty. The subject of the conversation is Ed, who found out this morning that he is leaving tomorrow. He is going back to Detroit, going back to work in the Steel Mill. He is happy and hopeful. He knows that his Union insurance won't pay for him to go

through Treatment again, and he feels as if this time it might actually
work, or he might actually work at making it work. He is anxious to see
his Sons. He has four of them. He knows that he has set a horrible example for them, and he wants them to see that he has changed for the better.
He feels that the change will make a positive difference in their lives, that
it will help prevent them from growing up to be anything like himself. Ed
is a hard man. Big, strong, tough as the material he works with, and I
have never seen him be vulnerable in any sense of the word, but as he
talks of his Sons, his eyes get soft and wet. He wants them to have a good
life, a life better than his life has been. He wants them to finish School
and stay out of Jail, go to College and get white-collar Jobs. He wants
them to have Families, and when they do, to have an example of how to
be a good man within those Families. He wants them to have everything
he never had, and he wants to stay sober so that he can give it to them.
He says he needs to do one thing, which is stay out of Bars. If he goes to
Bars, he knows he will drink. If he drinks, he knows he will fight. If he
fights, he knows he'll be in trouble. His Union won't support him if he
gets into trouble again. He wants to set an example for his Children so
they don't end up like him. He knows this may be his last chance. He is
happy and hopeful.

We finish eating. As we walk out of the Dining Hall, I look through the glass
at the table where Lilly was sitting. Lilly is not there. The table is empty. I
don't know why, but she was looking at me as if she wished I were dead.

We walk through the Halls together. Matty and Ed and Ted discuss the absence of Leonard and Miles at dinner. They laugh about what they might
be doing together. A Mobster and a Judge. Ed says he saw them sitting on
the benches in front of the Lake, that they looked deep in conversation. Ted
says Leonard is asking Miles for some sort of Immunity in relation to something that Leonard has done. Matty says whatever they're doing it ain't
none of our business. We split up and they go to the Lecture and I go to
Joanne's Office.

Joanne is sitting behind her desk. I say hello to her, she says hello to me.
My Mother is sitting on the couch. She stands, says hello, gives me a hug.
I hug her back. I am still not comfortable touching her, and I am still not
comfortable having her touch me, but I know it's better if I let it happen.
She hugs me tight. I wait. She lets go of me. I feel better.

Where's Dad?

My Mother speaks.

He had a call he had to make for work. He'll be here as soon as he's
done.

Everything all right?

I think so.

I look at Joanne.

What are we doing tonight?

We're going to talk about the source of your addiction and what the root causes might be.

Do we wait for my Dad to do that?

Yes.

What do we do till then?

Your Mother was just telling me a story.

About what?

The first time she really believed you might be in trouble.

I look at my Mother.

When was it?

Do you remember when I found that bag of marijuana in your jacket pocket?

I chuckle.

Yeah.

Why are you laughing?

I don't know.

It wasn't funny, James.

I know, Mom.

Joanne speaks.

Did you find it funny, James?

Sort of.

Why don't you tell me your version of it.

I look at my Mother, she looks tense. I wait for a moment, collect my memories, speak.

I was fourteen. I had been away at Soccer Camp the Summer before. I had met this Girl there, I think her name was Emily, and we spent all of our time at the Camp sneaking away and smoking dope. When we left, we wrote each other. She was sort of a female version of me, which meant the letters were pretty explicit about drugs and drinking. One afternoon I came home from School and went to my Room and a bunch of my stuff, stuff that I kept hidden, including Emily's letters, was sitting on my dresser. I knew I was in trouble and I was pissed my Mom had gone through my shit, so I went back downstairs to find her and get it over with. When I walked into the Kitchen, she was standing there holding a bag of dope that she found in the pocket of my coat. She asked what's this and I asked her where she got it and she said don't talk back to me

young man and I said tell me where you got it and I'll tell you what it is
and she said stop mouthing off young man and I laughed.
I look at my Mother. Her face is white beneath her makeup. I look back
to Joanne.
She held the dope in front of me and she screamed **what is this where
did you get this you tell me right now.** I laughed and she kept screaming. I got sick of her screaming and I was pissed about the invasion of my
privacy, so as she was holding the bag up, I reached out and I snatched it
from her hand. She was shocked, and as I put the bag in my pocket, she
reared back to slap me. I saw it coming, so when she swung I grabbed her
hand. That made her swing with the other hand and I grabbed that one
too. I had both of her hands and she was struggling and screaming and I
was laughing. I guess I was laughing because a bag of dope didn't seem
like such a big deal to me and it was ridiculous to watch her freak out
over it. She couldn't hit me because I had her arms, so she tried to kick
me. As she did, I let go of her hands and she lost her balance and fell to
the floor and she started crying, crying really hard. I turned around and
walked out the front door. I could hear her crying as I did, but I didn't
want to deal with it, so I just walked out. When I came home a few
hours later my Dad screamed at me and grounded me for a month.
I look at my Mother. She is staring at the floor. Joanne speaks.
That's an awful story, James.
I know.
How did it make you feel as you told it?
Part of me still thinks it's funny, but more of me is just ashamed and
embarrassed.
How do you think it makes your Mother feel?
I look at my Mother. She is staring at the floor and she is trying not to
cry.
I think it probably makes her feel pretty awful.
Why?
Because it must have been humiliating. Trying to confront your Kid
about drugs and having him laugh at you and trying to discipline him
and ending up in a heap on the floor.
Joanne looks at my Mother.
Is that true, Lynne?
My Mother looks up, lips quivering.
Yes.
Do you think that was what the incident was really about, drugs and
discipline?

I speak.

No.

What do you think it was about?

It was about control.

Why do you think that?

Going through my shit and reading my private letters was about knowing what I was doing so that she could control me. Trying to make me tell her what was in the bag when she already knew what was in it was about control. When she fell after she hit me, she wasn't upset because she didn't land her shots, she was upset because she knew, at that point, I was out of control.

Joanne looks at my Mother.

Do you think that's a valid interpretation?

My Mother stares at the floor, thinks. She looks up.

I was upset about the drugs. It was upsetting reading those letters and find-ing out about some of the things he had been doing, especially after we sent him to that Camp to try and get him away from some of that stuff. When I actually found the bag in his coat, I was scared and horrified. He was four-teen. Fourteen-year-old Boys shouldn't be carrying around bags of drugs. To a certain extent, though, he's right about the control. His Father and I were always trying to control him, mainly because he had always been so out of control.

There is a knock at the door. Joanne says come in and the door opens and my Father steps into the Office.

My Mother stands and gives him a hug. I do the same. My Father sits next to my Mother. He holds her hand and he looks at Joanne.

Sorry I'm late.

We were talking about an event that happened when James was fourteen, and that discussion led to one about the issue of control. The goal of this evening's session is to try and get some idea of a root cause for his addic-tion. I'm sensing that there may be some connection between the issue of control and the root cause.

What was the incident?

My Mother speaks.

When I found that bag of marijuana in his coat pocket.

Which time?

The time I fell trying to slap him.

My Father nods.

That was bad. What does control have to do with it?

Joanne speaks.

James said he thought the incident had more to do with control than
with drugs.

My Father turns toward me. He looks confused, slightly angry.

That sounds a bit ridiculous, James.

I speak.

Not to me. Going through all my stuff and reading my letters and hunt-
ing through my jacket is about trying to find out what I'm doing so that
Mom could try to control it.

There were drugs in there. Your Mother had every right to go through
your jacket. You were fourteen years old.

That's fine if that's what you think, but spying on me and sneaking
around through my private shit was about controlling me, which is something you guys always tried to do.

My Father's voice rises.

You've been out of control your entire life. We're your Parents, what did
you expect us to do?

My voice rises.

Leave me be. Let me live my own life.

When you were fourteen? Where do you think you'd be if we'd done
that?

Where the fuck am I now? It couldn't be much worse than this.

Parents don't leave Children alone, James, they raise them. That's all your
Mother and I tried to do with you.

You tried to micromanage me and keep track of me every second of every
day and make me do what you wanted me to do.

My Father clenches his jaw just like I clench my jaw. He's angry, very angry, and he starts to speak. Joanne cuts him off.

Just a second, Mr. Frey.

He takes a breath and he nods. She looks at me.

Why do you think it didn't work?

Same reason that if you keep a dog on a short leash it's more aggressive.
Same reason if you keep a Prisoner in solitary for too long they become
violent. Same reason Dictatorships usually end in Revolution.

Those are nice examples, but what's the reason?

I didn't want to be controlled, so I did everything I could to try to break
the pattern of it, which made them want to control me more.

Joanne looks at my Parents.

Do you think there is any validity to what he's saying?

My Father speaks.

No.

My Mother speaks.

Yes.

My Father looks at my Mother.

Why do you think that?

You know I always worried about him, even when he was an Infant I worried. I probably tried to keep him too close because I didn't want him to get hurt.

Joanne speaks.

You have another Son, right?

My Mother nods, my Father says yes.

Did you raise him the same way?

My Father nods, speaks.

Yes.

My Mother speaks.

No.

What was the difference?

I was much more careful with James than I was with Bob. I knew we weren't going to have any other Children, and I wanted James to be perfect and healthy and safe. I can't say it any other way. I wanted him to be safe.

That's natural, but do you think you tried to keep him too safe?

My Father speaks.

Too safe? Is that possible with a Child?

Joanne nods.

Yes, it is.

My Mother speaks.

How?

Everyone has boundaries. They're different for every Person, but we all have them. When they're crossed or violated, it is usually upsetting. If they are crossed or violated repeatedly, especially in the case of a Child, who usually has no way of controlling whether someone crosses or violates his boundaries, it can result in negative behaviors, the easiest example being the resentment of authority.

My Father speaks.

That sounds absurd to me. Children's boundaries are set by their Parents, and the Child learns to respect them, not the other way around.

Joanne speaks.

Not necessarily.

What do you mean?

Children learn more in the first two years of their life than they do in all of the rest of their years combined, even if they live to be a hundred. Most behavioral patterns, including our personal boundaries, are set during those first two years. Sometimes the pattern of establishment of those behaviors and boundaries is disrupted.

By what?

Generally by abuse.

My Father flares.

If you're suggesting—

Joanne holds her hand up.

I'm not suggesting anything, and when I brought up the possibility of abuse with James, he very adamantly insisted that he had not suffered from any. I'm telling you how this sometimes happens.

My Mother speaks.

We did protect James more than our other Son, but I think we had good reason, and I don't think we violated anything.

Joanne looks at her, waits for her to continue.

Bob is three years older than James. Just after Bob was born, my Father retired, and after he retired he started drinking heavily. It was very difficult for my Mother and my Brother and my Sister and me. We tried to stop him, but he just told us to leave him alone, that he had spent his whole life taking care of us and now he wanted to be left alone. I had heard about Alcoholism being passed from generation to generation, so when James was born I was scared to death. I don't know if it was female intuition or what, but for some reason I didn't worry about Bob, I just worried about James.

I speak.

Grandpa was an Alcoholic?

My Father looks at my Mother, my Mother speaks.

I don't know if he was an Alcoholic, but he had a drinking problem.

Joanne speaks.

Did you not know that, James?

My Father speaks.

It's not something we have ever really spoken about.

Why?

It was a very sad and devastating situation. We try to remember Lynne's Father as he was for the greater part of his life, which was a kind and gentle and generous man, rather than what he was near the end of it.

Joanne speaks.

As Lynne mentioned, it has been proven that there is a link between the disease of Alcoholism and genetics. Don't you think it might have helped

James to know that he might have, and in my opinion, most probably does have, a genetic predisposition toward addiction?
I speak.
I don't think knowing about my Grandfather would have made any difference. I didn't drink and do drugs because of some genetic flaw.
Joanne speaks.
Why are you so quick to dismiss what has been proven empirically to exist?
I think it's bullshit. People don't want to accept the responsibility for their own weakness, so they place the blame on something that they're not responsible for, like disease or genetics. As far as studies go, I could prove I was from Mars if you gave me enough time and enough resources.
My Mother speaks.
It certainly might help explain a lot of these things for us.
I think it's interesting that Grandpa had a drinking problem. I'm surprised to learn it, because I have only heard great things about him. I think it sucks, and it must have been awful for everyone to have to deal with him, just like it has been awful to have to deal with me, but I won't blame him or his genes for my problems.
My Father speaks.
What's your explanation?
I was weak and pathetic and I couldn't control myself. An explanation, especially a bullshit one, doesn't alter the circumstances. I need to change, I have to change, and at this point, change is my only option, unless I am ready to die. All that matters is that I make myself something else and someone else for the future.
Joanne speaks.
Don't you think knowing why you are the way you are might help you in the process of that change?
I think I do know why.
Would you like to share your ideas with us?
Not really.
Why?
Because it will hurt and upset my Parents, and I think I've done enough of that.
My Mother speaks.
I think we'd like to hear, James.
My Father speaks.
We definitely would.
I look at them, take a deep breath, speak.

I've always felt these things. I don't think there are any words that describe them exactly, but they are a combination of rage, anger, extreme pain. They mix together into what I call the Fury. I have known the Fury for as long as I can remember. It is the one thing that has been with me throughout my entire life. I am starting to learn how to deal with it, but until recently, the only way I knew was through drinking and drugs. I took something, whatever it was, and if I took enough of it, the Fury would subside. The problem was that it would always come back, usually stronger, and that would require more and stronger substances to kill it, and that was always the goal, to kill it. From the first time I drank, I knew drinking would kill it. From the first time I took drugs, I knew drugs would kill it. I took them willingly, not because of some genetic link or some function of some disease, but because I knew they would kill the goddamn Fury. Even though I knew I was killing myself, killing the Fury was more important.

I look at my Parents.

I don't know why, and I don't know if it matters, but whenever you are near me, the Fury gets worse. Whenever you have tried to control me or baby me or take care of me or stop me, the Fury has gotten worse. Whenever we talk on the phone or I hear your voices, the Fury gets worse. I'm not saying you're to blame for it, because I don't think you are to blame. I know you did the best you could with me and I know I'm lucky to have you, and I can't think of anything in my background that would have caused it. Maybe the Fury is genetic, but I highly fucking doubt it, and I won't accept disease and genetics as the cause of it anyway. It makes it too easy to deflect the responsibility for what I have done and what I have done knowing full well I was doing it. Each and every time, I knew full fucking well, whether it was take a drink or snort a line or take a hit from a pipe or get arrested, and I made the decision to do it anyway. Most of the time it was to kill the Fury, some of the time it was to kill myself, and eventually I didn't know the difference. All I knew was that I was killing and that at some point it would end, which would probably be best for everyone involved. For whatever it is worth, I feel it now, sitting here with you, and I will feel it tomorrow morning when I see you again. I will feel it the next time we speak, and the time after that and the time after that, and if there is an explanation for why I am the way I am or for who I am, it is that there is a Fury within me that is uncontrollable without drinking or drugs. How do I get better? I take responsibility for myself and I learn to deal with myself and I learn to control the Fury. It might take a while, but if I hold on long enough and I don't accept excuses for failure or deflect what is essentially a problem I have caused, I can do it.

My Mother and My Father stare at me. My Mother looks as if she's going to cry, my Father looks pale, as if he has just seen a terrible wreck.

My Mother starts to speak, stops, wipes her eyes. My Father just stares. Joanne speaks.

Not discounting other factors, I would say there may be some validity to your theory, but I am curious where you think this Fury comes from.

I don't know.

She looks at my Parents. There are tears on my Mother's face, my Father still stares. My Mother looks at me, speaks.

Why didn't you tell us this before?

What was I supposed to say?

Do you hate us?

I shake my head.

What did we do?

You didn't do anything, Mom. This isn't your fault.

She wipes her face. My Father stares.

I'm sorry, James.

Don't be sorry, Mom. I'm the one who should be sorry.

There is a long silence. My Father looks at Joanne, speaks.

Could this feeling, or set of feelings, have been brought on by a Medical Condition?

Did James have a Medical Condition as an Infant?

He had ear problems.

Were they properly diagnosed and treated?

My Mother speaks.

We didn't know.

How did you not know?

My Mother looks at my Father and she takes his hand. She speaks.

We didn't have much money when the Boys were first born. Bob was a Lawyer, but most of his salary went to paying off his school loans. Bob Junior came out healthy and he was a happy child. He was very quiet and very calm. When James was born, he was the opposite. He screamed and screamed and screamed, and no matter what we did, we couldn't get him to stop. It was awful screaming, long and loud and piercing, and I can still hear it in my memories. We went to the Doctor, and we got the best one we could afford.

The Doctor told us that there was nothing wrong, that James was probably just a vocal child. We went home and the screaming continued. I'd hold James, Bob would hold James, we tried giving him little toys and feeding him more, and nothing worked. Nothing could make him stop. The tears start flowing. My Mother grips my Father's hand, my Father watches her as she speaks. I sit and I listen. I have never heard about my screaming before, though it does not surprise me. I have been screaming for years. Screaming bloody fucking murder. My Mother cries as she continues.

It went on for almost two years. James just screamed and screamed. Bob started doing well at his Firm and got a raise, and as soon as we had some extra money, I took James to see a better Doctor. As soon as he looked at him, he told me that James had terrible infections in both of his ears that were eating away his eardrums. He said James had been screaming for all that time because he was in tremendous pain and that he had been scream-ing for help. He recommended surgery, and just before he turned two, James had surgery on both of his ears, which was the first of seven surgeries that he would have on them. Obviously we felt terrible, but we didn't know.

The tears turn into sobs.

If we had known we would have done something.

Sobs.

But we didn't know.

My Father holds her.

He just screamed and screamed and all that time we didn't know that he was screaming because he hurt.

My Mother breaks down, burying her face in my Father's shoulder and shaking and trembling and quivering. My Father holds her and he pa-tiently waits for her, stroking her hair and rubbing her back. I sit and I stare, and though I have no memory of what she's talking about, I do re-member the pain. That is all that remains. The pain.

My Mother stops crying and she pulls away slightly just slightly from my Father. She looks at me.

I'm sorry, James. We didn't know. We really didn't know.

I reach out and I put my hand on one of my Mother's hands.

You got nothing to be sorry about, Mom. You did the best you could.

She pulls away from my Father completely and she stands and she takes two steps toward me and she puts her arms around me and she hugs me. She hugs me strong and tight and I return her hug and I can tell that she is trying to express her remorse and sadness. In a way this hug is her apol-ogy, though none is needed.

She lets go and she sits back down next to my Father. Joanne waits for a moment to see if any of us are going to speak. We don't, so she does.

Do you remember any of that, James?

I remember the operations, only because I had them until I was twelve, but I don't remember any of the early stuff.

Was there any long-term damage from them?

I have thirty percent hearing loss in my left ear and twenty in the other.

Why didn't you tell me this before?

I don't think it's that big a deal.

It helps explain, or perhaps, entirely explains, why you say your first and earliest memories are of rage and pain.

Why do you think that?

When a child is born, it needs food and shelter and a sense of safety and comfort. If it screams, it is usually screaming for a reason, and in your case, it seems you were probably screaming because you were in pain and you wanted help. If those screams went unheeded, whether consciously or unconsciously, they might have ignited a fairly profound sense of rage within you, and might very well have led to some long-term resentments. That rage would help explain both your feelings of what you call the Fury, and also your particular feelings of it in regards to your Parents and in regards to issues of control with them.

I sit and I think. I try to decide if I am willing to accept genetics and ear infections as an explanation for twenty-three years of chaos. It would be easy to do so. To place myself on a pedestal away from what and who I am and to write it all off because of my Grandfather's genes and a Doctor's incompetence. It has been twenty-three years of chaos. Twenty-three years of Hell. I could let it all go with the simple acceptance of that which has been presented to me. I could let it all go.

I look up. My Parents are watching me, Joanne is watching me. They are waiting for a response. I take a breath and I speak.

It's an interesting theory. It probably holds some weight. I can accept it for what I feel it is, which is a possibility. I won't accept it as a root cause, because I think it's a cop-out, and because I don't think it does me any good to accept anything other than myself and my own weakness as a root cause. I did everything I did. I made the decisions to do it all. The only way I'm going to get better is if I accept responsibility for the decision to either be an Addict or not be an Addict. That's the way it has to be for me. I know you're going to try and convince me otherwise, but you shouldn't bother.

Joanne chuckles, my Mother and Father stare at me. I look at Joanne and I speak.

Why are you chuckling?

She smiles.

Because you are the single most stubborn Person that I've ever met.

I just won't let myself be a victim.

What do you mean by that?

People in here, People everywhere, they all want to take their own problems, usually created by themselves, and try to pass them off on someone or something else. I know my Mother and Father did the best they could and gave me the best they could and loved me the best they could and if anything, they are victims of me. I could say I'm flawed in my genetic makeup, that I have this disease and my addictions are caused by the presence of it, but I think that's a load of shit. I'm a victim of nothing but myself, just as I believe that most People with this so-called disease aren't victims of anything other than themselves. If you want to call that philosophy stubbornness, go right ahead. I call it being responsible. I call it the acceptance of my own problems and my own weaknesses with honor and dignity. I call it getting better.

Joanne smiles.

Despite the fact that I can't really endorse or condone your philosophy, I am gradually becoming a Believer.

I smile.

Thank you.

My Father speaks.

James.

I turn toward him and my Mother. They are smiling at me.

I have never been more proud of you than I am this moment.

I smile.

Thanks, Dad.

My Mother speaks.

Me too, James.

Thanks, Mom.

Joanne looks at her watch.

I think we've done some exceptional work tonight and it's getting late.

I stand.

Let's get out of here.

My Parents stand. My Mother speaks.

Can we have another hug before we go?

I step forward, put one of my arms around each of them, and they each put one of their arms around me. We pull each of us pulls and we hug each other the three of us hug each other it is strong and easy and full of something maybe love. The Fury flares and I am momentarily uncomfortable, but the strength I am giving and the strength I am taking kills it. Easily and quickly. The giving and taking kills it.

We separate. My Parents are still smiling. I say good-bye to Joanne and she says good-bye to me. I open the door and I wait. My Parents say good-bye and thank you to Joanne and she smiles and says no problem. They walk out and I follow them. We say good-bye outside the door and they go one way and I go another.

I walk back to the Unit. I know my way the walk is automatic. I am tired and I'm ready for bed. I don't want to deal with anything or anybody. I don't want to think about Prison or genetics or ear infections. I don't know about one and the other two don't matter. I want to sleep. Close my eyes and sleep.

I get to my Room open the door walk inside. Miles is in bed he is already sleeping. The light on my nightstand is on I turn it off get under the covers. They are warm. The pillow is soft.

I am tired.

I go to sleep.

There are hands shaking me gently shaking me. I hear my name James James James I am being shaken. I hear my name. James.

I open my eyes. It is dark I can see the blurred shape shaking me and saying my name. I blink once. Twice. It is dark. I can see.

Miles is standing above me. He sees my eyes I see his eyes. He lets me go. I sit up.

There's a young lady at the window for you.

What?

A young lady is at the window. She's asking for you.

I lean forward, look around him. I see an outline through the glass.

Fuck.

Miles laughs.

Women are difficult. They become more so if you ignore them. I'd suggest you go speak to her.

Fuck.

I push away the covers, Miles steps back. I drag myself from my bed and I walk to the window and I open it. A rush of a cold wind slaps me in the face. I stick my head out the window. Lilly is standing in the shadows. She speaks.

I need to talk to you.

Right now?

Yes.

Can't wait till morning?

I need to talk to you.

Hold on.

I step away from the window and I close it. I turn around and Miles is smiling at me.

You knew it couldn't wait till morning if she woke us up in the middle of the night.

I thought I'd try.

I put on my pants.

There's no use trying with them. You just do.

My shoes.

That'll be my Policy in the future.

Hank's jacket.

It's the best way.

I walk back to the window.

Sorry you got woken up.

Miles smiles.

Don't get caught.

I smile.

I won't.

I open the window, get hit by the cold the cold the cold. I climb through and I close the window behind me. Lilly is in the shadows. I walk toward her.

Hi.

That's all you've got to say?

What's that supposed to mean?

You think you can say hi to me and everything will be cool?

What are you talking about?

I stop walking and I stand in front of her. I can see swollen eyes and the stains of tears. I see her rear and swing. One step back and she misses.

What the fuck is your problem?

She regains her balance and she steps forward and she pushes me.

Fuck you.

I laugh. She pushes me again.

You think this is funny?

She pushes me again.

Fuck you.

Her voice is getting louder. She pushes again.

Fuck you.

She rears back.

FUCK YOU.

She swings. I grab her arm. She swings with the other. I grab that one. She struggles and she clenches her teeth and I hold her arms and I drag her away from the Building, trying to be gentle, but using enough strength to move her. She says let me go let me go you fucking Asshole let me go. I ignore her. I walk slowly backward, holding her arms and gently pulling her into the darkness.

Fifty feet away we're safe. I keep pulling, she keeps struggling and swearing and calling me names. A hundred feet away we're safer. The darkness is darker. The sound carries less. I stop walking and pulling, but I don't let go. She struggles. I put my arms around her and I hold her tight.

Calm down.
No.
I'm not letting go of you.
I'll make you.
She struggles more. I hold tighter. Her body is against mine, her arms are pressed against the flesh of each chest. I hold her and she struggles. I wait and she swears. When she stops after a few moments she stops I hold her still. She breathes. Deep heavy breaths. In the silence of night. In the darkness where we're safe.
Her breathing slows slows slows. I lay my head on her shoulder. When she is breathing normally I speak.
You all right?
No.
What's wrong?
You're an Asshole.
Why am I an Asshole?
You talked to him. Why didn't you show up?
When?
You talked to that Motherfucker on your Unit.
I don't know what you're talking about.
Where were you today?
When?
At three o'clock.
In a session at the Family Center.
You were supposed to be with me.
I didn't know that.
You had three plates at lunch. Three o'clock.
I didn't know we were doing that today.
Why'd you think I was staring at you during dinner?
I had no idea. I thought you looked upset, but I didn't know why.
Why didn't you call me?
You always call me.
So what?
I don't have the number.
That's bullshit.
No, it's not.
That's an excuse. You should have called me.
Give me the number and next time I will.
She pushes herself away from me slightly away but she keeps her arms around me. She looks down at the ground and at the blackness near her

feet. She looks up. Clear water blue into pale green. She smiles, barely smiles, not a happy smile but a smile of regret. Of sadness. A smile of mistake and of misunderstanding. She speaks.

I'm sorry.

Why?

I got scared.

Why were you scared?

I was scared you were leaving me.

I'm not going to do that.

I was scared after I told you those things about me that you didn't want to see me anymore. Then I thought somebody on your Unit told you something else.

Those things don't bother me. Nothing I hear is going to bother me.

I thought they did, and when you didn't show up, I thought I knew for sure.

The only thing you need to know for sure is that I'm not leaving.

She smiles. This time it's a real smile.

Ever?

Yes. Ever.

You're sure?

I am.

I don't want to be alone anymore, James.

You won't be.

I cried all day.

Don't cry again. Just think of the word ever.

She smiles brighter, wider, a smile more full of what she is, which is beautiful. Inside and out. The smile. Her. Beautiful. She leans forward and she steps to her toes and she closes her eyes and she kisses me. Long and sweet and slow. I could keep kissing her forever.

We separate. I tell her we should go. Not back, but farther into the darkness. We start walking, hand in hand, slow steps, there's no hurry. The Woods are alive at night. Twigs cracking, leaves rustling, branches swaying. Moon sitting, clouds drifting. Shadows dancing and threatening and disappearing. Small animals fighting and chattering and foraging for food. Small animals hiding. The living Wood.

As we walk we talk. Lilly needs to talk about her feelings about her worries about her fears. I let her. I encourage her. I listen to her. Though the stains of tears have been wiped away from the softness of her cheek, the cause of her tears remains alive and full not faded not yet. She talks softly and easily and without hesitation. She talks of her feelings of being left in the past. By her Father and by the Boy in Chicago and by everyone she has ever cared about in her entire life. They left her and they never called and they never sent a letter, never showed her that they loved her, never came back. Not once. Not ever.

She talks about the desertion. How each time it broke her heart. How with each break it became harder to heal. How with each time she healed, it became harder to love again. How each time hope faded into desolation. Into loneliness and despair. Into self-hatred and self-loathing. At the beginning there was hope. It faded. At the end there was nothing.

She talks about me in relation to her life. She is seeking freedom. That is all she wants, all she desires, all she hopes to achieve. Freedom. Not just from chemicals but from the cycle of loving and losing, risking and failing, returning to that which she abhors each time returning. She thought she had lost me earlier today. With that she thought she began to lose herself. To feel doors closing on the Prison of self-destruction. She wanted to fight it but she can't fight it all. Not chemicals and her past and the prospect of a dim, solitary, isolated future. She started to need. Need the crack. Need the pills. Need something to kill the pain. She thought about leaving and she almost left. She imagined herself walking out. She was going to go to the Bus Station in Minneapolis and panhandle money for a ticket back to Chicago. Panhandle or worse. When she got to Chicago she was going to go see her Grandmother and say good-bye. Good-bye to the only Person who ever cared about her. Good-bye. There are other ways to achieve freedom. Good-bye.

We stop walking. We sit on a bench, the carved wooden bench. One of the smaller Lakes is frozen in front of us. Frozen dark silent unmoving content. We sit on the bench and I hold Lilly's hands in my hands. I keep them warm. I tell her I'm glad she didn't leave. More than glad. I tell her that if she had left I would have followed her. I would have found her, I will not let her say good-bye to me or to her Grandmother or to life. It is all we have and it is not to be wasted. We have wasted too much she and I and the others like us. Wasted far too much. We have to hold on to what we have left. Fight for it. Cherish it. Try to survive it. Try to love it. I would have followed her. I'm going to hold on to her. I will fight for her. Cherish her. Try to survive myself. Try to survive myself so that I can love her. I hold her hands in mine. I keep them warm.

We stand and we start walking. Hand in hand we walk as if we're normal People living normal lives, in love. Just walking. The Trail leads us along shores of ice through dead yellow grass to the wooden Elevated Walk and up. We stop in the middle and we smoke cigarettes. We stare at the darkness stare across the waters of the Swamp. There is no other just us. We stare at the water. We are holding each other's hands. There are no words. None necessary.

We finish smoking start walking back down into the Wood. The circle around the Land of the Clinic is ours and only ours we are completely alone. Just walking. Like normal People. Walking up the grass of the hill we sit on the cold ground at the top looking down at the concrete and steel reminders of our pasts. Halls too bright too white the Halls of Hell for some, purgatory for others, redemption for few. The Buildings are quiet, imposing and well lit. I don't want to go back. Going back means leaving her hand her body her eyes her lips her pale skin her hair long and black her hair long and black. Going back means leaving her. I don't want to go.

We lean to the ground holding hands our legs wrapped together. We look toward each other. She smiles and I smile. I speak.

I'm glad you knocked on my window.

I am too.

I wish we could do this every night.

We can.

We have to be careful.

They won't catch us.

They know we're doing something.

They won't catch us.

I hope not.

How are your Parents?

They're good.

How has it been with them?

Very good.

You're getting along?

For the first time ever.

Are they being cool?

More than I imagined they could be.

What's your Dad do?

He's a Businessman. Works eighteen hours a day and travels a lot.

What's your Mom do?

Travels with my Dad.

How long have they been married?

Twenty-eight years.

Are they in love?

Very much so.

That's incredible.
It is.
I want to meet them.
They want to meet you.
You told them about me?
Yes.
What'd you say?
I told them I met a Girl.
What else?
That she was beautiful and that she understood me.
What else?
I pause, smile.
Why are you smiling?
I just am.
What else did you tell them?
I told them I loved her.
She smiles.
What?
I told my Parents I loved her.
She smiles wider.
No you didn't.
I smile wider.
I did.
You told them you loved me?
Yes.
Tell me.
Is that what you want?
Tell me.
I smile. I stare. I am holding her hand and my legs are wrapped with
hers. My eyes are inches away. Inches. From clear water blue in the dark-
ness. They cannot be dimmed even in the darkness they cannot be
dimmed. I stare and I smile and I speak.
I love you.
She smiles. With her lips, her teeth, her eyes, her shaking hand. She
smiles and I say it again.
I love you.
I say it again.
I love you.
I say it again.
I love you.

And I do. I love her. This Girl who said hello to me as I stood in line for medicine. This Girl with addictions to crack and pills. This Girl who used to sleep with men for money and hitchhiked across the Country on her back. This Girl who has been through things of which she cannot speak. This Girl with nothing. This Girl with nothing but her own strength and a desire to be free. With nothing but a beating heart that is scared to be alone. With nothing but clear blue eyes that see through me and understand me. With nothing but open arms ready to receive me. To stand by me. To walk with me. To love me. I love her. Lilly. The Girl with nothing and everything. Lilly. I love her.

A tear appears. She smiles. She leans forward kisses my lips softly kisses me and as our lips touch barely touch she whispers.

I love you too, James.

Our lips barely touching she whispers.

I love you.

Whispers.

I love you.

We lie together. Smiling and holding on to each other and the night and the moment. We stare into each other's eyes and softly kiss speaking and saying more with the movement of our lips and the tips of our fingers than words will allow us to say. Words can't say this. The one word love means too little for what it is. It means everything and that is still not enough. It doesn't communicate even a fraction of the feelings involved. Love. The word is not enough for what it is. Love. Love.

The Sun starts to rise. Behind us the light streams in thin white and yellow and pink lines. I don't want to leave. I could lie here and die happy. I could die in this love happy and without the need for anything more. I don't want to leave. I know by the way Lilly holds me tighter with each moment a little tighter that she does not want to leave. We have no choice. We have to go back.

I pull away and I tell her we have to leave and she says she knows and we kiss one last time slow and deep the clock is ticking. We untangle each other from ourselves and it takes a second and a century and we stand. I hold her hand in my hand I look into her eyes and I stare. I don't see what I saw when I stared into the Arctic eyes in my final moment of impotence. There is nothing saying go away, I don't want you. In Lilly's eyes her beautiful clear water eyes there is what I have sought and never found, wanted and never had, hoped for and never discovered. Love.

I step back and I step away. Our eyes are still locked, our hands still

touching. I take another step. Our fingers touch, one finger from each of
our hands. I smile again and I speak.
Ever.
She smiles.
Remember that when you feel scared or vulnerable or you don't think
things are going to work out.
She smiles wider.
Ever.
One more step and I'm away our fingers apart. I turn and I start walking
down the hill. I want to look back, but if I do I won't keep going. I know
it's time to return. My wounds aren't healed and I need to heal them. If I
am to survive to live to love completely I need more time just a little
more time. If I look back I'll go back. To her to her arms to the safety
and comfort within. It is not time. Not yet.
I reach the bottom of the Hill. I walk across the wide expanse of dead
grass in front of the Buildings. I open the sliding-glass door and I step
into the Unit. Leonard is doing jumping jacks in the middle of the
Lower Level. I ignore him. I turn and I look back through the glass
toward the Hill. Lilly is still there. Sitting on the ground smoking a cigarette. Staring down at me. The smoke drifts off one hand and she
raises it. Holds it in the air. She can see me. I raise one hand and press
it against the glass. Hold it. We stare at each other we are too far away
to see anything but outlines. It doesn't matter.
I lower my hand. She lowers her hand. I stand for a moment. I can hear
Leonard finishing his jumping jacks behind me. When he does, I step
away from the window and I turn around.
Leonard is bent over, his hands on his knees. He is wearing a bright red
sweat suit and there are beads of perspiration dripping off his forehead.
He looks up at me and speaks.
Hey, Kid.
Hey, Leonard.
How's your Girl?
I smile.
Very good.
You have a good night?
Yeah.
You in love?
Yeah.
You tell her?

Yeah.

He smiles. Large and wide.

That's beautiful.

I smile again. Large and wide.

Yeah.

He takes his hands from his knees, stands.

How things been with your Parents?

They're good.

You getting along?

Yeah, we are.

He smiles.

Good, 'cause you'll regret it if you fuck this up with them. Family is the most important thing you'll ever have.

I hear you.

I'm proud of you, Kid. It seems like you're doing all the right things.

I'm trying.

You keep this up and I'm not gonna have to watch out for you anymore.

I didn't know I asked you to watch out for me.

Doesn't matter if you asked me or not. All that matters is that I'm doing it, whether you like it or not.

I laugh.

I'm gonna go shower, get ready for the day. Meet me here in twenty minutes. We'll have coffee and get breakfast.

Okay.

He walks away. I walk to my room. I open the door Miles is not here nor is his clarinet nor is the copy of the *Tao*. I take off my clothes walk to the Bathroom turn on the shower get under the water wash myself. The water is hot, but not too hot. It is comfortable. It feels good.

I turn off the shower step out of it walk to the sink and I brush my teeth and I shave. I look at the scar where there once was a hole. It is pink, lighter than the rest of my skin, it is healing. I look at my nose, there is a slight bump along its ridge, it is healed. I look at the area around and beneath my eyes, the swelling is gone, the yellow fade of damage is gone. There are gray rings beneath but they are from lack of sleep not injury. My eyes have healed. On the outside.

I start to look up at them. The whites are white and lined with the pink run of thin veins. I follow the veins to the edge of the green. It is pale like a faded olive with small dots of brown spread few and far between. I stay at the edge of the green, hold there. I can see into myself and I am com-

fortable with what I see. It is not too deep. The depths are where reality
lives. On the edge there are only flashes of it. I start to move up, move
deeper, see more. Moving becomes harder and the edge disappears into
the black of a pupil surrounded. The black where all is revealed. I see it
for the slightest second, I see the deepest black surrounded by pale green.
I look away.

I walk out of the Bathroom. I put on my clothes and I leave my Room.
Bobby and the man I know but not from where are sitting at a table on the
Upper Level. They are staring at me. I ignore them. I get a cup of coffee and I
take a sip. It's hot, it burns my mouth, and it is strong. I feel it immediately. It
makes the night and the weariness of a night without sleep disappear. My
heart starts beating faster. Even weak drugs make the weariness of a night
without sleep disappear.

I turn around. Bobby and the man are still staring at me. I start to walk
past them when the man speaks.

You don't remember me, do you?

I stop and I turn around and I look at him. He is wearing black again.
Black sweatpants with white stripes down the sides and a black T-shirt.
His hair is short and dirty and spiked, his face is marked with acne scars.
His eyes are dull and brown and his arms are lined with purple-black
tracks.

No, I don't.

I told you to remember me, I'm disappointed you don't.

Sorry.

I hear you're with Lilly.

Where do you hear that?

Does it matter?

No.

Then don't ask me.

Where do I know you from?

I met you a few weeks ago.

I was here a few weeks ago.

So was I.

I step forward, stare at the man, search my memory. Although it is dim
and obscure, it comes. I remember watching television. I remember him
dragging me across the floor. I remember him whispering in my ear. I remember him telling me he could have hurt me. I was drugged and helpless. He could have hurt me.

I remember now.

He smiles.

Good Boy.

Don't call me that.

You gonna do something if I do?

I might.

After your last performance, I'm real scared.

I step forward.

Try me now.

He smiles.

I'm not here to fight you.

Then what do you want?

To tell you about Lilly.

What do you want to tell me about her?

Some things you should know.

What?

He leans back and smiles and lights a cigarette. I stand and I wait. Bobby is staring at me and smiling like a strangler whose hands have found a neck. I feel a presence near me and I look to my side and I see Leonard standing a few feet away. Although he hasn't heard the conversation, I can tell by his expression that he knows something unpleasant is about to happen. The man looks at me and he speaks.

I know Lilly from home. She used to run around with my best Buddy and he used to share her. He'd bring her to parties and get her all wasted and put her in a room and let guys fuck her if they gave him drugs. She loved it because it meant free rock and a handful of pills and a night full of dick, which, as I'm sure you know by now, she loves more than anything.

He stares at me. He laughs.

I did her a few times myself. She has that nice little body and those big, fat lips and she knows how to use them, and she'll let you do just about anything to her. Her Boy, my Buddy, got in a jam with a Dealer. You could say he overextended his credit. The Dealer agreed to let him off the hook if he gave Lilly to him and my Buddy made the deal. He didn't really give a shit about her, I guess because it's hard to respect a whore, so without her knowing why, he took her to the Dealer's House. When they got there, she started smoking crack and took a bunch of Valium and got all trashed. Then the Dealer's friends came over.

Bobby laughs. The man smiles and takes a drag of his cigarette and he stares at me and I stare back. I can feel the Fury rising. Unlike most of the episodes with it, it is not directing its rage and anger and urge to destroy at me, but at him. I can feel it. The Fury rising.

From there it got ugly. Fifteen guys got in line and they put Lilly face-down on the floor and they started fucking her. They fucked her mouth, fucked her pussy, fucked her in the ass, fucked her everywhere and in every way you could imagine. All fifteen of them fucked her, a few more than once, and not one of them wore a rubber. They came all over her. On her back and her stomach, in her hair and on her face, in every fucking hole she's got.

Bobby laughs again.

About two guys in she tried to get up and leave, but they wouldn't let her. They held her down and they laughed at her and they fucked her. One after another after another, and she couldn't do a damn thing about it, and after they were done, and she was screaming and crying and going fucking crazy, she tried to gather up her clothes, but they wouldn't give them to her. They gave her a trash bag instead, one of those big, black plastic ones, and they cut two armholes in the side, and they made her put it on. Then the Dealer opened up the door and he grabbed her by the hair and he threw her out, just like a piece of fucking garbage.

Bobby laughs louder, bangs his hand on the table. The man looks at him and smiles, looks back at me.

From what I know, she came up here straight after that. Jumped in a car with her batty old Grandma and drove as fast as she fucking could. I think she met you a few days later. If I were you, I'd be careful. That Girl's got some dangerous shit floating around inside of her, and if she hasn't already, she'll probably give you something that'll make your goddamn dick fall off.

The man smiles at me. He stubs out his cigarette in an ashtray. I hear Bobby laughing, and out of the corner of my eye, I see him raise his hand. The man chuckles and hits it, as if receiving thanks for the words he has spoken. I clench my jaw. I stare at the man. The Fury is up. It is at full strength I want to kill kill kill. I don't care that Lilly has done whatever she has done. Her sins, if there are any, are not to be judged by me. I care that this man has defiled her. Not in body, but in name. I care that he has spoken of her as if she were a piece of meat, as if she were less than human, as if she were something to be degraded and debased by him and others. The Fury is at full strength. I want to kill kill kill. I step forward.

Why'd you tell me that story?

Because I felt like it.

Because you felt like it?

Yeah.

Lilly's had a brutal fucking life. She doesn't need to have you talking shit about her.

You gonna give me a fucking Lecture?

Did it make you feel better about yourself to tell me that?

What?

Did it make you feel like more of a man, like you had some power over me or her?

Fuck you.

Did it make you feel like you were different from her, even though you know you're not, or did it make you feel good, even though deep inside you feel like a piece of shit?

Fuck you.

Did it?

Fuck you.

I step forward.

Last time we met, you let me slide. I'm gonna let you slide now. But if you ever speak of her again, I will find you and I will fucking destroy you.

You threatening me?

I'm warning you.

I'm real scared.

Try me now.

Fuck you and your dirtbag whore. Fuck you both.

Bobby laughs. The man stares at me and I stare back. I drop the cup of coffee I am holding in my hand it hits the ground it distracts him and as soon as he looks I'm on him. I grab his hair and jerk his head back and press my thumb into his neck just below his Adam's apple. I press hard. The flesh is soft and my thumb sinks deep and he starts gagging, choking, losing breath, suffering. Out of the corner of my eye I see Bobby step out of his chair and start to move I see Leonard step forward and push him and I hear something I don't know what I hear. Leonard says something and Bobby immediately stops. I see Leonard lean toward Bobby and I see his mouth move more words that I cannot hear. Bobby sits down.

I press. Into the soft flesh. I look into the man's eyes. I let him know that I could kill him. He is gagging. Choking. Losing breath. Suffering. He is helpless. He knows it and I know it. His life is in my hands. I am looking into his eyes. I speak.

If you ever say another thing about her, I will kill you.

I press harder.

I will fucking kill you.

I press harder.

I will fucking kill you.

I let go. Step away. The man starts coughing. Clutching his throat.

Breathing and taking as much air as he can as fast as he can. He's hacking, spitting, gagging. I could have killed him. I wanted to kill him. I take two steps toward Bobby, who is sitting on his chair. He is pale, white, gray, sick, as if the Reaper has told him the end is coming. I spit in his face. I wait for a reaction, but there is none. He just stares straight ahead. I don't know what Leonard told him, but I know there will be no more words. There will be no words from either of them.

I walk out of the Unit and I walk down the Hall. I'm shaking with rage and the afterburn of fear. I'm shaking with horror and the residual rush of violence. I'm shaking with adrenaline. I'm shaking with the Fury like I have never felt it before. The Fury raised to defend someone I love. Greater than I have ever felt it before.

I want a door. I see a door. I hit the door and I'm out the door. Into the cold, gray morning. Into the wet, heavy air. I clench my jaw my fist the muscles in my chest. I clench everything tight. I breathe through my nose as deeply as I can. The wet, heavy air. I can feel it soaking into my cells I can feel my cells draining it. I can feel my cells draining me.

The door opens and Leonard steps out. He doesn't say a word just lets me breathe. The breathing empties me and the need to clench fades. The Fury fades. I have done what I could what I felt was right. The violence was unfortunate but the unfortunate was necessary. Sometimes skulls are thick. Sometimes hearts are vacant. Sometimes words don't work. The violence was necessary.

I take a last breath the final the deepest and I let it out. I look at Leonard and he speaks.

You okay?

Yeah.

You know what they said doesn't matter.

I know.

And you know it probably isn't true.

It's true. I know it's true.

How do you know that?

I just know it is.

Doesn't matter anyway.

I know.

That you love her is all that matters.

Yeah.

Don't forget it, Kid. Love is all that matters.

I nod.

Yeah.

He puts his hand on my shoulder.
I'm proud of you for what you did in there.
I guess.
You gave him a chance and then you let him off. Those are two things I
never do. You also sent the message, crystal fucking clear.
I chuckle.
What'd you say to Bobby?
I told him my name. My full name.
I laugh.
That's it?
Leonard nods.
It's more complicated than you think, but yeah, that's it.
Thanks for backing me up.
Always.
I owe you one.
You don't.
I do.
He shakes his head.
You don't.
I motion to the door.
Let's go to breakfast.
We walk back inside through the Halls down the Corridor. I look for
Lilly she is not there. We get in line a plate of eggs and beans we find our
friends. They have heard about my confrontation, I don't want to talk
about it. We talk about Ed's departure. Ted is near tears. We write down
our names and our addresses and our phone numbers on a piece of paper.
Only Miles and Leonard have permanent ones. The rest give what we can
and hope that they work. We hope that Ed will survive long enough to
call. We wish him luck. We tell him everything is going to be okay.
We finish. I have watched for Lilly and she hasn't come. My friends go
to the Lecture, I go to Joanne's Office. The door is cracked and it is
open enough so that I can hear voices. I walk in, my Parents are on the
couch, they rise to greet me. We hug each other and we sit down. I say
hello to Joanne and she speaks.
There's been a change of plan.
What?
My Father speaks.
We're having to leave early.
Why?
Business emergency.

Same thing as yesterday?

Yes.

I look away for a moment and the Fury flares. As has been the case throughout my life, my Father's job comes first before everything always. I stare at the wall the white wall I do not like it but I cannot change it. The white wall. Nor can I change my Father or his position he has always done the best he could for all of us. Me and my Brother and my Mother. He has always done the best he could and he has given us plenty. He is what he is, he does what he does. I cannot change it and after all they have given me, all they have forgiven me, I can forgive this and accept them leaving early. My Mother speaks.

We're sorry, James.

Don't be sorry, Mom.

We wanted to stay for the whole time.

I'm lucky to have Parents willing to come here at all.

She smiles. It is an insecure smile, one looking for validation.

Are you sure?

I nod.

Let's do what we can with the time we've got.

Joanne speaks.

Normally we wouldn't deal with this right now, but your Parents and I would like to talk about the future.

It's very bright.

Is that a joke?

Yes and no.

Why yes?

Because I'm going to Prison.

We don't know that for sure yet, but okay. Why no?

Because I'm starting over and I'm thankful for the chance.

So what do you do when you leave here?

I go and I do my time and I keep to myself. I try to survive and I try to remain human. I get out and I get a job and I see what happens.

How do you stay sober?

I'll be locked up and I won't have any money. Shouldn't be that hard.

You can get drugs in Prison.

Maybe, but I don't want them.

You think it will be that easy?

I think I'll have more serious worries than staying sober.

Joanne speaks.

What if you don't go to Prison?

I'll move to Chicago and I'll get a job and I'll try to be happy.

What about a Halfway House?

No.

Why?

We've talked about this already.

Joanne looks at my Parents. My Parents look at each other. My Father speaks.

Don't you think that type of environment might be good for you?

I don't believe in Higher Powers and the Twelve Steps or anything related to them, and that is all they teach in Halfway Houses. It'll be a waste of my time.

My Mother speaks.

If you don't believe in those things, how are you going to stay sober?

Every time I want to drink or do drugs, I'm going to make the decision not to do them. I'll keep making that decision until it's no longer a decision, but a way of life.

What if you can't do that?

As soon as I get out of here, I'm going to go find a way to test myself, either in the presence of alcohol or drugs or both, to make sure that I can.

Joanne takes a deep breath, shakes her head.

I have been trying to talk James out of this idea. It's an incredibly risky plan, and the probability of relapse is astronomical. The stakes are way too high.

My Father speaks.

I don't like the idea either, James.

My Mother speaks.

I don't either.

No offense to any of you, but this is entirely my decision.

My Father speaks.

What if you relapse?

I won't.

What if you do?

I won't.

Why are you so confident?

I just believe, simple as that, and I don't want to spend the rest of our time together trying to persuade you. Whatever is in the future is in the future and will be handled as necessary. Let's move on.

My Mother looks at my Father, my Father looks at Joanne. My Father nods, Joanne speaks.

Let's talk about your relationship.

I look at my Parents, they look at me.
How is everyone feeling about it?
My Father speaks.
Very positive.
My Mother speaks.
Much better.
I speak.
We're getting there.
Joanne smiles. It is a big, genuine smile. She looks at my Father.
Why?
I feel like I haven't known James for a very long time, if I ever knew him at all. That has been very difficult, being a Father to a Son who was essentially a Stranger. I have never understood why he has been the way he has been or why he has had all the problems that he has had. I have never understood why he hasn't let his Mother and me into his life and why he seemed to harbor such intense anger toward us. For me, the best part of this experience has been the feeling that I have gotten my Son back, gotten to know who he is and why he is that way, and I have started to come to terms with our past and his past. I'm hoping that past is behind us.
Joanne nods, looks to my Mother. My Mother smiles.
I feel the same way as Bob about not knowing James, and as hard as it has been to learn about him and some of the things he has done, I'm happy that at least we know. He also seems less angry since he's been here. Even over the course of the past few days, he seems less angry. It has always been difficult dealing with that anger and knowing he was so angry at us and not understanding why. I feel like there is a connection between us now, like we are actually a Family, and I haven't felt that for a long time.
Her eyes start to tear. She looks at me.
I'm proud of you, James. I want you to stay alive and be happy and that's it. However you want to do it, just stay alive and try to be happy.
Thanks, Mom.
Joanne looks at me.
James.
I take a deep breath.
I didn't want you guys to come here. I didn't want you to see me here in the state that I was in and I am in, because, on a certain level, I'm ashamed to be here. I know I've always been a disappointment to you. I think I've always kept things from you because I knew if you knew them, they would hurt you. I knew what I was doing was wrong, and if you

knew, you would have tried to change me, and I didn't want to change. It was good admitting all of that shit to you. I think you were amazingly cool with everything while you have been here. I was expecting yelling and screaming and Lectures, and I was expecting you to try and impose a bunch of Rules on me, which I wouldn't have accepted. I'm happy there wasn't any of that, and I'm happy that you came.

My Parents both smile. Joanne smiles.

How do you see your relationship functioning from here?

I speak.

I think it's important that my Parents leave me alone. When I say that I don't mean that I don't want them in my life, because I do, but I would like my life to be my own and I need to be entirely responsible for what it is and what it becomes.

I look at my Parents.

I won't hide things from you, but if I tell you I don't want to talk about something, leave it alone. When I make mistakes, I don't want to be lectured about them. I don't want you to give me money anymore. I want to support myself in whatever way I can, and I want to have to live on that. The last thing, and most important thing, is if I relapse, you can't Bail me out again. This is my last chance. I need it to be that way because if I know there's a safety net, I'll use it. If I know there's not, the decisions I'm going to face are going to be easier for me to make because I'll know that if I make the wrong one, there will be no coming back.

My Parents stare at me. Joanne stares at me. My Father speaks.

I think leaving you alone will be hard for us because you're just starting to come back to us. I think, though, that we can try. I think it will be important for you to define, as we go along, what leaving you alone means. If it means not talking to you or not keeping in good touch with you, I don't like that. If it means talking and being honest about what's going on in your life, but trying to reserve judgment and trying to let you make your own mistakes, I think it is a good idea. If you don't want money from us anymore, that's fine, but the idea of not helping you if you stumble is one that scares me. We've learned here that most People do stumble and do relapse, and I don't like the idea of not trying to help you if that happens. We want you to live a productive life. We don't care if it takes fifty times in places like this to make that happen.

My Mother speaks.

I just don't want you to hide things from us anymore or think that you can't share things with us. Your Father and I only want the best for you, and want you to be happy in your life, and whatever we need to do to help make that happen, we'll do. All I want is to be a part of your life and have you include us in it. I can tell you that if you do relapse, I'm going to continue to try and help you. Like your Father said, if it takes fifty times, that's fine. I'll be here fifty times.

Joanne speaks.

After Prison, what are you going to do once you're on your own?

I'm going to go to Chicago. I'm going to get a job. I'm going to try and survive and be happy. That's all I really want, to survive and be happy.

My Father speaks.

Why Chicago?

I motion toward Joanne.

I don't know if I can talk about it in front of her.

Joanne laughs.

Go ahead, there aren't many Rules we haven't already broken.

I smile.

I'm going to Chicago because Lilly, that girl I told you about, is going to be in Chicago. I want to be with her.

Joanne shakes her head.

Is there anything I can say?

I shake my head.

No.

My Father speaks.

What's she going to be doing in Chicago?

She's going to a Halfway House.

My Mother speaks.

You wouldn't want to go with her?

No.

My Father speaks.

What will she do if you're in Jail?

I haven't talked with her about it, but I'm hoping whichever one of us gets out first will find a place for both of us to live.

Joanne speaks.

And then what?

We'll live with each other and help each other. We'll do the best we can for each other.

My Mother speaks.

That sounds nice.

I think it will be.

Are you going to get married?

You're way ahead of yourself, Mom.

She smiles and she laughs and my Father squeezes her hand. Joanne smiles, though I can see her trying to hold it back. She looks at her watch, speaks.
I think it's about time.
My Father looks at his watch, nods.
It looks like it.
He stands, my Mother stands. My Father looks at Joanne.
Before we leave, I just wanted to say thank you. This would not have been the experience it has been without you, and we, as a Family, owe you a great amount of credit for that. If there is anything we can ever do to repay you, please do not hesitate to ask.
Joanne smiles.
After seeing you together a few days ago, seeing you today is all the thanks I need.
My Mother speaks. As she does, her eyes start to tear.
Thank you, Joanne.
Certainly, Lynne.
My Mother walks around her desk and Joanne stands. They hug each other strong and true in the way that only women can hug each other. There is no hesitation between them and there is no distance. No emotional distance, no physical distance, no distance of any kind.
They separate and my Father shakes Joanne's hand and he thanks her again and I thank her and I walk with my Parents to the Room in the Family Center where they have been sleeping. We get their bags and we get their jackets. We walk back through the Halls to the Front Entrance of the Clinic. We step outside and there is a Car waiting. A long, black Car with black windows. We set down the bags. My Father speaks.
This has been a great experience. I am very proud of you for being here and for trying as hard as you are. Obviously there are still some problems and some issues to be worked out, but I feel very good about everything. Please call us when you hear from the Lawyer and please call us if you need anything or we can help in any way and please call us just to say hi and let us know how you're doing.
I will.
I love you, James.
I love you too, Dad.
A tear appears in the corner of my Father's eye. He doesn't wipe it and it runs down his cheek. He steps forward and he hugs me and I hug him. There is discomfort and the Fury, but I ignore them.
We separate and my Mother steps toward me. Her eyes are tearing again I

used to hate her crying I don't now. She feels and she cries. It is to be admired. She puts her arms around me I put mine around her. We hug each other she holds me like I am her Baby. I am not anymore, but I still am. We hug each other and I fight the Fury. It cannot beat me or control me right now. My Mother hugs me in a way that lets me know I am forgiven and that she wants me to live and be happy. I hug her in a way that lets her know I am trying to be different and I am trying to be stronger than my rage. We are trying to forgive.

We separate and she looks at me and she tries to speak, but she can't. My Father opens the door of the Car and she steps toward it and she sits down on the black leather seat. She is crying and she is smiling. She raises a hand to say good-bye. I raise mine.

My Father, who is standing next to the door, looks at me and speaks. Keep up the good work.

I will.

He climbs into the car next to my Mother and he shuts the door. The Car pulls away down the wooded drive that leads in and out of the Clinic. I can't see through the darkened windows, but I know my Parents are watching me and I stand and I watch them. We are a Family saying good-bye. For now good-bye.

When the Car is gone from view and my Parents away, I turn and I go back into the Clinic. It is time for lunch, so I walk to the Dining Hall. I get a tray and a plate of French-bread pizza and a glass of red fruit punch and I see my friends in one of the corners. I sit down with them.

They are talking about fighting. My fight this morning and the Heavyweight Championship, which is a few nights from now. They ask me what happened this morning I tell them it was not really a fight it was more of a discussion that got heated. Leonard laughs. They ask me what the man said to me and I tell them I don't want to talk about it. They ask me if I am going to go after him again and I tell them that I hope that the entire situation goes away.

We talk about the real fight. Leonard and Matty know the most about it, so they do most of the talking. Matty likes the smaller of the Heavyweights, who is still a very large man, Leonard likes the bigger Heavyweight, who is massive. The men have fought twice previously, with each of them winning one of the fights, and they don't like each other or respect each other, and each have promised a knockout this time. We want to see the fight. All of us want to see it. We want to see it because we like sports and we like boxing, because all of the newspapers and television sports shows have been running stories about it, because it will be something to talk about after it is over, and mostly we want to see it because it would allow us, if only for a couple of hours, to feel normal.

In here, anything resembling normalcy is coveted. The phone is always busy because men want to be in contact with the normal outside world. Letters are eagerly awaited and opened because they are physical contact with it. Television is watched and newspapers are read obsessively because they give us glimpses, magazines are thumbed until the pages fall apart. Our Jobs here, as stupid and menial as they may be, allow us to pretend that we are, if even for just a few minutes a day, just like other people. That is why the Jobs get done. Not because we are told to do them, for most of us have spent our lives doing everything but that which we have been told to do, but because the Jobs make us feel normal. Normal people have Jobs. For a few minutes a day, we get to pretend.

All of us started out normal. All of us started out as functioning human beings with the potential to do almost anything we wanted, but somewhere along the paths of our lives, we got lost. Though we are here at this Clinic trying to find our way back, we all know that most of us will never get there. Things like the fight allow us to dream, and take us away from here, and allow us to imagine what the normal World must be like and how normal people must live in it. Normal men would make plans with their friends to watch the fight. They would choose a location with room to sit down and a large television. They would show up. They would have some food and a few drinks before the fight began, and they would be able to stop drinking before they blacked out or became violent. They would have their favorite fighter. They would be able to talk and they would debate with each other about his strengths and weaknesses. They would be conscious enough to watch the fight, and they would cheer or groan depending on the outcome. When it was over they would go Home and they would be in a condition to walk or to drive, and if they were lucky, they would have a Wife to kiss or a sleeping Child to check, and they would go to bed. When they woke the next day, they would remember the night before, and they would continue with their life. Their normal, beautiful life. Everyone here, male or female, Crackhead or Drunk or Junkie, rich or poor or black or white, would give everything we have ever had and everything we will ever have, if only we could be normal. Things like the fight, the silly, stupid, soon forgotten fight, would afford us the opportunity. We want to watch it. We would love to watch it. We would give anything to watch it, but the television here will not carry it. It requires a special cable system with a special box. The type available in the outside World.

We finish eating. We stand and we put our trays away. We walk to the Lecture and we sit in the back row. I look for Lilly she is not here. I wish she were so that I could watch her instead of listening to the Lecture. So I could look at her and let time fade away. So that she could look at me and I could feel the love I felt earlier. In her arms. In her eyes. In her words. I want it again.

A male Doctor wearing glasses and khakis and a white lab coat steps in front of the lectern and he starts speaking. The subject is the concept of cross-addiction. In the simplest terms, cross-addiction means that if you're Addicted to one substance or means of behavior, a substance such as heroin or means of behavior like gambling, you are Addicted to all substances and means of behavior. Recovery from any of them means abstinence from all of them. If you use or do something other than your drug of choice or behavior of choice, you will most likely become addicted to it, and you will also most likely relapse back to the original addiction. The Doctor talks about being constantly and consistently self-aware in order to guard against the perils of cross-addiction. He says smoking cigarettes and drinking coffee are fine, because they are more habit than addiction, but beyond them, be careful how you eat, how you conduct yourself sexually, be careful not to gamble or spend too much money shopping, be careful of linking yourself to people who do these things, stay away from places where they are done, and be on constant alert. For the rest of your life. Constant alert.

Though fundamentally sound in theory, in its practical application, what this Doctor is saying is too absurd to be taken seriously. Any Idiot, especially an Addicted Idiot, knows that if you do drugs or drink when you're trying to stay sober, even if that drug or drink is not your chemical of choice, then you are probably going to get hooked on it. Any Idiot, especially an Addicted Idiot, knows that once you cross the line from use to abuse, and from abuse to addiction, that you can't go back and start over with something else. To suggest that having sex or eating is dangerous and should be monitored is ridiculous. To suggest that buying something or spending money will lead me back to smoking cocaine is fucking dumb. To state that I need to be on guard against all manner of potential addiction all the time everywhere I go for the rest of my life is pathetic. I won't live that way. It is fucking pathetic.

The Lecture ends and the Patients clap. I stand and I follow the rest of the men out of the Lecture Hall. We walk back to the Unit. As I pass my Room, I see a note on the door that says James Call Urgent and there is a number. I don't recognize the number and I have never dialed it before, but I know it is a local number because of the area code. I take the note and I walk to the phone. The men are getting ready for the afternoon Session, so there is no line.

I open the door and I sit down and I dial the number. It rings once twice three times it rings. On the fourth ring a woman answers she says the name of Lilly's Unit. I ask if Lilly is there. The woman asks who is this and I tell her a friend. I hear her drop the receiver. I wait a moment or two a couple of moments pass. I hear the receiver move I hear someone picking it up. I hear her voice. She's been shattered. Shattered.

What's wrong?

Where have you been?

I was at the Lecture.

I've been trying to call you.

I just got the message.

I need to see you.

What's wrong?

I need to see you.

Tell me what's wrong.

She starts to cry.

My Grandma.

What's wrong?

My Grandma.

What's wrong with her?

She breaks down and she starts to sob. It is heavy, horrible sobbing, the kind that hurts the body, that comes when the heart is overwhelmed. I can see her. Sitting in the Phone Booth eyes swollen, body shaking, tears running down her face.

I need to see you.

What's wrong?

My Grandma.

Her voice breaks.

My Grandma's going to die.

What?

She starts crying again.

I need to see you.

We can't right now.

Why?

We'll get caught.

I need to see you.

Wait till it's dark.

I need to see you now.

What happened with her?

Please.

She's crying. Crying. I know I shouldn't go, but the sounds of her tears hurt me wreck me destroy me she's crying. I know she needs me. It shouldn't matter what or when or where we are, nothing should matter but her. She needs me. I told myself I would do anything for her. She's crying and she needs me.

Meet me in the Clearing.

When?

I'll leave as soon as we hang up.

Okay.

If you're there before me, just wait. I'm coming as fast as I can.

Okay.

Everything is going to be all right.

It won't.

It will.

She's going to die, James.

We'll get through it. Everything is going to be all right.

I love you.

I love you too.

She hangs up and I hang up. I open the door of the Phone Booth and I step out. The men have gathered on the Lower Level, the chairs are in a semicircle, and Lincoln is preparing to start the afternoon Session. He looks at me and he speaks.

You joining us?

I need to go outside, take a walk.

You think you can just skip things when you want to skip them?

I don't want to, I need to.

Why?

Because I do.

Answer my question?

I need to go outside. Why is it your business?

Because I'm the Supervisor of this Unit.

Then supervise it. I'm going for a walk.

I open the sliding-glass door and I step outside and I start walking. I don't pay any attention to my surroundings. I walk quickly I know my way. I don't want her alone. She needs me.

I step into the Clearing she is there. Eyes swollen. Cheeks stained. Hands shaking. She has been crying for so long that she doesn't know she's crying anymore. She's crying.

She steps forward and I step forward and she's in my arms and I am holding her. She lays her head on my shoulder and she cries. She shakes. She
holds me squeezes me presses herself against me as if I can absorb what
she feels as if I can take it away. I can. I can absorb what she gives me
take it from her and make it mine and let go of it. I can. I will take it and
make it mine. Give it to me. I'll let go of it. I can let go of it.
I guide her to the ground hold her let her cry. I whisper in her ear it's
okay it's okay it's okay. The words are nothing, just simple words, but
they calm her down because she has never had someone tell her it's okay
before and she has never believed it. It's okay it's okay. I hold her in my
arms and she believes me. It's going be okay.
She calms down and she stops crying. She stays against my shoulder. I
speak.
What happened?
She has cancer. It's in her bones and her blood. There's no cure.
You found out this morning?
Yes.
How long has she had it?
They found it last week. She was feeling sick, but she thought it would go
away. She collapsed at work.
Why didn't she tell you earlier?
She didn't want to worry me.
Why'd she tell you this morning?
It's worse than she thought. She figured the sooner the better.
How long's she got?
Anywhere from two weeks to six months.
I hold her tighter.
I'm sorry.
She holds me tighter.
She's all I've got.
You've got me.
I'm scared.
Don't be.
What are we going to do?
Get through it.
How?
When I can I'll come to Chicago and we'll get a place together and we'll
be fine.
She pulls away slightly and she looks at me.
You're going to come?

As soon as I can.
When you leave here?
No.
Where are you going?
I'm going to Prison.
What?
I'm in some trouble. I'm going to have to go away for a while. I don't know for how long right now, but as soon as I'm done, I'll come to Chicago.
What'd you do?
I got in a fight with some Cops and I was drunk and I had some drugs on me.
Why didn't you tell me?
I didn't want you to worry until I knew what was happening.
You should have told me.
I know. I'm sorry.
How long will you be away?
I don't know yet.
You should have told me.
I'm telling you now. I'll come as soon as I can.
You're all I've got, James. In the whole goddamn world, you're all I've got.
You've got yourself.
I wish that were enough, but it's not.
You may surprise yourself.
I've been alone my whole life. I can't do it anymore.
You're not going to have to.
She's dying, James.
Everything is going to be okay.
I hear a noise. I turn toward the green. The noise is louder approaching fast. We start to stand, the noise is louder. Footsteps on leaf and dirt and broken branch we're tangled and having trouble standing. It's louder and we're up. It's louder and I look at Lilly. Louder and she takes my hand. It's just outside the Clearing. She kisses me. It's coming through. She looks me in the eye. It's through. She says you're all I've got.
The noise stops. I turn around. Lincoln is standing a few feet away from us. He speaks.
Ken took over for me. I thought I'd come see how you're doing.
I'm doing fine.
No, you're not. You're not even close.

Depends on how you think of it.

I think of it according to the Rules of this Institution. You obviously don't.

No, I don't.

Let's go, and not a word while we're walking back.

I turn to Lilly, who is staring at Lincoln. Her stare is a mixture of defiance and fear and rage. Lincoln stares back at her and he tries to step between us. We are still holding hands and she pushes him away. He grabs her wrist and she holds my hand tighter and she stares at him and she speaks.

I'll keep my mouth shut, but I'm not letting go.

You're in no position to be making demands.

It's not a demand, it's the way it's gonna be.

You broke the Rules, now you deal with it.

Fuck you and your Rules, I am dealing with it.

She stares at him and he stares back. I watch her and I am proud of her she breaks my heart I love her. They stare at each other. Her eyes are stronger than she knows. Lincoln can see what I can see she is not letting go of my hand. He can talk all day, try to pull us apart for as long as he wants, she is not letting go of my hand.

Follow me.

He turns and he starts pushing through the green and we follow him. We hold hands and we stare straight ahead. Lincoln is moving quickly. He gets to the Trail and he stops and he waits for us. When we're a few feet behind him, he starts walking again. The Trail leads us back to the green grass separating the Buildings from the Wood. As we get closer, we turn and we stare at each other. There are no words we just stare at each other and with each second Lilly's eyes soften. They start to tear. I don't want her to cry I don't want her to go I don't want her to be in trouble. I'll take the blame if necessary they can kick me out and I'll wait for her and I'll be fine. She's crying. Not sobbing just tears down her cheeks more tears. I wish I could take them and make them mine I don't want her to cry not now not ever not ever again. She's crying.

We reach the door. Lincoln opens it and we step inside. All of the men turn and stare. Lincoln closes the door and he steps in front of us and he speaks.

I'm taking her to her Unit. Go to your Room and wait there. It may be a while.

I nod.

Let's go.

I look at Lilly and she looks at me. I pull my hand away and I put my arms around her. I whisper in her ear.

I love you. Remember that. I love you.

She holds me until Lincoln puts his hand on her shoulder. She steps away and he waits for her and she turns and they start walking up the stairs and I follow them. Everyone is staring at us. Ken and the men. Staring. We enter the Hall I hate it fucking hate it they walk in front of me and I watch them. I stop walking when I reach my door, I just stand and I watch them. Lilly is a few feet in front of Lincoln. As she walks, she stares straight ahead. He stares at her back. There are no words. The Hall is silent.

As they near the end of the Hall, Lilly turns around and she looks back at me. All I see are her eyes, deep water blue and defiant, broken and lost, her eyes staring back at me. They are wet with tears. I don't want to lose them they turn the corner and they're gone. I stand at my door hoping she'll come back, hoping this is all a nightmare, hoping for the sake of hoping. I stare down the Hall at the unforgiving white walls. Nothing changes.

I open my door and I step inside my Room. It is quiet and empty, exactly as it was when I left it this morning. I look at my bed and I think about sitting on it. I look at the Bathroom and I think about a shower. I look at the window and the gray light coming through it and I think of climbing out of it. I look at the walls. I would like to destroy them. I can only wait. For my fate to be decided, for Lincoln to come back. I can only wait.

The substance of what has happened sinks into me. Not gradually, but all at once. I have broken one of the Cardinal Rules of this Institution. I have broken it with impunity. I have fallen in love with a Girl, a beautiful and profoundly troubled Girl who is alone in the World and who has said she cannot live without me. I don't want to stay here without her and if I leave, I have nowhere to go. She has nowhere to go. We could go back to her Grandmother, but her Grandmother will be dead soon. We can't go to my Family, I have burdened them too much. We could run, but there's nowhere to run. I am wanted, and sooner or later, I'll get caught. When I am, I'll be sent away, and it will be for far longer than three years. We are both Addicts. We both need to be here. We're going to get kicked out. Both of us. Kicked out.

I think back on what has happened. I try to see what I did wrong. I try to rethink what I have done and find a way that would have allowed me to avoid this situation. I could have ignored her the first day. I could have thrown away the note she gave me. I could have not spoken to her or not responded to her. I could have not called her back earlier or not left the Unit or not stayed in the Clearing when I met her. I didn't do any of these things. If I had, I would not be in trouble, not be facing what I am. I don't want to accept what has happened. I want to go back. I want to change it. Fuck me. We're fucked.

I sit on my bed light a cigarette take a drag, a deep drag, as deep as I can take. I stare at the floor. My thoughts slow. I know I can't change what has happened and I don't regret it. I did what I did and I would do it again. I love her and love is more important than Rules or Regulations. I have learned more from it than I have from them. I have become better because of it. Fuck the Rules and Regulations.

I take another drag. My thoughts slow more. Two streams run simultaneous to each other. Drink. Lilly. Drugs. Lilly. Get fucked up. Lilly. They are independent of each other and they are intertwined. One is an overwhelming need for self-destruction, an overwhelming need to kill what I feel with chemicals. The other is of Lilly and where she is what she's doing what she's thinking is she okay. Who is with her and what are they saying to her. They overlap and run together because I need her and her absence and the pain I know she's feeling fuels the need to kill what I feel.

I stand up. I sit down. I stand up. I sit down. My mind is telling my hands to go to take action to facilitate leaving here my mind is telling my hands it is time to leave. I sit on them. I sit on my hands. I feel like a complete Asshole, a weak pathetic Fuck. My mind is telling my hands to leave to get something anything to leave to get destroyed. I am sitting on them. I am sitting on my hands. I'm a weak, pathetic, Addicted Fuck. My heart is telling me stay. To wait. To hold on. To have strength. To sit on my goddamn hands and defy them. Strength comes in defiance. Defy your mind your feelings your addictions. Defy them, you Motherfucker, defy them.

I sit on my bed sit on my hands close my eyes breathe let myself feel everything. I test my will. Can I sit and stay. Can I hold on. Am I strong enough. What the fuck am I doing. When will this end. End soon. Please. Hold the fuck on. End soon.

I sit and time stops disappears moves fast and slow each second more and less than a second. My hands shake beneath me. My eyes are closed and I am breathing slowly. Thoughts and feelings of panic and self-destruction and endurance and self-will run through and through and through.

Sit.

Stay.

Leave
No.
Drink.
Smoke.
Panic.
Panic.
Leave.
Stay.
Fucked.
Fucked.
Run.
Run.
Run.
Caught.
Eight years.
Maximum Security.
Lilly.
Where are you.
Lilly.
Where are you.
Use.
Drugs.
Drink.
Alcohol.
Kill.
Yourself.
Now.
No.
Without time. On my hands. Fighting myself. The thoughts change.
Use.
Fucking.
Drugs.
Drink.
Now.
You.
Motherfucker.
We.
Are.
Stronger.
Than.

You.

Will.

Ever.

Be.

Over and over. Over and over. Time has disappeared. I sit on my hands. I fight myself. Over and over. I fight myself. Over and over.

I start to cry. Not sobs just tears streaming down my face through my closed eyes. Tears from effort and tears from stress and tears from fear this is a fucking nightmare. Worse than a nightmare. Tears from holding on and tears from fighting and tears brought on by the prospect of death and by the prospect of a return to my old life. There are tears of love. Lilly's love and the love of friends and Family love. There are tears because the Fury and the fear and the addiction want to beat me and I will not let them. They want to beat me and I will not let them.

Time is gone.

I cry.

It's a fucking nightmare.

Worse.

Please end.

Please end.

Please end.

I hear the door. I open my eyes. It is dark now the gray is gone. The simple sound breaks the cycle. The simple sound of a door. Miles turns on the light sees me sitting there looks surprised.

Are you all right, James?

No.

Is there anything I can do for you?

No.

Have you been here since this afternoon?

Yeah.

Why are you sitting on your hands?

I don't trust them.

I know that feeling.

Yeah?

I don't sit on them, though. I squeeze them together.

I smile and I move my hands and I wipe my face and I set my hands on my lap. They are crossed with lines and they are blue from lack of blood. I shake them and they hurt. They tingle. They sting.

They okay?

I look up.

They hurt.
Try warm water.
That works?
Very well.
I nod and I stand. Miles walks to his bed and he sits down on it. I go into the
Bathroom turn on the warm water put my hands in it and it burns them. Not
because the water is warm but because my hands are cold. It stings them. The
tingling feels like a nest of needles trying to escape. I hold them and they
slowly warm. Go from blue to gray to white to pink to yellow to beige. I flex
my fingers and they flex as they should. The pain goes away. I flex them and
they're fine.
I walk out of the Bathroom. Miles is sitting on the edge of his bed wait-
ing for me.
Are you going to Dinner?
I'm supposed to stay here.
For how long?
I don't know.
Would you like me to get you something to eat?
Sure.
What would you like?
Whatever's easy.
Okay.
Thank you.
Anything I can help you with?
You know what time it is?
He looks at his watch.
Six-fifteen.
Thank you.
I walk to my bed. He stands and he walks to the door.
If you're not here when I get back, I'll leave whatever I bring you on your
nightstand.
Thanks, Miles.
He walks out, closes the door behind him. I lie down on my bed I am
cold I start to shake I climb under the covers. I curl into myself and I
close my eyes and I bury my face into my chest and into the bed. I fall
into a sleep where I am not asleep. A state of heavy consciousness neither
aware nor unaware. My body relaxes my body shuts down my body rests.
My mind slows, holds images, wishes, mistakes, reality. They are like
thick surreal photographs. I look at them in my mind and they sit there. I
am sleeping but not I'm not asleep. I am aware and unaware.

The door opens again I open my eyes. I lift my head and I see Lincoln standing under the door frame. There is light behind him he speaks.

Time to get up.

Okay.

Come to my Office when you're ready.

Okay.

He turns and he leaves and he closes the door as he goes. I get out of bed and I walk to the Bathroom and I turn on the water and I splash some of the water over my face. It runs down my cheeks and over my lips and into my mouth and it tastes good. I lean over and I take a sip. Another another another. Straight from the faucet. It's good.

I leave my Room and walk through the silent Hall. The Unit is empty, the men at Dinner. I go to the coffee machine and I get a cup and I take a sip and it immediately wakes me.

As I walk down the stairs, I start to get nervous. The coffee burns my stomach and I can feel my blood moving through my veins. My legs are unsteady, and I think about each step. In front of the other. In front of the other.

I cross the Lower Level walk into the short Hall leading to Lincoln's Office. The Hall is dark, though there is light at the end where his door is open. I think about each step. As I enter his Office, I have to think about each step. He is sitting behind his desk.

Shut the door.

I turn and I shut the door. I turn back and he motions to a chair across from him. I sit and he leans back in his chair and he stares at me. I stare back.

If it were up to me you'd be gone. I don't like your attitude, and I don't think you've made much of an effort, and I think your continued resistance to what we try to do here, which is help People, has been detrimental to both the Unit and to yourself.

He stares. I stare back.

That being said, you're being given another chance. If you behave and work hard and follow the Rules, you will be able to stay until your Program runs its course. If you violate any of the Rules, even something as simple as not doing your morning Job or saying anything more than hello to any woman not on our Staff, you will be asked to leave. You think you can do that?

I smile. I'm relieved.

Yes, I can. Thank you.

Don't thank me, I wanted you out. Thank Joanne. Just like before, she's the one who saved you.

Thanks anyway.

You can go now.

He looks down at some papers on his desk. I wait. When he looks up, I speak.

Is Lilly staying?

No, she's not.

My relief disappears.

You kicked her out?

Panic returns.

When we told her she wouldn't be allowed to see you anymore, she walked out.

You didn't stop her?

When people want to leave, we let them leave. Our Job is to help people who want to stay and be helped.

What if I told you I knew where she was going?

Doesn't matter.

I know where she's going. I could get her and bring her back.

He chuckles, and instantly the panic is gone. The Fury rises.

Why's that funny?

We discourage relationships because they generally turn out this way. People think they can solve each other's problems, and it's just not the case. I hope this will teach you a lesson.

What's that supposed to mean?

We know what we're doing here. We have Rules for a reason. Maybe you'll listen a bit better from now on.

Fuck you.

What did you say?

She's a Person, not a fucking lesson.

What did you just say to me?

I said fuck you, you fucking Asshole. She's not a fucking lesson.

One more remark like that and you're out of here.

You think I want to stay here now?

If you want to stay sober you will.

I'm not gonna stay in a place where Assholes like you say that their Job is to help People, but when someone needs help most, you deny it to them because they believe in something different than you or need a different kind of help than what you think is right.

Do what you need to do.

I will, and I'm gonna stay clean doing it, if for no other reason than to be able to come back here and show your self-righteous ass that your way isn't the only way.

Good luck.

Fuck you.

I stand and I leave. I walk through the Unit and I go to my Room. I grab the little book the *Tao* put on my warmest clothes a sweater two pairs of socks another pair of socks over my hands. It's cold I can see it through the window. I leave my Room good-bye good-bye good-bye. I walk through the Halls I will never have to see these fucking Halls again fuck you good-bye. I walk through the Reception Area hit the Front Door I am out of the Clinic. Fuck you and good-bye. I am out.

I start walking. It's cold and dark, there's no light and no Moon. I follow the road the one road in the one road out. I see the outlines of trees and the mist of my breath. I hear rocks and gravel crush beneath my feet. I don't remember coming in, it was so long ago, but I know this road ends on a larger road. There will be Cars on the larger road. I will try to get a ride. Locals will know where I'm from and they won't pick me up, but Trucks might pick me up or People passing through on their way somewhere else might pick me up. My face is healed. I don't look like the image of an Alcoholic and a drug Addict and a Criminal anymore. I look normal though I'm not. A Truck might pick me up or someone passing through might pick me up. The locals won't get near me. They will know what I am.

The road curves away and the last light of the Clinic disappears behind me. It is pitch black and it is quiet and I like it. I have been away from the night and from the darkest darkness for too long. I know them well I am Home now and the feelings of Home and the Fury of Home come back to me. They all come back.

There is noise behind and noise ahead. The noise behind is a Car or Truck coming down the road, coming toward me. The noise ahead is the noise of vehicles moving fast on a long smooth road. I want the noise ahead. That is noise I need. I am through with all that behind me. Fuck you and good-bye. I start running. I am out of shape and the cold air burns my lungs. I run along the edge of asphalt and the trees, I run as fast as I can knowing the distance I need to cover. It is not far. Not far, but far for me. Each deep breath of the cold black air hurts my lungs. I'm twenty-three. I can hardly run.

I make it to the larger road. The lights of passing vehicles streak across long, wide fields. I know the nearest City is to the west. Lilly is in the City and the west is to the left. I sprint across the road and I turn left and I start walking. I watch for a vehicle and I wait to lift my thumb.

A white Van pulls up at the end of the road leading to the Clinic and

flashes its lights. Whoever is in the Van can go fuck themselves. It pulls
out and it makes a left and it drives toward me.

As it approaches, the window on the passenger's side slides down. The
Van pulls alongside me and I feel someone staring at me they wait for
me to acknowledge them. I don't. I walk with my eyes fixed and focused. The City is somewhere in front of me. Above the murmur of the
engine, I hear a voice.

Hey, Kid. You forgot something.

It is a voice I know, a voice I like, a voice I trust, a voice that held me
when I couldn't stand. I look at the Van and I look through the lowered
window. Lincoln is sitting in the passenger's seat. He is staring at me.
Hank is sitting in the driver's seat. Hank is holding his coat. The coat he
lent me the coat I left in my Room. He is smiling at me.

You're gonna freeze your ass off without this.

I smile.

How you doing, Old-Timer?

Good. How you doing?

I'm in a hurry.

Where you going?

To find a friend.

Jump in and get warm for a minute.

I don't mind the cold.

Jump in.

No thanks.

Lincoln speaks.

Get in.

I stop walking and Hank stops the Van. I stare at Lincoln and he stares at
me.

I'm not going back.

Get in the Van.

Fuck you.

You want to find her?

Yeah.

Then get in the goddamn Van.

I stare at him and he stares at me. His eyes are cold and dark and dull,
but there is truth in them. I step toward the door and he reaches over his
shoulder and he unlocks it. I open it and I step inside the Van and I close
the door behind me. The heaters are blowing and it is warm. Hank tosses
me his jacket and I put it on. He speaks.

Where we headed?

Bus Station in Minneapolis.

We in a hurry?

I look at Lincoln. He stares straight ahead.

What time did she leave?

He speaks monotone.

About four.

I look at Hank.

Yeah, we're in a hurry.

He smiles and the Van jumps as he drops his foot. The Cornfields become a dull ugly blur, the wind becomes a shriek, the Road a cylinder of moving light and yellow lines leading toward finding Lilly. I sit and I stare out the window and I smoke cigarettes. Lincoln stares straight ahead, taking deep breaths through his nose and occasionally cracking his knuckles. Hank finds a country-western station on the radio and he sings along with every song. If he doesn't know the words, he makes up his own, usually having to do with hockey or fishing. There is no conversation.

The glow of the City rises. We pull off the Highway and down an Exit Ramp into a crowded center of towering steel and glass. People hurry through the streets, the Restaurants and Bars are crowded and busy. Cars honk and Trucks sit waiting on Loading Docks, Cabs search for Passengers. Hank makes a turn and we pass a huge Sports Arena with a flashing sign announcing Game Night. We pull around a jammed Parking Lot, and the far side of it, next to a boarded Building and run-down Motel, is the Bus Station.

The last quarter mile takes an hour, a week, a year, a lifetime. I know we're moving quickly, but quickly isn't good enough. My legs are bouncing up and down and I am anxious and nervous and scared. I feel the way I felt when I was ten and I borrowed my Father's watch without asking him. I lost it on a Beach. I discovered the loss on my bike ride home and I returned to the Beach and searched the sand for hours and hours. I searched on my hands and knees. I feel the way I felt when an ounce of cocaine disappeared in my Room. I tore the Room apart flipped the bed emptied drawers went through all my clothes. I went through everything. I never found the watch. I found the cocaine.

As we pull up to the Entrance I open the Van door before it stops. I hit the ground running. I push past the men standing outside with cups begging change. I ignore the smell of piss and smoke. I push open the doors they are old and heavy and I'm inside the Station.

It is a typical inner-city Bus Station. There is one giant Room with dull fluorescent lights hanging from wires, Ticket Windows built into three

walls, multiple Exits leading to the buses, Aisles of worn wooden benches
bolted to the floor. It is not crowded, but it is not empty. There are drug
Dealers, pimps, homeless men and women sleeping on benches, drifters,
runaways. I am at ease among them.
I start scanning the benches. I want to find her, I don't care how or
where, I just want to find her. I walk up and down the Aisles. I pull blankets off bodies. I roll people over so I can see their faces. I look in sleeping bags, I offer smokes for information. I can't find her. I get nothing,
nobody knows a thing. I can't find her.
I go to the Ticket Windows. I go to all three of them. The Clerks are bored
and annoyed, busy watching black-and-white televisions with poor reception. I describe her to them and I ask if they have seen her. They say they
have not. I ask again, but the game shows and the soap operas are too important for them to care. They say they have not seen her. They tell me without
looking at me.
I walk back to the Entrance. I know she is either here or she has been
here. I know someone has seen her. I examine each person examine them
closely. She would avoid the pimps because she could make her money
without them. The Dealers I have seen don't deal what she uses they offered me pot or meth or low-grade smack. Her goal would be to get high
or get Home. I know she is either here or she has been here. I know
someone has seen her. I know. I stare. I know. Stare.
I keep looking, looking, looking. My eyes settle on two Boys sitting on a
bench. They are about twelve. They are wearing huge baggy jeans, thick
down jackets that hide their bodies, hats on backward with the brims facing down. The bench is in front of a Bathroom and provides views of the
entire Bus Station. I watch them. They are what I think they are. I know
what they're doing.
I walk across the Room. As I approach the Boys, they pretend not to notice me, but I know they are looking at me as carefully as I am looking at
them. I stop in front of the Bathroom door. As I do one of them quickly
and briefly looks at the other. The other acknowledges the look. The
looks let me know I'm right.
I open the door. It immediately smells like piss and shit and human rot.
Two steps through a short, dark, dirty Hall and there is another door. I
open it and the smell is stronger. I step into a foul Bathroom. Cracked,
stained tiles cover the floor. They were once white, but now they're
brown. Shattered mirrors hang above sinks filled with stagnant water.
Urinals run along one wall. All of them are full of yellow piss, in one lies
a disintegrating shoe. I look at a line of Stalls. None of them have doors,

there is graffiti covering the beaten wood walls. I see a pair of shoes be-
neath the last in the line. They are new shoes, expensive basketball shoes.
I speak.
What's up?
I hear a voice. Deep and thick like a sledgehammer with Ghetto inflec-
tions.
What do you need?
I need to talk to you.
I hear a chuckle. I hear movement. I see the shoes step forward and I look
up and I see a man emerge from behind the wall of the Stall. He is about
twenty. His head is shaved. He has a thin goatee and he wears the same
style of clothing as the Boys on the bench. He looks at me, top to bot-
tom, sizes me up. He speaks.
What's up?
I'm looking for someone. Hoping you can help me.
Who you looking for?
A Girl. A young, white Girl. Long black hair and blue eyes. She was
wearing an Army coat.
His head stays still, but his eyes move quickly and unconsciously to the
upper left.
I ain't seen her.
I stare at him.
Yes, you have.
He starts walking toward me.
You calling me a Liar?
I don't move.
I'm not calling you anything.
His voice rises.
You calling me a motherfucking Liar?
Where is she?
He takes another step forward. His eyes slide quickly to the left and back
at me.
I don't know.
We're face-to-face, inches apart. I can feel his breath on my cheeks. I
stand my ground, but keep my hands at my sides.
Tell me where she is.
He smiles. It is not a friendly smile.
Why you gotta find this Girl?
She's in trouble. She needs help.
What do I get if I tell you what I know?

The satisfaction of knowing you did the right thing.
He chuckles.
That ain't worth much to me.
I don't have anything else.
You gotta give me something.
Like what?
How much money you got?
None.
You got a gun?
Nope.
You got a car?
I laugh.
I don't have shit, man.
He laughs and he looks away. He looks back, looks me up and down, and
he stares in my eyes. I hold his stare, but not in an aggressive way. I hold it
passively and in a relaxed manner, without fear and with patience.
How you know to come in here and find me?
Because I saw your Boys out front.
And how'd you know I'd have the rock?
Because I used to smoke the rock and I used to sell the rock.
And now you trying to help this Girl get off it?
Yeah.
I lost a Sister to it once.
I'm sorry.
I knew better than to try and make her quit.
You should have tried.
Can't nobody quit. The shit's too strong.
Doesn't mean you can't try.
Do what you gotta do, but there ain't nobody that can quit the shit.
Tell me where she is.
His stare narrows and it takes on an edge of potential violence. I wait and
I stare back.
You bust me, or get me busted, or fuck with me in any way, and I'll kill
you.
That's fine.
I'll fucking kill you.
That's fine.
She was in here a couple of hours ago with some old white man. He
didn't look like he smoked, but she was all shaking and shit and had them
greedy eyes that Baseheads got. The old man bought two fifties and I

think they went to that empty Building down the Street. There's a busted-down door in the back and a buncha Baseheads do their cooking up on the third floor. If she ain't there, I can't help you.

I nod.

Thank you.

He stares.

Don't come back here.

I won't.

I turn and I walk out the door, across the Station and toward the Entrance. Hank is waiting for me.

I think I found her.

Where?

Down the Street. In that boarded Building.

How do you know that?

A Dealer told me.

We walk outside to the Van, which is waiting at the Curb. He gets in the Driver's seat and I get in the back. Lincoln sits staring out the window. Hank starts the Van and whips it around and we roar down the Street toward the Building. It looks as if it was once an Apartment Building. It is five floors high with windows regularly spaced along each of its sides. All of the windows are now covered with boards. A rubbled Stoop leads to a Main Entrance, which has also been boarded up. There is scrawled graffiti everywhere, most of it illegible, and there are piles of garbage on what used to be the Lawn.

Again, I am out of the Van before we stop. I run around the Building, looking for a back door, a loose board on a window, something, anything. I see a set of stairs leading downward, a door at the bottom. There is a board covering the door, but it looks loose, looks like it will move. I walk down the stairs, step around and over broken glass dirty cans empty bottles pieces of loose foil covered with burn marks lost syringes used matches and shattered lighters. I reach for the board and I push it aside. I step into the Building.

The Building is a wreck, a wretched fucking wreck. There is trash everywhere, there are soiled mattresses lying in the Halls and in Rooms. Polluted pipes are dripping some foul liquid. I hear rats in the walls and I see their shit piles in the corners, a smell that resembles rotten eggs and death permeates the air and makes me wince, cringe, want to hold my breath. I move quickly, driven by the stench and the shit, through a Hall and up the first set of stairs that I find.

It is pitch black in the stairwell, so I walk carefully. I step on a can and it collapses beneath my foot. I hear rats scurry away I hear them chatter and squeak. I put my hand on a Rail, but the Rail is covered with something thick and wet and cold, so I move it. At the top of the first flight there is an empty garbage can that has been lit on fire. I can see outlines of soot and shades of ash. I step around it. I keep going up.

It gets cleaner as I go higher, though it is still disgusting. At the top of the second flight, I start to hear sounds of human activity. Footsteps, muffled voices, deep inhalations, deep exhalations. The hiss of a butane torch. There is laughter, but it is not happy laughter. It is a high, scratchy cackle, like the laugh of a Witch. It echoes, echoes, echoes.

I get to the third floor. I step into a Hall that leads to my left and to my right. To my left, a strong male voice screams who the fuck's there, Motherfucker, who the fuck's there. I start walking toward it. It screams again you best tell me who the fuck's there. I don't say a word. I walk, tense up, prepare to fight. It screams I'll fuck you up, Bitch, fuck you up. I walk closer, prepare.

It becomes quiet, but for the butane hiss. I know the voice came from a Room two doors down. My fists are clenched, my jaw tight, my muscles twitching.

I step around a corner and into the Room. Against the far wall is a gaunt old man who looks like a ghost. His hair is matted, his skin is a gray of unknown race, a color that comes from months without cleaning. He is smiling without teeth and he is clutching a pipe, a long thin glass pipe red hot and flaming. I see the pipe burning his hand. The butane torch is in his other hand he is pointing it at me like a gun. The smell of crack, like bittersweet peppermint gasoline, drifts through the Room. The smell taunts me and it enrages me I would love to taste that smell, but I want Lilly more than the great and terrible rock. As I stare at the man he speaks.

I ain't got no rock. I ain't got none.

I step back.

I ain't got none, I ain't got none, don't take my rock, don't take it.

I step through the door.

There ain't nothing here, Motherfucker, there ain't nothing for you, you dirty white Devil you dirty white Pig.

Away and back. About halfway to the stairwell, just as his voice fades, the man starts screaming who the fuck's there, Motherfucker, who the fuck's there. I ignore him. Who the fuck's there, Motherfucker, who the fuck's there?

I move down the other Hall. Beneath the screams I hear new noise.

Another hiss, the cackling laughter, creaking floorboards, inhalation and exhalation. I push open another door. I see three women and a man sitting on the floor in the middle of a Room. Their eyes are all wide and empty. One of the women is inhaling from a pipe. She sucks so hard her cheeks are caving in. She finishes and she passes the pipe to the woman next to her, who takes it and holds the torch to its tip and inhales. I don't say a word to them, they don't say a word to me. I want that pipe I would die for that pipe hold on get away. As I reach for the door, I hear the cackle. I shut the door and keep moving down the Hall.

It is quiet. The man has stopped screaming. The only noise is of my feet stepping on old boards, faded newspapers and shards of glass. I look into each Room, but they are all empty. I fight the urge to go back for some rock the urge is growing stronger each second. As I near the end of the Hall, I hear a man's voice saying oh Baby, yeah Baby, suck it Baby, suck that big fat dick. Under the voice I hear spit on flesh moving back and forth, back and forth. The Fury flares to full strength and I remind myself I am here to retrieve, not to hurt. I am here to retrieve and get out. My urges are growing. Retrieve and get out. As fast as I fucking can.

I get to the end of the Hall and I stand in front of a door. Behind it I hear oh yeah, you little Whore, just like that take it all take it all, you little Whore. I open the door and I step into the Room and she's there on her knees, her face buried in an old man's crotch. There is a pipe and torch on the floor next to her.

He looks over says what the fuck she looks up and gasps. In her eyes is the greedy need, the desperate insanity, the awful shame and the complete obsession of crack. She falls back away from the man whose khakis are at his ankles he yells what the fuck are you doing in here. I ignore him and I step toward her I am here for her. He reaches for a bottle I see it out of the corner of my eye and I stop and I turn around and I take one step toward him. He's within striking distance and he has a bottle in his hand. I strike. A quick hard backhand across one of his cheeks. It stuns him and I take another step forward. He shrinks against the wall and I stare at him.

I'm not here to hurt you.

He stares back at me. His eyes are wide. He's scared.

Get your shit and get the fuck out of here.

He starts pulling up his pants, looking around the floor for whatever he has with him. I turn back to Lilly, who is clutching the bag of crack and the pipe and crawling backward into a corner. I reach toward her with one hand.

Come here, Lilly.

She crawls backward, shakes her head.

Come on. We're going Home.

She crawls into the corner, clutching her gear. She shakes her head.

We're going to leave that shit here and we're going Home.

She clutches, shakes her head, her eyes are gone, she is gone. She speaks.

No.

I step toward her.

Yes.

Behind me I hear the old man walking out. She shakes her head.

Get away from me.

I'm not leaving without you.

She screams.

Get the fuck away from me.

I step forward.

No.

She huddles deeper into the corner, clutches the bag and the pipe.

Get the fuck away from me.

I step forward, lean over, put my arms around her. She struggles, tries to push me away, tries to fight. I hold on tight, stand straight, pull her up with me.

Come on.

She's grunting, growling, struggling, fighting. I know it's the drug the crack the rock that's fighting me, I know it's not her. I know if I hold on long enough, I'll beat it.

Come on. We're going Home.

She tries to push.

You can fight me all you want, but we're going Home.

She tries harder. Harder. Harder.

I raise my voice.

Stop fucking fighting me. We're going Home.

There is a last burst of anger and fear and punching and pushing and she stops. Goes limp. I feel the pipe and the bag against my chest. I feel them fall away, hear them hit the floor. I think about picking them up the urge is so fucking strong I hold on to her. I hold on until it goes away. Hold on. She starts crying against my shoulder weeping. She has broken the drug

has broken I stay still for a moment to make sure. I hold her and I turn
her and I start walking toward the door. We get into the Hall start moving toward the stairwell. The Ghost is screaming again and the cackling
has returned. I hold Lilly and she cries and we start down the stairs walking slowly and carefully if I let her go she will fall. She is broken and lost
and high, she doesn't know what's happening. If I let her go she will fall.
We get to the bottom of the stairs walk through the Basement the smell
the smell we walk up the stairs back into the night. We walk around the
Building. The Van is out front. Hank steps out and he comes around to
meet us.

She all right?

No.

He opens the door.

We'll get her back fast.

I lift her inside.

Thank you.

He shuts the door. I sit down with Lilly in my arms and she cries against
my shoulder. Lincoln turns around and he looks at us.

Crack?

Yeah.

He nods and without another word, he turns back around. Hank opens
the Driver's door and he gets behind the wheel and he starts the Van and
we pull away from the Building.

Hank drives as fast as he can within reason. Lilly starts to come down from
the crack. She shakes and sweats, fades in and out of consciousness, fades in
and out of sanity. When she's conscious her eyes are wide and nervous. They
can't stay in one place and she blinks and her whole face moves as she blinks
blinks blinks. She babbles about her bag of crack and a large fire and a man
from Atlantis who is coming to get her. When she is not babbling, she is crying. When she's unconscious, she twitches and moans as if small bursts of
electricity are blasting through her body. Her legs shake and extend, her arms
quiver, she holds on to my shirt so tightly that she tears it. Occasionally she
swears, like someone with Tourette's, saying fuck you or Motherfucker or
goddamn fucking Bitch. I sit and I hold her. I respond to her words, though
I know she can't hear me. Even if she's awake, nothing registers, except that
she was high and now she's not. She's coming down. I hold her. I just want
to get her back.

We pull off the Highway and onto the Road that leads back to the Clinic.
There is a spark of recognition Lilly knows where we are. She grabs on to
me and I can feel her fingernails breaking through the flesh of my arms

and she looks into my eyes and her eyes are filled with fear fear fear and for
the first time since we have been in the Van she says something that makes
sense.

I'm scared.

There's nothing to be scared of.

I'm scared, James.

Everything's going to be okay.

I didn't mean to do it.

I know you didn't.

I just couldn't stop myself.

It's over.

I'm so scared.

We're Home now. Everything's going to be okay.

We pull in front of the Entrance to the Clinic. The Van stops. Hank and
Lincoln get out, Lincoln opens the back door and I help Lilly from the
seat and hold her as we step out. Lincoln speaks.

We'll take her from here.

Where's she going?

Detox.

How long?

Probably a day.

Take good care of her.

We will.

He reaches toward us, Lilly holds tighter. I tell her it's okay it's time to go
I tell her I love her. She starts crying. I gently push her toward Lincoln
who holds her up on one side as Hank walks to the other. When she is
gone from me and safe in their arms, I look at Lincoln.

Thank you.

He nods.

Go to bed. Sleep in tomorrow if you want, come to my Office when you
wake up.

Okay.

Hank speaks.

And don't worry about her, she's going to be fine.

I start to break down.

Thank you both so much. Thank you.

Lincoln nods, Hank says no problem. They turn and start walking Lilly,
who is incoherent and babbling again, toward the Medical Wing of the
Clinic. I watch them and the tears flow and I fight the sobs. I know she's
in good hands and I know she's going to be fine, but seeing her this way

breaks my fucking heart, destroys me, makes me want to die so that somehow she can live. I watch them walk away and I cry.

They disappear into the Medical Unit. I stand alone in front of the Entrance with my face in my hands and I cry. It is cold and dark and it's the middle of the night and there's nothing I can do but cry. I let myself. For her and for her pain and for the World that we have created together. I would give my life if it could somehow make her better. I would have given it earlier tonight, I would give it in the future. If it would make any difference, I would give her my life. I know it won't make a difference. I cry.

I stop crying and I turn and I walk inside. There is a woman at the Front Desk we say hi to each other and I head back to the Unit. The Halls are empty and silent, everyone is asleep, and when I get to my Room, I open the door and I quietly step inside. Miles is in bed and the lights are out. I get undressed and I climb under the covers of my bed.

I start crying again.

Softly crying.

I think of Lilly and I cry.

It's all I can do.

Cry.

I am sitting in the Room with Lilly. I have a loaded pipe in one hand, a bottle of Thunderbird in the other. A torch sits on the floor between my feet. I smoke and drink until I meet oblivion. I love it and I hate it.

The old man is with us. He is pleasuring himself with Lilly. I sit and I watch. I sit and I smoke. I sit and I drink. I care only about the pipe. I care only about the bottle. I am helpless. I love it and I hate it.

The dreams are real, or as real as dreams can be, and in them I see and I hear and I feel and I touch. Inside and out. Images like running film, sounds like a stereo. The crack and the wine in my body are real, the crack and the wine in my mind are real. I fade in and out, between consciousness and unconsciousness, between sanity and insanity. I love it and I hate it. I love it and I hate it.

I give up on sleep. I get out of bed. I walk to the Bathroom. I get in the shower and I wash off all of the dirt from yesterday. I am in the shower for a long time.

I get dressed and leave my Room and get a cup of coffee and walk down the stairs toward Lincoln's Office. There is a Group Meeting in the Lower Level, and as I pass by it, I can feel the stares of all the men. I don't look at them. I don't acknowledge them.

I walk past the Phone Booth down the short Hall. The door is open, Lincoln is sitting at his desk reading the Blue Book, the *Big Book*, the Bible of Alcoholics Anonymous. He looks up at me as I come in and he speaks.

Have a seat.

I sit across from him.

You sleep well?

No.

Bad dreams?

Yeah.

I thought you'd have them.

Why?

Because you were near it.

That what happens?

It does to me, even after fourteen years.

I guess that's the price I'll pay.

I guess it is.

Lincoln stares at me for a moment. Unlike at most of our meetings, his stare isn't loaded with anger and judgment. He holds up his book, speaks.

You ever read this?

Yeah.

What'd you think?

I didn't like it. Didn't ring true for me.

Last night made me think a lot about it.

Why?

Because you aren't supposed to be able to do what you did.

Because that book says so?

No, because my belief in this book says so.

I don't believe in it, so I'm not bound by its Rules.

Whose Rules are you bound by?

My own.

And what are those?

Just one rule: Don't do it. No matter what happens, no matter how bad I want it, don't do it.

You think that's gonna work?

I do.

In the long term?

I do.

I tried that way.

How'd it go?

I failed three times with it.

What happened?

I was Addicted to speed. I'd use, go to a Treatment Center, get some days under my belt, refuse to listen to what I was being told. I thought I was stronger than my addiction, and when I got out, the first time I was near it, I used it.

How'd you get sober?

I finally gave up. I came here, I listened, I did what I was told, I turned my will over to God as I understand him, I worked the Twelve Steps.

That's what saved me.

That's a good thing.

Yeah, it was.

He smiles, looks at me for a moment. He looks down at his book and back at me.

I didn't think you would do it last night.

No?

I hear a lot of shit talking in here, and most of it turns out to be just that, shit talking.

I wouldn't have been able to live with myself if I hadn't done something.

For whatever it's worth, and considering our relationship up till now it might not be worth much, I'm proud of you.

Thank you.

I wouldn't have been able to do it. I wouldn't have gone after her, I wouldn't have gone into that Bus Station, and I sure as hell wouldn't have gone into that Building.

Why do you say that?

You risked your life last night, maybe in more ways than you know, to save someone else. I save People, or at least I try to save People, but it's controlled and it functions under a System that doesn't force me to risk anything. I don't know what you saw last night, or who you dealt with, but I can imagine what it must have been like, and I know it wasn't easy. I don't think I would have done it.

I assume you risked your Job coming to pick me up.

Maybe, but I did it because if you were willing to risk what you did, risking my Job wasn't that big a deal.

It was a big deal, and I owe you for it. I owe you huge.

You do two things and we'll call it even.

What?

I'd like to get along for the rest of the time you're here. I know I'm going to make an effort, I'd like you to also.

I smile.

No problem. What's the second?

You said last night you were going to prove me wrong.

Yeah?

Do it. Prove me wrong.

I smile.

I'm sure as hell gonna try.

He stares at me.

Do more than try.

I stare back, nod.

I will.

He stands.

Shake my hand?

I stand.

Absolutely.

He reaches and I reach and our hands meet. We hold strong and firm we stare into each other's eyes and there is a bond of respect. We let go and I speak.

Am I allowed to ask how she's doing?

She's okay.

What's going to happen?

They're going to keep her on the Medical Unit for today. She'll start the Program over and work her way through it again. We're trying to get hold of her Grandmother because our Rules state that when a Patient leaves, if they come back, they have to pay for another term. You're still not allowed any contact with her, but I'll give you updates if you want them.

I do.

Consider this your first.

If you see her, will you tell her I love her.

He smiles.

I will.

Thank you.

You should get back out.

Okay.

Come find me if you ever need anything.

I will. Thank you.

He nods.

Thank you.

I turn and I walk out. I walk down the short Hall and I walk into the Unit. The Group Session is breaking up, the men are starting to go to the Dining Hall for lunch. I see Leonard and Miles and we walk to the Dining Hall together. Along the way they ask me where I've been and I tell them and they are both stunned. By Lilly's actions and by my actions, that I found her and I brought her back and that Lincoln and Hank helped me do it. They ask me if it was hard and I say yes. They ask if I would do it again and I say yes, and I would do the same for either of you. As we get our trays and our food, today's special is Spanish rice and pork cutlets, they ask about how Lilly is doing and what's going to happen with her. I tell them, though I leave out the part about the money

because it isn't my place to talk about it. They tell me if they can do anything to help to let them know. I thank them.

We sit at a table in the corner with Ted and Matty. Matty has a stack of
newspapers in front of him and he is looking for articles on tonight's
fight. Most of the papers are picking the larger Heavyweight to win,
though Matty still thinks he's going to lose. As he reads the articles he
talks about the writers, most of whom he knows from his days as a
fighter, and he calls the ones he doesn't agree with names like feckhead,
grasshole or kicksucker. We know this is part of his ongoing attempt to
quit swearing and it makes all of us laugh. Leonard asks him why he
doesn't just use the real words and Matty says that he's been three days
without the Devil's talk and he ain't gonna start with it again just because
of some gosh darn fight.

After lunch, we go to the Lecture. We play cards in the back row. Leonard
wins all of the money, but he gives it back when we're finished.

As we walk out of the Lecture, I see Ken standing outside the door with
Randall, the Lawyer who has been working on my case. I look at Randall,
speak.

Any news?

Can you talk in Ken's Office?

I say yes and we walk to Ken's Office. With each step my feet get heavier
and a sense of dread begins to consume me. I watch Ken and Randall in
the hope that some manner of expression in one or both will give me a
clue to my fate, but there's nothing. We walk and my feet get heavier and
the dread grows. It feels as if I'm walking to my cell right now.

Ken opens the door and Ken sits down behind his desk and Randall and
I sit across from him. Randall is holding a file on his lap and he opens it
and he looks at me and he smiles. I am expecting the worst, so his smile
annoys me. He speaks.

I almost don't want to know, but I'll always wonder if I don't ask.

He waits for some sort of response. I stare at him. I'm scared and annoyed
and I wish he'd get on with it. He smiles again.

Who are your friends?

What?

Who did this for you?

I have no idea what you're talking about.

He laughs.

Just tell me.

I start to get angry.

I don't know what the fuck you're talking about.
Ken speaks.
Calm down, James.
Stay the fuck out of it, Ken.
Randall looks at me.
We got an offer this morning for three to six months in County Jail and
three years Probation. All of the felonies have been changed to misde-
meanors, and if you get through Probation cleanly, they'll be wiped
from your Record.
I smile.
No fucking way.
He nods.
Yes. Yes fucking way.
I laugh.
What happened?
The Prosecutor said they had encountered some problems, that there
were some issues with missing evidence, and that he had received a couple
of phone calls on your behalf. When I pressed him for details, he
wouldn't give them to me.
I laugh again. I am overjoyed.
When do I go?
You want to accept?
Fuck yeah.
Given the sudden change, you might have a chance at Trial.
I just want this to be over.
I understand. I'll get the paperwork started.
When will I have to go?
I believe you'll have to turn yourself in within the next ten days.
I smile.
Fuck yeah.
Ken speaks.
I can't believe you're this excited about going to Jail.
I'm excited because three to six months in County is a fucking cake-
walk.
It's still Jail. You'll still be locked up.
But it's not Prison. In County, I'll be with a bunch of drunk drivers and
wife beaters and pot Dealers. I won't have any problems with them.
It's still Jail.
It'll be a cakewalk.
Randall speaks.

Do you have any idea how this happened?
I smile.
I have an idea.
You mind sharing it with me?
I don't think the People I'm thinking of would appreciate it if I did.
I understand.
He closes his file, stands.
I'll bring the paperwork by when I get it.
I stand.
Thank you very much for all your help.
I think there are some other people you may need to thank more than me.
I will, but I'm thanking you as well.
Certainly.
We shake hands and Randall leaves and I sit back down. Ken looks at a file for a moment, then at me.
I went over your Program with Joanne this morning and we think you're ready for the final two steps that we cover here, which are Step Four and Step Five.
It doesn't matter that I haven't done the other ones?
Will you ever do them?
No.
Then let's talk about Four and Five.
Okay.
Step Four, we made a searching and fearless moral Inventory of ourselves.
Step Five, we admitted to God, to ourselves and to another Human Being the exact nature of our wrongs.
My Confession.
Yes.
Except for the God part, it sounds fine.
We recommend that when you do your Inventory you write everything down.
Okay.
And we recommend that when you do your Admission, you do it with a Priest.
Why?
They have experience doing it. They tend to reserve judgment and they tend to be objective. Most people think it's the best way.
I look down, think, remember. I take a deep breath.
Ken speaks.

I can try to find someone else.

It's fine.

When will this happen?

Depends on how long it takes you to do your Inventory.

I'll be done by tomorrow.

It usually takes people three or four days.

I know what I need to say.

Don't make a joke out of this, James.

I won't. I promise.

Are you comfortable doing Step Five day after tomorrow?

That sounds good.

I'll schedule a Room for you. Think about whether you would like a Priest or not.

A Priest is fine.

If you have any questions, come find me.

Okay.

I stand and I thank him and I leave. I walk back to the Unit, where Lincoln is leading a group on Relapse Prevention and the Recognition of Triggers. He is standing in front of a blackboard speaking. The men are spread out in front of him on the couches and the chairs.

I look for a place to sit. On one of the couches there are two spaces on either side of one man. He is a new man, a man I have never seen before now. He has long, stringy hair that has been dyed black. He is wearing black leather pants and a black T-shirt that has a picture of a skeleton on it. His left arm is missing, and his right arm has been freshly amputated just above his elbow. What remains of it is covered in bandages and rests in a plastic splint that emerges from beneath his shirt. It holds the arm above his chest and parallel to the ground. There is a red snake tattooed around the width of his neck and the bottom of his eyelids appear to have been tattooed black. His eyes themselves are a dull brown. They stare straight ahead. They are motionless. There is nothing in them.

I look for another place, but there isn't one. I sit next to the man and I try to pay attention to what Lincoln is saying, but I can't do it. I am uneasy next to this man and I stare at him out of the corner of my eye. I look at the stump of his right arm. The bandages are clean, but beneath their edges, his skin is light blue covered with greenish black spots. I look at his neck and I follow the snake around it. The snake's head is on his Adam's apple and its jaw is wide and hissing, I see its tail disappear down his back. I look at his face. His skin is pale yellow, the sign of a fading jaundice, there are small scars on his cheeks, as if he has cut himself with shards of glass or a razor blade, and there are the remnants of holes in his eyebrows, lips, nose and ears, as if his face was once pierced.

Worse than anything I can see is what I can smell. The man smells like he is rotting, like there is something inside of him that is either dying or dead, like whatever it is has been there for a long time. I can almost see the smell, and when he exhales and his breath leaves his body, there is another equally foul smell. It is sour and slightly chemical, old and incredibly dirty. It is as if he brushed his teeth with a mixture of raw sewage and motor oil. It is as if the last time he did so was years ago.

I am not the only one who notices the smell. I am not the only one staring at this man. Everyone in the Room, including Lincoln, is drawn to his presence. Some, like me, watch him from the corner of their eyes. Some stare directly. Those sitting nearest him wince at the smell or wave the air in front of their faces in an attempt to make it go away. Those sitting farther away shift in their seats, lean at awkward angles, sniff the air as if checking to see if what they think they smell is what they actually smell. It is. It is fucking awful. There is something dead in him and it is slowly decomposing.

Before the Session ends, Lincoln tells us that we have the rest of the afternoon off and that dinner tonight is on the Unit at six-thirty.

Someone asks why and he says wait and see and he releases us. Most of the men get up quickly. They leave the Room or walk to some part of it where the smell isn't as bad. I stand and I walk over to Leonard and Miles, who are sitting together against one of the walls. As I approach them, they look up at me. I smile and I speak.

Thank you both very much.

They look at each other. They look confused. They look back at me and Leonard speaks.

For what?

I was just with the Lawyer who has been dealing with my shit.

Miles speaks.

And?

I smile again.

Three to six months in County Jail. I have to report within ten days.

Leonard smiles, Miles speaks.

Are you happy with that?

I nod.

Yeah, I'm very happy.

Miles nods.
Good.
I think you two had something to do with it, so I want to say thank you.
Leonard looks at Miles, Miles looks at Leonard. Leonard speaks.
Did you do something?
Miles shakes his head.
No. Did you?
Leonard shakes his head.
No, I didn't do anything.
Miles smiles.
And if you had, considering our positions on the opposite ends of the legal spectrum, you certainly wouldn't have discussed it with me.
Leonard smiles.
No fucking way. I get nervous discussing the weather with you.
Miles laughs. I speak.
Is that how we're playing this?
They both look at me. They are both smiling. Miles speaks.
Consider yourself a very fortunate young man, James.
Leonard nods.
Very fucking fortunate.
I smile.
Thank you.
Miles stands and says he needs to make some phone calls, Leonard stands and says he has some business to take care of before tonight. I walk up the stairs and I go to my Room and I open the door and I sit down on my bed and I pick up my book. I have missed it my little Chinese book. Forty-four. What is more important, fame or integrity. What is more valuable, money or happiness. What is more dangerous, success or failure. If you look to others for fulfillment, you will never be fulfilled. If your happiness depends on money, you will never be happy. Be content with what you have and take joy in the way things are. When you realize you have all you need, the World belongs to you.
Thirty-six. If you want to shrink something, you must first expand it. If you want to get rid of something, you must first allow it to flourish. If you want to take something, you must allow it to be given. The soft will overcome the hard. The slow will beat the fast. Don't tell people the way, just show them the results.
Seventy-four. If you understand that all things change constantly,

there is nothing you will hold on to, all things change. If you aren't afraid of dying, there is nothing you can't do. Trying to control the future is like trying to take the place of the Master Carpenter. When you handle the Master Carpenter's tools, chances are that you'll cut your hand.

Thirty-three. Knowing other people is intelligence, knowing yourself is wisdom. Mastering other people is strength, mastering yourself is power. If you realize that what you have is enough, you are rich truly rich. Stay in the center and embrace peace, simplicity, patience and compassion. Embrace the possibility of death and you will endure. Embrace the possibility of life and you will endure.

This little book feeds me. It feeds me food I didn't know existed, feeds me food I wanted to taste, and have never tasted before, food that will nourish me and keep me full and keep me alive. I read it and it feeds me. It lets me see what my life is in simple terms, it simply is what it is, and I can deal with my life on those terms. It is not complicated unless I make it so. It is not difficult unless I allow it to be. A second is no more than a second, a minute no more than a minute, a day no more than a day. They pass. All things and all time will pass. Don't force or fear, don't control or lose control. Don't fight and don't stop fighting. Embrace and endure. If you embrace, you will endure.

I set down the book and I close my eyes. I don't feel peace and I don't feel chaos. I don't have hope nor do I lack it. I am not anxious and I am not in a hurry. What I feel isn't time slipping away it is simply time passing as it does and as it should pass. What is going to happen is going to happen. It is simply life and the events that occur during the term of life. Just as I am accepting that I am on my bed right now in this moment unmoving and still my eyes closed and my body quiet, I will accept the events of my life as they come. I will deal with them. Good and bad they will both come. I will accept them in the way that I am accepting myself right now. Let them come.

I open my eyes and I pick up the book and I read more. I read words like harmony, contentment, humility, understanding, intuition, nourishment. I read words like open, fluid, receptive, balanced, core. I read that if you close your mind in judgments and traffic in desire your heart will be troubled. I read that if you keep your mind from judging and aren't led by the senses your heart will find peace. I read close your mouth, block your senses, blunt your sharpness. I read untie your knots soften your glare settle your dust. I read that if you want to know the World, look inside your heart. I read that if you want to know yourself, look inside your heart. I

set the book down I set it against my chest. I close my eyes my bed feels
warm and soft against my back. I don't move I just lie there warm and
soft against my back. Quietly breathing.
Thinking.
Not thinking.
Of me.
Of the World.
As it is.
The bed is soft and warm against my back.
I lie there.
The door opens I hear it. It has been a while I don't know how long. I
hear the door and I open my eyes and Miles comes in his eyes are
swollen. I sit up.
What's going on?
He walks to his bed, sits down.
I've been on the phone with my Wife for the last hour and a half.
How'd it go?
He looks down and he shakes his head. I stand up and I walk over to him
and I lean over and I put my arms around him and I hug him. He hugs me
back and he starts crying. I don't know what to say, so I say nothing. I hug
him and I let him hug me and I hope that somehow and in whatever way, I
am helping him. I don't know what his Wife said, but I know he needs
help. His crying becomes sobbing becomes violent sobbing. He squeezes
me tight. I have my arms around him they are my only weapon against his
grief. We sit and he cries and I hold him. Whatever has happened has happened he'll talk about it if he wants to talk my arms are my only weapon.
We sit and Miles cries.
Violent sobs become sobs become crying. He stops. The Room is silent.
It is getting dark the Sun is down the last streaks of fading light slip
through our window. He pulls away and he asks me if he can be alone. I
stand and I leave the Room. I close the door behind me.
I walk into the Unit, and it is a madhouse. There is a man in a blue jumpsuit
installing a cable box on top of the television. There are other men dressed in
white pants and white shirts and white shoes setting up banquet tables. Most
of the men of the Unit are standing in small groups talking about what's going on and why these people are here. I hear one of the men ask the
Cableman why he is here and the Cableman says I am not at liberty to discuss it. I hear another ask one of the Caterers and the Caterer says I am not
at liberty to discuss it.
I get a cup of coffee light a cigarette look for somewhere to sit down. I

want to sit down alone. As I start to look for an empty chair, a man steps
from the Phone Booth and calls my name. I say what and he tells me I
have a phone call. I ask him who it is and he says he doesn't know.
I walk to the phone step into the Booth pick up the receiver.
Hello.
Hi, James.
My Mother and Father both say hello. The connection is distant. There is
a slight echo and a slight delay.
Hi.
My Mother speaks.
We wanted to apologize, James.
For what?
For having to leave early. We feel terrible about it.
Don't.
Are you sure?
Yeah. I appreciated you coming at all.
My Father speaks.
Thank you, James.
Sure.
Any news?
I heard from Randall.
My Mother speaks.
What'd he say?
Three to six months in County Jail in Ohio. Three years Probation. If I
stay out of trouble, my Record gets cleared.
My Father speaks.
That's great news. How'd it happen?
I chuckle.
I'm not sure.
My Mother speaks.
Why are you laughing?
I'm just happy. This is a big load off my shoulders.
My Father speaks.
When do you go?
Sometime in the next ten days.
When are you leaving there?
I don't know, but soon.
There is silence. I can feel my Parents thinking about me, their youngest
Son, sitting in a Jail cell. The silence is dense, and it is punctuated by deep
breaths and footsteps. I hear my Mother start to cry and the echo doubles,

my Father is standing with her. He asks if he can call me back and I tell
him yes and he tells me he loves me and I tell him I love him and we hang
up.

I open the door of the Phone Booth and I step back into the Unit. The
banquet tables have been set up and they are covered with white table-
cloths, white plates, forks and knives and glasses. I don't see the Caterers,
but I know they are nearby because of the smell, which is of rich, strong,
hot food. The smell makes me instantly hungry instantly ravenous. I want
it right now. Ten heaping plates of it right fucking now.

I walk up to the Upper Level. I stand with Matty and Ted. I ask them if
they know what's going on. Matty says no, but he's hungry and if he don't
get some gosh darn food soon he's going to go fricking crazy. Ted just
shrugs and says he has no idea.

Lincoln walks into the Unit, looks around and speaks.

Everyone here?

The men look at each other. A voice I don't know replies.

Miles isn't here.

Another Voice.

And Leonard isn't here.

Lincoln speaks.

Anyone know where Miles is?

I speak.

In our Room. I don't think he wants to be disturbed.

He nods, speaks.

Anyone seen Leonard?

The men look at each other.

Anyone?

They shake their heads.

Anyone?

Lincoln smiles, raises his voice.

Leonard.

He does it again, but louder.

Leonard.

He yells.

LEONARD.

Down one of the Halls, music starts playing. It is the theme song from a famous boxing movie about an unknown Palooka from Philadelphia who almost wins the Heavyweight Championship. All of the men smile, a few
laugh. The music comes closer, gets louder, and everyone turns toward a
doorway through which Leonard, in a bright white suit, comes bursting

out. He has a small boom box in one of his hands, the other is raised in a
fist above his head.

There is cheering, laughing, a few men throw candy wrappers or pieces of
paper at him. He stands next to Lincoln, turns off the boom box, motions for silence. When it comes, he speaks.

We have cause for celebration, my friends.

There is more cheering. Leonard waits for it to stop and he speaks
again.

Early yesterday, I was told by our friend Lincoln that tomorrow, I will be
set free. In honor of that, and in honor of all of you, and in honor of this
place, tonight we feast.

More cheering. Leonard and Lincoln smile. When the cheering stops,
Leonard speaks.

I've had steaks and lobsters brought in from Minneapolis, we'll have apple
pie and ice cream for dessert, and in between, we will watch the World
Heavyweight Championship.

The men go wild, cheering and yelling and clapping. They start rushing
down to thank Leonard and Lincoln and shake their hands. As they do,
the sliding-glass doors open and the Caterers start bringing in large plates
of porterhouse steaks, boiled lobsters, baked potatoes and huge bowls of
Caesar salad. They set them on the banquet tables and lines form immediately.

I stand on the Upper Level and I watch the madness. I watch men get
food huge piles of food. I watch Leonard work the Room, saying eat all
you want, have a good time, this is a celebration. I watch Lincoln observe
like a proud Father. I watch the men devour the food as if they haven't
eaten in years. They are all Addicts and Alcoholics and the food is their
fuel. I watch some go back for seconds, I watch some go back for thirds. I
want food myself but watching this is beautiful.

For the first time since I have been here, and it feels as if I have been here
forever forever for fifty fucking years forever, everyone on the Unit is smiling and everyone seems happy. Men are talking and laughing and interact-
ing with each other. Not one word of what they are talking about and
laughing about has anything to do with addiction or Alcoholism or the
loss of Job and Family. Men are moving around, breaking down the barri-
ers of the small groups we congregate in, the small cliques that exist within
the Unit, and the movement has nothing to do with anything other than
having a good time. Our pasts are nonexistent, our futures but a distant
fear. Our anger and our hatred, our failure and our shame, our regret and
our horror and the humiliation we all live with has been forgotten. The

fact that not a single one of us is healthy in mind or in body or in any identifiable way is completely ignored. Right now we are like men all over the Country all over the World eating and having fun getting ready to watch the fight. We are not in a Treatment Center and we are not fucked up. We are men eating and having fun and getting ready to watch the fight. I want food myself, but watching this is beautiful. Beautiful.

I hear someone call my name once twice. I look over at one of the couches Leonard is calling my name. He motions to an empty place next to him and tells me he's been saving it for me, I should get some food and enjoy the night. I smile and I start walking toward the banquet tables. As I pass a table just before the stairs I see the Man with No Arms. There is no one near him. He is sitting alone.

Hey.

He looks up at me. His eyes are dead.

You want me to get you some food?

He stares at me.

I'll bring you a plate of whatever you want. Help you with it if you need the help.

He laughs.

Fuck you, man.

What?

This is all bullshit, man. This whole fucking thing.

What's that supposed to mean?

This is all pretend. Most of these fuckers are going to be dead or using within the next six months. This is all a fucking joke.

You want some food or not?

I want some fucking smack. You get me that?

Sorry.

I start to walk away.

I want some fucking smack, Motherfucker. You get me that?

I walk down the stairs. I ignore him. As I get in line to get some food, I hear him push his chair away and say fuck you, fuck all of you. I get a plate and a huge porterhouse and a bright red lobster and a baked potato. I cut the potato open and I cover it with slices of butter and a spoonful of sour cream. I don't bother with the salad. At the end of the table there is a cooler filled with soda and I take a can of root beer. Root beer will be fine.

I sit down next to Leonard and I start eating. As I do, I listen to him and Matty and a Pediatrician who is Addicted to Xanax and a Corporate Lawyer who is a Crackhead talk about the fight. Matty is still rooting for

the smaller of the men, Leonard for the bigger. The Doctor talks about
the blows to the head that both men have taken and the seriousness of
the blows relative to their size. He predicts the larger man will win. The
Lawyer says the smaller. He feels it in his gut.

I eat slowly. I start with the steak, cut it into pieces, cut those pieces into
smaller pieces. I eat the pieces one at a time, occasionally putting some
potato on top, occasionally dipping my fork into the butter and sour
cream. I hold each bite and I let it dissolve. I let the flavor of the rare red
meat sink into my tongue, I let the juices fill my mouth. It is a fight not
to eat more, to eat three or four pieces at a time, to eat five steaks or
maybe ten or as many as I can get, but it is not a difficult fight. What I
am eating is better than any meal I can remember having eaten at any
point in the distant past. What I have is all I need. I am happy with it.

I finish the steak, start breaking apart the lobster. I pull off its upper shell,
pull the tail away from the torso. I cut open the soft underbelly of the tail
and remove the meat in one thick piece. I hold it in my hand and I dip it
into what remains of the butter. I take a bite. I hold the bite and I let it
melt and I swallow it. I do it again and again. When I'm done with the tail,
I break apart the claws. I pull out the meat and I eat it. The claws are as
good as the tail.

I finish and I am happy and I am full. I stand with my plate and I look at
the banquet tables there is more food on them. I don't take any. I will resist my urge to eat everything I see, to eat myself into a coma, to eat so
that I no longer feel anything, to eat until I'm beyond feeling anything.

I clear the scraps from my plate put the plate in a bin with other plates. I
get a new plate with a new steak and a new lobster and a new potato. I
want it so bad goddamn I want want want it. I walk to my room. I knock
on the door, there is no answer. I open the door and I step inside. Miles is
lying on his bed with his face in his pillow. I don't want to disturb him. I
set the plate on his nightstand and I walk out. I close the door behind me
and I go back to my seat.

I look around me. I look at the other men, the bulk of whom are still eating. Most have food spread across their faces and down their shirts, most
have forgotten their forks and knives, most are eating with their hands.
They are tearing the steaks apart and stuffing them into their mouths,
tearing the lobsters apart and stuffing them into their mouths, holding
the potatoes in their fingers and eating them like apples. As they chew,
they keep their mouths open and they stuff more food in before they
swallow what they are already chewing. In the brief moments between
bites, they wipe away the mess with the sleeves of their shirts, with the

backs of their hands, with paper napkins so covered with stains that they are starting to disintegrate. They lick their fingers and their lips, lick the backs of their hands, lick the bones of the steaks, suck on the broken shells of the lobsters.

I laugh at what I'm watching. It is like something from Rome. An orgy of food and an excess of need and desire. An orgy of gluttony and greed and hunger. No one cares what they look like or how they are acting they just want more more more. No one cares about their addictions the addictions they are here to deal with and learn to control. The addictions have been unleashed. The food is a drug, a drink, a chemical, a substance. No one cares that they are getting all they can handle, that they have more than they need. If they could, the men would eat the furniture, the bookshelves, the plates, the napkins, the banquet tables, the coffee machine. They would tear up the floor eat the carpet, the glue, the nails, the floorboards. If it wasn't going to broadcast the fight, they would probably eat the television. No one cares what they are eating. They just want fucking more.

Leonard checks his watch. He stands, his white suit covered with stains, and he announces that it is getting close to fight time. The men rush down to get whatever seats are still available near the television, they rush to the banquet tables for a final frenzy of food. Lincoln walks over and he tells Leonard that he has to go Home. Leonard stands and thanks Lincoln for allowing this to happen and then announces Lincoln's departure to the rest of the men. Lincoln walks out to a chorus of cheers.

As soon as he is gone, Leonard pulls out a huge roll of cash and a notebook and he announces that he is open for business. Men rush over and start placing bets, so many bets that Leonard can't keep track of them. Fifty bucks, ten bucks, a pair of shoes worth fifteen bucks, a watch, a gold necklace, a bracelet, the orgy continues. One man wants to bet his wedding ring, but Leonard won't let him.

I turn my attention to the television. Various experts are making predictions about the outcome of the fight. Matty, who is sitting on the other side of Leonard, talks to the men on the television in his way of pseudo cursing, calling them either smarty-pants Mofos or pantywaist Fruckers. Someone tells him he should give it up and just start swearing again and he tells them no way no way, I ain't ever gonna fricking swear again.

The Commentators announce that it is time for the fight and the Room becomes quiet and all the men focus on the television. The fighters make their way to the Ring. The larger man, who is the Challenger, enters first. He is about six foot five, weighs around two hundred and forty pounds, and has a body like a bear, which has thick layers of muscle and a thin layer of fat. The smaller man, who is the current Champion, is six foot three and two hundred and twenty-five pounds. Unlike his opponent, there is not an ounce of fat on his body and his dark skin glistens as if he's been carved out of polished steel. Both of them are covered with beads of sweat, which indicates that they are warmed up and ready to fight. It is going to be a fun night.

After the National Anthem and the introductions, the bell rings, starting the first round. Rounds in boxing are three minutes long with one-minute breaks in between each of the twelve rounds. In most fights, the fighters spend the first two rounds feeling each other out for their respective strengths and weaknesses. They then spend the rest of the fight avoiding the other's strengths and exploiting his weaknesses. There is none of that bull-shit in this fight. The fighters rush toward each other and immediately start throwing huge dangerous punches. The only apparent strategy is to try and destroy the other fighter as soon as possible. About thirty seconds into the fight, the smaller man lands a right hand directly on the larger man's jaw. The larger man's legs shake and he stumbles backward. The smaller man pursues him, traps him against the Ring ropes, and spends the next minute mercilessly pounding the larger man's ribs, stomach, shoulders and jaw. When the smaller man's arms tire, and he can no longer throw punches, the larger man starts his counterattack. He pushes the smaller man back and starts beating him in the same way that he was just being beaten. At the end of the round, both men stumble back to their corners. I am on my feet cheering and yelling the entire time, as are most of the men on the Unit. The next four rounds follow the same pattern as the first. The bell rings, the fighters meet, they try to knock each other out. There is no defense and no strategy. Both of their faces start to swell, both start bleeding from their mouths, from their noses and from cuts above their eyes, both start to accumulate welts from the ropes and leather burns from the gloves on their chests, backs, and shoulders. Nobody in the Unit sits down the entire time.

Whether they will admit it or not, all men love fighting. Watching it or engaging in it ignites in us our true selves, the selves that have been di-luted by thousands of years of culture and refinement, the selves that we are constantly told to deny for the greater good. To stand alone in front of another man and to either hurt him or be hurt is what men were built to do. Boxing allows us to live with the most base of those instincts, and to still feel a sense of what it is like to fight.

The sixth round starts. Both men look exhausted, as if their bodies don't want to fight anymore, but their minds and their hearts won't let them stop. They walk methodically to the center of the Ring and start slowly circling each other. They each throw a couple of harmless jabs, straight punches with their weaker arm designed more to keep an opponent away than to hurt him, and then the smaller man strikes. He throws a wide, winging left hook that lands directly on the larger man's jaw. The larger man goes down, as if his legs have been swept from beneath him, and he lands on his back, his eyes straight toward the ceiling. The Unit goes crazy. Men are screaming and shaking their fists, some yelling stay down, some yelling get up, and above all of them I hear Matty hollering he's gonna do it, my man is going to do it.

The larger man sits up, shakes his head, and at the count of nine, he stands. The Referee asks him if he's okay and he says yes, though it is clear he is not, clear that he is barely conscious. The Referee motions for the men to start fighting again and they both warily step forward. Matty is screaming for the smaller man to hit him to knock him out one shot will do it just knock him out, but the smaller man can't do it. It is as if his last punch, that last beautiful hook, took as much out of him as it took from his Opponent. For the rest of the round they paw each other, both too exhausted to throw real punches.

In between the rounds, Matty stands and he starts pacing. Leonard tells him to sit down but Matty can't do it. He is shaking his head and kicking the floor, imploring the smaller fighter to come out and ruin the larger fighter. When the bell rings, he's screaming come on, you Bastard, come on.

The round starts slowly, but about thirty seconds into it, as the fighters stand in the middle of the Ring, the larger man throws a straight right hand that connects on the smaller man's nose. There is an explosion of blood as the nose breaks and the smaller man falls to his knees. From there he falls facedown on the canvas.

The Room erupts. Most of the men are yelling get up get up, a few are high-fiving each other and saying it's over. At the count of eight the smaller fighter struggles to his feet and the Referee asks him if he's all right and through the blood on his face and the blood in his mouth he says yes. The Referee steps aside and the larger man steps forward and drills another perfect right hand into the smaller man's nose. The smaller man falls backward, through the ropes, and onto the Ring apron. His eyes are closed and he is not moving. The fight is over.

Men cheer yell swear throw empty soda cans at the television get up and walk away. Amid all of the noise, I hear one thing above everything else.

It is Matty screaming fuck fuck fuck fuck. He is staring at the television in utter disbelief, just staring and screaming fuck fuck fuck fuck fuck. Leonard stands and he puts his arm around him and he says it's just a fight, it's not a big deal and Matty stops screaming and he says I know, but when the guy I want to win doesn't fucking win, it breaks my fucking heart. Leonard says he knows the feeling and he gives Matty a hug. They separate and Matty says fuck at the television one more time and Leonard starts walking around the Room settling his various bets. He had most of his money on the larger man, but in a gesture of goodwill he waives all the bets that he has won, and he pays on all of the bets that he has lost. I stay up late talking with Matty and Ted and Leonard and other men who come and go. We talk about the fight and we let Matty do most of the talking. Any pretense of him not swearing is gone gone gone. We eat apple pie and ice cream, we smoke cigarettes and drink coffee. We watch the highlights of the fight on the News and we relive the experience of watching it again and again. No one goes to sleep. The Unit is crowded at two o'clock in the morning. Tomorrow we go back to reality. Everyone stays awake because no one wants the night to end.

At about four in the morning, I get off the couch and I walk to my Room. I open the door it is dark and quiet Miles is asleep. I climb into my bed and I put my head down and I think of Lilly. I think of her sleeping in the Medical Unit and I think about how close she is to me and I think about how far away she is from me how far away. She is in the Medical Unit and it is close, but a World away. I miss her. I miss her. Tonight was one of the best nights of my life. Food and friends and a fight. Things I love with people I love. It was almost perfect.

Almost.

I miss Lilly.

I miss Lilly.

I miss Lilly.

I wake. I don't remember falling asleep and I don't remember sleeping. There were no dreams. No dreams.

I get out of bed. There is Sun coming through the window. Bright Sun. I don't remember the last time I saw the Sun.

I go to the Bathroom and I shower and I brush my teeth and I shave. I avoid the mirror. I don't look at my eyes and I don't look at myself. I shower brush my teeth shave.

I get dressed and I leave my Room. I walk into the Unit, men are doing their jobs. I look at the Job Board to see if I have one and my name is listed beneath the word Greeter. I laugh. I am the Greeter, it is my job to greet. It makes me laugh.

I walk to breakfast the Halls are bright I don't care about the Halls anymore. They are what they are I can't change them.

I get a tray and a plate of waffles and a cup of coffee and a jelly donut. I walk into the Dining Room. I see my friends sitting at a table in the corner. They are always in the corner.

I sit down. Miles, Leonard, Matty and Ted. There is a new man sitting at the end of the table away from us. I look at Leonard motion toward the man and Leonard shrugs. I am now the Greeter. I decide to greet the man.

I move to the end of the table. I sit across from the man. He is old, probably in his late sixties. He has short gray hair that is thick for his age, and though it is messy and spiked, it could be easily straightened with a comb. He is very thin and gaunt. His skin is covered with liver spots, his veins bulge beneath the skin of his hands. He is staring at his plate. He is slowly eating a wet pile of scrambled eggs and cheese. I speak.

Hi.

He looks up. He has sharp blue eyes, one of them is bruised and black. He has a long thin nose and thin lips. The area above his upper lip and beneath his nose is covered with bleeding blisters.

What do you want?

His voice is lean and stiff, like the snap of a ruler on a desk.

I'm the Greeter. I came to greet you.

Go greet someone else.

I laugh.

Go away.

I laugh again.

Go away, you Little Fucker.

I reach across the table. Offer my hand.

I'm James.

He doesn't take it.

Go away, James. You Fucker.

Why don't you come sit with me and my friends.

I motion toward the other end of the table. My friends are watching me. The man looks at them, looks back at me.

I'd rather be alone.

No, you wouldn't.

Yes, I would.

If you really wanted to be alone, you'd be sitting at an empty table.

The man stares at me and I stare back. He's tense, I'm not.

You're a Little Fucker.

I smile.

I know.

My name is Michael.

Nice to meet you, Michael.

He stands and he moves toward the other end of the table and I follow him. We sit and I introduce him to everyone. At first he is quiet. He sits and he listens to us talk. We are talking about the Man with No Arms, who left this morning and said he was going to find some smack he didn't care that he didn't have arms he just wanted some fucking smack. He starts asking questions, about the man, about us, about what we do and why we are here. We answer his questions and we start asking him questions. At first he doesn't reply, but after a few minutes he says what the fuck, you're going to find out anyway. He tells us that he is a high-level Administrator at a large Catholic University in the Midwest. He tells us that he has been married for fifty-one years and that he has seven Children. He tells us that after the last of them was born, his Wife stopped having sex with him because she didn't want any more Children and because she believed that sex was intended for procreation and procreation alone. He tells us he started seeing hookers. Not expensive ones, but Girls off the street. He tells us that he became Addicted to them and to the danger of being with them and to the danger of getting a disease from them. He tells us that one of the hookers gave him some crack and he started smoking it and he became Addicted to it. His addictions became part of each other. He needed hookers and he needed crack. He couldn't have one without having the other and he needed them both all the time. He needed hookers and crack every single day. He got caught when a Student at the University who was also a hooker recognized him and tried to blackmail him. He decided it was time to stop so he went to a Priest and he confessed. The Priest told him to tell his Wife and his Wife forgave him on the condition that he stop doing it. He couldn't stop. He did it that day and again the next day. He left his Wife and he spent eight days in a cheap Motel with all of the hookers and crack that he could afford to buy. He smoked so much that he burned his mouth with his pipe. When he ran out of money he went home and his Wife was waiting for him. She called the Priest the same Priest. The Priest drove him here. He arrived four days ago and he has been at the Medical Unit being detoxified.

We laugh at him and we laugh at his story. At first he is angry and confused by us and our laughing, he doesn't understand it. We continue to laugh. We start telling stories of our own. Matty talks about smoking with a hooker who burned his testicles with a butane torch. Ted talks about smoking with his Momma and going line-dancing with her while they were high. I talk about getting drunk with a hooker and passing out and waking up in an alley without my pants and without my shoes and finding my empty wallet jammed between my ass cheeks. We tell stories and we laugh at each other and Michael the Catholic comes to understand that we are not laughing at him, but with him. That we are the same as him and that we are as awful as he is and that we are not judging him. He starts laughing. We are all awful. It is easier to laugh at ourselves than cry at ourselves. We are all awful.

We finish eating and we put away our trays and we go to the Lecture. It is about drugs and alcohol in the Workplace. Michael is the only one of us who pays attention, the rest of us play cards. When the Lecture ends, Leonard gives envelopes to Matty and Ted and Miles. He tells them to open them after he's gone. He tells me to meet him at his Room at eleven o'clock.

We walk out of the Lecture Hall and Joanne is waiting for me near the door. She asks me to come to her Office. We walk through the Halls and when we get there, she sits on the couch and I sit on the chair. We both light cigarettes. She speaks.

Heard you were in a Crackhouse the other night.

I was in a place where a bunch of people smoke crack, but it wasn't a Crackhouse.

What's the difference?

Crackhouses usually have a supply on hand and they're usually run by someone and kept secure by them. This was just a deserted old Building where people go smoke.

What was it like?

It smelled bad.

That's what you remember?

No.

She nods and she waits for me to offer more. When I don't, she speaks.

Were you near it?

Yeah.

How close?

Touched it and could have done it.

Did you want to?

Very badly.

Why didn't you?

I made a decision not to.

Simple as that?

Simple as that.

You make it sound easy.

It wasn't.

You think you'll be able to do it in the long term?

It'll be harder than it was the other night, but I do.

Why will it be harder?

I love Lilly more than I love getting fucked up. That made the decision whether to help her or take care of myself an easy decision to make. When I'm alone with it, be it the rock or the bottle, it will be more about me and whether I want to take care of myself or not.

Which do you think it will be?

You know what I think.

She smiles.

I saw Lilly this morning.

Where?

I went down to the Medical Unit to check on her.

How is she?

All things considered, she's good. I think she's more worried and embarrassed than anything else.

What's she worried about?

Her Grandmother, and finding the money to stay here.

Is there any kind of Aid she can get?

There is, though it usually takes a while to work it out. We're trying to rush it through.
Will she get to stay?
I hope so.
What if she doesn't?
I don't know.
I look away. I stare out the window behind Joanne's desk. It is bright and sunny outside, like a morning in Spring. A morning full of life, a morning full of new beginnings. I could still run. Run from jail and run from my past. Run with Lilly run until we're safe and run until we find ourselves a life. Running is still an option, but I don't want to run. I have run my entire life I am tired of running. I stare out the window, but the window is without answers. They will come in time. It is a morning full of new beginnings.
What are you thinking about?
Answers.
You have any?
No.
You will. Answers always come.
I'm starting to learn that.
She lights another cigarette. I light another cigarette.
I want to talk to you about your Inventory and the rest of your time here.
Okay.
Ken told me you think you'll be finished with the Inventory by the end of the day.
Yeah.
That's pretty quick.
I know what I need to say.
The idea of this is to clear your conscience so that you can start your life over without guilt, regret and shame. You think you'll be able to achieve that with what you want to talk about?
I do.
Ken said you might have issues doing this with a Priest.
It might be uncomfortable for him.
The Priests who do this hear some pretty awful things. Whoever you have, I'm sure he'll be able to handle it.
If you say so.
Is it something you want to talk about with me?

No.

Does this have anything to do with the way you feel about God?

Whatever's happened between me and any Priest has nothing to do with my feelings about God.

Are you sure?

Yeah.

Fair enough. When do you want to do it?

As soon as possible.

First thing in the morning?

Yeah.

I'll schedule a Room and a Priest. I'll make sure the Priest will be able to deal with whatever you have to say. Come by my Office after breakfast and I'll walk you over.

Thank you.

After you're through, your Program is basically finished.

What's that mean?

It means it will be time for you to leave.

When?

The day after tomorrow.

I smile.

Excellent.

Do you have any plans?

Maybe see my Brother for a couple of days. Then I'll go down to Ohio and do my time.

I hear you're happy with the outcome of that situation.

Yeah, I am. Very happy.

Any worries?

No, I just want to be done with it.

What are you going to do about Lilly?

Hopefully she'll be here. Since I won't, I'm assuming I'll be able to speak with her and we'll figure something out. If she doesn't stay here, we'll figure something else out.

Like what?

I don't know. I'm hoping she stays here.

She nods, waits for more. When I don't give more, she speaks.

Come find me if you have any questions while you're doing your Inventory.

I will.

I stand and I leave. On my way out I look at her clock, it's almost eleven. I make my way back to the Unit and I knock on Leonard's door. He says who is it and I say James. He says come in and I open the door and I step inside.

There is a small, black leather suitcase sitting on the floor next to the door, an open garment bag is spread across his bed. He is carefully filling the garment bag with precisely folded shirts. He speaks.

How ya doing, Kid?

I sit on the edge of the bed.

Good. How are you?

I'm happy to be leaving.

What are you gonna do with yourself?

Got one of my boys picking me up and we're gonna drive back to Vegas. Probably stop and see Mount Rushmore and Old Faithful and a few of the sites along the way.

I chuckle.

Sounds cool.

You got any plans yet?

Looks like I'm getting out day after tomorrow. I'm going to try to get hold of my Brother and spend a few days with him. After that, I go down to Ohio.

You worried about Ohio?

No.

I probably don't need to tell you this, but if anybody fucks with you, go after them. Just showing them you're willing to fight will keep them away.

I'm hoping to avoid that shit, but I'll do whatever I have to do.

He smiles.

You're a good Kid.

I laugh.

Thanks, Leonard.

He finishes packing the garment bag and he closes it. He reaches into his back pocket and he pulls out his wallet and he removes a small card like a business card. He sits on the bed across from me and he hands me the card.

Those are all my numbers and the places where you can get hold of me.

I take it.

If you ever need anything, doesn't matter where you are or what you need, you find me and I'll take care of you.

I look at the card, look up at Leonard.

There are five different last names on here, Leonard.

He smiles.

I use different names in different places. The numbers correspond to
the names. The Vegas number is the best, but they can find me at any
of them.

I put the card in my pocket.

Thank you, Leonard.

He nods.

I also heard Lilly was having some financial issues. I don't want you to
worry about them anymore. She is going to stay here and she is going
to be fine.

I smile.

What?

He smiles.

Love is a beautiful thing, Kid.

You shouldn't have done that, Leonard. You—

Say thank you, Kid.

I smile.

Thank you, Leonard. Thank you so much.

He nods again.

One last thing.

What?

Before I say this, I want to say that I mean no disrespect to you or your
Family or your Father, so if you feel or you think he'll be uncomfortable
with what I'm going to tell you, let me know.

Okay.

He takes a deep breath holds it for a moment, exhales. He looks as nervous as I've ever seen him.

I have always wanted to be married. I have always wanted to have
Children. More specifically, I have always wanted to have a Son. I have
been thinking about this for a while now, basically since the first day I
met you, and I have decided that from now on, I would like you to be
my Son. I will watch out for you as I would if you were my real Son, and
I will offer you advice and help guide you through your life. When you
are with me, and I plan on seeing you after we both leave here, you will
be introduced as my Son and you will be treated as such. In return, I ask
that you keep me involved in what you are doing and allow me to take
part in it. Outside of here, I see our relationship functioning, to a certain
extent, just like it did in here. We are friends, we trust each other, we help
each other make it through shitty times, we enjoy the good times together. If there are ever issues with your real Father, I will insist you defer
to and respect him before me and over me.

Is this a joke, Leonard?

He shakes his head.

No, not even close.

You want me to be your Son?

He nods.

Yes.

You sure about that, Leonard? I'm kind of fucked up.

I know what your problems are, Kid. Believe me. But if I had a Son, I would want him to be like you.

I smile.

Sounds cool to me.

You sure about that, Kid?

Yeah.

I'm kind of fucked up.

I laugh.

Doesn't bother me.

He laughs.

Good.

He stands.

Now pick up one of these goddamn bags and walk me out of here. This isn't gonna be all fun and fucking games.

I laugh and I stand and I pick up the suitcase. Leonard grabs his garment bag and he puts it over his shoulder and we walk out of the Room.

We walk through the Halls. He asks me to say good-bye to everyone for him tells me he didn't want to do it himself. He doesn't like good-byes and he has said too many of them in his life. He asks me to give Miles and Matty and Ted the number on the card that corresponds to his real name and I tell him I will and he asks me not to show the card to anyone else. I tell him I will keep it safe and I will keep it private.

We walk through the Lobby of the Clinic and past the Receptionist and through the front door. There is a large, white, brand-new Mercedes-Benz sitting at the curb. The Driver's door opens and a tall, thick man in a black silk suit steps out. The man has a long, deep scar along one of his cheeks and he looks like a bear. A mean bear. A bear who would eat a person alive if given the chance. Leonard smiles.

Snapper.

The man speaks.

Hey, Boss.

They hug and they separate. Leonard speaks.

Thanks for coming.

Of course.

This the new Car?

Yeah, you like it?

I do. It's white and it's new. Just what I wanted.

Good.

Leonard turns to me, motions me forward.

James.

I step toward him.

This is the Snapper. He's one of my closest friends and an Associate of mine. They don't call him the Snapper 'cause he likes fish, so be careful. Snapper, this is my Son, James.

We shake hands. The Snapper looks at Leonard.

This the one you told me about?

Leonard nods.

Yeah, and he's a whole lot meaner than he looks, so you be careful too.

The Snapper laughs, looks back at me.

Nice to meet you, Kid.

Yeah, you too.

Leonard opens the back door of the Car and throws his garment bag onto the backseat. He motions for me to bring the suitcase and I step forward and toss it onto the backseat. Leonard shuts the door and he turns to the Snapper.

Let's get this show on the fucking road, Snap.

You got it, Boss.

The Snapper walks around the Car and sits down behind the wheel.

Leonard turns back to me.

You need anything, you call me. Don't forget that.

I won't.

It's been great getting better with you. I'll be in touch soon.

Thanks for everything, Leonard. In a lot of ways, you saved my life.

Thank you.

He smiles.

You saved your own life.

I smile. Leonard steps forward. He puts his arms around me and he hugs me. I put my arms around him and I hug him. He lets go and he steps away and he looks in my eyes and he speaks.

Be strong. Live honorably and with dignity. When you don't think you can, hold on. I'm proud of you and you should be proud of yourself.

I look back. In his eyes.

I'll miss you, Leonard.

We'll see each other soon, my Son.

I nod. I force myself not to cry. Leonard turns and he opens the passenger door of the Car and he sits down and he shuts the door and the Car pulls away. I stand and I watch it. As it drives down the Road leading in and out of the Clinic, the passenger's window goes down and a fist, a tight, closed fist, emerges from it. The fist is held high in the air. As I watch the fist and Leonard and all that they represent to me drive away, I almost start to cry. Leonard and his fist. I almost start to cry.

I stand there looking down the Road after the Car is gone. I stand there for five minutes looking down the Road. It is hard to imagine that Leonard is gone. Strange and kind and vicious and magnificent Leonard. Satan and Saint. I am going to miss him. I am going to miss him.

I turn and I walk back into the Clinic. I make my way to the Dining Hall. I get in line and I get a tray and a plate of tuna noodle casserole. The meals are starting to repeat themselves. I have had tuna noodle casserole before. I hope I don't ever have it again.

I sit down alone at an empty table. I start eating. I can't tell which part is tuna and which part is noodle and which part is casserole. I eat anyway. One bite after another. I fill my stomach. I miss Lilly and I miss Leonard. I am alone at an empty table. I fill my stomach. One bite after another.

I finish my plate. I start to stand I want another plate I want forty or fifty plates I want a fucking vat of this tuna noodle bullshit. I see Miles walking toward me he is smiling. I sit back down. I still want more. More more more.

Hello, James.

Miles sits down across from me.

Hi.

He puts a napkin on his lap, picks up a fork.

How are you today?

I'm okay. You?

I have some good news.

What?

My Wife called me this morning.

What'd she say?

She said she stayed up all night thinking about us and she spent a long time sitting and staring at our Baby and she decided to give me a second chance. She is going to come here and enroll in the Family Program and we are going to try and work things out between us. There are no guarantees, but we're going to try.

I smile.

That's great. Quite an improvement over yesterday.
To say the least.
I don't know if congratulations is the right word, but congratulations.
He smiles.
Thank you, James. Thank you.
We don't speak anymore. We just sit. He eats and I stare across the
Dining Hall. It's comfortable. Relaxing. Pleasant. To sit and not talk. To
sit and stare at nothing. To sit and let the mind shut down. To just sit.
There is no awkwardness and no anxiety. Miles is in his World and I am
in mine. We just sit.
Miles finishes eating and he stands and he waits for me to notice him
standing. When I do, I stand and we put our trays away. We walk
through the Halls and Miles goes to the Lecture and I don't. He asks why
I'm not going and I tell him if I am leaving in two days I don't want or
need to sit through any more Lectures that I have been lectured enough.
He laughs and I walk back to the Unit and I go to the Telephone Booth.
I call my Mother and Father. They are on the other side of the World and
it is the early morning there. My Father answers the phone. He sounds as
if he's asleep. I ask him if I should call him back and he says no, hold on
for a second. I wait. My Mother picks up the phone and says hello and
she also sounds as if she's asleep. My Father picks up another phone.
There is an echo and a delay.
I tell them I am leaving in two days. They are both surprised. My Father
asks me if I am ready to leave and I tell him I feel ready, but that I won't
know how ready until after I'm gone. My Mother asks what that means
and I tell her I won't know how much better I am, if I am better at all,
until I am in the outside World. My Dad asks what that means and I tell
him that it's easy to stay sober in here because there is nothing to tempt
me. He asks me if I am ready to deal with temptation and I tell him I believe that I am, but that I won't know until I leave. He sighs as if he is
frustrated. My Mother sighs as if she is frustrated.
I ask them how they are and they say they are fine. I ask them how Tokyo
is and my Mother says they wish they were closer to me so that they
could offer me more support. I tell her that they have done more than
enough. My Father tells me he's worried about me and I tell him he
shouldn't be, that I have never felt better or stronger in my life. He says
that is reassuring. He doesn't sound as if he thinks it's reassuring.
They ask me what my plans are and I tell them I'm going to call Bob and
try to spend a couple of days with him and then I am going to go to
Ohio and start serving my time. They ask me how I'm going to get there

and I tell them I'm probably going to take a Bus. They offer to get me a Plane ticket and I say thank you, but no. My Mother asks me if I need anything and I tell her no. My Father asks me to call them when I am with Bob and I tell them I will. He tells me to be careful. I tell him I will. My Mother tells me to be careful. I tell her I will. They tell me they love me and I tell them I love them and we hang up.

I call my Brother. He is not home, so I speak into his answering machine. I tell him that I'm being released the day after tomorrow and that I would like it if he could come pick me up. I tell him that if he can't, not to worry about it, that I'll find my way. I ask him, whether he picks me up or not, if I can stay with him for a couple of days, if I can sleep on his couch or on his floor or wherever there is space. I ask him to call me back. I leave him the number. I hang up.

I step out of the Phone Booth and I walk to the shelves where I found the crayons for my coloring book. Next to the crayons there is a small stack of yellow legal pads. Next to the pads is a coffee mug full of pens. I take a pad and a pen and I walk to the Upper Level and I get a tall cup of coffee steaming hot and black. I put the pen in my pocket and I carry the pad in one hand and the coffee in the other and I walk back down the stairs. I open the sliding-glass door with my foot and I step outside. The Sun is shining. Bright and high, though not warm. A slow breeze moves the air like a whisper. I walk across stiff grass frozen now and for the term of Winter. I walk toward the Lake it is hard and still and it is covered in a shell of ice. I sit down on one of the benches the middle bench and I take a sip of the coffee and I light a cigarette. I look at the pad and the pad is yellow and empty. I start thinking back across the length of my life. I start thinking about all that I have done and all that I have done that was wrong. I start young, or as young as I can remember. I was bad even then, as young as I can remember. I start writing.

Ran over a Nursery School Teacher with a Big Wheel. I did it on purpose. I was four. Hit a boy with a bookbag full of books and broke his nose. His name was Fred. I was six. Dug a hole and tricked a boy named Michael into climbing into the hole. I put a board over the hole and I sat on it for three hours. He cried and cried and cried. I laughed. I was seven. Put a boy named David in a coatbox at my Parents' Church. Put a padlock on the box and flushed the key down the toilet. Got permanently banned from Sunday School. I was seven. Stole a pack of menthol ciga-rettes from my friend Clay's Mother. Smoked them and threw up. Stole another pack. Threw up. Stole another pack. I was eight.

As I write the wrongs of my early childhood, most of them make me laugh. They were stupid, the actions of a kid who didn't know any better, or who didn't give a fuck if he did know better. I write four pages of them. Things I did. They make me laugh.

I start writing again from the age of ten. The age when I started to lose control. Thinking back it seems like maybe I didn't do the things I did, that someone else did them and I just watched. I wish it were so. I started to lose control at ten.

Snuck out of the house and got drunk. Stole liquor from my Parents more times than I can count or remember. Stole a stack of porn magazines from my neighbor's garage. Caused a traffic accident by egging a random car. I watched the aftermath from the top of a tree. No one was hurt, though there was bent steel. Got caught mooning the Principal of my School on a Friday night while I was supposed to be in my bed. Was dragged home by the Principal while my Parents were having a dinner party. I ruined the party and humiliated my Parents. I stole a bag of pot from my friend Sean's Father. I stole a pipe from Sean's Father. I stole a bottle of pills from Sean's Father. I smoked the pot in the pipe and took all of the pills. They made me vomit. I did it again the next time I was at Sean's House.

Three more pages. Filled with stolen chemicals and stupid pranks. Sometimes I got caught, most of the time I didn't. At twelve the memories start to lose themselves in the haze of liquor and drugs. At twelve my life was blurred. Attacked a kid in a hockey game. He wasn't looking and I blindsided him. I knocked him out and I stood over him and I laughed. I filled a Teacher's mailbox with bags of dog shit every night for three weeks. I lit a Boy Scout Leader's tent on fire while on a camping trip. I got thrown out of the Troop. I filled the gas tank of a neighbor's car with sugar and wrecked his engine. I stole liquor and drugs from wherever I could find them whenever I was near them.

Five pages covering three years. Hurt People who didn't deserve to be hurt. Hurt People who did deserve it. Started to contemplate death, started to realize I was fucked, started to hate myself. I did what I did because I hated myself.

At fourteen I stole a moped and pushed it off a cliff. I took a sledgehammer to a sculpture in a neighbor's lawn. I blew up a mailbox two mailboxes four mailboxes ten. I learned the strength of words and I used them. I called a girl a fat wench. I told a pregnant Teacher I hoped her Child was born dead. I asked a Doctor's Wife if she knew her Husband was having an affair. She had been mean to my Mother and I didn't want to let this woman get away with that. Her Husband was having an affair. The Marriage fell apart.

At fifteen I sold drugs to Kids. I sold them alcohol. They were my age, but they were still Kids. Most of the time I ripped them off, took too much of their money or sold them oregano. Sometimes I pissed in the bottles before I gave them the bottles. I destroyed a drive-in sign at a local fast-food Restaurant. I took a hammer to it in the middle of the night because the Manager had kicked me out of the place while I was drunk. I snuck out of my House. I snuck out the Car. I got drunk and I did drugs. All the time.

Sixteen and seventeen and eighteen take up five pages. More of the same. Drinking and drugs. Sneaking out and vandalizing. Saying things to hurt People if they hurt me or hurt someone around me. I trashed the yard of a local Christian Youth Group Leader when he tried to recruit me. I trashed it every Friday night for eight straight weeks. I stole the mail of a neighbor who had bad-mouthed me. I stole it to get all of his Personal information and I signed him up for twelve credit cards and wrecked his credit rating. The level of my addictions grew, the level of my self-hatred grew, the level of my destruction grew.

Nineteen and twenty. Six pages. My first years at College. I cheated on a Girlfriend once twice three times got caught every time. Told her I would change it wouldn't happen again. I knew it would. I did it to another Girl. To another. Lying became part of my life. I lied if I needed to lie to get something or get out of something. I cheated at School. I took money from my Parents and I spent it on drugs. I took more money and I bought more drugs. I terrorized a Kid named Rob because I heard him say something about her with the Arctic eyes. I vandalized his Car and his Room. I taunted him and threatened him and intimidated him. I made his life miserable. I never told him why I was doing it, I just did.

Twenty-one. Three pages. Drank smoked got arrested doled out a beating or two took a beating or two cheated lied deceived used women slept with prostitutes took more money wasted more money my best friends were drugs and alcohol those who tried to stop me were told to fuck off and leave me alone. I made a Girl snort lines off my dick. She was a cocaine Addict and I traded drugs for her body. She let me do whatever I wanted and I did too much too often. Drugs and her body. I held a gun to a man's head. It was an unloaded gun but he didn't know it was unloaded. He was on his knees begging for his life. I did it for a drug Dealer who wanted to test me and I needed his trust because I needed his drugs.

The man had stolen from the Dealer I pulled the trigger of the unloaded gun the man pissed in his pants and pissed on the floor. The Dealer rubbed his face in it and I watched.

Twenty-two. Two pages. My arrest the arrest in Ohio. The arrest I will pay for with time in a cell. A Girl in Paris claimed I was the Father of her Child. I wasn't. I hadn't been able to stay erect with her I had never been hard inside of her. She was begging and crying for me to take responsibility for the Child, but I wasn't the Father, so I threw her out of my Apartment. In a Bar two days later one of her Girlfriends came after me with a bottle and I floored her. When she got up I kicked her in the ass and told her if she came near me again I'd beat her silly. Another Girl I knew carried me back to her Apartment one night after she found me passed out in the Street. I vomited and pissed on her couch and on her floor. When I woke up I took a bottle of vodka and I walked out. I never saw her or heard from her again. I hit a man with a chair at a Bar in London. He had spilled a drink on my table and I hit him when his back was turned. I didn't bother waiting around to survey the damage. I never bothered waiting around to survey the damage.

I finish writing. The coffee is gone and I have smoked a pack of cigarettes. I look at the stack of paper, count the pages, there are twenty-two of them. Twenty-two pages filled with my wrongs, my mistakes, my lapses in judgment and my bad decisions. Twenty-two pages filled with my anger, rage, addiction, self-hatred and Fury. Twenty-two pages documenting my disgraceful, embarrassing and pathetic life. Twenty-two pages.

I read the pages. Slowly and carefully I read them. As I do, I think about whether I am leaving anything out is there anything I have forgotten is there anything I'm scared to face or acknowledge, is there anything I am scared to admit. I want to come to terms with my past and leave it behind me is there anything I have forgotten left out is there anything that scares me. There is one thing. One thing that haunts me from page one to page twenty-two. I have never spoken of it. I have never told another Person what I did to that man, how violently out of control I was, how badly I hurt him. It haunts me.

I pick up the pen and I pick up my stack of yellow paper and I fold it in half. I place the stack in my pocket I pick up the pad and the pen and I stand and I walk back across the grass the Sun is starting to fall. The breeze is starting to pick up. It is no longer singing it is screaming, screaming bloody murder. I open the sliding-glass door and I walk to the shelves. I put the pad and the pen in their proper place.

The Unit is crowded with men relaxing before dinner. I don't speak to any of them. I walk up the stairs and I go to my Room and I walk into the Bathroom and I stand before the mirror. I have written the wrongs of my life they are in my pocket I want to see if I can face myself. I put my hands on the sink. They shake against the white porcelain. I start to look up toward the mirror. I can see my lips quivering. I get to my nose to the black lashes beneath my eyes I go to the bottom of my eyes. To the pale green. To the dirty green. To the green that is impure. I am staring at the bottom of the green there is only one thing keeping me from looking into my own eyes. Looking into my own self. Looking into the past that is mine and that is in my pocket. That Motherfucker in Paris. There is only one thing.

I let go of the sink and I turn and I walk out of the Bathroom. I walk to the Dining Hall and I eat dinner with Miles and Michael. After dinner I go to the Lecture, but I don't listen to it. After the Lecture, I go back to my Room. I try to read, but I can't.

I climb into bed and I try to sleep.

There is one thing.

That haunts me.

Still.

I sleep through the night. Without interruption, without the aid of chemicals. It is the second night in a row I have slept without interruption and without drugs and alcohol. It is a new record.

When I wake it is morning early morning. Not dark, but not yet light. It is gray. Gray like fading sadness, gray like rising fear. Not dark, but not yet light.

I get out of bed. Miles is asleep I walk quietly to the Bathroom. I shower and I shave and I brush my teeth. I get dressed and I leave the Room.

I get a cup of coffee and I sit down at a table and I drink the coffee and I smoke cigarettes and I watch the men do their morning Jobs. One cleans the Kitchen, one takes out the garbage, one vacuums the floor. I see a man carrying the supplies for the Group Toilets. They seem so long ago. The Group Toilets. Roy. So long ago.

I finish the coffee. I walk through the Halls to the Dining Hall. I get another cup of coffee and I look for a table. Matty is alone in the corner I sit with him.

He stares at his food. I can see his eyes they are bloodshot and swollen. A fork shakes in his hand. A glass shakes in the other. He stares at his food. I speak.

You okay, Matty?

He shakes his head.

What's wrong?

He shakes his head.

Is there anything I can do?

He shakes his head.

Do you want me to leave?

He shakes his head.

I sit with him. I sit with him and I sip my coffee. He sits and he stares at his food. His hands shake and he doesn't speak. He just stares at his food. I finish my coffee and I stand and I ask him if he needs anything. He looks up at me and he speaks.

Don't leave.

I sit back down.

Okay.

He looks at me. His eyes are bloodshot and swollen.

I need someone to sit with me.

I'm here.

He looks at me. His eyes are bloodshot and swollen.

It's over, James.

What do you mean?

My fucking life. It's fucking done.

What are you talking about?

He sets down his fork, releases his glass. His hands continue to shake.

I found out my Wife started smoking.

Started smoking what?

He starts to break down.

The fucking rock.

He stops himself.

Shit, Matty. I'm sorry.

He shakes his head.

She had never done it before. She was supposed to take care of our Kids until I got out of here. She got all fucking curious about what the shit was and why it did what it did to me and she went out and she fucking tried some.

How'd you find out?

My Grandma called me. Said she went by the house and found the Kids alone. They hadn't been fed in a couple of days and our little one was sitting on the floor in a dirty fucking diaper. She waited there till my Wife came back and when she did, she was all fucked up and babbling and shit and she said she'd been out smoking.

I'm sorry, Matty.

Ain't your fucking fault.

What are you gonna do?

I don't fucking know. My fucking Wife has always been the one that held us together while I was out fucking up, and if she's on the shit, things are gonna fall the fuck apart. You can't have Kids or have a Family with two Parents that are Rockheads, and I probably won't be able to stay clean if she's fucking smoking.

What about getting her some help and going back to boxing?

Look at me, James, I can't fucking fight no more. My body is wrecked, my head is all fucked up. I wouldn't last thirty fucking seconds in a Ring with the worst fucking fighters in the World. And as much as I want her

to get help, we spent the last chunk of my fighting money paying for me to come here and we ain't got nothing else. We ain't got fucking shit.
Can I do anything to help?
Not unless you got a big-ass chunk of money sitting around that you want to give me.
I don't.
I'm fucked, James. It's all over.
Something will work out.
I seen too much of the fucking rock to believe that bullshit. I'm gonna die, she's gonna die, and our Kids gonna grow up to be just like us. We're all fucked. Totally fucked.
He stands.
I gotta go for a fucking walk.
He picks up his tray.
Thanks for listening to me.
He walks away. I watch him. I pick up my coffee cup and I stand and I walk to the conveyor and I set my cup on it. I walk down the Glass Corridor separating men and women. I see Miles and Ted walking toward me. They are close together and their heads are turned down. Their lips are moving, but barely. Miles looks up at me and he gives me a slight nod acknowledging me and he continues speaking to Ted. They walk past me. I leave them alone.
I go back to my Room. I open the nightstand next to my bed. I take the stack of paper the twenty-two pages and I put them in the pocket of my pants. I leave my Room and I walk through the Halls. They are gray like the morning like fading sadness like rising fear. I am aware of them, but they don't bother me. I know them too well. They don't bother me.
I knock on Joanne's door she says come in. I open the door and I step inside. She is sitting behind her desk, reading the paper, drinking coffee, smoking a cigarette. She speaks.
How are you?
I'm good.
You ready?
Yeah, I'm ready.
Anything you want to talk about before we go?
No.
She sets down her paper, stubs out her cigarette.
After lunch today, I need you to come back here. Ken and I want to go over some things with you.
Is everything okay?

We have a Recovery Plan we'd like you to follow after you leave here.

Anything in it I'll actually do?

Probably not, but it would be irresponsible not to present it to you.

Okay.

You want to go?

Yeah.

She stands. We walk out of her Office and through the Halls. The Halls are still gray, though a few shades darker, like deeper sadness, like greater fear. We do not talk as we walk, and with each step, the memory of that night grows stronger. I just wanted to be alone. I was crying. He came to me and I destroyed him. His spilling blood. I fucking destroyed him. We stop at a door. A sign on the door reads Father David, Chaplain, Religious Services. Joanne knocks on the door a voice says come in. She tells me to wait for a moment and she opens the door and she walks inside and she closes the door behind her.

I stand and I wait. I start to shake my hands and legs and lips are shaking. My heart is shaking. If they were part of me, the Halls would be black. With sadness and fear. With the darkest darkness that lives within me. They would be jet fucking black. I am shaking.

The door opens. Joanne steps out and she stands in front of me. She speaks.

He's ready for you.

All right.

I told him there might be some uncomfortable moments. He said it's probably nothing he hasn't heard before.

We'll see.

Good luck.

Thank you.

She reaches out and she puts her arms around me and she hugs me. She speaks.

You'll feel better when it's over.

I nod. She lets go of me. I reach for the door my arm is heavy. I pull the door it weighs a thousand pounds. I open it and I don't want to go in I don't want to do this. Joanne is standing behind me and I turn and I look at her and she smiles and her smile allows me to step forward. Into the Office. I close the door behind me.

A Priest sits behind a desk. He is wearing black he is wearing a white collar. He is old, in his seventies, he has gray hair and dark brown eyes. A Crucifix hangs on the wall behind him, a worn leather Bible sits on top of a stack of papers. It is the first time since that night that I have

been in the presence of a Priest. As I stare at him, the Fury rises. He
stands and he looks at me and he speaks.
Hello, my Son. My name is Father David.
All due respect Sir, but I'm not your Son. My name is James.
Hello, James.
Hello.
Would you like to sit down?
He motions to a chair on the far side of his desk. It is across from him. I
sit down.
Thank you.
He sits in his chair.
You're here for your Fifth Step.
I don't believe in the Steps. I'm here to make a Confession.
Are you a Catholic?
No.
I can't take a Confession unless you are a Catholic.
Would you like me to leave?
Are you comfortable calling this a conversation?
Yes.
Why don't we do that.
Thank you.
Do you have any questions before you start?
No.
Do you have any concerns?
No.
You should be reassured that whatever you have to say this morning will
never leave this Room. It is between you and me and God.
I don't believe in God, Sir.
Then it will be between you and me.
Thank you.
Would you like to begin?
Yes.
Take as much time as you need.
I take a deep breath. I pull the twenty-two pages of yellow paper out of
my pocket and I set them in my lap. I look at them. They contain every-
thing I can remember except for one thing.
I start reading. I read slowly and methodically. I read every word and I re-
count every incident. Each page seems as if it takes an hour. As I move
through them, I feel better and I feel worse. Better because I am finally
admitting my sins and I am finally taking some form of responsibility for

them. Worse because as I speak of them, I relive them in my mind. Each and every one of them. I relive them in my mind.

When I am done reading I take another deep breath. I look at the pages and I fold them and I put them back in my pocket. The Priest speaks.

Are you finished?

I shake my head.

No.

It looks like you have read all that you have written.

There was one thing I didn't write about.

Would you like to tell me about it?

Yes.

Take as much time as you need.

I look down. I look at my hands they are shaking. I feel my heart it is beating hard it is scared. I am scared. I take another deep breath I take another. Another. I am scared of speaking scared of the memory. I am scared.

I look up. Into the eyes of Father David. They are deep and dark and in them I do not see what I saw that night. In the eyes of this Priest there is only peace and serenity and the security of his belief. Not what I saw that night. I take another breath, one last breath. I exhale. I speak.

Eighteen months ago in Paris, I beat a man so badly that he may have died. The man was a Priest.

I take another breath.

Right after my arrest in Ohio, while I was sitting in Jail, I started thinking about my life. I was twenty-two years old. I had been an Alcoholic and drug Addict for a decade. I hated myself. I didn't see a future and the only thing in my past was wreckage and disaster. I decided that I wanted to die. When I got out, and jumped Bail, I flew back to Paris. When I got to my Apartment, I drank a bottle of whiskey and wrote a note. All it said was Don't Mourn Me. I left it on top of my bed and I went out and I started walking toward the nearest Bridge. A lot of Parisians kill themselves that way, by throwing themselves into the Seine. You jump, hit the water, and you either die on impact or you drown.

As I was walking, I started crying. Crying because I had wasted my life and made such a mess of it, and crying because I was happy it was finally going to end. I also started getting scared. Scared because killing yourself isn't an easy thing to do, and I knew that when I did it, everything was over. I don't believe there's a Heaven or anything resembling it. Life just ends.

I take a breath.

I saw a Church and I was getting so scared that I was having trouble

walking. I figured I could go inside and it would be quiet and empty and
I could sit by myself and think. I found an empty pew and I sat down
and I just cried. For a long time. I just sat there by myself and cried.
I take a deep breath. The Fury that faded while I have been speaking
starts to rise again.
After a while, a man, dressed like you, approached me and asked me if I was
all right. I told him no. He introduced himself as a Father. He told me that
he had a lot of experience counseling young People and that if I wanted to
talk to him about my troubles we should go back to his Office and talk. I
said no, I'd like to be alone. He sat down next to me and said we should go
back to his Office. He told me that he was sure he could help me, just come
back to my Office, just come back to my Office. I figured it couldn't hurt, so
I went.
I take another breath. The Fury has risen. I speak.
His Office was one of a series of Rooms behind the Altar. When we got
there, the Father locked the door behind us. I should have known right
fucking then, but he was a Priest, and it didn't cross my mind. I sat down
on a couch and he sat down next to me and he asked what was wrong
and I told him. I told him about my addictions, about the shitty life I
had led, about the disaster I had just run from and about my plan to kill
myself. The whole time I talked, he sat and stared at me and pretended to
be listening. When I finished he reached over and put his hand on my
thigh and said you have come to the right place, I believe I can help you.
I didn't like his hand there, so I moved it. He put it back and he said although God has sent me to you, there is something you must give me in
return. I moved his hand off again and I asked him what and he put his
hand back and he put it higher on my thigh and he said I know you are
upset and confused right now, but you must not resist or fight God's will,
we were put together for a reason, and he started moving his hand up my
thigh toward my crotch. I moved it away and told him not to do that
again. He said okay, but he put it back and this time he put it on my
crotch and he started to reach for my face with his other hand. As he did
he said you must not resist God's will, my Son.
I stare at Father David. The Fury is up up up. I feel what I felt that night.
The urge to kill, destroy, annihilate.
I didn't give that Motherfucker a chance to touch my face. I hit him on the
point of his chin and I heard a crack and the blood started to flow. I stood
up and hit him again. I did it again and again and again. I don't know how
many times I did it, but at a certain point all I could see was blood. After I
was through with his face, and after he was knocked out, I pulled him off

the couch and I spread his legs. I spread them so I could kick him and I did. I kicked him about fifteen times as hard as I fucking could. I kicked him to the point that he was moaning, even though he was unconscious. Then I turned and I unlocked his door and I walked out and I went to the nearest Liquor Store and bought as much whiskey as I could with the money I had with me and I found an alley and I sat there and I got fucking drunk till I passed out. When I woke up the next morning, I went Home. For the next few days, I kept expecting the Police to come see me or to arrest me, but it didn't happen. I checked the Papers for a couple of weeks to see if there was some mention of what I had done, but there was nothing. I can only imagine that the Priest had done to others what he had tried to do to me, and that if he lived through what I did to him, and I think he did, he knew if he went to the Police I would tell them why I did it, and if they looked into my claims, there would have been others to substantiate them.

Father David looks away from me. He takes a deep breath and shakes his head. I keep speaking.

I don't know if I lost the courage to kill myself or I gained the strength not to, but I didn't do it. I kept living and drinking and doing drugs and fucking up. Eventually I ended up here. Unlike the rest of what I told you about, I don't feel regret or remorse about what I did to that Priest, and to be honest, I think he deserved it. But it has haunted me. At that moment when I was kicking that Priest I could have killed him, and I wanted to kill him, and knowing that I was capable of doing that and willing to do it and out of control enough to do it, scared the shit out of me. I don't want to be that way again, and I think talking to you about what I did and confessing it, if that's even the right word, will help me to prevent something like that from happening again. Now that I have, and now that I have told you everything else, I'm finished.

Father David stares at his desk. I stare at him. I wait for him to speak, but he doesn't. He just stares. I stand.

Thank you for listening to me.

I walk toward the door. As I reach for the knob, I hear him speak.

James.

I turn around.

I'm sorry.

You didn't do anything.

I'm sorry anyway.

Thank you, and thank you again for listening to me.

I open the door and I step into the Hall and I close the door behind me. I take a deep breath and I let it out slowly. As it leaves me, so does everything I wrote, everything I said, everything I have done. It's gone. All of it. It's fucking gone.

I walk back to the Unit. My step is light and easy, I have a smile on my face. I go to my Room and there is a note on my door that says call your Brother at work. Beneath the writing there is a number.

I take the note and I walk to the Phone Booth and I step inside and I shut the door. I dial the number wait while it rings. A woman answers I ask for Bob Frey she says just a moment, please. My Brother picks up and he says hello. I say what's up, Motherfucker, and he laughs and he says congratulations, you're getting out. I say thank you and I ask him if he can pick me up and he says yes, he's taking a few days off and he's hoping that I'll stay with him. I tell him that sounds good. He tells me my friend Kevin wants to come up from Chicago to see me and he asks if that would be okay. I tell him it would be great and he says he'll call him. He asks me what time he should come and I say ten-thirty or eleven or whenever he can get here. He says he'll see me at ten-thirty. We hang up.

The men are leaving for lunch and I follow them. As I walk toward my Room I see Miles stepping out of it. He turns to me and smiles.

Hello, James.

He shuts the door, starts walking with me.

Hello, Miles. How you been?

Busy.

With what?

My Wife is coming tomorrow. Doing all of the things we're expected to do here. And I've been trying to help Ted.

What's up with Ted?

Ted is looking at Life-No-Parole in Louisiana. I have been trying to help him avoid it.

Any luck?

No, I'm afraid I can't help him. The Girl's Father wants him put away.

Fuck. Does he know?

Yes.

What's he say?

He wants to stay here for as long as he can, and then he thinks he can hide with Relatives in Mississippi.

What do you think about that?

I think it is very sad.

We enter the Corridor between the men and women. Miles nudges me and he motions toward the Women's Section. I look over and I see Lilly. Her back is to me and she is sitting at a table with three other women.

Her hair is in a ponytail and she is wearing a T-shirt. Her arms look too thin, as if she has lost a lot of weight.

I smile. I see one of the women say my name and I wait for Lilly to turn around I hope she will turn around, but she doesn't. One of the women sitting at her table is the Supervisor of her Unit.

As I get in line, I stare at her. As I get my food, which is a turkey pot pie, I stare at her. As I walk through the Dining Room toward the table in the corner, I stare at her. I want her to turn around, I want to see her face. She doesn't.

I sit down. Miles sits with me. We are joined by Ted and Matty and Michael. Neither Ted nor Matty speak a word. They just stare at their plates and eat. Miles and Michael talk about their Children. I stare at Lilly's long black hair and her arms that look too thin.

When she stands to take her tray to the conveyor, I stand as well. I walk slowly and I try to time my arrival so that it coincides with her arrival. I know if I speak to her or try to get her to acknowledge me I will get her in trouble, so I'm not going to try. I just want to be near her. Near enough to feel her presence. Near enough to see the details of her face. Near enough to smell the scent of her hair. I just want to be near her.

She arrives at the conveyor and she places her tray on it. The other women are behind her, and I am behind them. When she turns around, she sees me and she smiles. It is a wide smile, a beautiful smile. I have missed that smile, I have missed it. I smile back, though what I want to do is put my arms around her and hold her and kiss her and tell her I love her. That's all I want to do. Put my arms around her and hold her and kiss her and tell her I love her.

The other women place their trays on the conveyor and they turn around and they walk away and Lilly walks away with them. I place my tray on the conveyor and I follow them down the Glass Corridor and into the Halls. At the entrance to the Lecture Hall, they turn and they go inside. I walk past to Joanne's Office.

The door is open when I arrive. I walk inside and Ken and Joanne are sitting on the couch. They are each looking at files that are sitting on their laps. I sit in the chair opposite them and I wait for them to finish. Joanne looks up.

We were just going over your Post-Treatment Plan.

How's it look?

Ken speaks.

If you follow it, it will serve you very well.

Joanne closes her file, sits up. Ken closes his file and he hands it to me.
I take it and I open it and I look at it. It is filled with AA literature and
schedules of AA Meetings in Chicago. I close it.
Looks good.
Joanne speaks.
You should take a little more time to look at it.
Why?
There's more in there than you think there is.
All I saw were things related to AA.
Ken speaks.
That's because we're recommending that you attend AA.
I look at Joanne.
I thought we were through with this bullshit.
Ken wanted to go over it again and I agreed that we should.
Why?
Ken speaks.
Because you won't stay sober without AA.
Why do you think that?
Because it is the only thing that works.
It might be the only thing that works for you, but it won't work for me.
Why?
I don't believe in the Twelve Steps. I don't believe in God or any form of
Higher Power. I refuse to turn my life and my will over to anything or
anyone, much less something I don't believe in.
Then what are you going to do?
I'm going to live my life. I am going to take things as they come and I
will deal with what is in front of me when it is in front of me. When al-
cohol or drugs or both are in front of me, I will make a decision not to
use them. I'm not going to live in fear of alcohol or drugs, and I'm not
going to spend my time sitting and talking with people who live in fear
of them. I am not going to be dependent on anything but myself.
Ken shakes his head.
That's a recipe for disaster.
I laugh at him.
I guess we'll see.
Joanne speaks.
I've said this before, James, and though I've been impressed by the way
you've come to terms with your addictions and your life, I feel it is my re-
sponsibility to say it again.

What?

The odds of someone with your substance abuse history staying sober without tremendous amounts of support, both in AA and therapy, be it Individual therapy or Group therapy, are a million to one. A million to one at best.

Those odds don't scare me.

Ken speaks.

A million to one, James.

It's a million to one that I'm here right now. A million to one doesn't scare me.

Joanne speaks.

I think it would make Ken and me feel better if you'd at least go over what's in the file with us.

Okay.

I open my copy of the file, they open their copies, and we start going over it. It has a small book on recovery in Jail, which is about AA programs in Correctional Facilities and working the Steps while incarcerated. It has a schedule of AA Meetings in Chicago and a list of phone numbers of the Groups. It has a small packet of literature on Rational Reaction Therapy and how to apply it in the outside World. It has a packet of information on a Facility in Chicago related to this Clinic and the Programs they offer for people who have been through Treatment. It has a copy of the Twelve Steps themselves. It has a copy of the Serenity Prayer.

As we go over all of it, Ken and Joanne dutifully explain everything and I dutifully listen to them. I figure I owe them the respect of listening to them. When we are finished, I am relieved. If all goes as I hope and I plan and I expect it to go, I will never have to listen to anything having to do with my own involvement with Alcoholics Anonymous and the Twelve Steps ever again.

I close my file. I ask Joanne if she minds if I smoke and she laughs and says she was about to ask me the same thing. We both light up. Ken stands and says he's going to go and I stand and I thank him for all of his time and all of his effort and I shake his hand and he wishes me luck and he tells me to call him if I ever have questions or concerns and I thank him again and he leaves. I sit back down and Joanne speaks.

You feeling good?

Yeah.

Excited?

Yeah.

You get hold of your Brother?
He's coming to pick me up in the morning. I think a friend of mine will be with him.
What are you gonna do?
Get a fucking cheeseburger.
She laughs.
If you had told me you wanted one I would have brought one for you.
You've done enough for me.
Will you come say good-bye in the morning?
Absolutely.
Good.
I put out my smoke and I stand and I thank Joanne and she says don't worry about it and I leave her Office. I walk back through the Halls and I go to my Room and I start gathering my things, though there is little to gather. A couple of pairs of pants. A couple of T-shirts. A sweater and a pair of slippers and a pair of shoes. Three books and a lighter. It isn't much, but it is mine, and it is all that I need. As I finish packing it into a small plastic bag, Miles walks into the Room. He is carrying a brown manila envelope.
There was something in the mail for you.
He hands me the envelope. I sit down on my bed.
Thank you.
As Miles unpacks and assembles his clarinet, I stare at the envelope. It is plain and brown. There is no return address and the postmark is from San Francisco. It is addressed to me here at the Clinic. The handwriting is simple and legible, the letters wide and loose and loopy. It looks like the handwriting of a woman. I think about women I know who live in San Francisco. There is only one and she wouldn't speak to me, much less write me a letter.
I open the envelope. I open it carefully along the ridge where it had been sealed before mailing. It tears slowly, and when I have it open, I reach inside. I feel a small stack of photographs. They are held together by a rubber band. I take them out of the envelope.
The first photo in the stack is a black-and-white photo of her. Her with blonde hair like thick ropes of silk. Her with blue eyes like the ice of the Arctic. She is standing in her Room, the Room where we first met, and she is smiling and she is holding a stuffed animal. I know this photo, and I used to have a copy of it. I used to carry the copy around with me in my wallet. I carried it before we were together, I carried it when we were

together, I carried it after we were apart. She is holding the animal, some kind of stuffed lion, in front of her chest. Her hair is down, she is not wearing makeup, and her smile is open and wide, as if the camera's shutter snapped just before she started laughing. She is beautiful in the picture. Absolutely beautiful.

I start looking through the rest of the pictures. There is one of us walking down a street together. We are holding hands and smiling. There is one of us lying together on a couch. I am asleep and she is kissing my cheek. There is one of us dressed in fancy clothes, her in a dress, me in a borrowed suit. We're toasting with glasses of champagne. There is one of us sitting in the Sun under a fading Fall tree. She is holding a book, I am smoking a cigarette. There is one of us kissing. Our eyes are closed, our arms are wrapped around each other, our lips have barely softly met. Her and me. We're kissing.

I put the photos back in a stack. I place the rubber band around them. I put them back into the envelope and I close the envelope. I stand and I walk out of the Room.

I go into the Unit down the stairs out the Door. I start walking along the Trail that leads to the Woods. It is cold and night is falling and I am not wearing a jacket. My teeth start chattering and my body starts shaking.

I enter the Woods. I walk along the Trail until it leads me to the point where I break off toward the Clearing. I push my way through the dense branches the dense Evergreen the dense undergrowth. I push my way into the clear.

I sit on the ground. The dirt is cold, the dead leaves frozen and stiff. I take the stack of twenty-two yellow pages I have been carrying around with me out of my pocket. I read them. I read them slowly. I read every word, relive every memory. I set them on the ground. I take the photos from the envelope and I take the rubber band from around them and I look at them. I look at them slowly. I look at every photo, I relive every memory. I set them, with the envelope, on top of the stack of yellow paper.

I take my lighter from my pocket. I draw my thumb along its flint. The lighter ignites and a small blue flame emerges from its tip. I put the flame beneath the yellow paper. I hold it there until the paper accepts it. The paper catches on its edge and the flame starts spreading. I put the lighter back in my pocket.

I sit and I stare at the pile as it burns. I sit and I stare as the yellow turns red with fire turns black with ash turns from ash to smoke and disappears. I watch the photographs catch and bend and crinkle and disintegrate. I watch her captured image disintegrate. I watch the times we had together burn away. I watch my memories of her burn away. I am through with them. Fucking through. It is time to say good-bye.

When everything has been burned, I stand and I put my foot on the pile of smoldering ash and I rub it into the dirt. I rub it until nothing remains of it and there is no sign of the fire. I rub it until it mixes with the Earth and it is black and it is gone.

Night has come and with it the darkness and the cold. I push my way back through dense branches dense Evergreen dense undergrowth. I meet the Trail and I follow it through the Woods. I cross frozen grass and I walk toward the lights of the Clinic. I arrive at the door and I go inside. The Unit is empty. I glance at a clock on the wall. It is time for dinner. I leave the Unit and I walk through the Halls toward the Dinning Hall. I am not hungry, and if I can, I will not eat another meal here, but I want to see Lilly.

I walk through the Corridor. I look directly into the Women's Section. I scan the tables for her, but she isn't there. I look closer. She isn't there. I look at the table where her Unit Supervisor is sitting, but she isn't there. As I turn toward the stack of trays, I see her walking toward me. She smiles and she brushes her hair away from her eyes. There are black circles beneath them, but the deep water blue is shining. I stop where I am and I wait for her, and as she passes, without saying a word, she gently brushes her hand across the skin of my forearm.

I turn and I watch her walk away. She does not look back at me. When she is gone, I glance toward her Supervisor, who sees my glance and frowns at me and shakes her head as if to say I saw what just happened don't do it again. I smile and I walk away.

I get a cup of coffee and I look for my friends. They are walking toward me and they are carrying their trays. Matty and Ted both look miserable. They grunt hello as they pass by me. Miles and Michael are just behind them, I turn and I walk with them to the conveyor. Miles speaks.

You're a little late.

I was busy.

Michael speaks.

Probably best.

Why?

It was a very depressing dinner.

What happened?

Miles speaks.
Ted found out he has to leave here in three days and Matty's Wife is missing.
Fuck.
Michael speaks.
It was very depressing.
Fuck.
They put their trays away. We walk through the Halls. They go to the Lecture and I go back to my Room. I sit down on my bed and I get my copy of the *Tao* and I climb under the covers and I start reading.
Seventy-nine. Failure is an opportunity. If you blame someone else you will never stop blaming. Fulfill your own obligations, correct your own mistakes. Do what you need to do and demand nothing of others.
Sixty-four. What is rooted will grow. What is recent can be fixed. What is brittle will break. Prevent trouble before it finds you, put things in order before they exist. The giant tree grows from a single seed. The journey of a thousand miles starts with a single step. If you rush, you'll fail. Hold on to things too tight and you'll lose them. Take action by letting action come to you. Remain as calm at the start as at the finish. If you have nothing, you have nothing to lose. Desire to not desire, learn to unlearn. Care for nothing and you will care for everything.
The words are as true now as the first time I read them. They don't tell me what to do or how to live or what not to do or how not to live, they simply tell me to be what I am and who I am and let life exist and exist within life. The words are true.
Twenty-two. If you want to be whole, you must first be partial. If you want to be straight, you must first be crooked. If you want to be full, first become empty. If you want to be reborn, you must first die. If you want everything, give everything up. If you don't display yourself, people will see your light. If you have nothing to prove, people will trust you. If you don't try to be something, people will see themselves in you. If you don't have a goal, you will always succeed.
Forty-one. When a superior man hears of the Tao, he begins to embody it. When an average man hears of the Tao, he believes in parts of it and he doubts in parts of it. When a fool hears of the Tao, he laughs at it. If he didn't laugh, it wouldn't be the Tao. It is said that the path into light is dark. That the path forward is backward. That true power seems weak, that true purity seems tarnished, that true resolve seems changeable, that true clarity seems obscure. The greatest art is unsophisticated, the greatest love indifferent, the greatest wisdom childish.

Miles walks into the Room. I close the book. He walks to his bed and he picks up his clarinet and he asks me if I mind if he plays it. I say please, I'd like it if you played. He picks it up licks his lips puts the reed to his mouth and he blows. I close my eyes. I hear long and slow. I hear short and fast. I hear a song that doesn't come from notes on a page but from a beating human heart. I hear sorrow and shame and hope and redemption. I hear a past that doesn't matter and the future that never comes. I hear harmony and simplicity and patience, I hear discipline and compassion. I hear it all now. In this moment in this Clinic in this Room in this bed with my eyes closed.

I hear it.

Right now.

The clock on Miles's nightstand reads three forty-seven. I am wide awake.

It feels as if there's a Phantom in the Room. A Phantom that wants to kill me. Slowly and painfully. Kill me.

I sit up. I look around the Room. It is dark, but I can see. Miles is asleep in his bed. The door is shut, the window is closed. Everything is as it was when I fell asleep. Though I know there is not, it still feels as if there's something in the Room.

I get out of bed. I walk to the Bathroom. I splash cold water on my face. I do it again and again. It doesn't make a difference. I still feel the Phantom.

I walk out of the Bathroom and I put on my clothes. I get Hank's jacket, a pack of cigarettes, my lighter. I leave.

I walk through the Unit. It is quiet and still everyone is sleeping. I go outside. I feel as if something is following me.

I walk to the benches in front of the Lake. I sit down on the middle bench. I light a cigarette and I stare at the frozen water. It is silent and black, unmoving. There are sticks and leaves trapped within it. Solitary bats dive along its surface.

The Phantom starts to take shape. It reveals itself as fear. I don't fight it or even try. I don't think I could fight it if I wanted to fight it.

I am scared. I don't know what I am scared of, I am just scared. As I sit and I smoke and I stare at the Lake, my fear starts to form itself.

I am scared. I am scared of leaving here. I am scared of losing the protection and security that exists within these boundaries. I am scared of going to Jail, I am scared of what is going to happen to me there. I am scared of alcohol and drugs and I am scared of drinking alcohol and using drugs. I am scared of what might happen if I do. I am scared of what might happen if I don't. I am scared scared scared. I am scared of everything. I am scared of sex, of a Job, of money, of having a place to live. I am scared of the thought of having these things, I am scared of the thought of not having them. I am scared of Lilly. I am scared of loving her and I am scared of letting her love me. I am scared of having her, I am scared of losing her, I am scared of living with her, I am scared of living without her. I am scared of having my heart broken. I am scared by her fragility and dependence. I'm scared of living. I'm scared of dying. I'm scared of living. I'm scared.

I sit and I stare at the Lake. I smoke. I watch the sky turn gray there is no Sun. I ask a bank of thick gray clouds what to do. I ask a bat what to do. I ask the grass, the ice, a frozen stick, a dead worm, the benches. Each of the benches. What do I do?

Fear is only fear. I already know that nothing can hurt me more than I have already hurt myself. I know there is no pain that I cannot endure. I know that by holding on each moment each hour each day the days add up each week each month if I hold on I will be fine. I know I am strong. I know I am strong enough to confront what I fear and I know I am strong enough to hold on until the fear goes away. I believe this in my heart.

I laugh. I laugh out loud. The answers to my questions are simple if I allow them to be simple. They are all in my lap I just need to look down. I am scared of everything. I am scared because I allow myself to be scared. There is nothing that should scare me. I laugh out loud because it is so simple. I shouldn't be scared of anything. I am not scared of anything. Simple as that. Not one fucking thing.

I stand and I walk back to the Unit. I open the door and I go inside. The men are awake now. They are doing their morning Jobs, reading the newspaper, drinking coffee and smoking cigarettes. I go over to the shelves and I tear a piece of yellow paper off one of the pads and I take a pen from the mug. I put them in my pocket and I go to my Room. Miles is standing by his bed. He turns around and he looks at me.

Hello, James.

Hi.

Are you excited to be leaving?

I smile.

I am. Are you excited to see your Wife?

I am very excited.

I hope it all works out for the two of you.

I have a feeling that it is going to.

I smile again.

Good.

I pull the pen and paper from my pocket.

I was wondering if I could get your address and phone number?

If I can have yours.

I don't really have either one.

When you get them will you give them to me?

Of course, but you'll hear from me before that.

I would hope so.

He takes the pen and the paper and he sits down on his bed. He puts the paper on his lap and he writes down his information. He stands and he hands the paper and the pen back to me. He speaks.

It has been an honor getting to know you, James. I appreciate everything you have given me. I'll always wish you the best and I'll always be there if you ever need help with anything.

That might be the first time anyone has ever said it was an honor getting to know me.

He laughs.

Thanks for all your help, Miles. Whether you admit it or not, I know you helped me in Ohio, and I'll always owe you for that.

He smiles.

You've been a great friend, and I'll miss you.

He nods again.

You too, James.

He reaches out his hand and I take it and we shake hands. We release each other's hands and we hug each other. We hold each other for a moment and Miles says good luck, James, and I say you too, Miles.

You ready for breakfast?

I nod.

Yeah.

We walk out. We walk through the Halls and we walk into the Glass Corridor separating men and women. I look for Lilly and she isn't there. We walk through the Corridor and Miles gets a tray and a plate of eggs and cheese and I get a cup of coffee. We walk over to our table, the table where we sit for every meal. The table in the corner.

I sit and I drink my coffee and I look for Lilly. Miles eats his eggs and cheese. Ted and Matty and Michael join us, and I ask them for their addresses and their phone numbers. Michael gives me both, Matty gives me his address, but no phone number, Ted doesn't have either one of them. I ask Matty to sign the bottom of the paper and he asks me why. I tell him I want his autograph and he laughs and he says it ain't worth shit no more. I tell him I want it because it is worth something to me. He smiles and he writes To James, the goddamn Middleweight Champion of the fucking Drug Center. I hope we live long enough to see each other again, that would be fucking nice.

Your Friend, Matty Jackson, former undisputed Featherweight Champion of
the World.
I take the paper and I put it in my pocket. When I am sure it is deep and
safe within, I take a sip of my coffee. I take a sip and I wait. I take a sip
and I wait.
I see Lilly walk through the Corridor. She is with her Unit Supervisor and
she does not look over at me. I watch her as she gets in line, gets a tray,
gets a cup of coffee and gets a donut. I watch her as she walks into the
Women's Section and she sits down at a table. I watch as her Unit
Supervisor makes Lilly sit so that her back is facing toward me.
I stand. I say good-bye to my friends. They ask me if they are going to see
me again and I tell them only if it's on the outside. I hug each of them. I
thank them for their friendship and I wish them luck and I tell them that
I hope everything works out for them.
I pick up my cup and I put it on the conveyor. I stand and I watch as it is
carried away to cleanliness. It is the last coffee mug I will use here. I say
good-bye to it. I turn and I start walking down the Corridor. My eyes are
on Lilly even though she can't see me. About halfway down the Corridor,
I stop walking and I turn and I stand in front of the Glass and I stare.
Lilly's table is about thirty feet away. There are four or five other tables
between me and it, there are about thirty tables in the women's Dining
Room. All of them are filled.
I stand and I stare. I stand and I stare. At the back of Lilly's head, at her
long beautiful black hair, at her hand as it brings her donut to her mouth.
A woman a couple of tables away from her motions toward me and the
rest of the women at that table turn and look at me. One of them says
something to a woman at the next table and all of the women at that
table turn and look at me. One of those women says something to Lilly's
Unit Supervisor, who looks up and glares at me. I don't move. I'm not going to move. I stare at Lilly's beautiful hair and beautiful hand. I smile because she's eating a donut and I think it's funny. The Unit Supervisor
motions for me to leave, but I am not moving. No fucking way.
Lilly sees her Supervisor glaring at me and motioning at me and she turns
around and she sees me. She smiles. I stare at her at her beautiful face at
her beautiful blood red lips at her beautiful skin so pale at her deep water
eyes. Those beautiful blue deep water eyes. She is all that I see. Beautiful
Lilly. She is all that I see. Beautiful Lilly.
She turns away. I see her Supervisor mouthing words, but I can't see what
she is saying. I see Lilly's jaw move, she's saying something back. The

Supervisor speaks again. I can't see the words, but I can see her face. She's angry and her anger is rising. I see Lilly say something back to her, I see Lilly stand and push her chair away. I see Lilly turn and start walking toward the entrance to the Corridor. I see her Supervisor stand and yell something at her. I see Lilly ignore her and keep walking toward the entrance to the Corridor.

I turn to her as she comes around the corner of the glass. I smile at her as she walks toward me. I start walking toward her. My heart is beating beating beating. I'm smiling and she's smiling. She starts walking faster toward me. She's beautiful so beautiful. Inside and out. I love her. Coming toward me. I love her.

I open my arms. She runs into them, into me. I close them around her close them tight hold her tight as tight as I can hold her. She closes her arms around me. There are no words. There is no noise. There is no one around us. I can feel her heart beating against my chest. I know she can feel my heart beating against her chest. Nothing else matters. Nothing else exists. Just her and me. Her heart and my heart. Her heart and my heart.

I kiss her neck, smell her hair, hold her body she's so small and thin I hold her body. I can feel her crying on my shoulder silently weeping her tears on her cheek her tears on my shirt. I whisper I love. I love you. I love you. I whisper I love you into her ear.

She pushes herself away, but not out of my arms. She pushes herself away so that I can see her face and she can see mine. She is smiling and there are tears streaming down her cheeks. Her lower lip is shaking and her eyes are more blue with the wetness contained. I smile at her. I speak.

I love you, Lilly.

I love you, James.

I'm going to miss you.

Where are you going?

I'm leaving in a little while.

Where?

I have to go to Jail in Ohio.

No.

It's only for a few months. I'm going to write you every day, and I'll call you whenever I can.

No.

You'll hear from me every day. In some form, you'll hear from me. When I'm done, I'm coming to Chicago.

I'm going to be alone.

No, you're not.

I am.

You're not.

You promise?

Remember the word.

What word?

Ever.

She smiles.

I like it, that word.

Remember it.

I'll miss you. I'm going to worry about you.

Worry about getting better. I'll be fine, and I'll come to you as soon as I can.

I love you, James.

I love you, Lilly. I love you.

She leans toward me and she closes her eyes. I close my eyes and I let her come. Our lips meet, softly, gently, slowly our lips meet and our arms are tight around each other and everything is good and safe and getting better. In each other's arms, everything is good and safe. Everything is getting better. Our lips separate. Our eyes open. I stare into deep water blue. She stares into pale green. I reach up with one hand and draw it down her cheek. As it slides off, I step back. Deep water blue into pale green. I smile. I turn around and I start walking away.

As I walk down the Glass Corridor that will lead me out of here, I know Lilly is standing in the space where I left her and I know she is waiting for me to turn around and say good-bye. I know if I do my heart will break. I know if I do I'll start crying. I know if I do it will be something I have never done before. Turn around and say good-bye.

The glass ends and the Halls start. I stop and I turn around and I look at Lilly. She is smiling and there are tears rolling down her cheeks. I say I love you, and though I know she can't hear me, I know she understands. She is smiling and crying. I lift one hand. I hold it in front of my chest and I say good-bye. She nods. I close my hand into a fist and I say get better. She nods. I stand and I stare at her and I smile. She stands and stares at me and she cries. I can see her eyes from here. I am going to miss those eyes. Deep water blue. I am going to miss those eyes.

I turn around, and I walk away, and the light of the glass Hall fades, though the image of Lilly does not. I will hold that image of Lilly beautiful Lilly standing alone and smiling and crying in my heart and in my mind for the rest of my life. Dearest Lilly.

I walk through the Halls and I go to my Room. I get Hank's jacket and the small black bag that holds my belongings. I leave the Room and I walk to Joanne's Office. I knock on the door. She says come in.

I open the door and I step inside. Joanne and Hank are sitting together on her couch. They are drinking coffee and Joanne is smoking a cigarette. Joanne smiles and she speaks.

Hi.

I walk to the chair opposite them.

Hi.

I sit. Hank speaks.

We've been waiting for you.

I had breakfast.

Joanne speaks.

How was it?

It was beautiful.

She smiles.

I've never heard anyone describe a meal here as beautiful.

I smile.

That's what it was. Beautiful.

Hank speaks.

You ready to go?

Yeah.

You scared?

I was earlier, but I'm not now.

Joanne speaks.

What were you scared of?

Everything.

And what happened?

I decided not to be.

Simple as that?

Simple as that.

I hold up Hank's jacket, toss it to him.

I brought your jacket back. Thank you for letting me use it.

He tosses it back to me.

I want you to keep it.

I toss it back to him.

Thank you, but no. I want you to keep it so when I come back to visit, I'll be able to wear it.

I'll make that deal on one condition.

What's that?

You come back here sober, as a Visitor, not as a Patient.
Have no doubt about that, Old Man.
He smiles.
That's my motherfucking Boy.
Joanne speaks.
Watch your mouth, Hank.
Hank turns to her.
I can swear around him now. He ain't a Patient anymore.
He's a Patient until he walks out the front door.
Hanks turns to me.
You care if I say motherfucking around you?
I smile.
I'd be fucking offended if you didn't.
Hank laughs, slaps his knee.
That's my motherfucking Boy.
I laugh. Joanne speaks.
You're all set to be picked up?
Yeah.
Have you checked out yet?
No.
You should get going.
I nod again.
I know.
She stands.
Give me a hug?
I stand.
Of course.
I step forward and I hug her. There is emotion in the hug, and there is re-
spect and a form of love. Emotion that comes from honesty, respect that
comes from challenge, and the form of love that exists between people
whose minds have touched, whose hearts have touched, whose souls have
touched. Our minds touched. Our hearts touched. Our souls touched.
We separate. Hanks steps forward.
I ain't much for words, Kid.
He puts his arms around me and he hugs me so hard that it hurts. My
arms are pinned to my sides so I can't hug him, but I don't think he needs
it. He lets go of me and he takes a step back and he puts one of his arms
around Joanne's shoulders. He speaks.
Make us proud, Kid.
I'll try.

Do better than try. I want you back here wearing that fucking coat in a year.

Joanne speaks.

Hank.

Hank looks at her.

He's not a Patient anymore.

Joanne shakes her head, turns to me.

Stay in touch.

I nod.

I will.

I turn and I walk out of the Office. I close the door behind me and I walk through the Halls. I go to the Administration Office and I sit with an Administration Officer and I fill out my release papers. When I am finished, I sign my name on the bottom of a page and I am done. The Officer tells me I am free to go.

I walk out of the Office and through a short Hall. I walk into the Lobby where I sat waiting with my Family in a different life. I say hello to the Receptionist and she says hello to me. Through the windows I see my Brother's gray Truck, which is the type of fancy passenger Truck common in the Suburbs, sitting in front of the Entrance. I open the Front Door and I walk out of the Clinic. I am free to go.

My Brother sees me coming and he opens the Driver's door and he steps out of his Truck. He is smiling. He speaks.

What's up, Buddy?

What's up, Motherfucker?

He hugs me. I hug him. A good strong fraternal hug. My friend Kevin steps out of the Passenger's door. He is my size, has short dark parted hair, and a newly grown beer belly. He sells commercial real estate for a living, but when he is not working, he dresses like a bum. He smiles and he speaks.

What's up?

Nothing. What's up with you?

Came to make sure you're okay.

I smile.

I am.

He hugs me. I hug him. My Brother speaks.

You ready to go?

Yeah, let's get out of here.

I pick up my bag and I open the door and I climb into the backseat. As I close the door, Bob and Kevin get in the front seats and Bob starts the

Car and we pull away. I turn around and I watch the Clinic recede into the distance from the back window. I am free to go. Free to go. Free.

When I can no longer see the Buildings, I turn around. Almost immediately, the Fury starts to rise. As if the walls of the Clinic kept it in check, as if my freedom is its freedom, as if my walking papers were its walking papers. The ascension is fast and brutal, and though I'm not shaking on the outside, I am shaking on the inside.

Kevin turns and he looks at me and he speaks.

How's it feel?

I see Bob looking at me in the rearview mirror.

I don't know.

Bob speaks.

What's that mean?

I don't know.

Kevin speaks.

What do you want to do?

I want to go to a Bar.

What?

I want to go to a Bar.

You're fucking kidding me.

No, I'm not.

My Brother Bob is looking at me in the rearview mirror. Kevin looks at Bob, Bob looks at Kevin. There is concern, dismay and shock on both of their faces. Bob looks back at me, shakes his head.

We're not going to a Bar.

You might not be, but I am.

You just got out of Rehab.

I'm going to a Bar.

You just got out of fucking Rehab.

I am going to a Bar. You can come with me or not, either way is fine, and you shouldn't waste your time trying to stop me. I'm going to a fucking Bar.

Bob looks at Kevin, Kevin at Bob. Kevin shrugs, Bob shakes his head. I light a cigarette and roll down the window. Even though it is cold, I like the air. It is free.

The drive takes an hour. No one speaks. Bob stares out the front window, Kevin stares out the front Passenger's window, I stare out my window. Occasionally I stick my head out and let the freezing air whip against the skin of my face. It hurts, but it feels good, and I do it because I can. I no longer have Rules and Regulations I have to follow, I no longer have

Counselors and Supervisors and Psychologists demanding answers, my schedule and my actions are once again my own. As it was before I went to the Clinic, and as it will be until the end, I answer only to myself.

We pull off the Highway and into the City. I look at the clock on Bob's dashboard it reads eleven-thirty. I ask him if he knows somewhere that is open now and he says yes. I tell him I'd prefer a place that serves cheeseburgers and has a pool table. He does not respond. He just stares out of the front window.

The Fury has risen. It is at full strength, it is beyond full strength. It is different now, at this moment, it feels different. It feels stronger, quieter, more patient. Simpler and more powerful. As if it is secure in its victory over me. As if the fight with me has fortified its might. As if it knows its time has come again, as if it is waiting to unleash itself.

I don't fight it. I don't challenge it. I sit and I wait and I anticipate my arrival in a place that feels like Home. I sit and I wait and I save myself for what is to come when I step inside a Bar. The Fury is stronger than it has ever been before. I sit and I wait for what is to come.

Bob pulls into a small Parking Lot. Next to the Parking Lot is a large brick Building. There are tall dark windows along the front of the Building. There is a neon sign that reads Billiards, Bar and Grill.

We get out of the Truck. I don't have any money, so I ask Bob if I can borrow some. He asks me how much I need and I ask him for forty bucks. He asks me why I need so much and I tell him because I do. He takes his wallet out of his pocket and he opens it and he gives me two twenties. I thank him.

We walk through the Parking Lot. We walk along a short stretch of Sidewalk. We come to the front door and I reach for it and I open it. I motion Bob and Kevin through, and after they have gone through, I follow them inside.

It is dark. There are tables in front of us, a long, worn oak bar runs the length of the wall to our right, at the end of the bar, and to the left, is a room with six pool tables. Next to the pool tables, a bored Waitress sits at her station watching a television that hangs from the ceiling. Behind the bar, a Bartender sits on a stool reading a newspaper. Neither of them look up.

I look at Bob and Kevin. I speak.

Why don't you guys go shoot some pool.

My Brother looks at me.

What are you going to do?

I need a couple of minutes alone.

His face is full with fear and disappointment. It is none of my concern. It is time for the reckoning. It is time for the Fury.

I turn and I walk to the bar. I pull out a stool about halfway down its length and I sit down. There are mirrors and bottles in front of me. The mirrors run from the ceiling down to a set of shelves. The shelves are lined with bottles. There are whiskey bottles, vodka bottles, bottles of gin. There are rum bottles, tequila bottles, bottles of strange liqueurs from foreign Countries. There are clear bottles and brown bottles, there are red bottles and blue bottles, there are multicolored bottles designed to please the eye. Some of the bottles are short, some are tall, some are wide, some are thin. They are all filled with alcohol. They are sitting in front of me. They are filled with fucking alcohol.

I look toward the Bartender. I speak.

Barkeep.

He looks up.

Yeah.

Give me a little help?

Sure.

He sets down his paper and he walks toward me. When he is standing in front of me, he speaks.

How ya doing today?

I'm not here to talk.

You in a bad mood?

I'm not here to talk.

What can I get you?

I look at the bottles. The beautiful bottles filled with alcohol. I let my eyes wander until they settle, avoiding the mirrors, avoiding myself. I stare at a black bottle. A thick black bottle with a thin neck that is filled with Kentucky Bourbon. It is the bottle the Fury most craves, the bottle with which it is most familiar. I point to it, stare at the Bartender, and I speak.

I want a glass of that. I want a big glass. Not one of those bullshit cocktail glasses, but a big fucking pint glass. I want it filled to the top.

That's gonna be expensive.

I set the forty dollars my Brother gave me on the surface of the bar.

Just bring it.

The Bartender stares at me like I'm crazy, like he's debating whether he is going to give me what I want. I stare back, let him know that I'm not leaving until I have it. He turns around. With one hand he reaches for a tall, thin pint glass, and with the other he takes the black bottle from the shelf.

I watch him pour the drink. As if in slow motion, I see every drop. When the glass is full, he turns around and he sets it in front of me.

Thank you.

I'll be down there if you need anything else.

Thank you.

He walks back to his newspaper. I stare at the glass. The Fury rises from its silent state it screams bloody fucking murder it is stronger than it has ever been before. It screams you are mine, Motherfucker. You are mine and you will always be mine. I own you, I control you and you will do what I tell you to do. You are mine and you will always be mine. You are mine, Motherfucker. I stare at the glass.

I put my hands on the bar. I put them on either side of the glass. They are not touching it, but they are close. Close enough so that when I decide, the glass will be within easy reach. I lean down. As my nose moves toward the strong brown alcohol, I can smell the fumes drifting from its shimmering surface. They enrage me. They make the Fury scream louder. They taunt me. They draw me closer.

I close my eyes. I stop moving when the tip of my nose hits the liquid. I close my mouth and I take a deep breath and it comes comes comes. With all of its strength. The beautiful aroma of oblivion. The foul stench of Hell. It makes me shudder, shakes me. Inside and out it destroys me and fortifies me. Though it has not met my lips or entered my body, I can taste it. Like sweet strong charcoal mixed with bitter gasoline. I can fucking taste it.

Time stops. I do not move. I sit with the tip of my nose in a glass filled with alcohol. I breathe. Deep thorough breaths. All the way in, all the way out. It ebbs when I inhale, ripples when I exhale. I can smell it and I can taste it and I can feel it. Inside and out.

The Fury screams pick it up pick it up pick it up. The Fury screams drink it drink it drink it. The Fury screams more more more more more. The Fury screams want need have to have can't live without I own you, Motherfucker, pick it up drink it give it to me or I will make you pay. More more more more more.

I open my eyes. I see the clear amber brown, the tip of my nose submerged, the rim of my glass. I start to slowly lift my head. I keep my eyes straight ahead, fixed and focused, they will not blink. The liquid disappears from view, the rim of the glass disappears. I see shelves and bottles, the edge of the mirror. I keep moving up I see the edge of my chin, my lips, my nose. I keep moving up. I see the edge of my eye, the lash, the white surrounding. I keep moving up. I see pale green. Straight ahead. Fixed and focused. They will not blink.

I look into myself. Into my own eyes. There is a glass of alcohol in front of me. Though I can no longer see it, I know it is there. I put my hands around it. My hands are on the glass. I look into myself. Into the pale green of my own eyes.

The Fury is screaming. Screaming like it has never screamed before. Its scream is stronger and more powerful, full of rage and need, of hostility and hunger. It is screaming for me to pick up the glass. Pick up the fucking glass.

I have a decision to make. It is a simple decision. It has nothing to do with God or Twelve of anything other than twelve beats of my heart. Yes or no. It is a simple decision. Yes or no.

I look into myself. Into the pale green of my own eyes. I like what I see. I am comfortable with it. It is fixed and focused. It will not blink. For the first time in my life, as I look into my own eyes, I like what I see. I can live with it. I want to live with it. For a long time. I want to live with it. I want to live.

The Fury screams bloody fucking murder. The Pale Green softly speaks. It says you are mine, Motherfucker. You are mine and you will always be mine. From this day forward I own you, I control you and you will do what I tell you to do. From this day forward, I make the fucking decisions. You are mine and you will always be mine. You are mine, Motherfucker.

I let go of the glass. I look at the Bartender. He is sitting on his stool and he is reading his newspaper. I speak.

Barkeep.

He looks up.

Yeah.

Dump this shit out for me.

What?

I motion to the glass.

Dump this shit down the fucking drain. I don't want it.

He stares at me for a moment like I'm crazy. I stare back and let him know I'm not. He stands and he starts walking toward me. I stand and I walk away. I leave the glass on the bar and the two twenties next to it.

I walk into the Room with the pool tables. My Brother Bob and my friend Kevin are finishing a game. There is one solid ball on the table,

one striped ball, and the eight ball in a corner. I sit down on a stool
along the wall. There is a table next to the stool and an ashtray on the
table. I light a cigarette.

As my Brother lines up a shot, he sees me sitting in the corner of his eye.
He looks up and he speaks.

You all right?

Yeah.

What were you doing over there?

Nothing.

Did you drink?

No.

Why'd you order one?

It was something I needed to do.

But you didn't touch it?

I touched it and I smelled it and I felt it, but I didn't drink it. I'm done
drinking. Won't ever do it again.

He smiles.

Congratulations, Buddy.

I smile.

Thanks.

As my Brother lines up his shot, I ask if I can play the Winner. Kevin
asks me how long it's been since I played and I tell him it's been a long
time. He asks me if I'm ready and I smile and I tell him that I am. He
asks me again he wants to make sure. I tell him yes, I'm ready.

Yes, I'm ready.

Michael returned to work at the University. Three weeks later he was arrested for Solicitation of Prostitution and Possession of Crack Cocaine. He died from a self-inflicted gunshot wound.

Roy attacked two Children with a baseball bat. He was sentenced to thirty to fifty years in an Institution for the Criminally Insane in Wisconsin.

Warren fell off the back of a fishing boat in Florida while he was drunk. His body has never been recovered.

The Bald Man started drinking eight weeks after he returned home. His Wife threw him out of their house and his whereabouts are unknown.

Bobby was found dead in New Jersey. He had been shot in the back of the head.

John was caught carrying fourteen ounces of cocaine in San Francisco. He is serving a life sentence without the possibility of parole at San Quentin State Penitentiary in California.

Ed was beaten to death in a Bar fight in Detroit.

Ted was captured by Authorities in Mississippi. He is serving a life term without the possibility of parole at Angola State Farm in Louisiana.

Matty was shot and killed outside of a Crackhouse in Minneapolis.

Miles is alive and well and continues to serve as a Judge. He is still married, had a second Child, a Daughter named Ella, and he has never relapsed.

Leonard returned to Las Vegas and retired. He subsequently died from complications due to AIDS. He was sober until he died. He never relapsed.

Lilly committed suicide by hanging in a Halfway House in Chicago. Her Grandmother had passed away two days earlier. She was found the morning James was released from Jail, and it is believed that she was sober until she died.

Lincoln still works at the Clinic.

Ken still works at the Clinic.

Hank and Joanne got married. Both still work at the Clinic.

James has never relapsed.

· · ·

Thank you Mom and Dad for everything, thank you Mom and Dad.
Thank you Brother Bob and Sister-in-Law Laura. Thank you Maya,
I love you Dearest Maya. Thank you Kassie Evashevski. Thank you
Sean McDonald. Thank you Nan Talese. Thank you David Krintzman.
Thank you Preacher and Bella my little Friends. Thank you Stuart
Hawkins, Elizabeth Sosnow, Kevin Yorn, Amar Douglas Rao,
Michael Craven, Quinn Yancey, Christian Yancey, Ingrid Sisson,
John Von Brachel, Helen Motley, Jean Joseph Jr., Joshua Dorfman,
Daniel Glasser, Marvin Klotz, Colleen Silva, Eben Strousse,
Chris Wardwell. Thank you Theo, Rigo, Jose and the Boys at the
Coffee Shop on the corner. Thank you Phillip Morris. Thank you
Andrew Barash and Keith Bray. Thank you Kirk, Julie, Kevin.
Thank you Lilly, Leonard, Miles, I love you and I thank you.